This book examines the ways in which the theory and data of social psychology can be applied to teaching, learning, and other experiences in schools. Its focus ranges in level from the individual (e.g., student attitudes and attributions), to teacher–student interaction, to the impact of society (e.g., racial and cultural influences on school performance).

The editor and distinguished contributors have two major purposes. The first is to illustrate the scope and sophistication of the emerging field known as the social psychology of education. The second is to provide solid, informed suggestions to educators for the amelioration of current educational problems. To that end, each author explicitly discusses implications for educational practice.

Psychologists and educational researchers will find *The Social Psychology of Education* a useful and comprehensive guide to an increasingly active new research area.

Robert S. Feldman is Associate Professor of Psychology at the University of Massachusetts, Amherst.

The social psychology of education

?

The social psychology of education

Current research and theory

Edited by

ROBERT S. FELDMAN

University of Massachusetts at Amherst

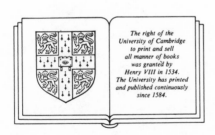

The right of the
University of Cambridge
to print and sell
all manner of books
was granted by
Henry VIII in 1534.
The University has printed
and published continuously
since 1584.

CAMBRIDGE UNIVERSITY PRESS

Cambridge
London   New York   New Rochelle
Melbourne   Sydney

Published by the Press Syndicate of the University of Cambridge
The Pitt Building, Trumpington Street, Cambridge CB2 1RP
32 East 57th Street, New York, NY 10022, USA
10 Stamford Road, Oakleigh, Melbourne 3166, Australia

First published 1986

Printed in the United States of America

Library of Congress Cataloging-in-Publication Data
Main entry under title:
The social psychology of education.

   1. Teacher-student relationships–Addresses,
essays, lectures. 2. Interaction analysis in education
–Addresses, essays, lectures. 3. Social psychology–
Addresses, essays, lectures. 4. Students–Psychology.
I. Feldman, Robert S. (Robert Stephen), 1947–
LB1033.S755   1986   370.19   85-30928
ISBN 0 521 30620 5

British Library Cataloging-in-Publication applied for

Contents

Contributors

Carol Ames
Institute for Child Behavior and
Development
University of Illinois

Brenda D. Baden
Institute for Child Behavior and
Development
University of Illinois

Daniel Bar-Tal
School of Education
Tel-Aviv University

Yaffa Bar-Tal
Everyman's University
Tel-Aviv

Marilynn B. Brewer
Department of Psychology
University of California, Los
Angeles

Jere Brophy
Institute for Research on
Teaching
Michigan State University

Harris M. Cooper
Center for Research in Social
Behavior
University of Missouri, Columbia

Vitaly Dubrovsky
School of Management
Clarkson University

Robert S. Feldman
Department of Psychology
University of Massachusetts,
Amherst

Donelson R. Forsyth
Department of Psychology
Virginia Commonwealth
University

Sandra Graham
Department of Education
University of California, Los
Angeles

Monica J. Harris
Department of Psychology and
Social Relations
Harvard University

David W. Johnson
College of Education
University of Minnesota

Roger T. Johnson
College of Education
University of Minnesota

vii

Neelam Kher
Institute for Management and
Labour Studies
Xavier Labour Relations Institute

Sara Kiesler
Department of Social Science
Carnegie-Mellon University

Martin L. Maehr
Institute for Child Behavior and
Development
University of Illinois

Norman Miller
Department of Psychology
University of Southern California

Robert Rosenthal
Department of Psychology and
Social Relations
Harvard University

Ronald D. Saletsky
Department of Psychology
Case Western Reserve University

Robert E. Slavin
Center for the Social
Organization of Schools
Johns Hopkins University

Howard A. Smith
Faculty of Education
Queens University

Karl A. Smith
College of Education
University of Minnesota

Lee Sproull
Department of Social Science
Carnegie-Mellon University

David Zubrow
Department of Social Science
Carnegie-Mellon University

Acknowledgments

In editing this book, I received enthusiastic cooperation – as well as scholarly, sophisticated, thoughtful manuscripts – from each of the chapter authors, and I thank them. I am also grateful to my ever – helpful secretaries, Kate Cleary and Jean Glenowitz. The staff at Cambridge University Press, particularly Susan Milmoe, and Mark Friedman were always encouraging. Finally, my family – who might be getting tired of being thanked, but I suspect not (and in any case like to see their names in print) – served always as my touchstone, and I thank them with love: Sarah, Josh, Jon, and Kathy.

ROBERT S. FELDMAN

Acknowledgments

Introduction: the present and promise of the social psychology of education

Robert S. Feldman

A decade ago, a person seeking to bridge the gap between social psychology and education would have been well advised to prepare for a long journey. Today, however, the gap largely has been bridged, as more and more researchers take up the byways that join the two disciplines. This volume is a testament to the burgeoning literature that encompasses the pathways linking social psychology and education.

Charting the present: the field of social psychology of education

A newcomer to the area of social psychology of education might wonder where the field fits in relation to other, more established disciplines. Is it merely social psychology applied to a particular area of interest? Or is it a subdiscipline of the field of education, looked at from the vantage point of the social psychologist?

The most appropriate answer to the question is that it represents an amalgamation of the two fields; it is not merely social psychology, nor is it simply education. Instead, the social psychology of education represents an interface of the two fields, which has produced a broad range of theories, research, and data that speak to the interests of educators and psychologists. Researchers in this area have both pushed the theoretical boundaries of the field of social psychology and produced solutions to difficult problems that have eluded solutions from people in other fields, to which the chapters in this volume attest. The oft-quoted words of Kurt Lewin, one of the towering figures of social psychology, are still appropriate: "there is nothing so practical as a good theory" (Lewin, 1951, p. 169).

Although a commonly agreed upon label has yet to evolve – the area has been variously (and somewhat inelegantly) referred to as "the social psychology of education," "educational social psychology," or sometimes

1

even "social educational psychology" – the degree of interest in the subject is substantial.

The number of publications relating to this area in scholarly journals is impressive. For example, a tally of the articles published in the last three years in the *Review of Educational Research* – the major review journal in the educational research field – shows that close to 40% relate directly to topics studied by social psychologists. Moreover, social psychology as a discipline is increasingly emphasizing applications, and education is one of those areas to which its theories are being applied with some frequency. For instance, a recent volume in the series *Applied Social Psychology Annual*, sponsored by the Society for the Psychological Study of Social Issues, was devoted to social psychology applied to education. A number of universities have instituted courses in social psychological factors in education. Also, the increasingly national interest in education has brought with it the realization that many educational issues ranging from the improvement of the quality of schooling to the introduction of technological innovations such as computers have important social psychological components. These examples provide evidence of the growing interest in the area.

This volume has two principal purposes. The first is to examine the major research areas within the social psychology of education. Each chapter presents an author's work that explicitly illustrates how social psychological theory has been used to guide research on a topic of direct relevance to education. Moreover, the range of work represented in this volume will expose readers to the dominant themes in the field.

A second purpose of the book is to provide solid, informed suggestions to educators regarding solutions to current educational problems. Each author was charged with providing as much practical, problem-solving advice for educational practitioners as possible. They have succeeded: The authors move beyond mere "window-dressing" statements and instead, while acknowledging the limitations of their research, elucidate the implications their results presently or at least potentially have for problems facing educators. The chapters here, then, provide information and guidance on both theoretical and applied levels.

The field of social psychology of education: an introduction

The current themes and areas of interest that characterize the field of social psychology of education are exemplified by the chapters in this volume. The major thrusts of the social psychology of education – as represented by the parts and chapters of this book - are best viewed within the broader context of social psychology. The following overview of this book serves as a framework from which to view the field of social psychology of education as well as its relationship to social psychology in general.

Part I: the individual in a social context

It seems somewhat curious that a field devoted to *social* factors in education should, at its most fundamental level, consider the individual. Yet social psychology has always been concerned to a large degree with people in contexts in which social interaction is merely a secondary consideration. Indeed, the field of social psychology has recently seen a resurgence of interest in the concept of self (e.g., Schlenker, 1985). It follows, then, that some of the most basic research being carried out in terms of social psychology of education employs the individual as the major focus of analysis.

Much of the current work within the field relating to the individual unit of analysis is based on attribution theory. Attribution theory is concerned with people's explanations of the causes of behavior - both others' and their own. Growing out of the rich social psychological tradition of person perception, attribution theory has focused on whether people attribute the causes of behavior to the situation or the individual, to ways in which responsibility for success or failure is determined and to how attributional decisions affect subsequent behavior.

Because attribution theory rode the zeitgeist of the 1970s into all corners of social psychology, it is not surprising that it also has had an important impact on research on the social psychology of education. In fact, it is hard to differentiate at which point some of the major theoretical expositions of social psychology leave off and the social psychology of education begins. For example, Bernard Weiner's influential theorizing and research on determining the causes of success and failure (Weiner, 1979, 1985) typically use an experimental paradigm related to *academic* success and failure.

The fruits of this tradition are borne out in the first two chapters in this volume. Forsyth's chapter (chapter 1) considers students' reactions to success and failure from an attributional perspective. He traces the development of attributions of an academic nature, how success and failure impact on the kinds of attribution that are made, the ways in which attributions determine expectancies about future performance, and how attributions affect future behavior.

Graham's chapter (chapter 2), which employs a more narrow and molecular view of attribution theory, uses an attributional approach to explain achievement motivation in black and white children. Her analysis suggests that teachers may communicate unintended messages to minority children, in which their expressions of sympathy for poor performance lead to attributions of low ability on the part of the children. Moreover, Graham suggests ways in which particular instructional strategies may communicate low ability attributions to children, thereby reinforcing poor performance.

Another major division of social psychology of education, which takes a primarily individualistic approach, is the study of attitudes. The study of attitudes comprises one of the oldest areas within social psychology, and it is not surprising that it has spawned a wide range of studies within the field. Research on teacher attitudes and student attitudes, the factors that produce such attitudes, and the impact that attitudes have on behavior have been thoroughly investigated (e.g., Brophy and Good's 1974 volume on teacher–student relationships).

Smith's chapter (chapter 3) in this volume addresses what is probably the most critical issue to grow out of social psychological research on attitudes: the nature of the relationship between attitudes and behavior. He reviews the background of the controversy that has been at the core of the study of attitudes and then applies his analysis to a classroom setting by examining the relationship between classroom behavior and student attitudes toward the subject matter being covered in the class. The work cited in Smith's chapter suggests that attitudes remains a fruitful and important area of study within the context of the social psychology of education.

Part II: teacher–student interaction

One of the core areas of social psychology of education concerns the relationship between teachers and students. Social psychological approaches take the view that the affective and cognitive qualities of the relationship between the two prime players in educational settings are crucial to the nature of ultimate success of the student's performance – and, in a sense, the success of the teacher's performance as well. The distinguishing characteristic of this kind of research is that it is assumed that the behavior of one individual has an effect on the other.

There are different kinds of research that fall under the rubric of teacher–student interaction. One key area is that of teacher expectation effects. Exemplified by the chapter by Harris and Rosenthal (chapter 4), this line of theory and research considers how teachers' expectations about their students are communicated to and affect the performance of their students. As an outgrowth of more theoretical work on self-fulfilling prophecies, this research has developed to the point where Harris and Rosenthal have been able to derive a four-factor theory and trace the degree of support for each factor, using a meta-analytic framework. Work on expectation effects has also been expanded conceptually to encompass how *student* expectations about a teacher's competence as a teacher are transmitted to the teacher and affect the teacher's performance, in a way analogous to the effects of teacher expectations (e.g., Feldman & Theiss, 1982).

Another level of teacher–student interaction is represented by nonverbal behavior. The role of facial expressions, paralinguistic cues, and body movements in the transmission of emotions and other kinds of communication is no less important in teacher–student contexts as it is in any other situation (Woolfolk & Galloway, 1985). In fact, social psychologists' concern over the affective quality of interaction has led them to attend particularly to the nonverbal context of teacher–student interaction.

Several chapters in this volume attest to the importance of nonverbal behavior. For instance, Harris and Rosenthal's chapter on the transmission of teacher expectations demonstrates the importance of the nonverbal channel of eye contact in mediating teacher expectations. Feldman and Saletsky's chapter (chapter 5) focuses directly on nonverbal behavior, considering its role in interracial teacher–student interaction. Their research suggests ways in which teachers may unwittingly communicate negative attitudes toward students of a different race during teaching interactions.

Some investigators have taken a more global approach to classroom interaction, a stance illustrated within the Bar-Tal and Bar-Tal chapter (chapter 6). They point out that classrooms represent social systems, with their own norms, roles, sets of beliefs, and interaction patterns. The actors within these social systems are influenced by each other, and the social system as a whole is greater than the sum of its individual parts.

Part III: cooperation and conflict in the classroom

Cooperation, bargaining, negotiation, and the resolution of conflict have always stood as a central topic within the field of social psychology.

Beginning with the classic studies of Sherif (Sherif et al., 1961), who studied intergroup conflict in a summer camp, studies of cooperation and conflict have evolved into sophisticated mathematical models of the processes underlying bargaining and negotiation (e.g., Miller & Crandall, 1980). During this evolution, several theories of cooperation and conflict have had enormous influence on social psychology: Thibaut and Kelley's social exchange theory (Kelley & Thibaut, 1978; Thibaut & Kelley, 1959), the prisoner's dilemma bargaining paradigm (Rubin & Brown, 1975), and the Deutsch and Krauss (1960) series of studies on cooperation and threat using the Acme-Bolt trucking situation.

Workers in the area of social psychology of education have been influenced by these works in a number of respects, and the area of cooperation and conflict in educational settings has become one of the most active areas within the field. One of the first researchers to build upon this tradition was Aronson, who devised what he called the "Jigsaw" team learning technique (Aronson et al., 1978). In this method, a group of students are each assigned a portion of a lesson to learn; they then must teach their portion to the other members of their group. The success of the group as a whole, as well as each individual, is dependent upon the success of the members in cooperating with each other in the teaching process. The technique has been successful in promoting cooperation among students of different races as well as enhancing group cohesiveness.

Slavin's chapter (chapter 7) in this volume summarizes the current status of work being carried out in this tradition. In his chapter, he discusses a number of techniques for using the benefits of cooperation in school settings, suggesting some very specific classroom interventions designed to enhance learning through the use of cooperative methods. He concentrates on the "Team Assisted Individualization" procedure, in which a complex system of team assignments are used to promote cooperative learning within the classroom.

Miller and Brewer's chapter (chapter 8) takes a more theoretical view of cooperative team techniques. In examining means of promoting positive interracial relations, they provide an elegant evaluation of four theoretical models that can explain the effects of structured intergroup cooperation. Their analysis, and the data that support it, have implications beyond just cooperative learning procedures, extending to such broader areas as homogeneous ability groupings and school desegregation.

In what at first glance seems to be a departure from much of the work in this area - which stresses the positive outcomes of cooperation -

Johnson, Johnson, and Smith (chapter 9) discuss the benefits of creating conflict and controversy within the classroom as a means of enhancing student achievement. They argue that appropriately controlled and structured conflict has the potential for enhancing both learning and social behavior. In actuality, their arguments are not as much at odds with the work on cooperation as it might first seem, because the conflict that works most effectively is that which occurs within the context of cooperation toward an interdependent positive goal. Cooperation, then, is necessary to make controversy effective.

Part IV: social aspects of motivation

Questions regarding the factors that enhance student motivation have played a prominent role in the social psychology of education. While motivation per se has not been a central topical area within the field of social psychology – except for some work on particular needs, such as the need for achievement and affiliation – motivational concepts are employed in a number of ways within the social psychology of education.

Motivational issues are central to a number of chapters in this volume. For instance, both Forsyth's and Graham's chapters in this volume (chapters 1 and 2) look at motivation from an attribution theory perspective, showing how attributions relating to the causes of school success can have a profound influence on motivational factors relating to achievement.

In Part IV of this volume, "The social aspects of motivation," several chapters address student motivation even more centrally than Forsyth's and Graham's. Ames (chapter 10) demonstrates how the learning environment of the classroom is a partial determinant of motivation. She discusses how the classroom environment and structure affect such motivational factors as the cognitive engagement of students, the value that is placed on achievement, student self-perceptions, and even the ways in which students think. The chapter suggests some specific means of enhancing long-term student achievement.

Chapter 11, by Brophy and Kher, reports research examining the ways in which teachers socialize a very specific sort of motivation – what the authors call "the motivation to learn." Here, the focus is on how teacher behavior can produce better and more motivated learners through the use of specific kinds of motivational statements. Building on social learning theory, expectancy x value theory, and work on intrinsic motivation (e.g., Bandura, 1977; Lepper, 1983; Parsons & Goff, 1980), they

suggest ways in training teachers to behave in a way that will socialize
and enhance student's motivation to learn.

The final chapter in this section, by Baden and Maehr (chapter 12),
draws upon a rich tradition both within traditional social psychology and
the social psychology of education of investigating the effects of
sociocultural diversity. They suggest that school culture has a powerful
effect on student motivation and performance, and their work suggests
how such culture can be modified to confront students coming from
diverse sociocultural backgrounds.

Part V: education, culture, and society

Whereas social psychology as a whole has generally shied away from
studying broad social trends and societal institutions, leaving that
approach to sociologists, investigators interested in the social psychology
of education have showed somewhat less hesitation in tackling some of
the broad social issues that are directly related to education. There are at
least two reasons for this. First, social psychologists of education are less
tied to traditional experimental techniques and procedures than are
workers studying more theoretical questions. Second, schools are
institutions, and it is difficult to grapple with some of the more profound
problems of education without taking an institutional and organizational
perspective as an important and necessary level of analysis.

The final two chapters in the volume take such a broader approach.
Chapter 13, by Dubrovsky, Kiesler, Sproull, and Zubrow, examines how
the introduction and use of computers varies within two different college
communities. They describe how the students in the settings are
socialized into the new culture that has arisen due to rapid technological
changes in society – what they call the "computing culture." They discuss
ways in which educational organizations can introduce novices most
effectively into this new culture.

Finally, chapter 14, by Cooper, examines a phenomenon that might be
called the social psychology of the social psychology of education. He
provides a case study of the ways in which the values and attitudes of
researchers in the field of social psychology of education influence their
interpretations of a body of research – in this instance, the reseach on the
effectiveness of desegregation. The topic of desegregation provides a
particularly apt example of social psychology of education: It
demonstrates a classic melding of findings and traditions taken from the
field of social psychology, and it applies them to one of the most difficult

and important educational issues facing society. Yet Cooper's paper also shows that some of social psychology of education is still "promise" as opposed to "reality"; even a panel of experts, using the most sophisticated methodological and analytic tools available to summarize a body of research, were unable to agree fully on the meaning and implications of previous research in the area.

Future prospects

If the present is represented by the chapters in this volume, what does the future hold in store for the field? There are a number of emerging trends that are likely to have wide impact on the future of social psychology of education. Three are substantive (an increasing emphasis on social cognition as a theoretical construct, the development of quasitherapeutic methods based on attribution theory, and the introduction of computers into schools), and one is related to the standing of social psychology of education relative to other subfields of social psychology.

Social cognition: understanding and organizing the world

If one were to identify the hottest topic in traditional, theoretical social psychology during the mid-1980s, it would likely be the increasing emphasis on social cognition. Social cognition is the area that investigates how people understand, organize, and recall information about the world. Encompassing some of the more traditional areas of person perception and attribution theory, it also is built upon more recent findings from the area of cognitive psychology.

The central concept of social cognition is the construct of *schema*. A schema is an organized body of information stored in memory (Fiske & Taylor, 1983; Rummelhart, 1984). The knowledge that is held in a schema provides a representation of the way in which the social world operates. Schemata also provide a means of categorizing and interpreting new information related to the information held in the schema; further, they allow people to organize behavior into meaningful wholes, forming personality types known as prototypes.

Because several of the most fruitful areas of interest to social psychologists of education are particularly amenable to analysis using constructs from social cognition, one prediction that can be made with some confidence is that the concepts of social cognition will become more prevalent in the field. For example, within an educational context, people can be viewed as holding schemata not only for salient objects in their environment – such as classroom, school, or lessons – but also for particular classes of people (teacher, principal, and student, for instance). Moreover, schemata and prototypes extend not just to others but to the self as well, and they are likely to have profound influences on student and teacher behavior within educational settings.

Development of attributional "therapeutic" treatments

Attribution theory, which, had such an important impact on social psychology throughout the 1970s, is likely to continue to have a major influence on the field. One outgrowth that is of particular relevance to the social psychology of education is the development of a number of quasitherapeutic interventions based on attribution theory (Försterling, 1985).

An excellent example of this, with a number of important implications, is seen in the work of Timothy Wilson and Patricia Linville (1982, 1985). In their studies, they devised a program for college freshmen to change the way they view the causes of their own school performance – in essence, modifying their attribution about the causes of success and failure. To do this, Wilson and Linville exposed students to information that demonstrated that difficulties in performance were due to temporary factors that were amenable to change, rather than to permanent, un-modifiable causes.

In the program a group of freshmen who reported difficulties with their first-semester performance were given information showing that most students' performance shows improvement over the course of their college careers. Actual videotaped interviews with upperclassmen were shown, which discussed how their grades had improved during their years in college. Compared to a control group who received no information, the students who received the positive information showed a significant response to the treatment. While 25% of the control group students had dropped out of college by the end of their sophomore year, only 5% of the experimental group had dropped out. In addition, the grade point average of students in the experimental group increased a mean of .34 points, whereas that of the control group declined by .05 points. Finally, students in the experimental group performed significantly better on a battery of test items than did those in the control group.

These results suggest a number of conclusions. First, attributions about one's self are amenable to change. Simply providing salient information about the nature and causes of performance – specifically, that it is brought about by unstable rather than stable causes – is sufficient to bring about improved performance. On a more abstract level, this work raises the possibility of extending social psychological research into the realm of educational "therapy." By modifying attributions relevant to the way in which individuals view themselves and the sources of their problems, it may be possible to systematically "treat," and ultimately alleviate, educational difficulties.

In sum, theory and research relating to attribution theory have the potential for making important contributions to teaching practice. We can predict that people in the field of the social psychology of education will make further use of this work in identifying ways of improving the classroom performance of students and their teachers.

Computers in the classroom

As Dubrovsky et al. point out in chapter 13, there is a technologial revolution in progress that has and will continue to have a profound impact on education. This revolution, the introduction of microcomputers into schools and homes, is a wave that started in the late 1970s and is continuing relatively unabated into the 1980s.

Although most of the research that is currently under way has been directed toward specific learning outcomes that are the outgrowth of working with computers, Lepper (1985) has pointed out that several social psychological issues are critical to understanding the changes computers have made in the schools. Among the major questions are how to harness the intrinsic motivation that sustains computer use in students, what is the relationship between positive affective qualities of computer software and instructional effectiveness, and issues of a broader social nature: how do computers affect social development, family relationships, and social equality across various segments of the population. Each of these issues has at its root a social psychological question, and it is likely that the field of social psychology of education will – or at least ought to – move toward incorporating questions such as these into the field.

Relating the social psychology of education to other applied areas of social psychology

The social psychology of education typically is considered in isolation from other applied areas of social psychology. Yet, if the field of social psychology is observed as a whole, it is clear that there is a general,

growing emphasis on applications of the theoretical underpinnings of the
field, in a variety of areas. Law, health, and the workplace are just some of
the areas to which social psychology is being applied with increasing
vigor.

What does this portend for the social psychology of education? It
suggests that social psychologists of education may come to see
themselves as more closely allied with social psychologists studying
applied research in other areas than with the parent field of social
psychology itself. Ultimately, this may lead to the development of a
general field of "applied social psychology." (Indeed, such an eventuality
may already be underway, as we see the continued growth and
development of series such as the *Applied Social Psychology Annual*, now
in its sixth volume). Although we may lament the specialization of the
field into applied and theoretical camps, the development of a sophisticated field related primarily to social psychological applications could
bring with it the promise of the development of innovative techniques
and procedures that may affect and improve the quality of not only the
social psychology of education but other applied areas as well.

Ultimately, of course, no one's prognostications are certain, and it is
important to reiterate that these are merely informed guesses. What is
certain is that the chapters in this volume represent the best of the current
research in the field of social psychology of education, and a wide variety
of audiences should find it of use. Quite apart from its appeal to scholars
and researchers directly in the area, it is likely that social psychologists
with an interest in applications and educational psychologists with an
interest in social psychology will find it useful. Moreover, because each
chapter addresses the practical implications of the work discussed, the
volume should prove invaluable to practicing educators. Both the present
and the promise of social psychology of education, then, are well
represented in this volume.

References

Aronson, E., Stephan, W., Sikes, J., Blaney, N., & Snapp, M. (1978). *Cooperation in the
classroom*. Beverly Hills, CA: Sage.
Bandura, A. (1977). *Social learning theory*. Englewood Cliffs, NJ: Prentice-Hall.
Brophy, J., & Good, T. (1974). *Teacher – student relationships: Causes and consequences*. New
York: Holt, Rinehart and Winston.
Deutsch, M., & Krauss, R. M. (1960). The effect of threat upon interpersonal bargaining.
Journal of Abnormal and Social Psychology, 61, 181 – 189.
Feldman, R. S., & Theiss, A. (1982). The teacher and student as Pygmalions: The joint effects
of teacher and student expectations. *Journal of Educational Psychology, 74*, 217 – 223.

Fiske, S., & Taylor, S. (1983). *Social cognition*. Reading, Mass: Addison-Wesley.

Fösterling, F. (1985). Attributional retraining: A review. *Psychological Bulletin, 98,* 495–512.

Kelley, H. H., & Thibaut, J. W. (1978). *Interpersonal relations: A theory of interdependence.* New York: Wiley Interscience.

Lepper, M. (1983). Extrinsic reward and intrinsic motivation: Implications for the classroom. In J. Levine & M. Wang (Eds.), *Teacher and student perspectives: Implications for learning*. Hillsdale, N.J.: Erlbaum.

Lepper, M. (1985). Microcomputers in education: Motivational and social issues. *American Psychologist, 40* 1 – 18.

Lewin, K. (1951). *Field theory in social science*. New York: Harper and Row.

Miller, C. E., & Crandall, R. (1980). Experimental research on the social psychology of bargaining and coalition formation. In P. B. Paulus (Ed.), *Psychology of group influence* (pp. 333 – 374). Hillsdale, NJ: Erlbaum.

Parsons, J., & Goff, S. (1980). Achievement motivation and values: An alternative perspective. In L. Fyans (Ed.), *Achievement motivation: Recent trends in theory and research*. New York: Plenum.

Rubin, J. Z., & Brown, B. R. (1975). *The social psychology of bargaining and negotiation*. New York: Academic Press.

Rummelhart, D. E. (1984). Schemata and the cognitive system. In R. S. Wyer, Jr., & T. K. Siull (Eds.), *Handbook of social cognition*. Hillsdale, N.J.: Erlbaum.

Schlenker, B. (Ed.). (1985). *The self and social life*. New York: McGraw-Hill.

Sherif, M., Harvey, O. J., White, B. J., Hood, W. E., & Sherif, C. W. (1961). *Intergroup conflict and cooperation: The Robber's Cove experiment*. Norman: University of Oklahoma Book Exchange.

Thibaut, J. W., & Kelley, H. H. (1959). *The social psychology of groups*. New York: Wiley.

Weiner, B. (1979). Theory of motivation for some classroom experiences. *Journal of Educational Psychology, 71,* 3–25.

Weiner, B. (1985). An attributional theory of achievement and emotion. *Psychological Review, 92,* 548–573.

Wilson, T., & Linville, P. (1982). Improving academic performance of college freshmen: Attribution theory revisited. *Journal of Personality and Social Psychology, 42,* 367–376.

Wilson, T., & Linville, P. (1985). Improving the performance of college freshmen with attributional techniques. *Journal of Personality and Social Psychology, 49,* 287–293.

Woolfolk, A. E., & Galloway, C. M. (1985). Nonverbal communication and the study of teaching. *Theory into Practice, 24,* 77–84.

Part I

The individual in a social and educational context

1   An attributional analysis of students' reactions to success and failure

Donelson R. Forsyth

Like it or not, evaluation is as much a part of education as is learning. In most schools and universities students are regularly tested and evaluated by their teachers, who communicate their appraisals in the form of a grade. When the papers are handed back, the grades are posted, or report cards are sent home, students find out if they have succeeded or if they have failed.

How do students react to these academic evaluations? According to a growing number of studies, the answer to this question depends upon their attributions: students' inferences about the causes of their performances and evaluations. Elaborating on theoretical foundations established by Heider (1958), Jones (Jones, 1978; Jones & Davis, 1965), and Kelley (1967, 1971), these investigations assume that students actively strive to understand the origins of their academic outcomes. They ask not only "What did I get on the test?" but also "Why did I get this particular grade?" In reviewing the results of these investigations, we will concentrate on four basic areas: (1) the nature and dimensionality of attributions formulated in academic settings, (2) the impact of success and failure on attributions, (3) the mediating role of attributions in determining expectations and affective reactions, and (4) the behavioral consequences of various types of attributions.

Attributions and academic outcomes

Students explain their educational outcomes through reference to a wide variety of causal factors. Although evidence indicates that Heider's (1958) classic foursome – ability, effort, luck, and task difficulty – are among the most frequently offered explanations of performance (Bar-Tal, Ravgad, & Zilberman, 1981; Elig & Frieze, 1979; Falbo & Beck, 1979; Frieze, 1976), additional factors are also sometimes suggested as causes. For example,

17

when Forsyth and McMillan (1982) asked 243 college students who had just received feedback about a course examination to describe "what you feel caused your outcome on this test," the students generated over 600 causes. Eliminating highly similar causes, these investigators then asked another group of 119 posttest-feedback students to rate the causal importance of the remaining 175 causes on a five-point scale ranging from "not at all causally important" to "very causally important." Through factor analysis, they then identified the causal factors shown in Table 1.1. The findings of similar investigations are also summarized in this table.

Attributions about outcomes can also be described in terms of underlying dimensions. Although students may attribute their outcomes

Table 1.1. *Unitary attributions in educational settings*

Forsyth & McMillan	Elig & Frieze	Bar-Tal, Goldberg, & Knaani
Good/faulty teaching methods	Motives of others	Teacher's instructional ability
Adequate/inadequate preparation	Effort	Effort for studying Preparation for test Effort during test
Test	Task difficulty	Test difficulty Attentive reading of test
High/low motivation	Intrinsic motives Stable effort Extrinsic motives	Interest in subject Will to succeed Will to prove to others
Personal problems	Personality Physical limitations Fatigue	Mood Self-confidence Health, fatigue Arousal during test
Knowledge	Ability	Ability Memory
Good/bad study habits	Ability/task interaction	Concentration during studying Learning conditions at home Studying load
Luck	Luck	Luck
Support from friends	Others' help	Help in home Cheating
Classroom atmosphere	Teacher's personality Teacher–student interaction	Like teacher
Good/bad textbook	—	Subject matter difficulty

Sources: Bar-Tal et al., 1984; Elig & Frieze, 1975; Forsyth & McMillan, 1982.

to a wide variety of specific, unitary factors like those shown in Table 1.1, many theorists believe that these causal factors are linked to a relatively small number of more fundamental cognitive dimensions. For example, Heider (1958) originally noted the perceptual importance of the inter- nality – externality, or locus of causality, dimension by proposing that ability and effort are both internal, dispositional causal factors, while luck and task difficulty are external, situational factors. However, just as luck is an external factor and ability is an internal one, luck also fluctuates more than ability, suggesting that a second dimension – stability of causes – should be considered when describing attributions (e.g., Frieze & Weiner, 1971; Weiner, 1972; Weiner et al., 1971). More recently, Weiner (1979, 1980) has also suggested that controllability may be the third dimension underlying unitary causal attributions. Although mood and effort are both unstable and internal, Weiner notes that mood is considerably less controllable than effort.

The descriptive adequacy of Weiner's three-dimensional theory (Brown & Weiner, 1984, Weiner, 1983; Weiner & Brown, 1984) has been supported in a number laboratory (Meyer, 1980; Weiner & Kukla, 1970; Wong & Weiner, 1981) and field (Bar-Tal, Goldberg, & Knaani, 1984; Forsyth & McMillan, 1981a; Hayamizu, 1984) studies. However, several investi- gators have suggested that other dimensions may also underlie unitary attributions. For example, when Wimer and Kelley (1982) asked subjects to describe their attributions about a number of events, they discovered five interpretable dimensions: internality (the Person), stability (enduring – transient), good – bad, simple – complex, and motivation. Similarly, when Kelley and Forsyth (1984) factor analyzed students' ratings of the causal importance of 70 unitary causal factors, they discovered five major factors: performance-inhibiting factors, performance-facilitating internal factors, performance-facilitating external factors, performance-inhibiting internal factors, and uncontrollable factors. Other theorists have proposed additional or alternative dimensions – including distinctive- ness, consistency, and consensus (Kelley, 1967, 1971); globality (Abramson, Seligman, & Teasdale, 1978); intentionality (Elig & Frieze, 1975); and achievement orientation, vitality, mastery, energy, attitude, and ability (Falbo & Beck, 1979) – prompting Wimer and Kelley to conclude cautiously that "people can make many possible attributional distinctions" (1982, p. 1161).

Attributions after success and failure

Despite some uncertainty regarding the dimensions underlying students' unitary attributions, the evidence is clear concerning one point: After failure students generally underscore the importance of external causes; after success they tend to emphasize the causal impact of internal factors. This pattern, which has been variously termed attributional asymmetry (Ross & DiTecco, 1975), benefectance (Greenwald, 1980), egocentrism (Forsyth & Schlenker, 1977), or egotism (Snyder, Stephan, Rosenfield, 1978), has occurred in a number of studies conducted in academic settings (see Bradley, 1978; Zuckerman, 1979). For example, Bernstein, Stephan, and Davis (1979) asked college students to describe the cause of their performance after three consecutive examinations. Despite fluctuation in performances and expectations, these researchers found that high-scoring students, relative to low-scoring students, felt effort and ability were more important whereas the ease of the test and luck were less important. Using a similar method, Kovenklioglu and Greenhaus (1978) found that success students emphasized the causal importance of ability and effort; failure students emphasized bad luck and the difficulty of the test. Arkin, Kolditz, & Kolditz (1983) found that test-anxious students who failed tended to blame their character; overall, however, successful students emphasized internal over external attributions, and failing students showed the opposite pattern. Forsyth and McMillan (1981b) found that low scorers' descriptions of their performance in terms of the three dimensions of Kelley's cube model (1971) placed them in the external attribution cells of the cube (high distinctiveness/low consistency/low consensus), whereas high scorers maintained that their performance was low in distinctiveness.

At least three perspectives can account for the impact of academic outcomes on attributions (Forsyth, 1980). First, a number of researchers feel that these attributional asymmetries are self-serving (e.g., Covington & Beery, 1976; Covington & Omelich, 1979; Miller, 1976; Wortman, Costanzo, & Witt, 1973). According to this view, when students succeed they can increase their confidence and sense of personal worth by attributing their performance to internal, personal, or dispositional factors. In contrast, when students fail, they can avoid the esteem-damaging consequences of their performance by denying responsibility for their performance – blaming their grades on such factors as the teacher, their home life, or the difficulty of the material.

Second, a logical, information processing explanation like that proposed by Feather (1969; Feather & Simon, 1971) emphasizes the relationship between anticipated grades and actual performance. According to this approach, if students' outcomes match their expectations – they expect to succeed and pass or expect to fail and flunk – then they tend to attribute their outcomes to stable, internal factors such as ability.

If, however, their outcomes violate their expectations, then they attribute their outcomes to unstable factors – for example, luck, mood, or a more difficult test. As Miller and Ross (1975) note, however, most students usually expect to do well because the covariation between (1) their own behavior and positive outcomes and (2) the environment and negative outcomes is attributionally salient. Thus, individuals tend to see themselves as the cause of positive performances; negative expectations are rare. Although it is likely that in instances of extreme and repeated failure a specific negative expectation will overwhelm the generalized positive one, Miller and Ross maintain that in most achievement situations success, and not failure, is expected.

Bradley (1978) has added a third possible explanation that emphasizes the interpersonal implications of attributions. Because students' performances are often public and the subject of considerable discussion, students attribute poor grades to external factors to avoid the embarrassment of academic failure and attribute good grades to their own effort or ability to create the impression of competence. Bradley (1978, p. 63) writes that attributions are "mediated by a desire to maintain or gain a positive public image (e.g., a public motive) rather than by a concern for one's private image."

These three explanations of the success–internal/failure–external pattern are not necessarily incompatible. As a functional approach to attributions suggests (Forsyth, 1980), in many instances students may become so personally involved in their academic performance that they would experience considerable anxiety if they felt their inability caused their failure or that a too-easy test caused their success. In such cases – when ego-involvement or need for achievement is high (Miller, 1976) – then attributions may be biased by self-serving motivations. However, students may also need to understand the causes of their outcomes if they are going to improve after a failure or maintain a level of success in the future. Therefore, they formulate explanatory, adaptive attributions that explain the outcome and suggest behavioral strategies for improvement or maintenance (Wong & Weiner, 1981). If students wish to project a public image of ability and competence, then they may wish to make certain that their teachers and classmates do not blame them for their failure but do credit them with their successes. When attributions fulfill an interpersonal function, then students can explain "What rotten luck!" or "The test was too hard" after failure and "I'm glad I worked as hard as I did!" or "Good, fair test" after success. This functional view of attribution thus suggests that, dependent upon the circumstances, all three processes can combine to determine attributions after success and failure.

Attributions and expectations

A number of studies based on Weiner's three-dimensional model of attributions indicate that students' attributions are systematically linked to their expectations concerning future performances. For example, in one study (Weiner, Nierenberg, and Goldstein, 1976) college students were told that they had correctly solved a sample problem from an intelligence test. When students were later asked to estimate how many additional problems, out of ten possible, they expected to solve successfully, those students who emphasized the causal importance of stable factors (task difficulty and ability) were more confident than those who attributed their past performance to unstable factors (effort and luck).

Although other studies have reported a similar impact of attributions to stable factors on shifts in expectations (Valle & Frieze, 1976; Weiner, 1974), field studies of students' expectations suggest that the significance of other attributional dimensions should not be underestimated (Bernstein et al., 1979; Forsyth, & McMillan, 1981a). For example, when Forsyth and McMillan examined the expectations of high and low scoring college students whose attributions varied across the internality, stability, and controllability dimensions, they found no effects of stability. Individuals who failed expressed the most negative expectations when they felt that their performance was caused by external, uncontrollable factors; however, individuals who succeeded expressed somewhat more positive expectations when they felt that their score was the product of internal, controllable factors.

In explaining their findings, Forsyth and McMillan argue that controllability may be more important than stability when students are concerned about maintaining or improving their current levels of performance. When success is produced by factors that students can control – effort, motivation, diligence – then they can assume that good scores will occur again. If, however, good grades are attributed to uncontrollable, external factors – an easy test, an excellent substitute teacher, or the topic – then successful students must wonder if they can maintain their high level of achievement. In contrast, if failing students believe that they can control the cause of the poor performance, then they expect to overcome these constraints in the future. If, however, they believe their grade was caused by external, uncontrollable factors – outside pressures or a poor teacher – then they pessimistically conclude that history will repeat itself.

In a related study, Forsyth and McMillan (1981b) found that expectations are also influenced by the attributional dimensions emphasized by

Kelley in his cube model of causal inferences (1967, 1971). According to Kelley, in most situations people formulate causal inferences by attending to three sources of information: distinctiveness, consistency, and consensus. Distinctiveness, in an educational context, is the extent to which a behavior is unique to a particular setting or is much like what occurs in many other settings. For example, if a student fails math, then the student can assess distinctiveness by considering whether his or her grades are low only in math, or if they are low in all subjects. Consistency is an assessment of behavior in similar situations in the past. Has the student always failed math, or does this outcome only apply to the present school, teacher, class, or unit? Consensus information is gathered by comparing personal reactions with other students' reactions. Are all the students in this class failing math, or is the student one of the few who is performing poorly?

To apply the model, Forsyth and McMillan asked students who had just received feedback concerning their scores on their third examination in a college course to estimate distinctiveness ("Is this grade typical of how you are doing in your *other classes?*"), consistency ("Is this grade about the same as your past grades on tests in this class?"), and consensus ("Do you think a very large proportion of the class got about the same grade that you did?"). Based on these responses, students were then assigned to one of the eight cells of the 2 (high vs. low distinctiveness) x 2 (high vs. low consistency) x 2 (high vs. low consensus) attribution cube.

When describing their expectations concerning the fourth test, students who received *A*s or *B*s reported more positive expectations than students who received *C*s or less. However, this impact of performance on expectations only held if students felt that consistency over time was high. If students earned a grade that they believed was inconsistent with their previous test scores, then the impact of both distinctiveness and consensus was more pronounced. High scoring students were still quite positive about their chances for a good grade, unless they also believed their score was highly distinctive (they were performing poorly in other classes) and low in terms of consensus (many other students in the course received lower grades). Such patterns would occur if students were attributing their performance to largely uncontrollable but personal factors, such as mood, inspired guessing, or extreme effort in this course alone. Among low scoring, low consistency subjects, expectations tended to be more negative if students felt their grade was similar to grades they had received in other classes (low distinctiveness) and relatively unique in comparison to other students' scores (low consensus). However, one group of low scoring, low consistency students – those who felt their outcome was low in distinctiveness but high in consensus – were quite positive in their expectations. Apparently they felt that the test was too difficult or that the material had been poorly covered, and that these factors would change in the future.

Attributions and affective reactions

After receiving feedback about their examination scores, students do not respond by just formulating causal analysis and revising expectations about future grades. They also experience a range of emotional reactions after the success or failure on the exams. In fact, outcome alone – irrespective of the students' attributions – has a major impact on their global emotional state. As commonsense experience suggests, relative to their successful counterparts, students who fail describe themselves as less relaxed, satisfied, content, elated, and pleasantly surprised and more unhappy, tense, incompetent, inadequate, upset, depressed, guilty, and hostile (Forsyth & McMillan, 1981a; McMillan & Forsyth, 1983). No matter what caused the outcome, students still experience a negative emotional state when they fail and a positive emotional state when they succeed.

Several theorists, however, have suggested that attributions can moderate affective reactions in some instances. For example, Weiner and his colleagues (e.g., Weiner, 1980; Weiner, Russell, and Lerman, 1978, 1979) have drawn a distinction between outcome-dependent affect and attribution-dependent affect. Using role-play methods in which subjects are asked to imagine or recall successes or failures on examinations, Weiner found that some affective reactions – such as happiness, confidence, depression, disappointment, disgust, and upset – were outcome-dependent; they were influenced only by the exam grade. Other affects, however, were associated with specific, unitary causes. Weiner noted that attributions to ability engendered feelings of competence and pride after success but feelings of incompetence, resignation, and unhappiness after failure. Effort attributions were associated with relief, satisfaction, and contentment after success but fear and guilt after failure. If a performance was attributed to the efforts of others, subjects reported feeling gratitude, thankfulness, and excitement when they succeeded but anger when they failed. Furthermore, attributions emphasizing luck were linked to feelings of surprise after both success and failure, although success subjects also reported feeling guilt and relief while failures felt sad and stupid.

These findings, however, have not gone unchallenged. First, when students' attributions and affective reactions are assessed immediately after they receive examination feedback in their classes, outcome tends to dominate their affective response; even those reactions that Weiner considers attribution-dependent – competence, fear, guilt, and surprise – are overwhelmed by the more powerful impact of outcome (Forsyth & McMillan, 1981a; Frieze, Snyder, & Fontaine, 1977; Kelley & Forsyth, 1984). Second, linkages between attributions and affects that Weiner considers outcome-dependent have been obtained in several studies (e.g., Forsyth & McMillan, 1981a; Kelley & Forsyth, 1984). For example, Forsyth and McMillan (1981a) found that, independent of outcome, students who felt that controllable factors caused their performance experienced more positive emotions than students who attributed their grade on an examination to uncontrollable factors.

Third, some of these studies report attribution-affect linkages that contradict those described by Weiner. For example, Bailey, Helm, and Gladstone (1975) found that attributions to the test after success resulted in as much positive affect as attributions to internal factors, such as ability or effort. Likewise, Covington and Omelich (1979, 1981, 1984; Covington, Spratt, & Omelich, 1980) have repeatedly maintained that individuals will experience greater pride after success and shame after failure when they feel their ability, rather than their effort, caused their outcome. In addition, Arkin, Detchon, & Maruyama (1982) found the following attribution-affect linkages: ability with interest (success) and shame (failure); effort and luck with joy (success) and distress (failure); and test difficulty with surprise (success) and fear (failure).

According to an attribution "network" model proposed by Kelley and Forsyth (1984) these empirical inconsistencies could be resolved if both attributions and affective reactions were conceptualized as multi-dimensional, dynamic processes. As summarized in Figure 1.1, the network model includes four primary components: attributional dimensions, unitary attributions, global affective reactions, and unitary affective reactions. Looking first at attributions, the model predicts that students' perceptions of their test performances are both dimensional and unitary. For example, after learning they have failed a test, students implicitly ask themselves such questions as "Was it something about me that caused my failure?" "Did something about this situation cause me to fail?" and "Did something beyond my control cause me to fail?" Furthermore, they also seek information about specific, unitary causes within these general attributional dimensions, including ability, effort, test difficulty, and luck.

Turning to affective reactions, recent studies indicate that emotions can also be conceptualized as unitary, discrete, monopolar states or as global,

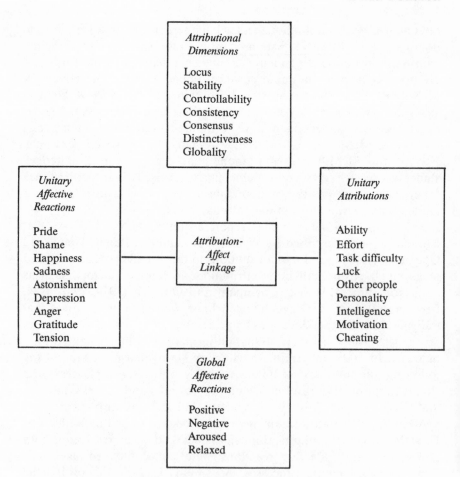

Figure 1.1. A network model of attribution-affect linkages in educational settings.

multidimensional reactions. For example, through factor analyses of self-reported affective states, several investigators have identified distinct emotional states, including sad, anxious, angry, elated, tense, relaxed, excited, and aroused (e.g., Izard, 1972; Nowlis, 1965). Other theorists, however, prefer to view emotions in dimensional terms. For example, Schlosberg (1952), by examining the errors that people make when inferring emotions from facial expressions, concluded that specific emotional states can be classified along two fundamental dimensions: pleasant–unpleasant and attention–rejection. Osgood, Suci, and

Tannenbaum (1957) argued that three dimensions account for the semantic meaning of most affective expressions: evaluation, activity, and potency. Russell (1978, 1979, 1980, 1983) has repeatedly argued that two dimensions are sufficient to describe affective experiences: pleasure – displeasure and degree of arousal. Moreover, Daly, Lancee, and Polivy's conical model (1983) is based on three dimensions: pleasantness, activity, and intensity.

The dimensional models and the unitary models complement one another (Russell & Steiger, 1982). Just as attributions can be described in both unitary and dimensional terms, unitary affective states can be linked to more global emotional dimensions. Although individuals may experience a global, dimensional reaction when they succeed or fail on a test, they may also describe this general emotional state with a discrete, unitary label, such as anger, depression, misery, happiness, bliss, or elation.

Applied to attribution-affect linkages, the network model posits complex interrelationships among both dimensional and unitary attributions and affective reactions. Although the temporal sequencing of cognitive and affective processes is the subject of considerable debate (Lazarus, 1984; Zajonc, 1984), one possible sequence might begin when students receive their grades on an exam. First, this information elicits a global affective reaction, which ranges from positive to negative and involves a degree of arousal or relaxation. At this stage, the emotional process is largely data-driven – a psychological reaction to valenced environmental stimuli.

Second, students formulate global attributional explanations for their outcomes. Although these attributional reactions include attributions to factors that vary in terms of such dimensions as stability, controllability, and globality, in this initial stage of cognitive processing students are primarily focused on facilitating–inhibiting factors and personal–nonpersonal factors.

Third, specific, unitary labels are then assigned to both the affective experiences and causal factors. At this point in the sequence, attribution-affect linkages are formed. For example, students who feel that their failure is due to inhibiting, nonpersonal factors will likely attribute their outcome to the instructor's poor teaching ability and experience anger. In contrast, students who feel that they, personally, controlled their performance will experience pride while attributing their outcome to effort. The direction of causality linking attributions and affects is not yet known, but a reciprocal model in which each influences the other should not be discounted (Stephan & Gollwitzer, 1981).

Several studies support these tentative predictions of the network approach shown in Figure 1.1. For example, Forsyth and McMillan (1981a) found that global affective reactions were linked to feelings of controllability; irrespective of performance, students who thought they controlled the causes of their outcome experienced a more positive emotion than students who thought their performance was caused by uncontrollable factors. Furthermore, the locus of the cause (internal or external) and the nature of the performance (success or failure) were linked to specific emotions: Students who believed their good performance was the product of internal causes felt more competent and adequate, whereas students who attributed their poor performance to internal factors felt more incompetent and inadequate.

Kelley and Forsyth (1984) also tested the multidimensional model. As described earlier, these investigators assessed a wide range of unitary causal forces, including ability, effort, task difficulty, and luck. They also measured affect using 28 unitary adjectives drawn from Russell's circumplex model (1980). These adjectives were selected to sample the affective space described by the model and included the words tense, bored, calm, astonished, and aroused. In addition, four items that Weiner (1980) feels are particularly important in educational settings – ashamed, competent, proud, and confused – were also included.

Through factor analysis, these investigators identified five factors underlying the students' responses to the 32 affect items: negative affect (frustrated, sad, miserable, depressed, angry, etc.), positive affect (glad, delighted, pleased, proud, happy, etc.), calm (calm, relaxed, at ease, tranquil), sleepiness (sleepy, drowsy, tired), and arousal (astonished, excited, alarmed, aroused). Furthermore, analysis of the attributions yielded five factors: inhibiting factors (poor teaching methods, poor preparation, poor textbook, poor test, low motivation, personal problems), facilitating personal factors (high motivation, good study habits, adequate preparation), uncontrollable factors (luck, help from friends, intelligence), external facilitating factors (good teaching methods, classroom atmosphere, good textbook), and personal limitations (bad mood, emotional problems; all items that loaded on the personal-limitations factor also loaded on the inhibiting-causes factor, suggesting considerable overlap).

These findings lend support to the "dimensionality" assumption: Both unitary affects and attributions are systematically related to fundamental affective and attributional dimensions. However, the dimensions that were obtained aren't completely consistent with previous empirical findings. For example, Russell maintains that affective dimensions are bipolar – they range from positive to negative – but Kelley and Forsyth identified independent unipolar dimensions – positive affect and negative affect. Similarly, a stability dimension was not identified in the attributions, although internality, controllability, and facilitative dimensions were in evidence.

Attributions and students' behaviors

Attributions also influence a range of academic behaviors, including examination performances, persistence at difficult intellectual tasks, and even attendance at study sessions. Looking first at the impact of attributions on examination performance, Bernstein et al. (1979) found that the more students attributed their grades on the first test in a course to their personal ability and the ease of the test, the lower their grade on the next test. According to Bernstein et al., these students may have become too complacent; by relying on their ability and assuming the test would be easy, they failed to study enough for the second test. Furthermore, Bernstein et al. found that students who attributed their performance on the second test to their effort when studying tended to earn higher grades on the third test. Although attributions and grades were not significantly related in a study conducted by Covington and Omelich (1979), attributions were correlated with expectations, which were, in turn, related to performance.

Recent conceptualizations of learned helplessness also underscore the impact of attributions on motivation, persistence, and performance (Abramson et al., 1978; Garber & Seligman, 1980; Wortman & Dintzer, 1978). Although Seligman (1975) originally proposed that students experience helplessness whenever their outcomes are independent of their behaviors, laboratory studies soon indicated that attributions mediate the relationship between noncontingency and helplessness. The reformulated model, as proposed by Abramson et al. (1978), hypothesizes that students who attribute aversive outcomes to certain causes are more likely to show signs of helplessness: motivational deficits, negative expectations about future performances, a depressed emotional outlook, and self-blame.

Global attributions imply to the individual that when he confronts new situations the outcome will again be independent of his responses. So, if he decides that his poor score was caused by his lack of intelligence (internal, stable, global) or his exhausted condition (internal, unstable, global) . . . he will expect that here, as well, outcomes will be independent of his responses, and the learned helplessness deficits will ensue. If the individual makes any of the four specific attributions for a low math score, helplessness deficits will not necessarily appear. (Abramson et al., 1978, pp. 57-58).

Some of the clearest support for an attributional model of learned helplessness comes from Dweck's studies of helpless and mastery-oriented students (Diener & Dweck, 1978, 1980; Dweck, 1975; Dweck & Bush, 1976; Dweck & Licht, 1980; Dweck & Reppucci, 1973; Goetz & Dweck, 1980). In one early project (Dweck & Reppucci, 1973) fifth graders were given insoluble problems by one female "teacher" and soluble problems by another teacher. When the teacher who originally gave the insoluble problems switched to soluble problems, a number of children continued to perform poorly; apparently they attributed their earlier failure to the teacher and the difficulty of the problems she assigned and thus became helpless. Furthermore, the children who evidenced the greatest helplessness were those who blamed their failure on lack of ability. Students who performed the best tended to emphasize the causal role played by effort.

In subsequent research Dweck and her colleagues have found that helpless children and mastery-oriented children behave similarly after successes, but when failure occurs they display dramatically divergent reactions. Among mastery-oriented children "effort is escalated, concentration is intensified, persistence is increased, strategy use becomes more sophisticated, and performance is enhanced" (Dweck & Licht, 1980, p. 197). In contrast, when helpless children fail, "efforts are curtailed, strategies deteriorate, and performance is often severely disrupted." In one demonstration of these differences, Diener and Dweck (1978) asked children who were failing on a cognitive task to "think out loud" about what they were doing. When they examined the content of these verbalizations, they discovered that 52% of the helpless questioned their ability, while none of the mastery-oriented students mentioned ability. In addition, mastery-oriented students emphasized effort and luck more than the helpless students. In a subsequent study, Diener and Dweck (1980) also found that helpless students, when given a series of tasks followed by immediate feedback about success and failure, underestimated their successes, overestimated their failures, and avoided attributing their performances to ability.

Dweck (Dweck, Goetz, & Strauss, 1980; Dweck et al., 1978) also believes that attributions may be partly responsible for certain sex differences in academic achievement. Dweck et al. (1978) found that males tend to be exposed to more negative feedback than females, but they tend to attribute this feedback to nonability factors such as the teacher's attitude or their own lack of effort. In contrast, failure feedback for females focuses on ability. In consequence, girls, more so than boys, tend to attribute their successes to external factors, while blaming themselves for their failures (Deaux, 1976). In some instances, girls also show decreased persistence after failure, impaired performance when threatened with failure, and more negative expectations when compared with boys (Dweck et al., 1978).

Ames and Lau (1982), in a study of help-seeking after failure on a test, also found sex differences; males, in comparison to females, were more likely to attend help sessions before the next examination. In addition, Ames and Lau discovered that attempts to seek help were also related to students' attributions to internal and external factors. Drawing a distinction between help-relevant and help-irrelevant attributions, these investigators predicted that low scoring students would be most likely to seek academic help when their attributions matched the following pattern: (a) relatively few attributions to overall ability (they are generally confident in their intellectual skills); (b) specific attributions focusing on their lack of understanding of key concepts or particular topics; (c) attributions to low effort in the form of lack of studying and preparation; and (d) an avoidance of help-irrelevant attributions, such as "ambiguous test questions" or "poor teacher." As predicted, 62% of the students who attributed their failure to help-relevant factors attended these sessions; only 43% of the failing students who blamed their outcomes on help-irrelevant causes sought help.

Changing attributions to improve outcomes

To summarize briefly, an attributional analysis of students' reactions to their educational outcomes assumes students implicitly identify the causes of their successes and failures. This attributional process results not only in attributions to specific, unitary causes such as ability, effort, task difficulty, and luck, but also in inferences about such attributional dimensions as internality and controllability. Students who perform well generally internalize their success while less successful students emphasize the causal significance of environmental factors, but this attributional pattern may be due to several interrelated processes, including self-serving biases, logical information processing, and self-presentational concerns. Attributions are also systematically linked to expectations about future performance in the course, as well as emotional reactions to examination feedback. According to a multidimensional model of attribution-affect linkages, these relationships occur at both the dimensional and the unitary affective and attributional level. In addition, attributions influence behavior, for certain attributional patterns lead to poor performance, reduced persistence, helplessness, and failures to seek academic help.

Given that attributions influence educational achievement (McMillan & Forsyth, 1981), educators should help their students arrive at the most adaptive, educationally beneficial causal conclusions possible. For example, the bulk of the evidence indicates that the student's first attributional inclination after failure – externalization – does not facilitate learning, help-seeking, or increased persistence. Also, while some students clearly take credit for their failures, when this self-blame reaches extreme levels, it can result in debilitating losses in motivation, persistence, and achievement. To counteract these "natural" attributional tendencies, educators should encourage students to explore the causes of their successes and failures, while guiding them toward achievement-promoting conclusions about causality.

What attributions promote academic achievement? Although additional research is needed, several studies suggest that attributions to controllable, unstable factors may facilitate academic performances after failure. For example, in one study Dweck (1975) identified 12 children who showed extremely maladaptive responses after failure: negative expectations about their performance, performance deficits following negative feedback, and low persistence on difficult tasks. She then trained six of these children to attribute their failures to a lack of effort rather than ability. For a 25-day period, these students worked on a series of arithmetic problems while the experimenter-teacher watched. While students received success feedback on most of the problems, at various intervals the teacher told the student he or she hadn't performed the problems quickly enough. In all cases, however, the teacher then stated "You should have tried harder." The remaining six students were exposed to success feedback only; they were never told that they failed.

Before the students' training, halfway through the experiment, and after the training the students' reactions to negative feedback were measured by asking them to solve sets of difficult math problems. As predicted, only the trained students persisted at these difficult problems, and when they did receive failure feedback they attributed their performance to a lack of effort. The students in the success-only conditions, in contrast, continued to show a severe deterioration in persistence when they learned they had failed.

Wilson and Linville (1982) have extended these findings to college students, but rather than trying to shift students from ability attributions to effort attributions, they sought to convince first-year college students that their grades were caused by unstable, rather than stable, factors. In a brief presentation, the subjects were told that, on the average, college students improve their grades during their educational careers. They were also shown videotaped testimonials of advanced students describing how poor first-year grades had improved over the course of their academic career. Relative to "untreated" students, the students who received the information (a) were less likely to drop out at the end of their second year, (b) achieved greater increases in their grade point averages, and (c) performed better on sample items from the Graduate Record Exam. Although the impact of this attributional intervention may have been due partly to regression toward the mean and attrition (Block & Lanning, 1984), the findings have been replicated (Wilson & Linville, 1985).

Other attributional strategies may be more effective after students receive success feedback. For example, in an elaborate study of math achievement in second-graders, Miller, Brickman, and Bolen (1975) assigned inner-city Chicago public school students to one of six experimental conditions: ability attribution, effort attribution, ability persuasion, effort persuasion, reinforcement, and a no-treatment control. Students in all but the last group were exposed to a series of verbal and written comments from their teachers, letters from the principal, and medals matched to their particular treatment. In the ability attribution condition, these messages reiterated the student's ability with such messages as: "You are doing very well in arithmetic" and "You are doing very good work." The achievement medal read "good student – math." In the effort attribution condition, the messages emphasized motivation – "You really work hard in arithmetic" and "You're working harder, good!" and the medal stated "hard worker – math." The messages in the ability and effort persuasion conditions were similarly phrased, but in every case they included a persuasive request such as "You should be doing well in arithmetic" or "You should work harder." The medals in these two conditions read "do better – math" and "work harder – math". Students in the reinforcement condition received a series of positive comments and awards ("very good," "excellent," and "math award"), while the students in the control group received no treatment whatsoever.

When students' scores on a math test given before, immediately after the eight days of treatment, and two weeks after the termination of the special treatments were compared, Miller and his colleagues found that only the students in the two attribution conditions showed improvement. Furthermore, the attribution treatment continued to produce increases in performance, while scores in the two persuasion conditions tended to drop once the experiment was terminated. Overall, the ability attribution treatment was the most effective, the effort attribution treatment was the next most effective method, the reinforcement and ability persuasion conditions were moderately effective, and the effort persuasion and control conditions were the most ineffective. These findings were recently replicated by Schunk (1983), who arranged for children who were deficient in subtraction skills to perform a series of workbook problems. Periodically during these exercises, they received attributional feedback that focused on the causal importance of (a) their ability, (b) their effort, or (c) their effort and ability. A control group that received no attributional information was also included. As in the Miller et al. study, the children given ability feedback performed best, whereas the children in the control condition performed worst. The students in the effort only and the ability plus effort conditions achieved intermediate scores.

These findings suggest that instructors must remain sensitive to students' attributional reactions to test feedback. In general, if students who do poorly in class conclude there is nothing they personally can do to change their outcomes, then their failure could undermine their motivation and satisfaction with self and school work. However, if the teacher encourages students to associate failure with factors that can be controlled, then the debilitating consequences of failure may be avoided. In contrast, by emphasizing the importance of internal factors as causal agents after success, teachers may further ensure continued success.

References

Abramson, L. Y., Seligman, M. E. P., & Teasdale, J. D. (1978). Learned helplessness in humans: Critique and reformulation. *Journal of Abnormal Psychology, 87*, 49–74.

Ames, R., & Lau, S. (1982). An attributional analysis of student help-seeking in academic settings. *Journal of Educational Psychology, 74*, 414–423.

Arkin, R. M., Detchon, S. S., & Maruyama, G. M. (1982). The role of attribution, affect, and cognitive interference in test anxiety. *Journal of Personality and Social Psychology, 43*, 1111–1124.

Arkin, R. M., Kolditz, T. A., & Kolditz, K. K. (1983). Attributions of the test-anxious student: Self-assessments in the classroom. *Personality and Social Psychology Bulletin, 9*, 271–280.

Bailey, R. C., Helm, B., & Gladstone, R. (1975). The effects of success and failure in a real-life setting: Performance, attribution, affect, and expectancy. *Journal of Personality, 89*, 137–147.

Bar-Tal, D., Goldberg, M., & Knaani, A. (1984). Causes of success and failure and their dimensions as a function of SES and gender: A phenomenological analysis. *British Journal of Educational Psychology, 54*, 41–61.

Bar-Tal, D., Ravgad, N., & Zilberman, D. (1981). Development of causal perception of success and failure. *Educational Psychology, 1*, 231–240.

Bernstein, W. M., Stephan, W. G., & Davis, M. H. (1979). Explaining attributions for achievement: A path analytic approach. *Journal of Personality and Social Psychology, 37*, 1810–1821.

Block, J., & Lanning, K. (1984). Attribution therapy requestioned: A secondary analysis of the Wilson-Linville study. *Journal of Personality and Social Psychology, 46*, 705–708.

Bradley, G. W. (1978). Self-serving biases in the attribution process: A reexamination of the fact or fiction question. *Journal of Personality and Social Psychology, 36*, 56–71.

Brown, J. & Weiner, B. (1984). Affective consequences of ability versus effort ascriptions: Controversies, resolutions, and quandaries. *Journal of Educational Psychology, 76*, 146–158.

Covington, M. V., & Beery, R. (1976). *Self-worth and school learning.* New York: Holt, Rinehart and Winston.

Covington, M. V., & Omelich, C. L. (1979). Are causal attributions causal? A path analysis of the cognitive model of achievement motivation. *Journal of Personality and Social Psychology, 37*, 1487–1504.

Covington, M. V., & Omelich, C. L. (1981). As failures mount: Affective and cognitive consequences of ability demotion in the classroom. *Journal of Educational Psychology, 73*, 796–808.

Covington, M. V., & Omelich C. L. (1984). Controversies or consistencies? A reply to Brown and Weiner. *Journal of Educational Psychology, 76*, 159–168.

Covington, M. V., Spratt, M. F., & Omelich, C. L. (1980). Is effort enough or does diligence count too? Student and teacher reactions to effort stability in failure. *Journal of Educational Psychology, 72*, 212–229.

Daly, E. M., Lancee, W. J., & Polivy, J. (1983). A conical model for the taxonomy of emotional experience. *Journal of Personality and Social Psychology, 45*, 443–457.

Deaux, K. (1976). Sex: A perspective on the attribution process. In J. H. Harvey, W. J. Ickes, & R. F. Kidd (Eds.), *New directions in attribution research* (Vol. 1, pp. 335–352). Hillsdale, NJ: Erlbaum.

Diener, C. I., & Dweck, C. S. (1978). An analysis of learned helplessness: Continuous changes in performance, strategy, and achievement cognitions following failure. *Journal of Personality and Social Psychology, 36*, 451–462.

Diener, C. I., & Dweck, C. S. (1980). An analysis of learned helplessness: II. The processing of success. *Journal of Personality and Social Psychology, 39*, 940–952.

Dweck, C. S. (1975). The role of expectations and attributions in the alleviation of learned helplessness. *Journal of Personality and Social Psychology, 31*, 674–685.

Dweck, C. S., & Bush, E. S. (1976). Sex differences in learned helplessness: I. Differential debilitation with peer and adult evaluators. *Developmental Psychology, 12*, 147–156.

Dweck, C. S., Davidson, W., Nelson, S., & Enna, B. (1978). Sex differences in learned helplessness: II. The contingencies of evaluative feedback in the classroom and III. An experimental analysis. *Developmental Psychology, 14*, 268–276.

Dweck, C. S., Goetz, T. E., & Strauss, N. L. (1980). Sex differences in learned helplessness: IV. An experimental and naturalistic study of failure generalization and its mediators. *Journal of Personality and Social Psychology, 38*, 441–452.

Dweck, C. S., & Licht, B. G. (1980). Learned helplessness and intellectual achievement. In M. E. P. Seligman & J. Barger (Eds.), *Human helplessness: Theory and application* (pp. 197–221). New York: Academic Press.

Dweck, C. S., & Reppucci, N. D. (1973). Learned helplessness and reinforcement of responsibility in children. *Journal of Personality and Social Psychology, 25*, 109–116.

Elig, T. W., & Frieze, I. H. (1975). A multi-dimensional coding scheme for coding and interpreting perceived causality for success and failure events. *JSAS Catalog of Selected Documents in Psychology, 5*, 313. (Ms. No. 1069)

Elig, T. W., & Frieze, I. H. (1979). Measuring causal attributions for success and failure. *Journal of Personality and Social Psychology, 37,* 621–634.

Falbo, T., & Beck, R. C. (1979). Naive psychology and the attributional model of achievement. *Journal of Personality, 47,* 185–195.

Feather, N. T. (1969). Attributions of responsibility and valence of success and failure in relation to initial confidence and task performance. *Journal of Personality and Social Psychology, 13,* 129–144.

Feather, N. T., & Simon, J. G. (1971). Attribution of responsibility and valence of outcome in relation to initial confidence and success and failure of self and other. *Journal of Personality and Social Psychology, 18,* 173–188.

Forsyth, D. R. (1980). The functions of attributions. *Social Psychology Quarterly, 43,* 184–189.

Forsyth, D. R., & McMillan, J. H. (1981a). Attributions, affect, and expectations: A test of Weiner's three dimensional model. *Journal of Educational Psychology, 73,* 393–401.

Forsyth, D. R., & McMillan, J. H. (1981b). The attribution cube and reactions to educational outcomes. *Journal of Educational Psychology, 73,* 632–641.

Forsyth, D. R., & McMillan, J. H. (1982, August). Reactions to educational outcomes: Some affective and attributional correlates. Paper presented at the annual meeting of the American Psychological Association, Washington, DC.

Forsyth, D. R., & Schlenker, B. R. (1977). Attributing the causes of group performance: Effects of performance quality, task importance, and future testing. *Journal of Personality, 45,* 220–236.

Frieze, I. H. (1976). Causal attributions and information seeking to explain success and failure. *Journal of Research in Personality, 10,* 293–305.

Frieze, I. H., Snyder, H. N., & Fontaine, C. M. (1977, August). Student attributions and the attribution model during actual examinations. Paper presented at the annual meeting of the American Psychological Association, San Francisco, CA.

Frieze, I. H., & Weiner, B. (1971). Cue utilization and attributional judgments for success and failure. *Journal of Personality, 39,* 591–606.

Garber, J., & Seligman, M. E. P. (Eds.) (1980). *Human helplessness: Theory and applications.* New York: Academic Press.

Goetz, T. E., & Dweck, C. S. (1980). Learned helplessness in social situations. *Journal of Personality and Social Psychology, 39,* 246–255.

Greenwald, A. G. (1980). The totalitarian ego: Fabrication and revision of personal history. *American Psychologist, 35,* 603–618.

Hayamizu, T. (1984). Changes in causal attributions on a term examination: Causal dimensions. *Japanese Psychological Research, 26,* 1–11.

Heider, F. (1958). *The psychology of interpersonal relations.* New York: Wiley.

Izard, C. E. (1972). *Patterns of emotions.* New York: Academic Press.

Jones, E. E. (1978). Update of "From acts to dispositions: The attribution process in person perception." In L. Berkowitz (Ed.), *Cognitive theories in social psychology* (pp. 331–336). New York: Academic Press.

Jones, E. E., & Davis, K. E. (1965). From acts to dispositions: The attribution process in person perception. In L. Berkowitz (Ed.), *Advances in experimental social psychology* (Vol. 2, pp. 219–266). New York: Academic Press.

Kelley, H. H. (1967). Attribution theory in social psychology. In D. Levine (Ed.), *Nebraska symposium on motivation.* Lincoln: University of Nebraska Press.

Kelley, H. H. (1971). *Attribution in social interaction.* Morristown, NJ: General Learning Press.

Kelley, K. & Forsyth, D. R. (1984, April). Attribution-affect linkages after success and failure.

Paper presented at the Annual meeting of the Eastern Psychological Association, Baltimore, MD.

Kovenklioglu, G., & Greenhaus, J. H. (1978). Causal attributions, expectations, and task performance. *Journal of Applied Psychology, 63*, 698–705.

Lazarus, R. S. (1984). On the primacy of cognition. *American Psychologist, 39*, 124–129.

McMillan, J. H., & Forsyth, D. R. (1981). The impact of social psychological factors on school learning: An overview. *Representative Research in Social Psychology, 12*, 20–31.

McMillan, J. H., & Forsyth, D. R. (1983). Attribution-affect relationships following classroom performance. *Contemporary Educational Psychology, 8*, 109–118.

Meyer, J. P. (1980). Causal attribution for success and failure: A multivariate investigation of dimensionality, formation, and consequences. *Journal of Personality and Social Psychology, 38*, 704–718.

Miller, D. T. (1976). Ego involvement and attributions for success and failure. *Journal of Personality and Social Psychology, 34*, 901–906.

Miller, D. T., & Ross, M. (1975). Self-serving biases in the attribution of causality. Fact or fiction? *Psychological Bulletin, 82*, 213–225.

Miller, R. L., Brickman, P., & Bolen, D. (1975). Attribution versus persuasion as a means for modifying behavior. *Journal of Personality and Social Psychology, 31*, 430–441.

Nowlis, V. (1965). Research with the Mood Adjective Checklist. In S. S. Tomkins and C. E. Izard (Eds.), *Affect, cognition, and personality*. New York: Springer.

Osgood, C. E., Suci, G. J., & Tannenbaum, P. H. (1957). *The measurement of meaning*. Urbana: University of Illinois Press.

Ross, M., & DiTecco, D. (1975). An attributional analysis of moral judgments. *Journal of Social Issues, 31*, 91–109.

Russell, J. A. (1978). Evidence of convergent validity on the dimensions of affect. *Journal of Personality and Social Psychology, 36*, 1152–1168.

Russell, J. A. (1979). Affective space is bipolar. *Journal of Personality and Social Psychology, 37*, 345–356.

Russell, J. A. (1980). A circumplex model of affect. *Journal of Personality and Social Psychology, 39*, 1161–1178.

Russell, J. A. (1983). Pancultural aspects of the human conceptual organization of emotion. *Journal of Personality and Social Psychology, 45*, 1281–1288.

Russell, J. A., & Steiger, J. H. (1982). The structure in persons' implicit taxonomy of emotions. *Journal of Research in Personality, 16*, 447–469.

Schlosberg, H. (1952). The description of facial expressions in terms of two dimensions. *Journal of Experimental Psychology, 44*, 229–237.

Schunk, D. H. (1983). Ability versus effort attributional feedback: Differential effects on self-efficacy and achievement. *Journal of Educational Psychology, 75*, 848–856.

Seligman, M. E. P. *Helplessness*. (1975). San Francisco: W. H. Freeman.

Snyder, M. L., Stephan, W. G., & Rosenfield, D. (1978). Attributional egotism. In J. Harvey, W. Ickes, & R, Kidd (Eds.), *New directions in attribution research* (Vol. 2, pp. 91–117). Hillsdale, NJ: Erlbaum.

Stephan, W. G., & Gollwitzer, P. M. (1981). Affect as a mediator of attributional egotism. *Journal of Experimental Social Psychology, 17*, 443–458.

Valle, V. A., & Frieze, I. H. (1976). Stability of causal attributions as a mediator in changing expectations for success. *Journal of Personality and Social Psychology, 33*, 579–587.

Weiner, B. (1972). *Theories of motivation: From mechanism to cognition*. Chicago: Rand McNally.

Weiner, B. (1974). *Achievement motivation and attribution theory*. Morristown, NJ: General Learning Press.

Weiner, B. (1979). A theory of motivation for some classroom experiences. *Journal of Educational Psychology, 71*, 3-25.

Weiner, B. (1980). The role of affect in rational (attributional) approaches to human motivation. *Educational Researcher, 9* (July-August), 4-11.

Weiner, B. (1983). Some methodological pitfalls in attribution research. *Journal of Educational Psychology, 75*, 530-543.

Weiner, B., & Brown J. (1984). All's well that ends well. *Journal of Educational Psychology, 76*, 169-171.

Weiner, B., Frieze, I., Kukla, A., Reed, L., Rest, S., & Rosenbaum, R. M. (1971). *Perceiving the causes of success and failure*. Morristown, NJ: General Learning Press.

Weiner, B., & Kukla, A. (1970). An attributional analysis of achievement motivation. *Journal of Personality and Social Psychology, 15*, 1-20.

Weiner, B., Nierenberg, R., & Goldstein, M. (1976). Social learning (locus of control) versus attributional (causal stability) interpretations of expectancy of success. *Journal of Personality, 44*, 52-68.

Weiner, B., Russell, D., & Lerman, D. (1978). Affective consequences of causal ascriptions. In J. H. Harvey, W. J. Ickes, & R. F. Kidd (Eds.), *New directions in attribution research* (Vol. 2, pp. 59-90). Hillsdale, NJ: Erlbaum.

Weiner, B., Russell, D., & Lerman, D. (1979). The cognitive-emotion process in achievement-related contexts. *Journal of Personality and Social Psychology, 37*, 1211-1220.

Wilson, T. D., & Linville, P. W. (1982). Improving the academic performance of college freshmen: Attribution therapy revisited. *Journal of Personality and Social Psychology, 42*, 367-376.

Wilson, T. D., & Linville, P. W. (1985). Improving the performance of college freshmen with attributional techniques. *Journal of Personality and Social Psychology, 49*, 287-293.

Wimer, S., & Kelley, H. H. (1982). An investigation of the dimensions of causal attribution. *Journal of Personality and Social Psychology, 43*, 1142-1162.

Wong, P. T. P., & Weiner, B. (1981). When people ask "Why" questions, and the heuristics of attributional search. *Journal of Personality and Social Psychology, 40*, 650-663.

Wortman, C. B., Costanzo, P. R., & Witt, T. R. (1973). Effects of anticipated performance on the attributions of causality to self and others. *Journal of Personality and Social Psychology, 27*, 372-381.

Wortman, C. B., & Dintzer, L. (1978). Is an attributional analysis of the learned helplessness phenomenon viable? A critique of the Abramson-Seligman-Teasdale reformation. *Journal of Abnormal Psychology, 87*, 75-90.

Zajonc, R. B. (1984). On the primacy of affect. *American Psychologist, 39*, 117-123.

Zuckerman, M. (1979). Attribution of success and failure revisited, or: The motivational bias is alive and well in attribution theory. *Journal of Personality, 47*, 245-287.

2   An attributional perspective on achievement motivation and black children

Sandra Graham

In 1969 Irwin Katz concluded a review of the literature on motivational processes in minority children with the following rather sobering lament: "It is all too obvious ... that psychologists have contributed little to the understanding of motivational problems of disadvantaged students. Scientific knowledge has barely advanced beyond the conventional wisdom of the teacher's lounge" (p. 23). Despite considerable progress in the field of motivation over the past 15 years, there may be some lingering truth to this critique. Personality approaches such as locus of control or self-esteem and behavioral orientations such as delay of gratification or reward preference have dominated the study of minority motivation since Katz's review, yet both research traditions continue to be hampered by methodological and conceptual inconsistencies. This chapter should dispel some of the cynicism implied in the opening quotation by presenting a social cognitive perspective on minority motivation.

Rather than focus on personality traits or situationally defined behavior as determinants of motivation, a social cognitive approach is concerned with people's cognitive representations of their environment: their perceptions, inferences, and interpretations of social experience. For example, a cognitive social psychologist might investigate how a student interprets her teacher's praise of a successful performance to infer personal competence: Did my teacher praise me because she believes me to be a capable student? Or does she simply want to protect my feelings because she does not think much of my ability? The particular cognitive representations addressed in this chapter are causal attributions, or inferences about why outcomes occur. Causal attributions are central to a theory of motivation that has proved to be exceedingly rich and applicable to a wide range of phenomena (see Weiner, 1985). A major goal of this chapter is to demonstrate how this theory can be a useful conceptual framework for investigating motivational patterns in minority populations.

39

The following section "Causal Attributions," begins with a brief overview of the major principles of an attributional model of motivation, principles that have been formalized in the work of Weiner and his colleagues (see Weiner, 1984; 1985). These principles form the base of a program of research that my colleagues and I have undertaken to examine motivational processes in minority children. The investigations presented here were conducted in a comparative racial framework – that is, we examine attributional patterns in black and white children who also differ in social class. Particular advantages of this approach are included as well as some general beliefs about how minority motivation might productively be studied. Finally, I describe some of the implications of our work for understanding attributional patterns of minority children in the classroom.

Causal attributions

"Why did I get a poor grade on the exam? Why didn't I make the team? Why doesn't my teacher like me?" The answers to such queries are causal attributions. As implied in these examples, some categories of experience are particularly conducive to causal search. For example, we are more likely to ask *why* following failure rather than success and in response to unexpected as opposed to anticipated outcomes (Folkes, 1982; Wong & Weiner, 1981). Causal search is therefore functional because it may impose order on a sometimes uncertain environment.

In achievement contexts, success and failure typically are ascribed to some ability factor that includes both aptitude and acquired skills, a motivation factor such as temporary or sustained effort, the difficulty of the task, luck, personality, and help or hindrance from others (see Cooper & Burger, 1980). Among these causal ascriptions, ability and effort appear to be the most dominant perceived causes of success and failure. When explaining achievement outcomes, individuals tend to attach the most importance to what their perceived competencies are and how hard they try.

What factors are known to influence attributions for performance? How do students know, for example, whether they failed a test because they are low in ability or because they did not try hard enough? Certainly an individual's knowledge about himself or herself, such as prior performance and typical effort expenditure on tests, are important sources of attributional information, as is performance relative to others. If an exam is easy and everyone but the student in question succeeds, that student is likely to question his or her ability. Attribution research has identified a number of cues such as prior performance history and social norm information that influence causal ascriptions (Kelley & Michela, 1980).

It seems reasonable to suppose that what a teacher communicates to students also will be an important source of information that students then use to infer self-ascriptions. Teachers no doubt often directly and intentionally tell students that they didn't try hard enough, for trying hard has moral implications and is certainly compatible with the work ethic espoused in school. On the other hand, one assumes that teachers do not intentionally tell their students that they are low in ability. Later on in this chapter I will return to this issue when I document how certain teacher communications might indirectly function as low ability cues.

Causal dimensions

What does it mean if a student attributes failure to, for example, low ability versus lack of effort, or success to an easy task rather than high aptitude? One's intuition suggests that it is more desirable to believe that successes imply personal competence and that failures are surmountable through individual effort. Indeed, if one surveyed a random sample of school-age children one would probably find near universal consensus that success due to high ability is preferable to success because of good luck and that failure attributed to not trying is more desirable than failure because of low aptitude. But why should this be so? What do these causal preferences mean in the context of an attributional theory of motivation?

It appears that meaning, or what a cause connotes in a particular context, can reveal something about the underlying properties of that cause. Three such properties, labeled causal dimensions, have been identified thus far: locus, stability, and controllability (Weiner, 1984). As its name implies, the locus dimension defines the location of a cause as internal or external to the individual. This causal property also has been captured in other motivation constructs such as locus of control (Rotter, 1966), the Origin-Pawn distinction (deCharms, 1968) and the notion of being intrinsically versus extrinsically motivated (Deci, 1975; Lepper & Greene, 1978). Among the dominant causes, ability and effort are internal because they reflect characteristics of the individual. Task difficulty and luck, on the other hand, are external or environmental determinants of outcomes. The stability dimension designates causes as constant or varying over time. Ability is stable in that one's aptitude for a task is relatively fixed, while effort and mood are unstable because individuals may vary from one situation to the next in how hard they try and in how they feel. Finally, the controllability dimension refers to personal responsibility, or whether a cause is subject to one's volitional influence. Effort is controllable because individuals are believed to be responsible for how hard they try. In contrast, aptitude and luck are generally perceived to be beyond one's personal control.

Causes therefore are classifiable within one of the eight cells of a locus x stability x controllability dimensional matrix. Ability is an internal, stable, and uncontrollable cause. This means that failure due to low ability is perceived as a characteristic of the failing individual, enduring over time, and beyond one's personal control. The dimensional placement of effort, on the other hand, indicates that this cause is internal, unstable, and controllable. Failure ascriptions to lack of effort, therefore, indicate a personal characteristic that is modifiable by one's own volitional behavior. These conceptual distinctions are central to the attributional model because causal dimensions are linked to a number of important psychological processes in achievement settings.

In attribution theory the causal dimension of stability is most closely linked to expectancy for success. Attributions for outcomes to stable causes lead to smaller changes in future expectations than do inferences to unstable causes. For example, when failure is attributed to low aptitude one is more certain of future failure than when the same outcome is ascribed to an unstable factor like temporary illness. Note that aptitude and illness, which differ on the stability dimension, are similar on the other two dimensions – both are generally perceived as internal and uncontrollable. Hence, causal stability rather than locus or controllability is the key mediating variable between inferences about the causes of performance and expectations for the future. These relations hold equally for both success and failure and are consistent with what is intuitively reasonable: If the causes of events are likely to remain unchanged (stable), then one has greater confidence that these events will be repeated in the future than if the causes are subject to change.

The controllability dimension of causality has distinct consequences for interpersonal evaluation. Consider, for example, how teachers might differentially evaluate their students based on the perceived causes of the students' successes or failures. A great deal of evidence documents that high effort is rewarded more than high ability following success and that lack of effort is punished more than lack of ability following failure (Harari & Covington, 1981; Weiner & Kukla, 1970; Weiner & Peter, 1973).

Furthermore, the most rewarded student is the individual who tries hard but has low ability (imagine the teacher's evaluation of the retarded child who works to capacity). In contrast, the least rewarded or most punished is the individual who has high ability but does not try (consider the teacher's reaction to the bright child who never completes assignments). Attribution theorists believe that the differences between ability and effort on the controllability dimension rather than, for example, on the stability dimension account for this differential use of reward and punishment. Recall that the controllability dimension connotes personal responsibility: Individuals "ought" to try and they tend to be rewarded and punished to the extent that they exercise this responsibility.

Causal dimensions and affect

In addition to expectancy and interpersonal evaluation, affect also plays a role in the attributional conception presented here, although the emergence of general principles linking particular feelings to specific causal ascriptions and dimensions is a recent development. In an early formulation of the attributional model, pride and shame were considered to be the only important achievement-related emotions and only the locus dimension was linked to these emotional reactions (Weiner et al., 1971). As it became apparent that this single linkage did not adequately capture the richness of affective life in achievement contexts, subsequent research began to identify a full range of emotions of increasing complexity that could be understood using attributional principles (see Weiner, 1982; Weiner & Graham, 1984).

The least complex emotions that individuals may experience following success or failure are outcome-dependent affects such as happy and sad. A student may feel happy when receiving an *A* on an exam whether that high grade was due to effort, luck, or help from others. Similarly, a student may feel sad when receiving a failing grade regardless of the particular cause of the failure. In contrast, a second cluster of affects in achievement contexts are linked to specific attributions. For example, following failure attributed to low ability, individuals often experience humiliation and embarrassment (Brown & Weiner, 1984). On the other hand, failure because of lack of effort tends to elicit guilt. In addition, specific emotions are linked to external causes of outcomes. Success ascribed to help from others gives rise to gratitude while failure due to others' hindrance leads to anger. And success or failure attributed to luck tends to elicit surprise. All of the emotions in these examples are attribution-dependent because they follow specific causal perceptions about why outcomes occur (Weiner, Russell, & Lerman, 1978, 1979).

Causal dimensions also play an important role in emotional reactions to success and failure. Each dimension, in fact, is related to a particular cluster of emotions (see Weiner, 1984). The locus dimension primarily is linked to pride and other esteem-related affects. We feel pride when we succeed because of our aptitudes, efforts, or personal characteristics, whereas negative self-esteem is the consequence of attributing failure to these internal factors. The stability dimension is linked to affects that implicate future expectations. For example, stable causes for failure give rise to hopelessness, apathy, or resignation – in other words, feelings associated with the belief that one's prospects will not improve in the future. The controllability dimension is linked to the specific emotions of sympathy, anger, and guilt (Graham, Doubleday, Guarino, 1984; Weiner, Graham, & Chandler, 1982). One feels guilty when the causes of personal failure are due to controllable factors. This includes not only lack of effort but also any other causal ascription that is subject to one's volitional influence. Sympathy and anger are emotions directed toward others that also are influenced by perceived controllability. We feel sympathy toward an individual whose failure is due to uncontrollable factors such as low ability but angry toward the person when failure is perceived as caused by controllable factors such as lack of effort.

Note how this analysis incorporates both self-directed and other-directed emotions. One might imagine a situation, for example, where a student does poorly on an exam because of some intentional behavior on his or her part (e.g., not paying attention). The teacher responds with anger and the student feels guilty. Alternatively, poor performance due to low aptitude leads to embarrassment on the part of the student and sympathy from the teacher. Thus, one strength of the attributional perspective presented here is that the psychology of emotions, or how one feels about oneself, and the social psychology of emotions, or how one feels about others, both fit the conception.

Summary

The major principles of an attributional theory of motivation have been presented. These principles address (1) the antecedents of causal search; (2) the dominant self-ascriptions for success and failure; (3) the underlying characteristics of these self-ascriptions, labeled causal dimensions;

and (4) the linkages between causal dimension and a number of psychological processes. The first of these principles indicates that one is more likely to ask *why* questions following failure rather than success and after unexpected as opposed to anticipated outcomes. Once a causal search is undertaken, the second principle identifies the dominant causal ascriptions for success and failure. In the achievement domain, ability (aptitude) and effort appear to be the most important factors, although other salient causes include task characteristics, teacher bias, mood, luck, and others' help or hindrance. These causes are then characterized along the three dimensions of locus, stability, and controllability (principle 3). Finally, the fourth principle indicates that causal dimensions are linked to important psychological consequences. The stability dimension is related to expectancy for success, the controllability dimension is linked to interpersonal evaluation, and all of the dimensions are uniquely related to a prevalent set of achievement-related affects that includes pride, guilt, gratitude, shame, anger, sympathy, and hopelessness. These psychological processes then influence a variety of motivational indicators including persistence, choice, and quality of performance.

The breadth of phenomena addressed by these principles sets the attributional model apart from other dominant motivational conceptions. While other theories are organized around a single cognitive construct such as expectancy (e.g., Rotter, 1966) or but a small set of emotions like pride and shame (e.g., Atkinson, 1964), the attributional theory presented in this chapter accounts for a wide range of cognitions and emotions with one set of interrelated constructs. Furthermore, the cognitions and affects encompassed by the theory might prove particularly useful for examining motivational processes in minority populations. A theory that deals so integrally with perceived control, interpersonal evaluation, expectations for success, and esteem-related affect must surely have particular relevance to minority populations. At least since the publication of the Coleman Report almost 20 years ago, these are the variables that most attracted the attention of researchers who seek to understand the psychosocial dimensions of the minority child's school experience. Since these school experiences so often are marked by chronic academic failure, theories guiding research with this population must explicitly address how individuals conceptualize and cope with failure. As indicated in the preceding sections, causal search and its subsequent impact on achievement strivings is most evident in situations of failure. Thus the theory has a particular concern with nonattainment of goals as well as some probable consequences of this

state such as low self-esteem, low expectations, and negative achievement-related affect.

A conceptual framework has been outlined, and in the process some of
my own biases have been disclosed. I now turn to the work that my
colleagues and I have undertaken to begin to examine motivational
processes of minority children within an attributional perspective.

Motivational patterns in black children: an attributional analysis

Before describing our research program, it is appropriate to comment on
the findings of other studies in this area, indicating how our perspective is
different from the prior work. Although the total number of studies is
surprisingly small, two methodologies generally have been employed to
investigate attributional patterns of black populations. One set of studies
has examined attributions of black students following success or failure
at a specific achievement task (Friend & Neale, 1972; Murray & Mednick,
1975). In general these studies suggest that blacks tend to rate external
factors of task difficulty (ease) and luck as the most important determinants of success and failure. It should be evident from the review in the
previous sections of this chapter that such an attributional pattern may
be maladaptive in certain respects. Attributions to external factors
mitigate personal responsibility for outcomes: one is not likely to
experience pride in success or believe that failure is surmountable
through personal effort.

A second type of study has employed a role-playing methodology to
examine black children's causal inferences about the outcomes of
hypothetical others (McMillan, 1980; Weiner & Peter, 1973). For example,
these studies have reported that disadvantaged minority children punish
hypothetical students less for lack of effort and reward them less for high
effort than do their white middle-class counterparts. The implicit
message in studies of this type is that minority children may attach less
value to effort as a cause for achievement outcomes.

Three of the aforementioned four studies (Murray & Mednick, 1975 is
the exception) were comparative in design – that is, the attributional
judgments of blacks and whites were contrasted and blacks were found to
endorse the less adaptive attributional pattern. These findings are
certainly compatible with the dominant view in the motivation literature
of blacks as more externally oriented than whites (e.g., Battle & Rotter,
1963) and less capable of sustained effort (e.g., Katz, 1969). In the one
recent investigation documenting no differences between blacks and

whites in their attributions for overall school performance (Willig, et al., 1983), the authors concluded that attributions may not be a relevant variable for studying motivational patterns in black children.

One possible drawback of these studies that might make such interpretations premature is their emphasis only on the content of causal inferences to the virtual exclusion of other important principles of the attributional model of motivation. Documenting similarities and differences between ethnic groups in the endorsement of particular causes has only limited value unless one also investigates the *meaning* of disparate attributions among the populations studied as well as the process of attributional reasoning that we described earlier. Suppose, for example, that we were to document that black children, relative to their white counterparts, are more likely to attribute their academic failures to bad luck. Recall from the earlier discussion of causal dimensions that we tend to conceptualize luck as an external, unstable, and uncontrollable causal factor. The instability of the failure attribution should lead to relatively favorable expectations for future success and there should be no undermining of esteem-related affect. But suppose that black students perceive luck as a relatively stable characteristic that is internal to them (e.g., "I'm always an unlucky person"). In this case, a child's perception of the cause might lead to low expectations for future success and enhanced negative affect. Thus the same luck self-ascription might have a different meaning for different students depending on how its dimensional properties are conceptualized. In our studies not only have we attempted to describe differences between ethnic groups in the content of attributions but also we have undertaken racial comparisons in the dimensionalization of causes and the linkages between causal thoughts and other achievement-related cognitions predicted by the attributional model.

A second point of departure between the work to be described here and earlier research in the area is that the failure to find differences between ethnic groups is not problematic to our conceptualization. Because all of our comparative racial research has been guided by the goal of investigating fundamental attribution principles, we interpret the presence of differences between blacks and whites as leading to theory refinement and the absence of differences as indicating theory generalization. In the following sections I examine the generality and possible refinement of principles related to the antecedents of causal attributions, the dominant perceived causes of success and failure, and the psychological consequences of causal ascriptions among black and white children.

Sympathy and anger as antecedent attributional cues

Our first comparative racial study examined the possibility that the emotions of sympathy and anger might be sources of attributional information. Why these particular affects? Recall from the earlier discussion of causal dimensions and affect that feelings of sympathy or anger toward others are in part determined by the perceived controllability of outcomes. Thus a teacher might feel sympathetic toward the handicapped child experiencing academic difficulty but angry toward the lazy student who just does enough to get by. We have documented linkages between sympathy and uncontrollable causes such as low ability and between anger and controllable factors such as lack of effort in a number of investigations with adults and children as young as five years of age (Graham, et al., 1984; Weiner, Graham, & Chandler, 1982; Weiner, Graham, Stern, & Lawson, 1982).

Now suppose that a teacher does react with sympathy or anger toward a failing student. What might these affective displays mean for the student to whom they are communicated? If feelings of sympathy and anger are determined by causal attributions and if these feelings are indeed communicated, then perhaps affects will function as attributional cues that students process and use to make causal inferences about themselves. In other words, a failing student might gain information about the causes of her own failure, such as whether that poor performance was due to low ability or lack of effort, based on the affective displays of teachers.

We investigated affects as cues guiding self-perception in a laboratory study involving failure induction (Graham, 1984). Sixth-grade participants were given four trials of repeated failure on a novel puzzle-solving task. Following failure, a female experimenter posing as a teacher conveyed either sympathy, anger, or no affective reaction. Children were randomly assigned to one of the three affect conditions. The affective cue consisted of the verbal label of the emotion and a set of predetermined nonverbal behaviors specific to each affect (see Graham, 1984, for details on the method). Children then reported their own self-ascriptions for failures in response to the question, "Why do you think you did poorly on these puzzles?" We anticipated that children would be more likely to believe that failure was due to low ability when sympathy was conveyed and that failure was caused by lack of effort when an experimenter communicated anger. Since causal attributions are believed to influence other achievement-related cognitions and behavior, we also investigated children's expectancies for success, their perceptions of competence, and their persistence at the puzzle-solving task in the face of failure. In sum, we predicted a cluster of cognitions and behavior that included sympathy, low ability, low expectancy, low competence, and low persistence that would contrast with linkages involving anger, lack of effort, high expectancy, high competence, and high persistence following failure.

As attribution theorists we assume that the function of affects as attributional cues will apply quite generally to a broad segment of the population. On the other hand, the specific theoretical linkages investigated here seemed particularly suitable for comparative racial study. We wondered, for example, whether disadvantaged black children, many of whom experience chronic failure in school settings, might be particularly susceptible to cues that convey low ability attributions for poor performance. Since there are no data bearing directly on this issue, our research participants included both black and white sixth-grade children. Furthermore, to avoid confounding race and social class (SES), within each racial group children also were designated middle- or low-SES according to a standard socioeconomic index. Thus there were two goals to this research. One purpose was to examine whether affects are sources of attributional information and within this theoretical context, the second goal was to investigate the attributional patterns of minority children following personally experienced failure.

We turn first to the attribution principle (the effects of affective cues) because the data were quite similar across all four demographic groups. Children reported their causal attributions in response to the affective cue by rating the extent to which their poor performance was due to low ability, lack of effort, a difficult task, or bad luck. The findings revealed no differences in task difficulty or luck attributions as a function of the emotional display by the experimenter. In other words, affective feedback provided no cues pertinent to external attributions for failure. This was in contrast to the two internal attributions that were influenced by the manipulation. As predicted, children were most likely to attribute their failure to low ability when the experimenter was sympathetic. Although the effort data were not as strong (there was a general tendency for participants in this study to perceive themselves as trying hard), children given the anger cue attributed their failure more to lack of effort than did children in the other two conditions. In sum, affective cues guided self-perception and this was particularly true for the sympathy–low ability linkage. Expectancy for success was also lower when sympathy was conveyed and there was a tendency for children given the sympathy cue to perceive themselves as less competent and to persist less on the puzzle-solving task.

S. GRAHAM

Having documented the generality of the attributional principle
guiding this research, we can now turn our attention to the race and class
effects that emerged in this investigation independent of the experimental
manipulation. Figures 2.1, 2.2, and 2.3 show attributions, expectancies,
and perceptions of competence on the task by demographic group.
Attributions were measured after the fourth failure trial, expectancies
were reported before each trial, and perceived competence judgments
were made immediately before and after the failure trials. What is most
striking in these figures is the distinctive motivational pattern displayed
by middle-class black children. Turning first to attributions (Figure 2.1)
middle-SES white, low-SES white, and low-SES black children did not
differ in their attributions to any of the four causes. When the affective
manipulation was not taken into account, these three groups basically
attributed poor performance on the puzzles to low ability and task
difficulty. In contrast, among middle-class black children the most
dominant self-ascription was lack of effort and these children were less

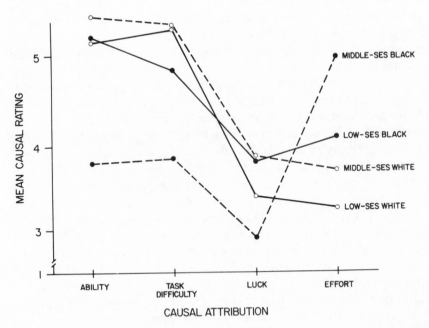

Figure 2.1. Causal attributions for failure within each race × SES group. (High
numbers indicate greater attributions to low ability, lack of effort, a difficult task,
and bad luck.)

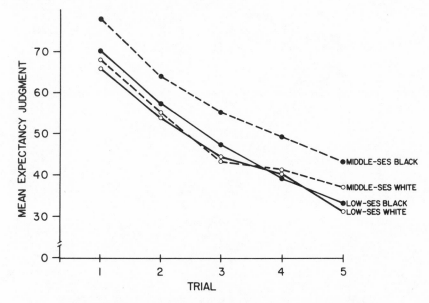

Figure 2.2. Trial-by-trial expectancies within each race × SES group. (Scales range from 0 to 100. High numbers indicate greater expectancies.)

likely than the other three groups to report that they were low in ability or that the task was too difficult. Similarly, middle-class blacks maintained consistently higher expectancies for success across failure trials (Figure 2.2) and they perceived themselves as more competent (Figure 2.3). Like their attributions, the expectancies and perceptions of competence of middle-SES black children were quite resilient even in the face of repeated failure. Adding performance to this distinctive pattern of achievement-related cognitions, our findings indicate that middle-class black children displayed greater persistence at the task than did any of the other three demographic groups. Such a systematic pattern of race and class effects has not previously been documented.

It is not at all clear why middle-class black children showed this particularly adaptive attributional pattern, although some speculations regarding their task focus have been offered (see Graham, 1984). What is clear, however, to the motivation theorist interested in comparative racial study is how infrequently research in this area has focused on economically advantaged populations. Middle-class blacks often have been ignored altogether in previous studies because many investigators

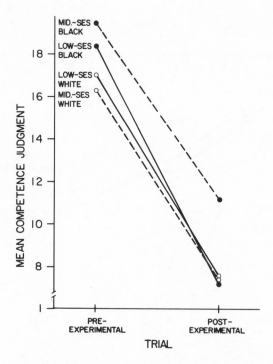

Figure 2.3. Perceived competence judgments within each race × SES group. (Scales range from 1 to 25. High numbers indicate perceptions of higher competence.)

erroneously compare low-SES blacks and middle-SES whites on the motivational variable of interest. Another possible reason for the neglect is that middle-SES blacks simply do not fit our dominant stereotypes of deviant minorities or special populations. One researcher, for example, justified his neglect of middle-class blacks by describing them as "uninteresting persons who present neither social pathology or remarkable success." (Fortunately I can no longer recall the exact source of this pernicious statement.) Furthermore, when a middle-SES black group has been included in comparative studies, investigators typically have highlighted an atypical motivational pattern among disadvantaged blacks while stressing the similarities between middle-SES blacks and whites (e.g., Havinghurst, 1976). The implicit message from studies of this type is that class is a more important factor than race in examining black–white differences in motivation, and that when SES is controlled, racial differences disappear (also see Yando, Seitz, & Zigler, 1979). These views, as well as the confounding of race and class in much previous research, have operated to obscure the black middle class as a potentially rich source of information about motivational processes of minority populations. Our findings indicate the need to look more closely at this demographic group to perhaps facilitate our understanding of the factors that influence positive self-perception and sustained achievement strivings among black children when failure is encountered.

The perceived causes of success and failure among black and white middle-school children

In our next investigation, we progressed from antecedents to actual causes and we shifted from a failure induction paradigm to retrospective recall in order to investigate the dominant perceived causes of achievement among black and white adolescents. Some researchers who question the generality of attribution principles with culturally diverse groups have argued that success and failure have different meanings for individuals who differ in ethnicity (e.g., Maehr & Nicholls, 1980). We wanted to explore this issue of meaning by examining how black and white children organize their causal world in response to success and failure. Our goal was to determine whether children who differ in race and social class report similar causes for personal success or failure and whether or not they perceive the underlying characteristics (dimensions) of these causes in a similar manner.

Our research participants were black and white seventh-grade students who again were designated as middle- or low-SES. Children first were instructed to recall a time when they did well or poorly on a school exam (outcome was a between-subjects factor) and to list all the possible causes that might explain why they succeeded or failed. A free-response format was used to avoid cuing children toward particular self-ascriptions. We then asked the participants to select the most important cause from their list and to rate that cause on the three dimensions of locus, stability, and controllability.

On the average children listed about three causes in both success and failure conditions. These causes were classified into categories (11 for success and 9 for failure) with 97% interrater agreement. The categories with greater than 5% representation among at least one of the four race x SES groups are shown in Table 2.1. This table also displays the proportion of children in each demographic group whose perceived most important cause was drawn from a particular causal category.

Table 2.1. *Perceived causes of success and failure within each race × SES group (in percentages and proportions)*

Causal Category	Mid-SES Black		Low-SES Black		Mid-SES White		Low-SES White	
Success								
Effort	52.2^a	$(.71)^b$	64.7^a	$(.81)^b$	46.3^a	$(.84)^b$	62.5^a	$(.80)^b$
Ability	10.1		5.9		8.8	(.04)	3.2	
Others' help	5.8		17.6	(.06)	3.8	(.04)	6.3	(.13)
Task ease	2.9		2.9		6.3		6.3	
Positive mood	5.8	(.04)	5.9		16.3		3.1	(.07)
Intrinsic interest	5.8	(.13)	2.9	(.06)	6.3	(.08)	3.1	
Extrinsic factors	8.7	(.04)	0.0		1.3		3.1	
Physiological condition	2.9		0.0		7.5		12.5	
Failure								
Lack of effort	39.4	(.83)	44.9	(.84)	37.7	(.64)	51.9	(.83)
Lack of ability	6.3	(.11)	8.7		9.1	(.12)	7.7	
Task difficulty	3.1	(.05)	5.8		5.2		1.9	
Negative mood	0.0		7.2	(.08)	11.7	(.08)	3.8	
Lack of interest	6.3		7.2		10.4	(.12)	11.5	
Poor strategy	6.3		11.6		11.7	(.04)	0.0	
Illness	9.4		1.4		0.0		5.8	
Home factors	6.3		10.1	(.08)	9.1		9.6	(.05)

Note: Columns of numbers may not equal 100% because not all causal categories are included.
[a]Percentage of total causes.
[b]Proportion of children selecting this category as the most important cause.

Among the causes for success, effort factors included both pretest preparation and concentration during the exam. The ability factor was captured by such self-ascriptions as "I'm smart," "I learn fast," and "I knew all the material." Others' help included extra assistance from one's parents, peers, or teacher. Positive mood state was defined by such statements as feeling "up," confident, relaxed, or calm. Extrinsic factors indicated a desire for approval from parents or teachers, and physiological condition was defined as having had a good breakfast on the morning of the test or having gotten enough sleep the night before.

It is evident in Table 2.1 that effort factors were by far the dominant self-ascription for success across all four demographic groups. In addition, there were specific causes more often reported by a particular race × SES group. For example, help from others as a cause for success was listed more often by low-SES black children than any of the other three demographic groups, whereas self-ascriptions to positive mood were most dominant among middle-class whites.

Turning next to the failure condition, Table 2.1 shows that lack of effort was also the dominant reported cause for doing poorly on an exam. Similar to the success factor, lack of effort included both inadequate preparation prior to the exam as well as inattentiveness (e.g., goofing off, daydreaming) during actual test taking. Note that lack of effort and low ability together represented approximately 46% to 60% of the listed causes in each demographic group. Among the other causal categories, home factors included family or personal problems such as an argument with a parent the night before the exam; poor strategies included careless mistakes, not checking one's answers, guessing, or not following the directions; and negative affect entailed reports of having been nervous, stressed, or under pressure.

Like success, some causes were more dominant among particular demographic groups. For example, middle-class whites were more likely to recall nervousness or stress as a cause for failure, whereas illness as a cause was most dominant among middle-class blacks. On the whole, however, the distribution of causes across race × SES groups was more even in the failure than in the success condition.

To examine the meaning (dimensional placement) of their dominant perceived causes, recall that we asked our research participants to select the most important cause for their success or failure and to rate that cause on the three causal dimensions. Following an explanation of each dimension, ratings were made on 9-point scales anchored at the extremes by "internal–external," "lasting–temporary," and "controllable–uncontrollable" for the locus, stability, and controllability dimensions, respectively.

Once again, there was great similarity in the judgments across the four race x SES groups. All children dimensionalized the most important cause for their success at a school test as relatively internal, stable, and controllable. In other words, they perceived their success as due to some personal characteristic, under their volitional control, and enduring over time. Given failure, the cause was perceived as somewhat less internal and controllable but considerably more unstable. Thus what most distinguished children's perceptions of success versus failure was the stability of the cause for success. Because we can assume that these ratings largely capture the dimensional placement of effort (see Table 2.1), it may be that the intention to succeed or the perception of oneself as "effortful" is a relatively long-lasting causal factor underlying success for all of these children. The possibility that effort may have stable properties has been documented in other recent investigations with adult subjects (see Dalal, Weiner, & Brown, 1984) and represents a refinement over prior conceptions of effort as unstable for both success and failure.

In sum, the children in this investigation employed a rather circumscribed set of causes when explaining prior success or failure at a school exam. Although some ascriptions were more prevalent among particular demographic groups, the clearest pattern to emerge was the importance of effort for success and lack of effort for failure across all demographic groups. Furthermore, the meaning (dimensional placement) of this cause was similar for all groups and is consistent with attributional principles. There appears to be a simplicity or economy quite prevalent in this culture in children's thinking about the causes of academic success and failure.

The consequences of causal ascriptions

In the next phase of this study we presented our research participants with hypothetical vignettes so that we could systematically examine some of the consequences of causal ascriptions (Graham & Long, in press). Children were asked to imagine that they succeeded or failed an important exam and this time a cause for the outcome was specified. For example, in the success condition children were told: "Imagine this situation. You just did well on an important test. You did well because you *tried hard*." Six causes for either success or failure were presented to the children in counterbalanced order. In addition to effort, these causes included ability, good or poor strategy, luck, task difficulty (ease), and help or hindrance from the teacher. As each cause was presented, children rated that self-ascription on the three dimensions of locus, stability, and controllability; they indicated their expectancy for success; and they estimated how much the teacher would reward or punish them for the outcome. Participants also indicated how they would feel about their performance by rating the intensity of six success- or failure-related affects. This particular set of questions was chosen so that the investigation could probe the linkages between causal dimensions and psychological processes predicted by the attributional model. For example, we were able to examine the relations between the stability of causes and expectancy for success, between the controllability of causes and interpersonal evaluation (teacher reward or punishment), and between the locus of causes and esteem-related affect.

The findings from this study – too numerous to report in their entirety here – will provide the reader with some insight into children's attributional reasoning processes, particularly concerning children's judgments about the causes of success. The data for failure tell a similar story and need not be presented here (see Graham & Long, in press).

The first question examined was how children dimensionalized the specified causes for success. Success due to ability, good strategy, and trying hard all were judged as internal, stable, and controllable. In contrast, a high score on an exam attributed to an easy test, help from the teacher, or good luck tended to be seen as external, unstable, and uncontrollable. The only difference in dimensional ratings as a function of race and SES was the finding that middle-class white children rated the external causes as more external, the unstable causes as more unstable, and the uncontrollable causes as more uncontrollable than did the other three demographic groups. These differences in the dimensional placement of causes take on additional meaning when we examine the particular consequences of each causal dimension. Take, for example, the hypothesized linkage between the locus of causes and esteem-related affect. The attributional model predicts greater pride and positive self-esteem for success attributed to internal rather than external causes. One might therefore anticipate that the lowest ratings of pride given external causes would be reported by the group who perceived these causes as the most external – that is, middle-class white children. The first panel of Figure 2.4 shows that this prediction is supported. This portion of the figure depicts reported likelihood of feeling proud as a function of the locus of causes for each demographic group. All children reported that they would feel less proud if they did well because of an easy test, lucky guessing, or teacher help, and this was particularly true for middle-SES white children. A similar pattern is evident in children's expectations for success as a function of the stability of causes (panel 2). Middle-SES whites who perceived the unstable causes as most unstable also reported the lowest expectancies when success was attributed to these factors. But note that the success expectancies among all four demographic groups varied as a function of the stability of causes, although the two black groups did not revise their expectancies downward as much when the causes were perceived as unstable.

The one dimension-consequence linkage that was not documented in all four race x SES groups was that between the controllability of causes and judgments of teacher evaluation (panel 3). Among low-SES black children in this investigation, the amount of praise they thought they would receive from their teacher did not vary as a function of the controllability of causes for success. Perhaps some cultural benefits about

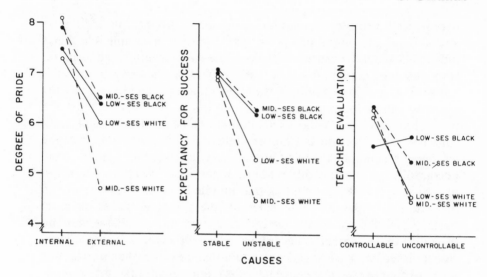

Figure 2.4. Ratings of pride, expectancy, and teacher evaluation as a function of causal dimensions, within each race × SES group. (High numbers indicate greater pride, higher expectancy, and higher perceived evaluation.)

the role of the teacher as a source of positive feedback mediates this linkage between controllability and teacher evaluation in a classroom setting. It may be, for example, that these children anticipate a moderate amount of praise or reward from their teacher whenever they do well, whether the causes of their success are internal and controllable factors like high ability and trying hard, or external and uncontrollable causes such as an easy test or extra help from the teacher. If this is so, one possible consequence is that positive teacher feedback might not be a source of information that the children then use to infer personal competence. I will return to this question of teacher feedback as a source of attributional information in the next section when I consider some specific classroom implications of the research described in this chapter.

Summary

We are really just beginning to explore how children who differ in race and social class perceive their causal world, but even these initial studies suggest some tentative conclusions. It appears that the principles of attribution theory apply quite generally to both black and white children. Each component of the attributional model that we examined in these studies was supported across four race × SES groups. When we examined antecedents of causal attributions, we found that sympathy and anger displays functioned as attributional cues in the predicted manner for all research participants. When we investigated the dominant perceived causes of success and failure, we found a prevalent set of self-ascriptions that were common to all four demographic groups. We also documented the overriding importance of effort as a cause for both success and failure among all of our research participants. Finally, when we examined the dimensional properties of causes as well as their psychological consequences, again we found more similarities than differences in the way children reasoned about attributional concepts. Thus, for example, we can reasonably infer that among both black and white children, expectations for future success are largely determined by how stable the causes of achievement are perceived to be, and that pride is a consequence of success ascribed to one's own personal attributes. Inasmuch as expectancy, or the likelihood of achieving an outcome, and affect, or how much one values that outcome, are among the most important determinants of achievement strivings, our findings support the belief that attribution theory provides a useful conceptual framework for examining motivational processes of minority populations.

What remains for future research is to identify how the specific attributions of minority children relate to these more generalized principles in actual achievement contexts. For example, recall that our findings indicated that low-SES black children were more likely than the other three demographic groups to report that help from the teacher was a dominant cause of success on a school exam. Since external attributions for success do not lead to enhanced pride in accomplishment, one wonders whether the classroom environments typically encountered by disadvantaged minority children are less likely to promote internal attributions for success, and hence the affects more uniquely linked to positive self-esteem. I believe that questions of this type offer a more fruitful approach to the study of black self-esteem in achievement contexts than personality approaches to the construct that continue to dominate the field.

Classroom implications

The arguments and evidence presented in this chapter admittedly are based on laboratory investigations. Nonetheless, there are classroom implications of this work for understanding motivational processes of minority children that I now will address.

Teacher affective communications to minority children

One implication of our research on affective displays of sympathy and anger is that these emotional cues can convey unintended attributional messages, particularly when the target of the emotion is perceived as low in ability. For example, in classroom contexts, a teacher who responds with sympathy toward a failing student is believed to be motivated by the desire to protect that student's self-esteem. But sympathetic displays in our investigation led to low ability self-ascriptions, which suggests that this affective cue may often undermine rather than protect the self-esteem of a failing student. On the other hand, we tend to think that teachers typically will avoid anger as an emotional reaction to failure because of its presumed threat to the self-esteem of the low ability student (see Leacock, 1969). But the attributional message conveyed by this emotion may have desirable consequences inasmuch as effort rather than ability is the inferred cause of failure.

Even though our investigation indicated that the effects of affective cues of sympathy and anger were similar across both black and white children, in classroom contexts it may well be that minority children are the particular targets of sympathetic cues from teachers. Empirical support for this belief is indirect but suggestive. First, there is evidence that teachers are more likely to believe that the failures of black students are due to factors such as bad heredity or low aptitude than they are to hold this attributional belief about comparable white students (e.g., Wiley & Eskilson, 1978). Teachers also have lower expectations for black than white students (Cooper, Baron, & Lowe, 1975; Rubovitz & Maehr, 1973; Taylor, 1979), and they are more likely to attribute the failures of low expectancy students to lack of ability (Cooper & Burger, 1980). Second, consistent with our belief that particular causal thoughts lead to specific affective reactions, there is evidence that teachers of minority children are perceived by observers as sympathetic and that being characterized in this manner is linked to low achievement among students. For example, following classroom observation of mainstreamed Native American children, Kleinfeld (1972) described a class of sympathetic teachers whom she labeled "sentimentalists." These teachers attempted to create a climate of emotional warmth for their low achieving students but accomplished little aside from establishing personal rapport. Consistent with our analysis, Kleinfeld (1972) summarized her findings with the observation that "sympathetic to the academic difficulties of native students ... sentimentalist teachers require very little and little learning occurs" (p. 335). Massey, Scott, and Dornbusch (1975) made similar observations in their study of low-income black high-school students in San Francisco. These researchers suggested that teacher sympathy and warmth were communicated through low academic standards and high grades for minimal effort. Even anecdotal evidence gathered by my colleagues and me from informal conversations with inner-city teachers indicates that these teachers often acknowledge feeling sympathetic toward their students. The question posed by our attributional analysis concerns what unintended messages to students are being conveyed by these feelings. Of all the subtle attributional cues in classroom contexts, the emotional reactions of teachers may be among the most important antecedents of perceived personal competence. And this may be particularly true when the emotion is sympathy and when the target of the emotion is the disadvantaged minority child.

Instructional strategies that communicate low ability

In classroom contexts there are widely practiced teacher strategies that appear to function, like sympathy, as indirect low ability cues. For example, there is evidence among both children and adults that praise for success at easy tasks and the absence of criticism for failure at these tasks can communicate to the recipients of this feedback that they are low in ability (Barker, 1984; Meyer et al., 1979). Other research in both laboratory and classroom settings documents that individuals who receive unsolicited help from the teacher are perceived by others and themselves as lower in ability than are students whom the teacher does not help (Meyer, 1982; Weiner, et al., 1983). Thus, some commonly accepted instructional practices such as the use of praise and the offering of help may have unintended negative consequences if they convey to students that they are low in ability.

Again, I want to argue that this analysis has particular implications for understanding motivational processes of minority children. If one takes a critical look at some prevailing pedagogical notions about educating disadvantaged minority children, it appears that teacher behaviors communicating low ability may be subtly incorporated into many programs for these children. Consider, for example, the direct instructional model, a widely adopted instructional approach for low-income minority children (see Rosenshine, 1979). According to Rosenshine, the principal components of this model are comprised of "simple questions, a high percentage of correct answers, help when the student does not know the answer, and infrequent criticism" (Rosenshine, 1979, p. 43). The close similarity between these instructional strategies and the behaviors believed to communicate low ability are apparent.

It is not only the behavior-analytic orientation of direct instruction models that may be sources of indirect low ability cues. Pedagogical notions about minimizing failure and criticism also are evident in some humanistic approaches specifically concerned with enhancing the self-esteem of minority children. For example, in one recent outline of humanistic objectives, specific teacher statements such as "you should be able to do that" and "you're wrong and you should do better than that" were judged to be inappropriate feedback to students following failure (Aspy & Hicks, 1978). These feedbacks were thought to be unduly critical and threatening to the self-esteem of a failing student. Yet *should* statements of this type that at one level appear critical are likely to function like the *anger* cues in our investigation of affective displays because they implicate effort rather than ability attributions for failure and they convey the expectation that one can do better in the future. Thus what some humanistic teachers view as esteem-threatening to minority children may, in fact, be esteem-protecting.

Like the direct instruction model, humanistic objectives have a good deal of intuitive appeal for educators concerned with the problem of chronic school failure among many disadvantaged minority children. The interpretation provided here is not meant to suggest that these instructional strategies always implicate one's ability and therefore should never be employed. Attribution principles applied to classroom contexts must not be taken so literally. Furthermore, the absence of criticism, the use of praise, helping behavior, and sympathetic affect probably often do neutralize some of the immediate impact of failure such as public embarrassment or frustration. Over time, however, or if indiscriminately adopted, these well-intentioned teacher behaviors are believed to have uncertain and sometimes negative consequences.

A final note

A major point I have attempted to make in this chapter is that we do not need alternative models to account for motivational processes of minority children. The most important determinants of achievement strivings, including self-esteem, perceived control, and expectations for success, all are amenable to the attributional perspective presented here. There is hardly a topic that has generated more concern among educators or remained as elusive as the problem of achievement and motivation in minority groups. The ongoing interchange between social psychology and education illustrated in this chapter has produced much of value to aid our understanding of this complex and pervasive problem.

References

Aspy, D. N., & Hicks, L. H. (1978). Research on humanistic objectives. In A. W. Coombs (Ed.), *Humanistic education: Objectives and assessment*. Washington, DC: Association of Supervision and Curriculum Development.

Atkinson, J. W. (1964). *An introducton to motivation*. Princeton, NJ: Van Nostrand.

Battle, E., & Rotter, J. B. (1963). Children's feelings of personal control as related to social class and ethnic group. *Journal of Personality, 31*, 482–490.

Barker, B. (1984). The influence of teacher feedback on perceived ability estimates in others. Unpublished doctoral dissertation, University of California, Los Angeles.

Brown, J., & Weiner, B. (1984). Affective consequences of ability versus effort ascriptions: Controversies, resolutions, and quandaries. *Journal of Educational Psychology, 76*, 146–158.

Cooper, H. M., Baron, R., & Lowe, C. (1975). The importance of race and social class in the formation of expectancies about academic performance. *Journal of Educational Psychology, 67*, 312–319.

Cooper, H. M., & Burger, J. (1980). How teachers explain students' outcomes. *American Educational Research Journal, 17*, 95–109

Dalal, A., Weiner, B., & Brown, J. (1984). Issues in the measurement of causal stability. Unpublished manuscript, University of California, Los Angeles.

deCharms, R. (1968). *Personal causation*. New York: Academic Press.

Deci, E. L., (1975). *Intrinsic motivation*. New York: Plenum Press.

Folkes, V. S. (1982). Causal communications in the early stages of affiliative relationships. *Journal of Experimental Social Psychology, 18*, 1982.

Friend, R., & Neale, J. (1972). Children's perceptions of success and failure: An attributional analysis of the effects of race and social class. *Developmental Psychology, 7*, 124–128.

Graham, S. (1984). Communicating sympathy and anger to black and white children: The cognitive (attributional) antecedents of affective cues. *Journal of Personality and Social Psychology, 47*, 40–54.

Graham, S., Doubleday, C. & Guarino, P. (1984). The development of relations between perceived controllability and the emotions of pity, anger, and guilt. *Child Development, 55*, 561–565.

Graham, S., & Long, A. (in press) Race, class, and the attributional process. *Journal of Educational Psychology*.

Harari, O., & Covington, M. (1981). Reactions to achievement behavior from a teacher and student perspective. *Amercian Educational Research Journal, 137*, 683–689.

Havinghurst, R. J. (1976). The relative importance of social class and ethnicity in human development. *Human Development, 19*, 56–65.

Katz, I. (1969). A critique of personality approaches to Negro performance with research suggestions. *Journal of Social Issues, 25*, 13–27.

Kelley, H. H., & Michela, J. (1980). Attribution theory and research. In M. R. Rosenzweig & L. W. Porter (eds)., *Annual Review of Psychology* (Vol. 31). Palo Alto, CA: Annual Reviews.

Kleinfeld, J. (1972). Effective teachers of Eskimo and Indian students. *School Review, 83*, 301–344.

64   S. GRAHAM

Leacock, E. (1969). *Teaching and learning in inner city schools*. New York: Basic Books.
Lepper, M. R. & Greene, D. (1978) *The hidden costs of rewards*. Hillsdale, NJ: Erlbaum.
Maehr, M., & Nicholls, J. (1980). Culture and achievement motivation: A second look. In N. Warren (Ed.), *Studies in cross-cultural psychology* (Vol. 3). New York: Academic Press.
Massey, G., Scott, M., & Dornbusch, S. (1975) Racism without racists: Institutional racism in urban schools. *Black Scholar*, 2–11.
McMillan, J. (1980). Children's causal attributions in achievement situations. *Journal of Social Psychology, 112*, 31–39.
Meyer, W. U. (1982). Indirect communications about perceived ability estimates. *Journal of Educational Psychology, 74*, 688–697.
Meyer, W. U. et al. (1979). The information value of evaluative behavior: Influence of praise and blame on perceptions of ability. *Journal of Educational Psychology, 71*, 259–268.
Murray, S. R., & Mednick, M. T. (1975). Perceiving the causes of success and failure in achievement: Sex, race, and motivational comparisons. *Journal of Consulting and Clinical Psychology, 43* 881–885.
Rosenshine, B. (1979). Content, time, and direct instruction. In P. Peterson and H. Walberg (Eds.), *Research on teaching*. Berkeley, CA: McCutchan.
Rotter, J. B. (1966). Generalized expectancies for internal versus external control of reinforcement. *Psychological Monographs, 80*(1, Whole No. 609).
Rubovitz, P., & Maehr, M. (1973). Pygmalion black and white. *Journal of Personality and Social Psychology, 25*, 210–218.
Taylor, M. (1979). Race, sex, and the expression of the self-fulfilling prophecy in a laboratory teaching situation. *Journal of Personality and Social Psychology, 37*, 897–912.
Weiner, B. (1982). The emotional consequences of causal ascriptions. In M. S. Clark & S. T. Fiske (Eds.), *Affect and cognition: The 17th annual Carnegie symposium on cognition*. Hillsdale, NJ: Erlbaum.
Weiner, B. (1984). Principles for a theory of motivation and their application within an attributional framework. In R. Ames & C. Ames (Eds.), *Research on motivation in education* (Vol. 1). New York: Academic Press.
Weiner, B. (1985). An attributional theory of achievement motivation and emotion. *Psychological Review, 92*, 548–573.
Weiner, B., Frieze, I., Kukla, A., Reed, S., & Rosenbaum, R. (1971). Perceiving the causes of success and failure. In E. Jones, D. Kanouse, H. Kelley, R. Nisbett, S. Valins, & B. Weiner (Eds.), *Attribution: Perceiving the causes of behavior*. Morristown, NJ: General Learning Press.
Weiner, B. & Graham, S. (1984). An attributional approach to emotional development. In C. Izard, J. Kagan, & R. Zajonc (Eds.), *Emotions, cognition, and behavior*. Cambridge, MA: Harvard University Press.
Weiner, B., Graham, S., & Chandler, C. (1982). An attributional analysis of pity, anger, and guilt. *Personality and Social Psychology Bulletin, 8*, 226–232.
Weiner, B., Graham, S., Stern, P., & Lawson, M. (1982). Using affective cues to infer causal thoughts. *Developmental Psychology, 18*, 278–286.
Weiner, B., Graham, S., Taylor, S., & Meyer, W. (1983). Social cognition in the classroom. *Educational Psychologist, 18*, 109–124.
Weiner, B., & Kukla, A. (1970). An attributional analysis of achievement motivation. *Journal of Personality and Social Psychology, 15*, 1–20.
Weiner, B., & Peter, N. (1973). A cognitive-development analysis of achievement motivation. *Development Psychology, 9*, 290–309.
Weiner, B., Russell, D., & Lerman, D. (1978). Affective consequences of causal ascriptions. In J. H. Harvey, W. J. Ickes, & R. F. Kidd (Eds.), *New directions in attribution research* (Vol. 2). Hillsdale, NJ: Erlbaum.

Weiner, B., Russell, D., & Lerman, D. (1979). The cognition-emotion process in achievement-related contexts. *Journal of Personality and Social Psychology, 37,* 1211–1220.

Wiley, M. G., & Eskilson, A. (1978). Why did you learn in school today? Teachers' perceptions of causality. *Sociology of Education, 51,* 261–269.

Willig, A. C., Harnisch, D. L., Hill, K. T., & Maehr, M. (1983). Sociocultural and educational correlates of success-failure attributions and evaluation anxiety in the school setting for black, Hispanic, and Anglo children. *American Educational Research Journal, 20,* 385–410.

Wong, P. T. P., & Weiner, B. (1981). When people ask "why" questions and the heuristics of attributional search. *Journal of Personality and Social Psychology, 40,* 650–663.

Yando, R., Seitz, V., & Zigler, E. (1979). *Intellectual and personality characteristics of children: Social class and ethnic group differences.* Hillsdale, NJ: Erlbaum.

3 Students' attitudes and class segment effects on patterns of classroom behavior

Howard A. Smith

The present chapter has three major objectives. First, some of the literature concerning the association between attitudes and behavior will be reviewed briefly, with the intent to sample current assumptions and findings, particularly those drawn from educational settings, rather than to provide a complete review of the topic (cf. Calder & Ross, 1973; McGuire, 1985). Second, some preliminary data involving the attitude-behavior relationship in the junior high school classroom will be discussed in the context of lesson subunits or segments (cf. Gump, 1967) derived from a single curriculum area, French as a Second Language (FSL). The focus of the accompanying analysis will be on the categories and durations of classroom behaviors displayed by students with differing attitudes toward FSL during various class segments. Finally, some implications of the research for classroom theory and practice will be outlined.

For more than two generations, social psychologists have tried to specify the nature of the association between expressed attitude toward an object or class of objects on one hand and the accompanying or subsequent behavior. This suggests that the attitude-behavior relationship has been judged to be an important one and to have significant implications for both theoretical and applied concerns. For example, determining whether attitude or behavior occurs first in a causal association is of major theoretical interest. From an applied perspective,

The major study from which these data were drawn was supported in full by Social Sciences and Humanities Research Council of Canada Grant No. 410-82-0348 to H. A. Smith and D. A. Massey. The Council's assistance is gratefully acknowledged.

An earlier version of this chapter was presented at the June 1984 meeting of the Canadian Society for the Study of Education in Guelph, Ontario. I thank Rod Clifton for his helpful comments following that occasion, and Robert Feldman for his capable editorial direction during preparation of the final manuscript.

knowing the order of occurrence of the two variables could have substantial influence on the type and structure of school experiences made available to learners.

In the educational setting, then, there are both theoretical and practical reasons for determining whether or when students' attitudes toward the subject matter are linked systematically with their classroom behaviors and for discovering what those relationships are. Although the range of acceptable behaviors is somewhat narrower in the classroom than in some other arenas, it is possible that students with highly positive attitudes toward a subject behave differently from fellow students with highly negative attitudes. Should this be the case, then it is important for teachers to become aware of these differences and to act upon the information available. As well, since both teachers and students influence each other through their behaviors (e.g., Arlin, 1979; Braun, 1976, Clark & Yinger, 1977; Winne & Marx, 1977), it follows that student behaviors accompanying different attitudes should result in varying classroom "personalities" and dynamics. If attitudes precede behaviors, then knowing a student's attitude may allow for prediction of his or her future conduct. On the other hand, if behaviors affect attitudes, then introducing appropriate task demands in the classroom should effect desired changes in student attitudes.

The attitude-behavior relationships notwithstanding, some recent work has stressed the significant effects of situational influences and contextual demands on individual behavior (e.g., Magnusson & Endler, 1977). Not only is the classroom a unique setting with some special characteristics (cf. Solomon & Kendall, 1979) but a variety of subsettings or lesson segments, each with its own concern and activity patterns, has been described (Gump, 1967, 1969). It remains to be determined whether attitudes toward a subject are strong enough to eclipse the contextual constraints on behavior that are imposed by these different class segments.

The basic theoretical framework of symbolic interactionism (e.g., Blumer, 1969; Denzin, 1978, McMillan, 1980a; Mead, 1934) underlies the present endeavor. Although details of symbolic interactionism will not be addressed in this chapter, several of its fundamental assumptions have guided the mode of investigation and influenced the choice of instruments used in the study. For example, this perspective underlines the importance of social interactions in the definition of self and the creation of personal attributes such as attitudes. As well, social interactions result in the meanings that became attached to attending symbols and behaviors. One implication of these assumptions is that the classroom is

68

H. A. SMITH

seen as an emergent social unit with both general and specific rules and roles.

Attitudes and the attitude-behavior relationship

Since research on the topic began, many definitions and perspectives have characterized the term "attitude." For example, a cognitive emphasis was favored by Rokeach (1968), who defined attitude as "a relatively enduring organization of beliefs around an object or situation pre-disposing one to respond in some preferential manner" (p. 112). Other researchers such as Fishbein and Ajzen (1975) and Lett (1977) have emphasized the affective dimension by advancing definitions such as the following: "the amount of positive or negative affect that one holds toward a specific social object or class of social objects" (Lett, 1977, p. 270). A third position was taken by Bagozzi and Burnkrant (1979) when their data supported a two-factor (i.e., cognitive and affective) model of attitude and implied that both factors should be assessed for an adequate measure of attitude. A fourth view is that attitudes consist of cognitive, affective, *and* behavioral components (e.g., McMillan, 1980b; Ostrom, 1969).

In order to be consistent with the theoretical and empirical foun-dations of the attitude measure used in the present study on second-language learning, the definition to be adopted here began with the general two-component model preferred by Bagozzi and Burnkrant (1979) and then incorporated the specific motivational characteristics derived by Gardner and Smythe (1981). The latter investigators con-sidered three highly related attitudinal/motivational clusters to be central to their notions: (a) integrativeness, involving affective reactions toward the target groups in question; (b) motivation, involving the three relevant aspects of drive to attain the goal of learning French, desire to achieve that goal, and positive feelings about the goal; and (c) attitudes toward the learning situation, involving student evaluation of the French teacher and the French course. In their test battery, Gardner and Smythe (1981) used the Likert scale (which measures cognitive components of attitude, according to Bagozzi & Burnkrant, 1979), multiple-choice questions, and the semantic differential technique (which measures affective com-ponents of attitude, according to Bagozzi & Burnkrant, 1979).

Two issues concerning the relationship between attitudes and behavior, which are of particular relevance here, have guided a number of investigations and will be summarized briefly. First, the prevailing but not unanimous view regarding their order of occurrence is that attitudes precede rather than follow expressed behaviors (e.g., Bagozzi & Burnkrant, 1979; Kahle & Berman, 1979). This particular ordering was demonstrated by Kahle and Berman (1979), who used cross-lagged panel correlations to support their assertions. As a result of demonstrating the significant influence of attitude, an individual characteristic, on behavior, Kahle and Berman also declared that their findings weakened the claims of situationists who argue that behavior is determined primarily by situational factors (e.g., Wicker, 1969). However, one possible methodological shortcoming in the Kahle and Berman study is that the behavioral measures consisted not of overt responses but of paper-pencil responses to questions concerning the subjects' activities during the previous 14 days.

Second, researchers who differ on the definition and composition of attitudes often agree that the relationship between attitudes and behavior is a most uncertain one (e.g., Ehrlich, 1969; Weinstein, 1972) and that measures of attitudes are not related systematically to single acts or behaviors (e.g., Bagozzi & Burnkrant, 1979; Fishbein & Ajzen, 1974; Lett, 1977). For example, Bagozzi and Burnkrant (1979) reported that both cognitive and affective measures of attitude can predict scaled, but not unscaled, multiple-act criteria. These investigators stated that, although individual attitudes could be related to single acts, the relationship should not be assumed. Hence, these and other data suggest that knowing one's attitude toward an object or class of objects is by itself a poor predictor of a future specific performance.

However, Crespi (1971) and Ajzen and Fishbein (1977) have provided important qualifications regarding this issue. After reviewing three areas (Gallup Poll preelection surveys, movie attendance, and consumer brand preference) in which a high correspondence between expressed attitude and subsequent behavior was observed, Crespi concluded that attitudes have predictable relationships to behavior when attitudes are treated as highly specific combinations of beliefs, preferences, and intentions *and* when subsequent behavior is highly institutionalized or routinized. This proposal has significant implications for the current investigation in which attitudes toward French as a Second Language (a specific combination of attitudinal dispositions) is related to behavior in the classroom (an institutionalized arena with a relatively narrow range of acceptable behaviors). In addition, Crespi's (1971) observations served to strengthen some of the claims of situationism (cf. Wicker, 1969).

In their comprehensive analysis of previous research, Ajzen and

Fishbein (1977) found that significant attitude-behavior relationships were obtained consistently when a high correspondence existed between attitudinal and behavioral components, that is, when the target and action elements in particular were equivalent for both attitudinal and behavioral entities. (For their purposes, Ajzen and Fishbein defined measures of attitude as measures which placed the individual on a bipolar evaluative or affective dimension.) This result held for both single-act and multiple-act criteria. In addition, Ajzen and Fishbein determined that attitude-behavior relationships were low and not significant under lack of correspondence and were inconsistent but normally low under conditions of partial correspondence. In other words, research that examines the association between attitude and behavior should ensure that both variables are concerned with the same target and involve the same actions in approaching or avoiding the target. Implications for the current investigation are that attitudes toward FSL should be examined in conjunction with behaviors that relate closely to FSL instruction and learning.

More recently, the views of Crespi (1971) and of Ajzen and Fishbein (1977) have been elaborated by investigators adopting either an individual (e.g., Snyder, 1982) or a situational (e.g., Abelson, 1982) emphasis. For example, Snyder (1982) outlined how attitude-behavior relationships vary among conditions for low self-monitoring and high self-monitoring individuals, while Abelson (1982) described three modes of attitude-behavior consistency which are dependent upon the situational context. In their review, Cooper and Croyle (1984) portrayed the perspective of researchers such as Crespi and Ajzen and Fishbein as methodological, and that of researchers such as Snyder and Abelson as mediational. In the study to be reported later in this chapter, mediational factors will be centrally involved but the important methodological issues raised by Crespi (1971) and by Ajzen and Fishbein (1977) will be addressed as well.

The attitude-behavior relationship in classroom research

The relationship between students' attitudes toward school matters and observed classroom behaviors (as opposed to their reports about behavior) has received little systematic attention to date, although related questions have been investigated (cf. Crano & Mellon, 1978; Early, 1968; Silberman, 1969). However, one study (Lahaderne, 1968) found no relationship between attitude toward school or the teacher and behavior as reflected by classroom attention or scholastic performance. In explaining her results, Lahaderne proposed that classroom constraints on the pupils were so strong that attitudes could not influence behavior. However, it is also possible that there was little correspondence in action, target, or specificity between the attitudes assessed and the subsequent behaviors measured (cf. Ajzen, 1982; Ajzen & Fishbein, 1977).

At least two studies with immediate implications for the present work have been conducted (Gliksman, 1976; Naiman et al., 1978). In his examination of nine Ontario intermediate grade classrooms, Gliksman (1976) proposed that the integrative motive affected students' active participation in the classroom (in the test battery used by Gliksman, the integrative motive comprised part of the attitude/motivation measure and consisted of four subscales that tested attitudes toward French Canadians, interest in foreign languages, integrative orientation, and attitudes toward European French people; see Gardner and Smythe, 1981, for a description of the test battery). In two related projects, each of which lasted several months, Gliksman obtained measures of attitude and motivation at the beginning of term and then rated the behaviors of students on the following variables: amount of volunteering (i.e., raising the hand), number of correct responses, and number of questions asked. He also split the integrative motive scores at the median to obtain an integratively motivated group and a nonintegratively motivated group. The former group of students volunteered more frequently, gave more correct answers, and were rated as more interested in class proceedings than the nonintegratively motivated students. However, both groups asked the same number of questions of the teacher. Hence, the results supported a clear relationship between the integrative motive and classroom behavior: The more integratively motivated students were more active and involved in FSL classes than the less integratively motivated students.

The second investigation to relate student attitudes toward FSL with classroom behavior was conducted by Naiman et al. (1978), who examined four classes in each of grades 8, 10, and 12 in the Ontario school system. These researchers used the same test battery as Gliksman (1976) and found highly significant correlations between assorted attitude/motivation indices and student hand-raising, student callouts, and student null responses (the latter was a negative correlation). The behaviors most highly associated with various scale values were student hand-raising (related to Integrative Orientation, Motivation, and Instrumental Orientation) and student null responses (related negatively to

Motivation). It appears that, even though hand-raising behavior has a high base rate in classrooms (cf. Fishbein & Ajzen, 1974) and is an important and well-known part of the classroom behavior code, varying amounts of hand-raising can be observed in students who score differentially on elaborated attitude measures such as the Attitude/ Motivation Test Battery, or AMTB (e.g., Gardner & Smythe, 1981). As well, other behavioral signs reflecting levels of student activity or involvement were related to attitude scores.

The classroom as a differentiated social setting

In the studies reviewed thus far, the classroom has been treated as a homogeneous entity in which the same rules of behavior are presumed to hold throughout the entire lesson. However, several researchers have demonstrated that different social structures and behavioral norms prevail at different times during each class period (e.g., Bremme & Erickson, 1977; Gottlieb, 1978; Gump, 1967, 1969). For example, Gump (1967, 1969) used comprehensive accounts of full-day activities in six third-grade classrooms to develop his notion of "segment." He defined a segment as an environmental section with its own business or concern, and found that each segment had its own activity pattern consisting of teacher and pupil actions and prescriptions. Gump also determined that pupils behaved differently in the different segments.

At the kindergarten/first grade level, Bremme and Erickson (1977) studied the "First Circle," a daily opening configuration in which students and teachers sat on a rug in a roughly circular arrangement to accomplish a variety of tasks such as taking attendance, sharing experiences and organizing the day's activities. The investigators reported that, during these sessions, different behaviors were manifested by both teacher and students during Teacher's Time and Students' Time. In addition, they found that student behaviors such as turning sideways and chatting with peers were acceptable during Students' Time but not during Teacher's Time. It was apparent from these results that not only did behavior shifts exist during First Circle but that socially competent 5- and 6-year-old children knew what "time" it was from appropriate reading of the teacher's verbal and nonverbal cues.

These studies demonstrated that the classroom is a complex social setting with rules and norms which vary according to the prevailing class segment. A major question remaining to be resolved asks whether student attitudes toward FSL are sufficiently robust to be reflected by differential behavior within and among lesson segments. The same question put in terms already mentioned asks whether student behavior is determined primarily by ongoing situational demands of the classroom or by individual factors such as attitudes (cf., Abelson, 1982; Kahle & Berman, 1979; Wicker, 1969). Accordingly, the prime objective of the investigation to be reported in detail here was to determine the behavior patterns of students with varying attitudes toward FSL within several segments of the typical classroom lesson.

Major premises of the present study

The findings reviewed previously provide substantial support both for the methodological proposals of Crespi (1971) and Ajzen and Fishbein (1977) and for the mediational notion that varying student attitudes toward FSL are reflected in differential amounts of classroom behavior. In fact, the stringent definition of attitude provided by Ajzen and Fishbein (1977) might be broadened somewhat and continue to yield significant relationships with behavior (cf., Gardner, Gliksman, & Smythe, 1978). Given the results of Gliksman (1976) and Naiman et al. (1978), it appears that the test battery used by these investigators to measure attitude/motivation toward FSL is appropriate for use when behavior in FSL classrooms is being observed. For at least some of the subtests, there appears to be a high correspondence between attitude and behavior insofar as the target and action elements are concerned.

The present study used videotaped observations of behavior rather than subjects' reports of their performance, since the subtle aspects of overt performance are more available to the observer than to the subject. Also, as most classroom behavior is relatively passive and accessible to videotaping techniques (with repeated viewing), student reports are not necessary in the first instance. However, student attitude was assessed by the usual paper-pencil approach required by the Attitude/Motivation Test Battery (Gardner & Smythe, 1981).

An additional consideration is that most research examining patterns of behavior has also featured dyadic interactions. The frequent use of dyads seems to have occurred for two main reasons: Most researchers studying behavior patterns have been interested primarily in the interaction between two persons such as a therapist and his or her client, and the resulting behavioral data has been presumed to be relatively easy to analyze. However, the dyad is an inappropriate model for the typical classroom situation, since the teacher rarely functions on the basis of a one-to-one relationship. In general, questions or exchanges directed at one individual are done in the public forum and are aimed, however indirectly, at the entire class in order to help guide instructional attention, consolidate learning, and ensure smooth class management. Therefore, when the focus of the study is on student behavior, it seems more appropriate to observe an individual student continuously, even when class attention is directed elsewhere, than to follow the teacher's interactions with successive students.

Two additional concerns involving the classification of student behavior deserve comment at this time. First, attempts were made to categorize student behaviors at about the same level of meaning as that characterizing teacher judgments concerning student involvement in class (cf. Lamb, 1979: Peterson, 1977). Accordingly, since teachers base their judgments on clusters of student behaviors (e.g., Clark & Yinger, 1977), the observation schedule used classified behaviors at higher levels of inference than was minimally possible. The negative effect of this decision was to increase the risk of reducing the reliability of observations. Second, the behaviors for each individual were rated continuously over a set period of time so as to provide a record of successive behaviors or, at the very least, the proportion of time spent in different activities. Because simple frequency counts are unable to represent behavior sequences and relationships (cf., Parke, 1979; Raush, 1969, 1979), frequency counts were used only when comparisons were being made with the results of previous experiments which have employed these counts.

The choice of FSL as the curricular subject of attention in this study was based on three factors: (a) little research has been done on FSL core programs (in which students receive brief periods of instruction several times a week), even though the core approach is the dominant mode of FSL instruction in Canadian schools, (b) research is required to determine why students in grades 7 and 8 in particular tend to behave negatively and to express negative attitudes toward French, and (c) with rare exceptions, previous studies of the FSL core program have not related student attitudes to the ongoing classroom behaviors associated with learning French, but have focused instead on the relationship between student attitude measures and accompanying achievement scores.

In sum, the major objective of the current preliminary investigation was to record the concurrent behaviors of students with varying attitudes toward FSL within different class segments. The research was observa-

tional and exploratory in nature rather than a test of specific hypotheses. Related studies (Gliksman, 1976; Naiman et al., 1978) have used frequency counts to determine that increased levels of behavioral activity such as hand-raising and callouts (i.e., student responds orally without the teacher's sanction) characterize students with more highly positive levels of attitude/motivation toward FSL. However, these studies have not investigated whether the behaviors emitted by students with highly positive, average, or highly negative attitudes toward FSL differ qualitatively over time, or how the respective behaviors differ from one class segment to another.

Method

Subjects. In the present study, the students consisted of those assigned initially to one sixth-grade class in each of three schools. The students were tested on their attitudes toward FSL in the spring term and then videotaped and retested at the grade 7 level in the fall. Also, all students returned permission forms that had been completed by their parents. A total of 95 students met all of these requirements.

The schools were located as follows: one in a city of 60,000 (urban public school, or UPS), one in an adjoining suburb (suburban public school, or SPS), and one near a small town about 30 km away (rural public school, or RPS). One FSL teacher in each of the schools taught grades 6 and 7 during both the spring and succeeding fall sessions when the study was in progress. Each of the three teachers was female and had from 5 to 10 years of teaching experience.

Procedure. In June of the school year, all students in the selected classrooms returned the parental permission forms and then were given the Attitude/Motivation Test Battery (Gardner & Smythe, 1981). In the second week of September, videotaping of the same students began and continued at the rate of one complete period a week per class for four weeks. Although by this time the students had been placed in grade 7, and sometimes were in different classes, they were being taught in each case by the teacher who had instructed them the year before. At the end of the videotaping, the AMTB was administered for a second time.

Three students were chosen from each grade 7 class in September on the basis of their *initial* (i.e., June) AMTB scores. One student per class was chosen on the basis of a very high (relative to the rest of the class)

Table 3.1. *Attitude/motivation indices of grade 7 students selected for present study*

Attributes	High AMI	Med AMI	Low AMI
RPS (n = 37; Spring AMI: x = 407.8; SD = 73.1)			
Sex	Female	Female	Female
AMI (Spring)	529	414	323
AMI (Fall)	530	343	322
Difference	+1	−71	−1
SPS (n = 43; Spring AMI: x = 394.3; SD = 70.3)			
Sex	Male	Female	Male
AMI (Spring)	501	403	198
AMI (Fall)	446	434	209
Difference	−55	+31	+11
UPS (n = 15; Spring AMI: x = 384.3; SD = 87.2)			
Sex	Female	Male	Male
AMI (Spring)	499	430	263
AMI (Fall)	484	402	248
Difference	−15	−28	−15

Attitude/Motivation Index, or AMI (Gardner & Smythe, 1981), one for a very low AMI, and one for an AMI in the average range. Characteristics of the nine students selected are summarized in Table 3.1.

When the data collection was completed, the focal individual coding method (Sackett, Ruppenthal, & Gluck, 1978) was used to view the selected students singly and repeatedly on videotape so as to categorize their classroom behaviors during particular continuous portions of class time. Usually, the three students in a given class were viewed during the following identical class segments: an opening (i.e., the initial period of student entry and preparation before the teacher successfully called the class to order), a transition (i.e., the time between the closing out of one part of a lesson and successful entry into the succeeding portion), an oral exercise (in which the major student task was to respond orally to teacher questions or statements), and a written exercise (in which the major student task was to write in exercise books or on the blackboard). A duration of up to two minutes was used for each segment. Unless the student was absent or not visible, each set of three students was viewed on four different videotapes representing the four weeks of videotaping.

Decisions were made, first, to use a functionally organized taxonomy (Rosenblum, 1978) and, second, to categorize student behaviors at about

Table 3.2. *Modified student behavior observation system (Adapted from Perkins, 1964)*

A. Work orientation

HIAC	High activity or involvement: reciting, laughing, hand-raising, verbal responding, or otherwise using large muscles; usually positive, work-oriented feeling.
REWR	Reading or writing: working in assigned area; active.
LISWAT	Interested in ongoing work: listening and watching–passive. Attending, looking at others' work.
WOA	Intent on work in another curricular area: school activity not assigned to be done right then.
WNA	Intent on work of nonacademic type: preparing for work assignment, cleaning out desk, opening book, goal-directed walking.

B. Mixed orientation

SWT	Social, work-oriented–teacher: discussing some phase of work with teacher
SWP	Social, work-oriented–peer: discussing or reacting to some aspect of school-work with classmate.

C. Social orientation

SFT	Social, friendly–teacher: reacting to or talking to teacher on subject unrelated to schoolwork (including carrying out instructions).
SFP	Social, friendly–peer: interacting with peer on subject unrelated to school-work. Laughing, whispering, fooling.
SUT	Social, unfriendly–teacher: diverting or rude remarks to teacher.
SUP	Social, unfriendly–peer: hitting, throwing things, negative remarks.
WDL	Withdrawal: detached, out of contact with people, ideas, classroom situation; day-dreaming, not attending, fidgeting, aimless walking, watching a social situation.

the same level of meaning as that used by teachers when making judgments about the nature of student involvement in class. As shown in Table 3.2, the instrument chosen for the study was a modified form of Perkins' Student Behavior Observation System (cf. Perkins, 1964; Simon & Boyer, 1974).

The procedure used to record student behaviors was as follows: The investigator sat at a computer keyboard and typed the letter representing the particular behavior which had just been observed on the videotape operating concurrently. The resulting computer generated display showed the sequence and durations of the behaviors registered during a particular segment. Usually, each segment was viewed about three times in order to obtain a stable measure of the durations. On another occasion, two other judges working together reached consensus on most of the segments used in this study; their data was used as a reliability check for the behaviors recorded by the single investigator.

Results

Since the Modified Student Behavior Observation System produced nominal data, an observer agreement index was the only form of reliability check possible (cf., Tinsley & Weiss, 1975). Application of Cohen's Kappa, the most highly recommended index of observer agreement (e.g., Hollenbeck, 1978; Tinsley & Weiss, 1975), resulted in $k = .72$, a level of agreement considered acceptable for the present work.

The method of data acquisition resulted in multiple timed-event discrete sequential data (e.g., Bakeman, Cairns, & Appelbaum, 1979), where events for the three students in each class constituted three parallel streams of behavior across the identical time units. For purposes of the current study, the percentages of time spent in each behavior category were determined and then used as the bases for subsequent analyses.

For each of the nine students, the mean duration of each behavior was determined for every segment. The resulting data constituted a 9 (students) x 4 (type of segment) array for each behavior recorded. Application of the Friedman two-way analysis of variance by ranks (Siegel, 1956) revealed that all but one of the following behaviors were unevenly distributed among segments to a highly significant degree ($p < .001$): HIAC, REWR, LISWAT, WNA, SFP ($p < .01$), and WDL (see Figure 3.1). Therefore, differing amounts of these behaviors characterized the various class segments. For example, openings manifested a high level of withdrawal (WDL), with lesser amounts of social, friendly interactions with peers (SFP), listening or watching (LISWAT), and preparing for work assignments (WNA). Transitions showed higher levels of LISWAT, WNA, SFP, and REWR (reading or writing). Oral exercises were characterized by extremely high amounts of LISWAT, whereas written exercises showed enhanced levels of REWR and LISWAT.

As shown in Table 3.3, the corresponding data were more equivocal when students were grouped by attitude toward FSL. According to results of the two-tailed sign test (Siegel, 1956) that was applied to the six behaviors represented in Figure 3.1, only three tests produced differences reaching acceptable levels of significance. All of these differences occurred among behaviors at transitions: high vs. low attitude students for SFP ($p < .02$), medium vs. low attitude students for SFP ($p < .02$), and medium vs. low attitude students for REWR ($p < .03$). That is, during transitions, students with the most negative attitudes toward FSL (the low group) showed significantly higher levels of SFP than students from the other two groups (high and medium), and significantly reduced levels of

Table 3.3. *Percentages of time spent on behaviors as a function of segment and student attitude*

Segment attitude	Behaviors							
	HIAC	REWR	LISWAT	WNA	SWP	SFT	SFP	WDL
Openings								
High			19.5	14.7		4.1	19.0	41.8
Medium			16.0	19.2		5.8	24.2	33.8
Low			20.3	10.1			13.0	56.5
Transitions								
High	1.5	25.2	36.6	20.5	4.1		5.4	6.7
Medium	2.2	23.7	41.5	27.5			2.2	2.2
Low		2.1	19.7	18.8	1.9		52.9	4.6
Oral ex.								
High	20.0		69.9	4.3			1.8	3.8
Medium	22.7	4.7	69.7				1.3	1.4
Low	10.7		74.2				9.2	4.0
Written ex.								
High	11.5	33.0	39.8	2.0	4.5		2.7	5.6
Medium	2.7	52.9	35.4	4.4			2.8	
Low		53.0	32.2	1.1			3.2	7.9

Note: Percentages of less than 1.0 (and of 1.7 for SWT with the low group in written exercises) have been omitted.

REWR when compared with the medium group. No other differences among the groups reached statistical significance despite the existence of several behavioral trends. However, more informal data suggested that the medium group was the most highly involved of the three groups in classroom proceedings and that students from this group were the most likely to be engaged in tasks assigned to them by the teacher.

The tendency for involvement by the medium group was confirmed by the kind of data usually obtained in previous studies, frequency counts of student hand-raising. For the 20 to 22 occasions involving oral or written exercises, the high group of students raised their hands 27 times, the medium group 54 times, and the low group 14 times. Analysis of variance indicated a significant group effect, $F(2,61) = 4.28$, $p<.02$, while the conservative Scheffe test revealed a significant difference between the means of the medium and low groups, $T(61) = 1.81$, $p<.05$.

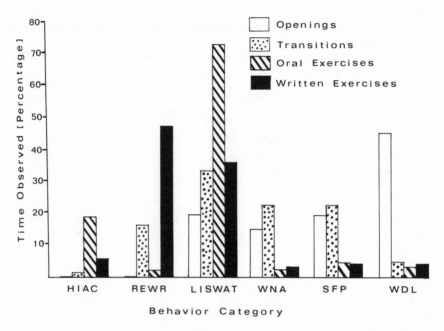

Figure 3.1. Percentages of time as a function of class segment and selected behavior category taken across subjects.

However, the varying levels of hand-raising were not reflected by the number of verbal responses produced by each group. Verbal responding, a variable usually under the direct control of the teacher, occurred as follows: seven responses from the high students, four responses from the medium students, and eight responses from the low students.

Discussion

When displayed as percentages of student time spent in each behavior category, data from the present investigation revealed that different behavior clusters characterized different class segments (see Figure 3.1). The results thereby supported earlier findings (Bremme & Erickson, 1977; Gump, 1967, 1969) and suggested that different rules of behavior hold within distinct class segments. For example, openings were defined by relatively enhanced levels of student withdrawal and by lesser amounts of peer interaction, listening and watching, and preparing for the ensuing work assignment. Transitions were characterized by higher amounts of listening and watching and by lesser amounts of peer interaction, preparing for the work assignment, and reading and writing. Oral exercises consisted of a very high amount (over 70% of the observed time) of student listening and watching together with a substantially reduced amount of high activity or involvement. Finally, written exercises featured a high level of reading and writing and a lesser amount of listening and watching. Hence, these data do not support studies that have treated the instructional period as a unitary phenomenon and that have obtained simple frequency counts of behavior across the entire lesson.

The second major set of findings from the current work involved the segment-related behaviors manifested by students with different attitudes toward FSL. The relevant time-based data revealed that, except for several group disparities during transitions, no differences in behavior patterns existed among the three groups of students. However, the meaning of these results is uncertain. It is possible that, except for transitions, the classroom constraints on behavior were strong enough to suppress any possible attitude-behavior discrepancies (Lahaderne, 1968). Or, similarly, it is possible that socially defined, or "scripted," classroom behavior outweighed that which was attitude-linked at the individual level (Abelson, 1982).

However, it is also possible that the small number of cases used here obscured most real differences in behavior which existed among the high-, medium-, and low-attitude groups. Karweit and Slavin (1982) reported that reliable data could be obtained with as few as three students per class, but the present work assigned the three students to three different attitude levels. It is conceivable that two students per attitude level (i.e., six students per class) would provide more stable data and a more substantial test of this third possibility. Accordingly, a replication study using the increased number of students is currently under way.

The accompanying supplementary data were less ambiguous. These results did not support completely those obtained in two earlier studies, which examined the attitude-behavior relationship using the AMTB (Gliksman, 1976; Naiman et al., 1978). Both of these investigations found more hand-raising, more interest, and more task-oriented activity in students with the more highly positive attitudes toward FSL. With three groups of students categorized by attitude toward FSL, the current work found the highest levels of activity and involvement in the medium-attitude students. That is, the data suggested a curvilinear relationship between attitude toward FSL as measured by the AMTB and amounts of positive behavior as reflected by the Modified Behavior Observation System.

It is unclear why the medium-attitude students were so actively engaged in FSL classes. The particular students examined did not have a history of superior achievement in FSL, because none of their stanine equivalent marks of the preceding grade exceeded those of the high-attitude group. (However, their marks varied consistently from 3 to 5 stanines above those of the low-attitude students.) It is possible that teachers were directing the bulk of their instruction toward the middle group of students and were using representatives of this group to signal what material evoked maximum student involvement and how quickly they should proceed through it. If the enhanced activity of the middle group is upheld in a replication study, then reasons for this state of affairs may deserve closer scrutiny.

A final observation to be made at this point involves the verbal response data. The high levels of voluntary behavior produced by the medium group were not reflected by the numbers of times that these students were called on by the teachers. It appears that teachers tried to obtain verbal responses from a majority of students during a single class period, even if most of the raised hands and other expressions of interest and involvement (especially those manifested by the medium group) were ignored in the process. The long-term effects on student attitudes of this specific teacher strategy remain to be determined.

In sum, results of the present study indicated significantly different behavior patterns within the class segments of openings, transitions, oral exercises, and written exercises. The major data set consisting of time-based behavioral records showed few substantial differences among attitude groups within segments. However, frequency data indicated more hand-raising among the medium-attitude students. Although the size of the three groups should be increased before firm conclusions can be drawn, these preliminary data tended to support researchers who have argued that behaviors are determined primarily by situational rather than by individual factors (e.g., Abelson, 1982; Wicker, 1969).

Implications for educational theory and practice

The current investigation provided two major findings – one strong and one weak – concerning classroom structure and mode of functioning. The stronger result was that different rules of behavior hold during various class segments. The weaker finding was that, within class segments, different patterns of behavior may be displayed by students with varying attitudes toward the subject. Therefore, because different segments are characterized by different constellations of teacher and student behavior, unqualified prescriptions concerning "appropriate" classroom conduct are bound to be overly simplistic. The situation is further complicated by student behavior patterns which may vary within the individual segments according to student attitude.

The traditional question of whether there is a relationship between attitude and behavior in the classroom was not resolved firmly. Student attitude toward a particular curriculum subject (FSL in the present case) was not related systematically to student behavior during lessons in that subject. The time-based results suggested that, in the absence of formal attitude measures, student attitude toward a subject could be inferred from behavior manifested only during transitions. At these times, students with very negative attitudes toward FSL seemed to engage in much higher amounts of peer interaction than students with medium or highly positive attitudes toward FSL. When compared with the middle group, the former students also manifested much less reading or writing activity. One possible reason for these results is that classroom constraints and demands are strong enough to obscure individual differences in attitude. However, it is also possible that group sizes were too small to detect other attitude-behavior relationships.

In the present study, the middle group of students was the source of several questions related to classroom procedures. As suggested by the hand-raising and supplementary informal data, these students appeared to be the most highly involved in the lessons. They seemed to display superior amounts of task appropriate behavior and raised their hands most often in response to teacher queries. Were the teachers adjusting the level and pace of their lessons to suit the middle-attitude (and often the middle-achievement) students? Will these students show a more positive attitude toward FSL in future? What will be the longer-term effects on the attitudes of students who are not now in the middle group? These questions aside, it was significant that teachers did not discriminate among the various student groups when calling upon them for oral responses.

The positive classroom contributions of the middle-attitude students in particular provoked several observations about the nature of the attitudes themselves. It is possible that the AMTB reflects qualitatively different attitudes toward FSL as scores on the test change significantly. That is, using Rokeach's (1968) typology of beliefs for illustrative purposes, students with high attitude/motivation indices (AMIs) may hold "primitive beliefs" about FSL that have been gained through direct outside experience with French and which are difficult to change despite a less than favorable classroom situation. Students with lower AMIs may have "inconsequential beliefs" about FSL that have been formed by classroom exposure to French, which are dependent upon the classroom context for maintenance and which are easily altered by situational circumstances. Clearly, these speculations cannot be resolved by the present study. However, the data do suggest that the most desirable educational goal for students (i.e., a set of firmly held positive attitudes toward FSL) may not be reflected by the classroom behaviors most preferred by teachers (i.e., the kinds of overt activity usually associated with significant lesson involvement and positive motivation).

In sum, the major contribution of the present paper was not to elaborate on the *Is* question mentioned previously (i.e., "Is there a relationship between attitude and behavior?") but to provide a preliminary description of the many relationships which have been presumed to exist between attitude and behavior in the classroom. Hence, the major issue being considered might be considered more appropriately as a *What?* query related closely to the *How?* question raised by Zanna and Fazio (1982): Given the demands and constraints of specific lesson segments (that were shown to exist), what is the nature of the association between student attitude toward the subject in question and patterns of student behavior? Because a somewhat ambiguous response was provided by the results reported here, more work is required to support the research assumptions and findings discussed in the chapter. Still, these findings provide further evidence for the importance of social psychological factors in determining classroom behavior.

References

Abelson, R. P. (1982). Three modes of attitude-behavior consistency. In M. P. Zanna, E. T. Higgins, & C. P. Herman (Eds.), *Consistency in social behavior: The Ontario symposium, Vol. 2* (pp. 131–146). Hillsdale, NJ: Erlbaum.

Ajzen, I. (1982). On behaving in accordance with one's attitudes. In M. P. Zanna, E. T. Higgins, & C. P. Herman (Eds.), *Consistency in social behavior: The Ontario symposium, Vol. 2* (pp. 3–15). Hillsdale, NJ: Erlbaum.

Ajzen, I., & Fishbein, M. (1977). Attitude-behavior relations: A theoretical analysis and review of empirical research. *Psychological Bulletin, 84*, 888–918.

Arlin, M. (1979). Teacher transitions can disrupt time flow in classrooms. *American Educational Research Journal, 16*, 42–56.

Bagozzi, R. P., & Burnkrant, R. E. (1979). Attitude organization and the attitude-behavior relationship. *Journal of Personality and Social Psychology, 37*, 913–929.

Bakeman, R., Cairns, R. B., & Appelbaum, M. (1979). Note on describing and analyzing interactional data: Some first steps and common pitfalls. In R. B. Cairns (Ed.), *The analysis of social interactions: Methods, issues, and illustrations* (pp. 227–234). Hillsdale, NJ: Erlbaum.

Blumer, H. (1969). *Symbolic interactionism*. Englewood Cliffs, NJ: Prentice-Hall.

Braun, C. (1976). Teacher expectation: Sociological dynamics. *Review of Educational Research, 46,* 185–213.

Bremme, D. W., & Erickson, F. (1977). Relationships among verbal and nonverbal classroom behaviors. *Theory into Practice, 16,* 153–161.

Calder, B., & Ross, M. (1973). *Attitudes and behavior.* Morristown, NJ: General Learning Press.

Clark, C. M., & Yinger, R. J. (1977). Research on teacher thinking. *Curriculum Inquiry, 7,* 279–304.

Cooper, J., & Croyle, R. T. (1984). Attitudes and attitude change. In M. R. Rosenzweig & L. W. Porter (Eds.), *Annual review of psychology: Vol. 35* (pp. 395–426). Palo Alto, CA: Annual Reviews.

Crano, W. D., & Mellon, P. M. (1978). Causal influence of teachers' expectations on children's academic performance: A cross-lagged panel analysis. *Journal of Educational Psychology, 70,* 39–49.

Crespi, I. (1971). What kinds of attitude measures are predictive of behavior? *Public Opinion Quarterly, 35,* 327–334.

Denzin, N. K. (1978). *The research act: A theoretical introduction to sociological methods* (2nd ed.). New York: McGraw-Hill.

Early, C. J. (1968). Attitude learning in children. *Journal of Educational Psychology, 59,* 176–180.

Ehrlich, H. J. (1969). Attitudes, behavior, and the intervening variables. *American Sociologist, 4,* 29–34.

Fishbein, M., & Ajzen, I. (1974). Attitudes towards objects as predictors of single and multiple behavioral criteria. *Psychological Review, 81,* 59–74.

Fishbein, M., & Ajzen, I. (1975). *Belief, attitude, intention, and behavior: An introduction to theory and research.* Reading, MA: Addison-Wesley.

Gardner, R. C., Gliksman, L., & Smythe, P. C. (1978). Attitudes and behaviour in second language acquisition: A social psychological interpretation. *Canadian Psychological Review, 19,* 173–186.

Gardner, R. C., & Smythe, P. C. (1981). On the development of the attitude/motivation test battery. *Canadian Modern Language Review, 37,* 510–525.

Gliksman, L. (1976). Second language acquisition: The effects of student attitudes on classroom behaviour. Unpublished master's thesis, University of Western Ontario, London, ON. (Canadian Theses on Microfiche No. 28231).

Gottlieb, J. (1978). Observing social adaptation in schools. In G. P. Sackett (Ed.), *Observing behavior, Vol. 1: Theory and applications in mental retardation* (pp. 285–309). Baltimore, MD: University Park Press, 1978.

Gump, P. (1967). *The classroom behavior setting: Its nature and relation to student behavior.* Lawrence: University of Kansas, Department of Psychology.

Gump, P. (1969). Intra-setting analysis: The third grade classroom as a special but instructive case. In E. P. Willems & H. L. Raush (Eds.), *Naturalistic viewpoints in psychological research* (pp. 200–220). New York: Holt, Rinehart and Winston.

Hollenbeck, A. R. (1978). Problems of reliability in observational research. In G. P. Sackett (Ed.), *Observing behavior, Vol. 2: Data collection and analysis methods* (pp. 79–98). Baltimore, MD: University Park Press.

Kahle, L. R., & Berman, J. J. (1979). Attitudes cause behaviors: A cross-lagged panel analysis. *Journal of Personality and Social Psychology, 37,* 315–321.

Karweit, N., & Slavin, R. E. (1982). Time-on-task: Issues of timing, sampling, and definition. *Journal of Educational Psychology, 74,* 844–851.

Lahaderne, H. M. (1968). Attitudinal and intellectual correlates of attention: A study of four sixth-grade classrooms. *Journal of Educational Psychology, 59,* 320–324.

Lamb, M. E. (1979). Issues in the study of social interaction: An introduction. In M. E. Lamb, S. J. Suomi, & G. R. Stephenson (Eds.), *Social interaction analysis: Methodological issues* (pp. 1-10). Madison: University of Wisconsin Press.

Lett, J. A., Jr. (1977). Assessing attitudinal outcomes. In J. K. Phillips (Ed.), *The language connection: From the classroom to the world* (pp. 267-302). Skokie, IL: National Textbook.

Magnusson, D., & Endler, N. S. (Eds.). (1977). *Personality at the crossroads: Current issues in interactional psychology.* Hillsdale, NJ: Erlbaum.

McGuire, W. J. (1985). Attitudes and attitude change. In G. Lindzey & E. Aronson (Eds.), *The handbook of social psychology: Vol. 2* (3rd ed.) N.Y.: Random House.

McMillan, J. H. (1980a). Social psychology and learning. In J. H. McMillan (Ed.), *The social psychology of school learning* (pp. 1-37). New York: Academic Press.

McMillan, J. H. (1980b). Attitude development and measurement. In J. H. McMillan (Ed.), *The social psychology of school learning* (pp. 215-245). New York: Academic Press.

Mead, G. H. (1934). *Mind, self, and society* (edited, with an introduction by C. Morris). Chicago: University of Chicago Press.

Naiman, N., Frohlich, M., Stern, H. H., & Todesco, A. (1978). *The good language learner* (Research in Education Series No. 7). Toronto: Ontario Institute for Studies in Education.

Ostrom, T. M. (1969). The relationship between the affective, behavioral, and cognitive components of attitude. *Journal of Experimental Social Psychology, 5,* 12-30.

Parke, R. D. (1979). Interactional designs. In R. B. Cairns (Ed.), *The analysis of social interactions: Methods, issues, and illustrations* (pp. 15-35). Hillsdale, NJ: Erlbaum.

Perkins, H. V. (1964). A procedure for assessing the classroom behavior of students and teachers. *American Educational Research Journal, 1,* 249-260.

Peterson, D. R. (1977). A functional approach to the study of person-person interactions. In D. Magnusson & N. S. Endler (Eds.), *Personality at the crossroads: Current issues in interactional psychology* (pp. 305-315). Hillsdale, NJ: Erlbaum.

Raush, H. L. (1969). Naturalistic method and the clinical approach. In E. P. Willems & H. L. Raush (Eds.), *Naturalistic viewpoints in psychological research.* New York: Holt, Rinehart and Winston.

Raush, H. L. (1979). Epistemology, metaphysics, and person-situation methodology: Conclusions. In L. R. Kahle (Ed.), *New directions for methodology of behavioral science, No. 2: Methods for studying person-situation interactions* (pp. 93-106). San Francisco: Jossey-Bass.

Rokeach, M. (1968). *Beliefs, attitudes and values.* San Francisco: Jossey-Bass.

Rosenblum, L. A. (1978). The creation of a behavioral taxonomy. In G. P. Sackett (Ed.), *Observing behavior, Vol. 2: Data collection and analysis methods* (pp. 15-24). Baltimore, MD: University Park Press.

Sackett, G. P., Ruppenthal, G. C., & Gluck, J. (1978). Introduction: An overview of methodological and statistical problems in observational research. In G. P. Sackett (Ed.), *Observing behavior, Vol. 2: Data collection and analysis methods* (pp. 1-14). Baltimore, MD: University Park Press.

Siegel, S. (1956). *Nonparametric statistics for the behavioral sciences.* New York: McGraw-Hill.

Silberman, M. L. (1969). Behavioral expression of teachers' attitudes toward elementary school students. *Journal of Educational Psychology, 60,* 402-407.

Simon, A., & Boyer, E. G. (1974). *Mirrors for behavior III: An anthology of observation instruments.* Wyncote, PA: Communication Materials Center.

Solomon, D., & Kendall, A. J. (1979). *Children in classrooms: An investigation of person-environment interaction.* New York: Praeger.

Snyder, M. (1982). When believing means doing: Creating links between attitudes and behavior. In M. P. Zanna, E. T. Higgins, & C. P. Herman (Eds.), *Consistency in social behavior: The Ontario symposium, Vol. 2* (pp. 105-130). Hillsdale, NJ: Erlbaum.

Tinsley, H. E. A., & Weiss, D. J. (1975). Interrater reliability and agreement of subjective judgments. *Journal of Counseling Psychology, 22,* 358-376.

Weinstein, A. G. (1972). Predicting behavior from attitudes. *Public Opinion Quarterly, 36,* 355-360.

Wicker, A. W. (1969). Attitudes versus actions: The relationship of verbal and overt behavioral responses to attitude objects. *Journal of Social Issues, 25*(4), 41-78.

Winne, P. H., & Marx, R. W. (1977). Reconceptualizing research on teaching. *Journal of Educational Psychology, 69,* 668-678.

Zanna, M. P., & Fazio, R. H. (1982). The attitude-behavior relation: Moving toward a third generation of research. In M. P. Zanna, E. T. Higgins, & C. P. Herman (Eds.), *Consistency in social behavior: The Ontario symposium, Vol. 2* (pp. 283-301). Hillsdale, NJ: Erlbaum.

Part II

Teacher–student interaction

4   Four factors in the mediation of teacher expectancy effects

Monica J. Harris and Robert Rosenthal

In the late 1950s a research program began that was designed to examine the processes by which a person's expectations about another may come to serve as self-fulfilling prophecies (Rosenthal, 1963). These early studies involved the social psychology of the psychological experiment, focusing on the effects of experimenters' expectations on the responses of their research subjects. The major conclusion from this research program was that experimenters can and often do exert subtle, unintended social influence on their subjects, eliciting responses that tended to confirm the hypothesis of the study (Rosenthal, 1966).

Later studies in this area explored the possibility that such unintended social influence could be operating within classrooms. Teachers no doubt hold expectations for their pupils' performance, but the question remained whether these expectations were merely accurate reflections of actual student ability or whether expectations acted as causal factors in determining student achievement. Experimental evidence that teachers' expectations can function as self-fulfilling prophecies with respect to the intellectual functioning of their pupils was first documented in *Pygmalion in the Classroom* (Rosenthal & Jacobson, 1968). Since the publication of that book, many other studies were conducted in attempts to prove or disprove the existence of teacher expectancy effects. Cumulative summaries of this research, now numbering over 400 studies, show not only that these interpersonal expectancy effects occur (with p vanishingly small) but that their magnitudes are of substantial practical importance as well (Rosenthal, 1969, 1976, in press; Rosenthal & Rubin, 1978).

The implications of this research on teacher expectancy effects are

This research was supported in part by a National Science Foundation graduate fellowship to the first author and a National Science Foundation grant to the second author.

91

serious because negative expectations can potentially affect literally hundreds of thousands of children adversely, particularly those of lower social classes or of minority ethnic groups. One compelling example of the practical importance of teacher expectancy effects is Rist's (1970) anecdotal description of the consequences of a tracking system employed in one urban elementary school. Children were classified into three ability groups *within the first week* of kindergarten, presumably well before the teachers could have assessed the students' academic potentials. Yet these students were maintained in the same tracks for the next 2 years. The moral appears to be that once a "Clown" (as the lowest ability group was named by the teacher), always a Clown. Rist wrote, "When a teacher bases her expectations of performance on the social status of the student and assumes that the higher the social class, the higher the potential of the child, those children of low social status suffer a stigmatization outside of their own choice or will. Yet there is a greater tragedy than being labeled as a slow learner, and that is being treated as one" (1970, p. 448).

Rist's quote emphasizes the importance of focusing on the *mediation* of teacher expectancy effects. It is the ways in which teachers communicate their expectancies to students that ultimately creates the self-fulfilling prophecy, and it is this mediation that ultimately is the focus of intervention. Hence, a more important and more interesting question in expectancy research concerns the question of process – that is, *how* teacher expectations about pupil performance are transmitted. In this chapter, we will outline one approach, based on a four-factor theory that has been proposed to account in part for the mediation of teacher expectancy effects (Rosenthal, 1973a, 1973b), and we will provide a meta-analytic summary of the available empirical evidence bearing on this four-factor theory.

Conceptualizing teacher expectancy effects

One useful model for conceptualizing teacher expectancy effects is the "ten-arrow" model shown in Figure 4.1 (Rosenthal, 1981). This model distinguishes between variables that *moderate* expectancy effects and variables that *mediate* such effects. Moderator variables are pre-existing variables such as sex, age, and personality that influence the size of interpersonal expectancy effects; mediating variables refer to the behaviors by which expectations are communicated. The basic elements of the model are (a) distal independent variables (e.g., stable attributes of the expecter and expectee), (b) proximal independent variables (the ex-

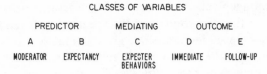

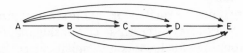

Figure 4.1. Ten-arrow model for the study of interpersonal expectancy effects. *Source:* Harris & Rosenthal (1985).

pectancy), (c) mediating variables, (d) proximal dependent variables (e.g., outcome measures such as achievement on tests, etc.), and (e) distal dependent variables (longer-term outcome variables). A useful feature of this model is that the 10 arrows of the model represent the types of relationships that can be examined in research on expectancy effects. These arrows are described in detail elsewhere (Rosenthal, 1981) so we will discuss here only the two links relevant to the topic of mediation: the B–C and C–D arrows. B–C relationships describe the effect the expectancy has on the expecter's behavior, the relationships most often investigated in research on mediation. Equally important to understanding mediation, however, are the C–D relationships between the expecter's behavior and outcome variables. Research bearing on the B–C link tells us which behaviors are induced by a given expectancy, but research bearing on the C–D link assures us that these behaviors affect the expectee so as to create a self-fulfilling prophecy. As is evident, the two types of relationships address different questions, making the B–C/C–D distinction critical. In the present chapter, we acknowledge this distinction by discussing results for the B–C and C–D links separately.

On the basis of the first 30 or so published studies relevant to mediation, Rosenthal (1973a, 1973b) proposed a four-factor "theory" of the mediation of teacher expectancy effects that describes four major groupings of teacher behaviors hypothesized to be involved in mediation. The first factor, *climate*, refers to the warmer socioemotional climate that teachers tend to create for high expectancy students, a warmth that can be communicated both verbally and nonverbally. The *feedback* factor refers to the tendency for teachers to give more differentiated feedback to their "special," high expectancy students. By differentiated, it is meant that the feedback will be contingent on the correctness or incorrectness of the student's response and that the content of the feedback will tend to be directly related to what the student has said. The *input* factor refers to the tendency for teachers to attempt to teach more material and more difficult material to high expectancy students. Lastly, the *output* factor refers to the tendency for teachers to give their special students greater opportunities for responding.

The four-factor theory is not a formal theory in the sense of providing a deductively derived network of hypothesized relationships. Rather, it is merely a convenient grouping of behaviors into molar categories, which are easy to understand but which are inductively derived and are not based on any prior theory of interpersonal behavior and influence. Although the four-factor theory is not a true theory, it nevertheless provides explicit, testable hypotheses about behaviors involved in mediation. Accordingly, a primary purpose of this chapter is to evaluate the current tenability and utility of the four-factor theory.

Meta-analysis and teacher expectancy effects

It has now been well over a decade since the four-factor theory of mediation (Rosenthal, 1973a) has been advanced, and a large body of research since that time now exists on the topic of mediation. A wide variety of behaviors has been examined as well as a variety of expectancy situations.

The question of exactly how expectancy effects are mediated is ultimately, of course, an empirical one. In an attempt to answer that question, Brophy (1983) provided a list of 17 behaviors that have been shown by various studies to be implicated in the mediation of teacher expectancy effects. These behaviors include variables related to patterns of reinforcement, frequency of interaction, assignment of class work, nonverbal cues, and so on, behaviors most of which could readily be classified into one of the four factors. Similarly, the four-factor theory predicts that behaviors related to the four factors will be important mediating agents of teacher expectancy effects. Still, it is not clear how to evaluate and weight which specific factors or individual behaviors have been best supported by this large body of earlier research.

Meta-analysis provides methods for integrating previous research on expectancy mediation. Meta-analysis is the quantitative combination and analysis of results obtained from a group of studies (Cooper, 1984; Glass, 1976; Glass, McGaw, & Smith, 1981; Rosenthal, 1969, 1980, 1984; Rosenthal & Rubin, 1978). The advantage of meta-analysis over traditional literature reviews is that it allows the estimation of an overall effect size and significance level for a variable of interest.

In this chapter, the variables of interest are specific mediating behaviors of teacher expectancies and the four factors of climate, feedback, input, and output. In a previous paper (Harris & Rosenthal, 1985), we presented a meta-analysis of 31 specific behaviors believed to be mediators of interpersonal expectations. In this chapter, we use meta-analysis to achieve two goals: (a) to offer an updated, more current meta-analysis (adding approximately 10% new studies), focusing particularly on the present state of research regarding the four-factor theory of the mediation of teacher expectancy effects; and (b) to discuss possible applications of this mediation research to education.

Method

Literature search

For this meta-analysis, manual and computerized literature searches of *Psychological Abstracts* were conducted, covering a span of time from the 1960s to 1983. In addition, many of the studies used in this meta-analysis were manuscripts that had become available through the "invisible college," that is, unpublished manuscripts, preprints, and doctoral dissertations. The literature search yielded a preliminary database of over 200 studies involving the mediation of expectancy effects. Most of the studies involved expectancies in an educational context, although the form of the expectancy manipulation was not constrained.

To be subsequently included in the meta-analysis, each study had to meet the following two criteria: (a) the study had to contain enough information to allow the estimation of significance level and effect size, and (b) the mediating variables examined in the study had to fall into one of 10 broad categories of behavior related to the four-factor theory. (This classification process will be described in detail later.) Several studies were excluded due to their anecdotal nature, rendering estimation of effect sizes impossible. Eighteen studies were not used because they dealt only with such nonspecific mediating variables as cheating, verbal conditioning, presence of audio versus video communication channels, and so on. The remaining studies excluded from the meta-analysis were ones addressing variables that were investigated by fewer than 13 studies; this included, for example, behaviors such as smiles, task-orientation, and so on.[1]

The primary goal of this meta-analysis was to discover the particular behaviors that are associated with teachers' expectations toward their students. We are *also* interested in the relationship between those behaviors and outcome measures such as student achievement. This latter issue has been a focus of intensive research in education for many decades. We do not claim to present here an exhaustive meta-analysis of all teacher behaviors that are related to student achievement and attitudes; such a review is beyond the scope of this chapter. Rather, our paper addresses the relationship between mediating behaviors and outcome measures that occur *within the context* of interpersonal expectancy research. The ultimate consequence of this limitation is that while we feel confident we have obtained a representative and fairly exhaustive sample of those studies examining the relationship between expectations and emitted behaviors, our conclusions about the relationship between the mediating behaviors and outcome measures must be restricted to studies within the expectancy domain.

Coding the studies

One coder (the first author) read each of the studies and extracted the following information: age, sex, and number of the expecters (teachers, experimenters, etc.); age, sex, and number of the expectees (students, subjects, etc.); whether the expectancy was experimentally manipulated or naturally occurring (nonexperimental); whether the study involved a B–C link (where the expectancy [B] is the independent variable and the emitted behaviors [C] are the dependent variables) or a C–D link (where the behaviors [C] are the independent variables and outcome measures [D] are the dependent variables); and all relevant results.

To be considered relevant, a result had to be a focused test (i.e., with one degree of freedom) of the relationship between expectations and behaviors, or between expectancy-induced behaviors and outcome variables. When focused tests of the hypotheses were not available in the original article, they were computed from the means, standard deviations, or mean squares that were provided (Rosenthal & Rosnow, 1985). A disheartening number of the studies (perhaps 10%) contained statistical errors, such as miscalculating degrees of freedom or applying inappropriate statistical tests. When such statistical errors in original analyses were detected, they were corrected before inclusion in the meta-analysis.

Classification of the mediating variables

After all studies had been coded, the results were sorted into categories of teacher behaviors. As noted earlier, many behavior variables were investigated by only a few studies. In order to achieve some level of stability, we used the rule of thumb that only variables represented by 13 or more studies would be reported in this chapter; these variables were also more clearly relevant to the four factors of climate, feedback, input, and output. There were 10 such behavioral variables, defined as follows. Unless otherwise noted, it is predicted that high expectancy students would receive more of that behavior than would low expectancy students.

I. *Climate*

    1. *Positive climate* – general positive attitudes, statements, or behaviors directed toward the student. This category includes such variables as "teacher warmth" and other global positive behaviors.

    2. *Negative climate* – general negative attitudes, statements, or behaviors directed by the teacher toward the student. High expectancy students are predicted to receive less negative climate than lows.

    3. *Eye contact or gaze* – instances when the teacher looks at the student or engages in mutual eye contact.

II. *Feedback*

    4. *Praise* – instances of positive feedback and positive evaluation directed by the teacher toward the student.

    5. *Criticism* – negative feedback or negative evaluation directed toward some characteristic of the student or the student's behavior. High expectancy students are predicted to receive less criticism than lows.

    6. *Accepts students' ideas* – a category of the Flanders (1970) classroom interaction coding system; it consists of instances when the teacher acknowledges, modifies, applies, compares, or summarizes what the student has said.

    7. *Ignores student* – instances of no feedback where the teacher does not acknowledge or respond to a student's statement or request. It is predicted that high expectancy students will be ignored less than lows.

III. *Input*

    8. *Input* – when the teacher presents more material or more difficult material to the student.

IV. *Output*

    9. *Asks questions* – frequency of any type of question asked by the teacher.

   10. *Frequency of interactions* – number of contacts, academic or non-academic, that the teacher initiates with a student.

Most of the studies included in the meta-analysis reported multiple results pertaining to several of the behavior categories. The results were analyzed separately by category; each study was allowed to contribute only one effect size per behavior category, thus satisfying the requirement of indepedence of effect sizes and probability levels (Rosenthal, 1984; Rosenthal & Rubin, 1984). In cases where studies reported multiple effect sizes with respect to a single category (e.g., various types of positive climate), the median of the relevant effect sizes was used in the meta-analysis. The use of the median is a robust procedure, but it is fairly conservative, serving to deflate somewhat our estimates of effect sizes (Rosenthal, 1984; Rosenthal & Rubin, 1984).

Results

Our analyses are divided into two major sections: First, we present the meta-analyses examining which behaviors are associated with higher or lower expectations (i.e., the B–C results). In a later section, we present the C–D results relating the mediated behaviors to outcome measures. Within these two sections, the results are broken down further by looking at behavior categories both individually and collapsed into the four factors of climate, feedback, input, and output.

Relationship between expectations and teacher behaviors:
The B–C link

The results of the meta-analyses for the ten behaviors individually are shown in Table 4.1. Column (1) shows the number of studies examining each behavior category; this number ranges from 13 for Eye Contact to 43 for Praise. Columns (2) and (3) show the combined standard normal deviates (Z) and their associated probability levels for each of the ten behaviors, obtained by the Stouffer method of adding Zs (Mosteller & Bush, 1954; Rosenthal, 1978, 1984).[2] All the combined Zs for the ten

Table 4.1. *Meta-analysis of ten mediating behaviors*

	(1)	(2)	(3)	(4)	(5) Experimental	(6) Experimental	(7) Non-experimental	(8) Non-experimental	(9) Experimental vs. nonexperimental contrast Z^a
Variable	No. of studies	Combined Z value	p	Combined effect size (r)	N of studies	Effect size (r)	N of studies	Effect size (r)	
Positive climate	34	7.61	<.0000001	.257	21	.208	13	.345	-1.361
Negative climate	17	5.10	.0000003	.282	9	.275	8	.290	-.097
Eye contact	13	2.42	.0078	.112	11	.141	2	-.055	.995
Praise	43	5.92	<.0000001	.128	17	.034	26	.189	-2.188
Criticism	32	3.92	.000045	.112	10	.006	22	.160	-1.992
Accepts ideas	14	6.43	<.0000001	.253	5	.362	9	.189	1.629
Ignores student	14	3.23	.00062	.197	5	-.047	9	.325	-2.939
Input	26	7.14	<.0000001	.259	19	.307	7	.122	1.800
Asks questions	35	6.69	<.0000001	.171	15	.138	20	.195	-.688
Frequency of interactions	36	4.70	<.0000013	.190	15	.112	21	.245	-3.740

Note: Positive Z and r values mean that the obtained result was in the predicted direction (see "Method").
[a]Positive Z means that effect sizes for experimental studies were larger than those for nonexperimental studies.

behavior categories were in the predicted direction and were highly significant, with probabilities ranging from $p = .00062$ for the Eye Contact to $p < .0000001$ for Praise, Positive Climate, Asks Questions, Input, and Accepts Students' Ideas. Consequently, it is extremely unlikely that any of these behaviors are implicated in the mediation of expectancies as a result of simple sampling variation.

More interesting, however, than the demonstration of the statistical significance of the combined results is the estimation of an overall effect size for all the studies of a given behavior. These combined effect sizes, indexed by the Pearson correlation coefficient, are displayed in column (4) of Table 4.1. These correlations range from .112 (for Eye Contact and Criticism) to a high of .282 (for Negative Climate). On the basis of the criteria set forth by Cohen (1977), these effect sizes can be considered as falling in the "small" to "medium" range. A simple, practical way of interpreting these effect sizes is given by the Binomial Effect Size Display or BESD (Rosenthal & Rubin, 1982a). The BESD is an intuitively appealing method of indexing the practical importance of a research effect that is easily understandable by researchers, students, and lay persons. The BESD essentially answers the question: What is the effect on the "success" rate of the institution of a new treatment procedure? As an illustration, an effect size of $r = .32$ (which accounts for "only" 10% of the variance) can be interpreted using the BESD as being equivalent to increasing the success rate from 34% to 66%. The control group success rate is computed as $(.50 - r/2) \times 100$, and the experimental group success rate is computed as $(.50 + r/2) \times 100$. The BESD thus conveys the real world importance of an effect size more clearly than do "percent of variance accounted for" measures (Rosenthal & Rubin, 1982a).

With respect to the present meta-analysis, the effect size with the lowest magnitude, $r = .112$ for Eye Contact and Criticism, can be interpreted in terms of the BESD as meaning that having high expectations for a student will be associated with an increase in the percentage of teachers showing or pupils receiving above average amounts of eye contact (or criticism) from about 44% to 56%. For the effect size with the largest magnitude, $r = .282$ for Negative Climate, the BESD shows that the percentage of teachers exhibiting or pupils receiving below average negative climate will increase from 36% for low expectancy students to 64% for high expectancy students. The other effect sizes can be interpreted in an analogous manner, and all are of sufficient magnitude to indicate a relationship of practical importance between expectancies and emitted behavior. The behavior categories with the largest effect sizes (all *rs*>.25) are Input, Negative Climate, and Accepts Student's Ideas; the effect sizes for Praise and Criticism, variables that receive much attention in research on teacher expectancies, are considerably lower.

Tests for heterogeneity of significance levels and effect sizes (Rosenthal & Rubin, 1979) were significant at $p<.05$ for all behaviors. Significant heterogeneity is common whenever many studies by different investigators utilizing different methods are examined, and it may be regarded as analogous to individual differences obtained within single studies.

One important question that can be answered by meta-analyses is whether effect sizes differ for studies of varying methodological quality. In the present meta-analysis, we examined the relationship between internal validity and effect size by comparing the combined effect sizes obtained for studies in which the expectancy was experimentally manipulated and those in which the expectancy was allowed to vary naturally (nonexperimental studies). The combined effect sizes computed separately for experimental and nonexperimental studies are presented in columns (6) and (8) of Table 4.1; the last column presents the Z for the contrast between these types of effect sizes (Rosenthal & Rubin, 1982b).

Table 4.1 shows that for 7 of the 10 behavior categories, effect sizes are smaller for experimental studies than for nonexperimental studies, suggesting that high internal validity *does* matter in this research area. Four of the contrasts testing the difference between effect sizes in experimental and nonexperimental studies are significant; these are the contrasts for Praise, Frequency of Interactions, Criticism, and Ignores Student. For each of these significant contrast Zs, there is more support for the hypothesis in the nonexperimental studies than in the experimental studies. The difference is particularly striking for the variables of Praise, Criticism, and Ignores Student, where the effect size for experimental studies drops close to zero. However, it is reassuring to note that of the three largest effect sizes (Input, Negative Climate, and Accepts Student's Ideas), there are no significant differences between experimental and nonexperimental studies, and for two of the categories (Input and Accepts Student's Ideas) the combined effect size is larger for experimental studies.[3]

The ten behaviors and the four-factor theory. The primary theoretical question of interest in this chapter concerns how the findings for these 10 behavior categories bear on the four-factor theory of the mediation of teacher expectancy effects. This question can be addressed by re-classifying the 10 behaviors into the four categories of climate, feedback, input, and output, and then deriving a combined significance level and effect size for each factor using the same meta-analytic techniques as above. In cases where a study contributed values to more than one behavior category within a given factor, the mean of those effect sizes or probability levels was calculated first, and that value was entered into the analysis, in order to preserve independence.

The results of this analysis are shown in Table 4.2. As can be seen, all four factors are extremely significant. In terms of effect sizes, Input appears to be the most important mediating factor in the transmission of expectancies. However, all four combined effect sizes are of substantial practical importance; even the lowest, Feedback at $r = .127$, is equivalent to an increase in the percentage of teachers showing (or pupils receiving) above average use of appropriate feedback from 44% for low expectancy students to 56% for high expectancy students. In short, the results of this meta-analysis provide strong support for the role of climate, feedback, input, and output as mediating factors induced by teacher expectancies.

Table 4.2. *Meta-analysis of the four factor theory: relationship between expectations and the four factors*

	No. of studies	Combined significance level (Z)[a]	Combined effect size (r)
1. *Climate* a. Positive climate b. Negative climate c. Eye contact	51	8.49	.229
2. *Feedback* a. Praise b. Criticism c. Accepts student's ideas d. Ignores student	50	5.90	.127
3. *Input* a. Input	26	7.14	.259
4. *Output* a. Asks questions b. Frequency of interaction	53	7.43	.185
Median	50.5	7.28	.207

[a]All entries are significant at $p < .0000001$.

Relationship between mediating behaviors and outcome variables:
the C–D link

Our earlier discussion of the ten-arrow model for the study of interpersonal expectancy effects emphasized the importance of learning
about all the links for a complete understanding of the processes
involved. With respect to mediation, it is not sufficient merely to
demonstrate that having high or low expectations for another person will
influence behavior in particular ways. We must also show that those
emitted behaviors reliably influence the behavior of the person of whom
the expectancy is held.

In this meta-analysis, the outcome measures that were used are broad
in scope, with the most common ones being student achievement on
some academic task, student attitudes, and observers' ratings of student
behavior. Studies that relate mediated behaviors to outcome measures are
unfortunately much less common in this research area; consequently our
conclusions must be based on smaller numbers of studies and are more
tentative. For example, for one of the behavior categories (Accepts
Student's Ideas), we were able to retrieve only a single study examining
the C–D link.

Table 4.3 presents the meta-analyses of the C–D link for the 10
behavior categories. Positive Z and r values mean that an increase in the
predicted direction of a given mediating variable is associated with better
outcomes. For example, the positive Z for positive climate means that
subjects who experienced more positive climates had better outcomes
(higher test scores, more favorable attitudes, etc.); similarly, the positive Z
for negative climate means that subjects who experienced *less* negative
climates had better outcomes. Table 4.3 shows that 8 of the 10 behavior
variables yielded a statistically significant combined Z. On the whole, the
effect sizes appear to be larger for the C–D analyses; four behavior
categories have a combined effect size of $r > .30$, in contrast to the B–C
analyses, of which none had an $r > .30$. Chi-square tests of heterogeneity
of effect sizes and probability levels showed significant heterogeneity for
6 of the 10 behavior categories: Praise, Frequency of Interactions, Positive
Climate, Criticism, Negative Climate, and Eye Contact.

In sum, we see that the following behaviors are most strongly and
significantly related to better outcomes: more positive climate, greater
input, increased eye contact, asking questions, and more praise. Interestingly, criticism appears to show very little, if any, relationship to
student outcomes, quite a counter-intuitive finding. Strong findings for
behavior categories with fewer than five studies (Frequency of Inter-

Table 4.3. *Relationship between mediating behaviors and outcome variables*

Behavior category	No. of studies	Combined significance level (Z)	p	Combined effect size (r)
Positive climate	17	10.16	<.0000001	.393
Negative climate	3	2.63	.0043	.357
Eye contact	7	4.81	.0000008	.316
Praise	13	4.18	.000015	.152
Criticism	7	0.38	.352	.059
Accepts ideas	1	2.33	.0099	.520
Ignores student	2	−.86	.804	−.228
Input	8	3.74	.000094	.279
Asks questions	6	3.15	.00082	.186
Frequency of interactions	3	2.36	.009	.214

Note: Positive values mean that the result was in the predicted direction.

actions and Negative Climate) can be taken as highly suggestive results deserving further research.

It is instructive to compare the results of the B–C and C–D analyses. A frequency count shows that for 7 of the 10 behaviors, the values of the effect sizes are larger for the C–D studies than for the B–C studies. Especially interesting are behavior categories that reveal conflicting results for the B–C and C–D links. For example, Ignores Student had a positive B–C effect size but a negative C–D effect size. The presence of such conflicting results warns against unequivocally accepting the results of B–C analyses as evidence for mediating factors without determining whether the given mediating variable has appropriate effects on subsequent behavior.

The ten behaviors and the four-factor theory. We are also interested in seeing how well the results of the C–D meta-analyses support the four-factor theory. To do so, we first employed the same behavior category reclassification that we employed earlier for the B–C results; we then computed a combined significance level and effect size in the same manner as before for each factor. These results are shown in Table 4.4. As can be seen, all four factors are statistically significant at $p<.005$.

However, the feedback factor has a very small combined effect size ($r = .075$), indicating that the appropriate use of feedback in this sample of studies is not very predictive of subjects' behaviors. The other three factors have quite substantial mean effect sizes. For example, the $r=.360$

Table 4.4. *Meta-analysis of the four-factor theory: relationship between the four factors and outcome variables*

	No. of studies	Combined significance level (Z)[a]	Combined effect size (r)
1. *Climate*	25	10.66[a]	.360
a. Positive climate			
b. Negative climate			
c. Eye contact			
2. *Feedback*	18	3.78[b]	.075
a. Praise			
b. Criticism			
c. Accepts student's ideas			
d. Ignores student			
3. *Input*	8	3.74[b]	.279
a. Input			
4. *Output*	7	2.93[c]	.156
a. Asks questions			
b. Frequency of interaction			
Median	13	3.76[b]	.218

[a] $p < .0000001$
[b] $p < .0005$
[c] $p < .005$

for the climate factor can be interpreted as meaning that experiencing more positive climate and less negative climate from the teacher will increase the percentage of students who score above average on outcome measures from about 32% to 68%. In sum, with respect to the relationships between mediating variables and outcome measures, there is evidence for substantial relationships for the climate, input, and output factors but evidence for only a small relationship for the feedback factor.

Conclusions, implications, and applications

Conclusions

The data from the studies examined in this meta-analysis support the general belief that teacher expectancies are mediated by identifiable behaviors. Furthermore, this mediation occurs in two stages, the first being the B–C relationships between expectations and emitted behaviors, and the second being the C–D relationships between the emitted behaviors and consequent outcome measures. To be considered a viable candidate as a mediating variable, a behavior must show a significant relationship for *both* the B–C *and* the C–D links. With this criterion in mind, we present the following summary of the ten behavior categories proposed to be important mediating variables in teacher expectancy effects. The behaviors are listed in order of the magnitude of the geometric mean of the B–C and C–D effect sizes. The geometric mean was employed specifically so as to give more weight to lower effect sizes, because even if the B–C effect for a variable were enormous, that variable could not play an important role in mediation unless the C–D effect also were substantial. Taking those considerations into account, then, here are the ten behaviors, followed by the geometric mean of the B–C and C–D effect sizes:

1. Accepting the student's ideas by modifying, acknowledging, summarizing, or applying what he or she has said. (.36)
2. Creating a warmer socioemotional climate; that is, acting in a more globally warm manner. (.32)
3. Creating a less negative climate; e.g., *not* behaving in a cold manner. (.31)
4. Providing more input by attempting to teach more material or more difficult material. (.27)
5. Interacting more often. (.20)
6. Engaging in more eye contact. (.19)
7. Asking more questions. (.18)
8. Praising more. (.14)
9. Criticizing more. (.08)
10. Ignoring the student more. (Geometric mean indeterminant due to negative effect size.)

This list illustrates that there is stronger empirical support for some variables, such as positive and negative climate and input, as mediators of teacher expectations than for others, such as criticism and ignores student. This is not meant to imply that those last two variables are not involved in the mediation of teacher expectancy effects, only that their role in mediation on the basis of both B–C and C–D relationships has not been satisfactorily demonstrated in these meta-analyses. These variables have received some support in the literature; at this point, further research is needed before we can say conclusively that they are or are not related to mediation.

Evaluating the four-factor theory

A major purpose of this chapter was to evaluate the available evidence bearing on the four-factor theory. Based on our meta-analytic results, a summary of the four-factor theory and its application to the entire mediation process is shown in Figure 4.2. As we can see, for B–C studies there was considerable support for the four-factor theory in terms of both statistical significance and practical importance. Teachers who hold positive expectations for a given student will tend to display a warmer socioemotional climate, express a more positive use of feedback, provide more input in terms of the amount and difficulty of material that is taught, and increase the amount of student output by supplying more response opportunities and interacting more frequently with the student. The C–D analyses supported the probable importance of these factors in affecting student outcomes, especially for climate, input, and output. While statistically significant, the effect size for feedback was quite low, indicating that its practical importance may not be great. In general, then, the four-factor theory proves to be a useful framework for conceptualizing broad classes of behaviors involved in the mediation of teacher expectancy effects.

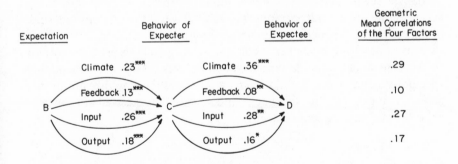

$$*p \le .005 \quad **p \le .0005 \quad ***p \le .0000001$$

Figure 4.2. Overview of the four-factor theory: correlations representing B–C and C–D links.

The role of feedback in mediation

The equivocal findings with respect to the feedback factor point out the curious results we obtained in general for praise and criticism variables. Praise and criticism were both significantly related to expectations, but this held true only for nonexperimental studies. When related to outcome variables, praise was significant and of practical importance but criticism was not.

Why were there no strong findings for praise and criticism as intuition would lead us to expect? One possible answer to this question may be that it is the *content* of the feedback that matters rather than its frequency, timing, or simple positive versus negative nature. In most situations, praise and criticism may refer to routine, almost mechanized, pronouncements of "Good" or "No, you're wrong." This kind of feedback is not informative to the student and consequently may have no impact on the child beyond the realization he or she got the answer right or wrong. Brophy (1981) supports this formulation by arguing persuasively that teacher praise does not function as a reinforcer, and that the meaning of praise depends in part on the context in which the interaction occurs.

Undoubtedly feedback becomes more salient to the student if the teacher takes time to explain *why* an answer was right or wrong; such statements with greater complexity and relevance to what the student has said would seem more likely to influence the child's self-image as well as his or her intellectual processes. The strong finding for the Accepts Student's Ideas variable supports this interpretation. By providing accepting feedback that expands and applies what the student has said, or by providing feedback for incorrect answers that discusses where the student went wrong, a teacher is communicating positive expectations for the student's intellectual abilities. Of course, this interpretation is highly speculative and needs to be tested by studies that would examine the actual content of the feedback and how it is related to teacher expectations and student outcomes.

Implications

What are some of the implications of the results of this meta-analysis? Perhaps the most obvious one is that expectations are mediated by a wide variety of behaviors, and, undoubtedly, there are other important mediating variables that are as yet unmeasured. The next question to be unraveled is what behaviors are most likely to be exhibited under which circumstances. We also need to develop typologies of teachers and other expecters; i.e., we will want to know how different types of teachers mediate expectancies in different ways. In terms of the ten-arrow model, this question would involve research on A–B–C relationships, an area typically neglected by research on expectancy effects.

Negative expectations. A concern similar in spirit to the one above is that while this review informs us considerably about the transmission of positive expectations, we know less about the mediation of *negative* expectations, or "Golem effects" (Babad, Inbar, & Rosenthal, 1982). There are obvious ethical reasons for not inducing negative expectancies in the field, but such experiments have been safely conducted in the laboratory. We need to explore the possibility that the processes involved in the mediation of negative expectations may be quite different than for positive expectations. Indeed, for intervention purposes, we may be even more concerned with understanding and eliminating Golem effects.

However, this last statement brings up an important issue. Brophy (1983) noted that some of the behaviors exhibited by teachers toward low expectancy students may be appropriate. Uniform behavior toward all students is an unrealistic and possibly unwise goal given the varying ability levels and academic needs of different students. By distinguishing between B–C and C–D relationships, the present meta-analysis allows an assessment of these concerns. We were able to determine whether behaviors associated with high or low expectancies actually were associated with corresponding good or bad student outcomes. Sometimes there were discrepancies; for example, as predicted, teachers ignored low expectancy students significantly more often than the highs, but examination of the C–D results revealed that being ignored actually appeared to have slight positive effects. This finding emphasizes once again the need discussed earlier for considering all elements of the ten-arrow model for understanding mediation.

Internal validity. One factor that should be taken into account when considering the results from the 10 behaviors is the experimental versus nonexperimental distinction. The conclusions throughout this paper were made on the basis of overall combined effect sizes. However, for some variables (most notably Praise, Criticism, and Ignores Student), the combined effect size for experimental studies was close to zero in contrast to the overall effect size. Consequently, care must be taken in drawing conclusions about these variables because there is no way of knowing what uncontrolled variables may be confounded with expectancy in the nonexperimental studies.

Research needs. The last important implication to be discussed here is the traditional plea for more research on mediation in general. Throughout this meta-analysis, our blocking variable of the number of studies examining a given behavior proved to be highly effective and a good predictor of effect sizes. As the number of studies investigating a variable decreased, our uncertainty about our conclusions for that variable increased. Many of our conclusions are based on very small numbers of studies, especially for the C–D studies. We need more studies that investigate a greater number of mediating variables as well as the interrelationships among those variables.

Applications

An important point to make about the list of 10 behaviors is that it is *not* meant to be a prescription for intervention. The results of a meta-analysis can be used to draw causal inference only when a substantial number of the studies to be combined are experimental (Rosenthal, 1984). In the present meta-analysis, this is frequently not the case, rendering causal inferences problematical. With respect to the B–C findings, the mediating behaviors are *dependent* variables; consequently, we cannot claim that manipulating those behaviors would necessarily lead to the desired effects. When we consider the C–D results we find that very few of the behaviors in those studies were experimentally manipulated, thus leaving us with the same problem of causal inference. Although unlikely, it is conceivable that some unmeasured variables or processes are associated with those behaviors and are the real mediators of expectancy effects. What is needed now is a research program in which these mediating variables are systematically manipulated and their effects measured. Once the variables have been shown to have strong causal effects, this information could be incorporated into future intervention programs.

   Although at this time our knowledge of teacher expectancy effects has not advanced to the point where a broad intervention program is justified, in recent years several experimental programs have been developed and tested. These programs were designed not to "eliminate" teacher expectancies, for such a goal would be both unwise and futile. Rather, the aims of intervention programs typically include making teachers aware of expectancy effects, identifying for teachers which of their behaviors communicate negative expectancies, and training in behaviors that communicate positive expectations. These programs wish to prevent teachers from developing negative expectations too hastily and to help teachers to communicate a confidence in the student that accurately reflects the student's actual ability and potential.

The first such program we will discuss is the Teacher Expectations and Student Achievement in-service training model (Kerman & Martin, 1980). The TESA workshops focus on three "strands": response opportunities, feedback, and personal regard. Within these three broad categories, 15 specific teaching behaviors are addressed, including such topics as equal distribution of reinforcements, proximity, higher level questioning, touch, praise, latency, and so forth. Workshops involve discussing expectancy effects with teachers and training them in each of the 15 skills. The TESA program has been evaluated recently in two doctoral dissertations. In a randomized experiment, Penman (1982) found that teachers who received the TESA training exhibited significant increases in positive interaction behaviors and decreases in negative behaviors toward low achieving students. A second dissertation confirmed these results and also showed that TESA training improved attitudes of teachers toward low achievers (Steeg, 1982). These promising results suggest that the TESA program may be an effective means of changing teacher expectations and behaviors in a positive direction.

In another doctoral dissertation, Sloan (1977) developed an intervention program aimed at changing teacher behaviors that convey expectations. This program involved four basic interventions: role-playing simulations that helped teachers understand what it felt like to be the recipient of negative expectations; discussion of teacher expectations and relevant mediating behaviors; feedback to teachers on classroom observations; and self-monitoring records for which teachers rated themselves with respect to given teaching behaviors. The four behaviors selected for intervention – smiling, substantive interaction, thought-provoking questions, and wait-time – were chosen on the basis of the four-factor theory. Analyses showed that the program was highly effective in increasing the frequencies of these teacher behaviors.

The last application program we will discuss is Project STILE (Student/Teacher Interactive Learning Environment), which is aimed at changing teachers' unequal interactional styles with their students. Project STILE is a long-term intervention program that includes the following aspects: (a) discussion of literature on teacher expectancy effects; (b) systematic and detailed feedback on teachers' interactions with different groups of students; and (c) mastery of skills through role-playing techniques that allow teachers to interact with students equitably regardless of the teacher's initial expectations or the student's academic standing (Banuazizi, 1981). Project STILE is different from other programs in that it also seeks to include parents as well as teachers in the intervention process. An evaluation of the project after two years of implementation found that teachers who participated in Project STILE exhibited an increase in the frequency of positive teacher behaviors compared to control teachers not in the program; reports from participants also showed that teachers believed Project STILE had a strong beneficial influence on their teaching (Greenfield, Banuazizi, & Ganon, 1979).

The successes reported in the various intervention programs described above are encouraging, and they illustrate how social psychological research on the four-factor theory can be fruitfully applied to education. At this time, more research on these and other intervention programs is needed; in particular, we need results from longitudinal studies demonstrating long-term positive effects from these types of programs. Most of the programs described are relatively simple and inexpensive to implement, and if effective, the cost-benefit ratio might be very advantageous.

Education constitutes one of the most important experiences a person encounters in his or her life. For too many children, school is a place where the teacher implicitly or explicitly tells some children that they are not capable of doing high quality work or that they will not achieve very much in life. For too many children, that message becomes a negative self-fulfilling prophecy. Research on the four-factor theory of teacher expectancy effects may one day help to change the message these children are receiving from their teachers and to increase the frequency of positive self-fulfilling prophecies.

Notes

1 Detailed information on the methods as well as results from behavior categories with fewer than 13 studies are reported in Harris & Rosenthal (1985). A complete list of references for the primary studies used in this meta-analysis is available from the authors.

2 All computations in the meta-analyses were carried out using a BASIC program written for a personal computer.

3 When the contrast comparing effect sizes from experimental and nonexperimental studies is considered for all mediating variables, not just those relevant to the four-factor theory, we find that the contrast is significant for 10 of 31 behaviors and for 6 of the 10 significant contrasts; effect sizes for experimental studies are larger than for nonexperimental studies.

References

Babad, E. Y., Inbar, J., & Rosenthal, R. (1982). Pygmalion, Galatea, and the Golem: Investigations of biased and unbiased teachers. *Journal of Educational Psychology, 74,* 459–474.

Banuazizi, A. (1981). An evaluation of the first year's activities of the National Demonstration Title II Project (Basic Skills Improvement Program) in selected elementary grades of Cambridge public schools. Final Report.

Brophy, J. (1981). Teacher praise: A functional analysis. *Review of Educational Research, 51,* 5–32.

Brophy, J. (1983). Research on the self-fulfilling prophecy and teacher expectations. *Journal of Educational Psychology, 75,* 631–661.

Cohen, J. (1977). *Statistical power analysis for the behavioral sciences.* New York: Academic Press.

Cooper, H. M. (1984). *The integrative research review: A social science approach.* Beverly Hills, CA: Sage.

Flanders, N. A. (1970). *Analyzing classroom behavior.* New York: Addison-Wesley.

Glass, G. V. (1976). Primary, secondary, and meta-analysis of research. *Educational Researcher, 5,* 3–8.

Glass, G. V., McGaw, B., & Smith, M. L. (1981). *Meta-analysis in social research.* Beverly Hills, CA: Sage.

Greenfield, D., Banuazizi, A., & Ganon, J. (1979). Project STILE (Student-Teacher Interactive Learning Environment). Evaluation Report.

Harris, M. J., & Rosenthal R. (1985). The mediation of interpersonal expectancy effects: 31 meta-analyses. *Psychological Bulletin, 97,* 363–386.

Kerman, S., & Martin, M. (1980). *Teacher expectations and student achievement (Teacher handbook).* Office of the L.A. County Superintendent of schools, Los Angeles, CA.

Mosteller, F. M., & Bush, R. R. (1954). Selected quantitative techniques. In G. Lindzey (Ed.), *Handbook of social psychology Vol. 1: Theory and method.* Cambridge, MA: Addison-Wesley.

Penman, P. R. (1982). The efficacy of TESA training in changing teacher behaviors and attitudes towards low achievers. Unpublished doctoral dissertation, Arizona State University.

Rist, R. C. (1970). Student social class and teacher expectations. *Harvard Educational Review, 40,* 411–451.

Rosenthal, R. (1963). On the social psychology of the psychological experiment: The experimenter's hypothesis as unintended determinant of experimental results. *American Scientist, 51,* 268–283.

Rosenthal, R. (1966). *Experimenter effects in behavioral research.* New York: Appleton-Century-Crofts.

Rosenthal, R. (1969). Interpersonal expectation. In R. Rosenthal & R. Rosnow (Eds.), *Artifact in behavioral research.* New York: Academic Press.

Rosenthal, R. (1973a). The mediation of Pygmalion effects: A four-factor "theory." *Papua New Guinea Journal of Education, 9,* 1–12.

Rosenthal, R. (1973b). *On the social psychology of the self-fulfilling prophecy: Further evidence for Pygmalion effects and their mediating mechanisms.* New York: MSS Modular Publication, Module 53.

Rosenthal, R. (1976). *Experimenter effects in behavioral research.* Enlarged edition. New York: Irvington.

Rosenthal, R. (1978). Combining results of independent studies. *Psychological Bulletin, 85,* 185–193.

Rosenthal, R. (Ed.). (1980). *New directions for methodology of social and behavioral science: Quantitative assessment of research domains* (No. 5). San Francisco: Jossey-Bass.

Rosenthal, R. (1981). Pavlov's mice, Pfungst's horse, and Pygmalion's PONS: Some models for the study of interpersonal expectancy effects. In T. A. Sebeok & R. Rosenthal (Eds.), *The Clever Hans phenomenon: Communication with horses, whales, apes, and people. Annals of the New York Academy of Sciences,* No. 364, 182–198.

Rosenthal, R. (1984). *Meta-analytic procedures for social research*. Beverly Hills, CA: Sage Publications.

Rosenthal, R. (1985). From unconscious experimenter bias to teacher expectancy effects. In J. B. Dusek, V. C. Hall, & W. J. Meyer (Eds.), *Teacher expectancies* (pp. 37–65). Hillsdale, NJ: Erlbaum

Rosenthal, R., & Jacobson, L. (1968). *Pygmalion in the classroom*. New York: Holt, Rinehart and Winston.

Rosenthal, R., & Rosnow, R. L. (1985). *Contrast analysis: Focused comparisons in the analysis of variance*. New York: Cambridge University Press.

Rosenthal, R., & Rubin, D. B. (1978). Interpersonal expectancy effects: The first 345 studies. *Behavioral and Brain Sciences, 3*, 377–386.

Rosenthal, R., & Rubin, D. B. (1979). Comparing significance levels of independent studies. *Psychological Bulletin, 86*, 1165–1168.

Rosenthal, R., & Rubin, D. B. (1982a). A simple general purpose display of magnitude of experimental effect. *Journal of Educational Psychology, 74*, 166–169.

Rosenthal, R., & Rubin, D. B. (1982b). Comparing effect sizes of independent studies. *Psychological Bulletin, 92*, 500–504.

Rosenthal, R., & Rubin, D. B. (1984). Summarizing effect sizes for multiple dependent variables from single studies. Manuscript submitted for publication.

Sloan, E. (1977). Interventions designed to effect conscious changes in teacher behaviors that convey expectations. Unpublished doctoral dissertation, University of Massachusetts.

Steeg, J. L. (1982). Behavioral and attitudinal changes of teachers toward low achieving students as a result of the TESA program. Unpublished doctoral dissertation, United States International University.

5 Nonverbal communication in interracial teacher–student interaction

Robert S. Feldman and Ronald D. Saletsky

When whites and blacks interact in an educational setting, the possibility for miscommunication is rife. Consider, for instance, the following example:

A black student shifts his eye gaze away from his teacher, toward the floor, as she asks him a question. Thinking at first that his behavior indicates that he doesn't understand the question, she rephrases it. The student continues to look down at the floor, although this time he mutters a cryptic "um-hum." Certain that the student is not attending to what she is saying, the teacher rebukes the student sharply, telling him that he should pay attention.

Although the situation described above seems, at first analysis, to be simply a case of a disinterested or unmotivated student, in fact the failure may be more on the part of the teacher than the student. It is likely, in fact, that this is a case of interracial miscommunication on a nonverbal level. For had the teacher understood more about the nature of black nonverbal behavior and how it differs from white nonverbal behavior, the scene might have had a more positive outcome.

In this chapter, we will review literature relating to the role of nonverbal behavior in interracial educational settings. We first will provide a theoretical and empirical context for understanding interracial interaction and nonverbal behavior. Next, we will discuss a series of studies that were designed to address directly how teacher–student racial characteristics affect nonverbal behavior and the nature of their interaction. Finally, the practical implications of the research findings will be drawn. The underlying assumption that runs through this chapter is the notion that nonverbal behavior represents an integral part of the communication process and that it plays an important role in social interaction in general.

Nonverbal behavior and interracial interaction: Theoretical background

The initial source of evidence bearing upon an understanding of racial factors in teaching interactions is related to work on the relationship between nonverbal behavior and interpersonal attitudes in dyadic interaction. In considering a dyadic situation, some theorists have suggested that the mere presence of a liked or disliked person can elicit an affect which is either positive or negative, respectively (Lott & Lott, 1968, 1969). Indeed, liked persons can act as effective positive reinforcers and disliked persons as negative reinforcers. Considering this work with evidence showing that nonverbal behavior is related lawfully to affective states (Ekman, 1982), these findings imply that the mere presence of an individual may be sufficient to evoke nonverbal behavior that is congruent with the attitude held regarding that individual. In fact, it may be possible that the immediate content of a dyadic interaction will be less influential in determining an individual's nonverbal behavior than the attitude the individual originally holds regarding the interactant, at least in cases where the prior attitude was strongly held.

The preceding theorizing relates quite directly to the case of white and black racial interaction if it can be shown that individuals have strongly held differential attitudes regarding persons of the same race compared with those of the other race. This possibility appears to be well documented by evidence of both an anecdotal and an empirical nature (Allport, 1954; Katz, 1976; Simpson & Yinger, 1975). Most of the research which has been carried out has focussed on white attitudes towards blacks, and findings indicate that – for the population as a whole – whites generally hold relatively negative feelings about blacks. For instance, Campbell and Schuman (1968) found in an extensive survey that most whites view blacks as lacking ambition and industriousness, and they blame blacks themselves for the existence of inferior black housing, employment, and education. More recent evidence still supports this view. For example, Hastings & Hastings (1984) found that most whites would object to having their children attend a school in which the majority of children were black, and 26% agreed that white people had a right to keep blacks out of their neighborhoods. A number of surveys have also shown that whites tend to resent economic advances in blacks (e.g., Ross, Vanneman, & Pettigrew, 1976). In general, then, there appears to be evidence to support the notion that whites hold differing – and more negative – views regarding blacks than towards whites (Crosby, Bromley, & Saxe, 1980).

There is also evidence showing that blacks hold differential attitudes towards blacks and whites. For instance, the Campbell and Schuman (1968) survey found that almost one-third of the blacks interviewed thought that whites were hostile and repressive, and another survey (Harris, 1971) showed that most blacks interviewed felt that whites had a "mean and selfish streak." Moreover, almost 60% of blacks interviewed in one survey said blacks were treated either not very well or badly in their community (Gallup Poll, 1981). Although there was some early evidence that blacks held more negative attitudes towards their own racial group than towards whites (e.g., Clark & Clark, 1947), this research seems largely contradicted by later findings (e.g., Hraba & Grant, 1970). The evidence now points to the conclusion that in general there is a tendency for blacks to have a more positive attitude towards blacks than towards whites.

Other research shows that attitudes relating to race are acquired quite early in a person's life and are strongly held (Katz, 1976). By the age of three or four years, children are able to differentiate between whites and blacks, and even at that age there seems to be some differential affective responses regarding same- and cross-race individuals. Moreover, some research suggests that the simple act of labeling a person as a member of an in-group or out-group is sufficient to produce differential attitudes and verbal behavior (Billig & Tajfel, 1973; Evans & Dovido, 1983), with members of in-groups being viewed significantly more favorably than members of out-groups. Therefore, we would expect that whites, viewing blacks as members of an out-group, would hold less favorable attitudes towards blacks than the white in-group members. Similarly, it could be expected that blacks would hold more positive attitudes towards members of their own in-group (i.e., blacks) than they would toward members of an out-group (i.e., whites).

In sum, there is a large body of theory and research that suggests, first, that nonverbal behavior reflects an individual's affective state and attitudes toward the person with whom he or she is interacting. This appears to be true even when the individual does not intend for the information to be communicated (Feldman & White, 1980; Zuckerman, DePaulo, & Rosenthal, 1981). Second, it is clear that both whites and blacks hold more positive attitudes towards members of their own racial group than towards members of the other racial group.

If we consider these findings together, we can hypothesize that attitudes and feelings about race will be elicited during interracial interaction and will be revealed nonverbally. We turn now to empirical work related to this hypothesis, beginning with research on differences in white and black nonverbal behavior.

Nonverbal behavior and interracial interaction: Empirical background

Even a cursory review of the research on black and white nonverbal behavior reveals a number of significant differences. For example, white and black North Americans show quite different patterns of behavior when they listen to one another. In a series of studies, LaFrance and Mayo (1976) found that while white and black listeners tended to spend the same amount of time gazing at a speaker's face when they were listening, the timing and sequence of gazing varied considerably. In addition, it has been found that black parents sometimes teach their children that looking an adult in the eye is a sign of disrespect (Byers & Byers, 1972). In contrast, white children are socialized to do just the opposite; looking away from a speaker is seen as disrespectful.

A further difference between blacks and whites relates to the use of "back-channel" behaviors, which are the short sounds that listeners make during conversation to indicate that they are listening to what the speaker is saying. The typical back-channel pattern for white listeners is to nod their heads, accompanying the nods with verbal responses such as "um-hum." Black listeners, in contrast, use *either* head nodding *or* a verbal response to indicate that they are attending to what the speaker is saying (Ericson, 1979). In a practical sense, this suggests that a black student who averts his eyes but who accompanies that behavior with a back-channel "um-hum" may be just as attentive as the white who gazes directly at the teacher.

Other research suggests that differences between white and black nonverbal behavior may be subtle indeed. For example, even the nature of head nods differs between whites and blacks. Erickson (1979) reports findings indicating that blacks tend to use "unaccented" nods, in which the head moves only slightly, while whites are more likely to use "accented" nods, which are more pronounced. Moreover, blacks may use slight, continuous unaccented head nodding throughout a conversation, a pattern which is not typically seen in whites conversing.

The examples we have cited of differences between white and black nonverbal behavior are in and of themselves obviously sufficient to provoke difficulties during the educational process. However, the problem is even more complex, for research has indicated that blacks and whites not only behave differently in a nonverbal level, but may interpret or *decode* nonverbal behavior in different ways. For example, Goldberg and Mayerberg (1973) investigated the reactions of elementary school-age children to a teacher. Black and white second- and sixth-graders evaluated a white female teacher who taught them a lesson while displaying either positive, neutral, or negative affective nonverbal behavior. Although white pupils in both grades rated the "positive" teacher more favorably, only the sixth-grade black pupils did so. Black second graders, on the other hand, rated the "neutral" teacher most favorably, suggesting that there are black and white differences in the nature of nonverbal behavioral decoding.

The differences that we have been discussing in white and black nonverbal behavior have clear applications to the scenario at the beginning of this chapter. Instead of assuming that the student's averted eyes indicated lack of understanding, a teacher more familiar with patterns of black nonverbal behavior might well have attributed the avoidance of eye contact while listening to a culturally learned behavior pattern having nothing to do with whether the student understood the question. The example illustrates, then, the possibility that differences in nonverbal behavior, both in terms of the kinds of behavior carried out and in terms of how such behavior is decoded, may occur between whites and blacks.

Interracial interaction

Although there is a fair amount of evidence indicating that there are general *differences* in nonverbal behavior between whites and blacks in their nonverbal behavior, there is considerably less work on interracial *interaction* and how such interaction affects nonverbal behavior. In fact, findings relating to interracial interaction probably are ultimately of greatest relevance to educators. It is clearly not sufficient to know simply that, say, blacks generally tend to use eye gaze when listening in a different fashion from whites; what may be even more crucial is whether eye gaze patterns differ in blacks according to whether they are listening to a white as opposed to a black. Although most of the work that has been done on this question comes from noneducational settings, the results have clear implications for educational questions.

Much of the research examining nonverbal behavior in interracial interaction has been predicated on the notion that nonverbal behavior is an unobtrusive measure of racism (Crosby et al., 1980). Typical of this type of work is a study by Weitz (1972), in which male white under-graduate subjects completed attitude scales toward blacks. The scale results indicated that the sample was very liberal, with subjects ranging from moderately to extremely liberal. Subsequently, in a different context, the same subjects were led to believe that they were speaking with either a black or white (bogus) partner over an intercom.

Judges then rated the subjects' speech along several dimensions to determine the subjects' feelings toward their partner at the other end of the intercom. In addition, subjects were asked to respond to several measures of behavioral friendliness, and to questions of how much they liked their partner. The primary dependent variable of interest in Weitz's study was voice tone. One clear result of the study was that subjects who claimed to be the most friendly were actually the least friendly in their tone of voice and other behavioral responses when they believed they were interacting with a black partner. With white partners, however, no such negative correlations emerged. Nonverbal behavior, then, appeared to be a reliable indicator of these white subjects' true feelings toward blacks.

Other experiments have examined black–white interaction in a face-to-face context. For instance, Fugita, Wexley, & Hillery (1974) observed the nonverbal behavior of white and black interviewees during an actual job interview as a function of the race of the interviewer. They found that white interviewees had greater eye contact with interviewers of both races than black interviewees and that black interviewers received fewer and shorter glances from both white and black interviewees. Thus, it appeared that the racial composition of the pairs did affect nonverbal behavior.

In a second experiment involving an interview situation, Word, Zanna, & Cooper (1974) found that white subjects, this time acting as interviewers, behaved differentially according to the race of their interviewee. The white interviewers tended to sit closer to white than black interviewees, and the interviewers showed a greater number of speech errors. There was also a difference in interviewer behavior on a combined measure of interpersonal distance, eye contact, forward lean, and shoulder orientation.

Another variable that has received attention is that of interpersonal distancing. For instance, Willis (1966) observed blacks and whites in various natural settings and found that whites consistently initiated speaking with blacks at a further distance than with other whites, a result supported by several other studies (e.g., Hendricks & Bootzin, 1976).

One study that examined nonverbal behavior in interracial interaction within an educational setting was carried out by Simpson and Erickson (1983), who studied teachers' nonverbal (and verbal) behavior in actual classrooms. Although student performance and achievement were not controlled experimentally and thus represent a potential confound, results showed that white teachers directed more nonverbal criticism toward black males than they did toward white males, as well as showing a number of sex differences in white and black behavior patterns.

In conclusion, there is evidence that white and black nonverbal behavior is affected by racial factors. However, there are some serious difficulties in interpreting these results, as well as in applying them to teaching situations. One problem concerns the standardization of verbal behavior and events within the setting. In none of the studies previously cited was the verbal behavior of subjects carefully controlled. Because verbal and nonverbal behavior can be correlated, differences in non-verbal behavior may be attributed simply to variations in verbal behavior. In addition, in many cases previous work has allowed subjects a fair amount of latitude in determining the nature of events within the interracial interaction. While such procedural techniques allow greater external generalizability, they also produce less internal validity. There-fore, more controlled experimental situations seem desirable.

A second problem with most of the previous research is that it has concentrated on white subjects' nonverbal behavior during same- and cross-race interaction. Work with black subjects has been minimal. Finally, most previous research has compared same-status and same-role interacting dyads. It is reasonable to assume that generalizations to teacher–student dyads, in which there is both status and role differential between the partners, is not necessarily warranted. Thus, in our studies, we have attempted to examine the nonverbal behavior of both white and black individuals in same- and mixed-race teaching situations. We have been careful to ensure that verbal behavior and events within the interactions were held constant.

Studies of black–white nonverbal behavior in an educational context

Despite the drawbacks of previous research, it does suggest that the nonverbal behavior of whites and blacks is affected by the race of the person with whom they are interacting. We assume that this phenomenon is reflective of the differential attitudes held toward same- versus cross-race individuals. From these assumptions, we hypothesized that attitudes and feelings about race would be elicited during an interracial teaching situation and are revealed nonverbally, independently of the verbal behavior of the interactants. Thus, even under conditions in which a same-race versus a different-race student was performing similarly in terms of success, leading the teacher to react in a verbally identical manner, we hypothesized that differences in nonverbal behavior would occur, reflecting the teacher's differential attitudes.

Nonverbal communication of affect in interracial dyads

In this experiment we set out to directly test the assumption that nonverbal behavior will occur differentially according to the racial composition of a dyadic interaction, independent of the nature of the verbal behavior (Feldman & Donahoe, 1978). Specifically, we hypothesized that the nonverbal behavior of whites would be more positive towards whites than blacks, and that blacks would behave more nonverbally positive towards blacks than whites. What is theoretically important is the assumption of independence between the verbal and nonverbal behavioral channels. Regardless of the verbal behavior in the situation, we expected that there would be differential nonverbal behavior.

Our general strategy was to devise a well-controlled situation in which the verbal behavior and events within an interaction were held constant and only the racial composition of the dyadic was varied. This entailed the use of a confederate to play the role of one of the interactants. In order to make the strongest test of the hypothesis possible, we devised an experiment in which the situation was unambiguously positive, and therefore only the subjects' attitudes toward the race of the confederate could result in differential nonverbal behavior.

In the study, white and black undergraduate subjects, acting as teachers, taught a lesson to a white or black student. The student was actually a confederate, whose verbal and nonverbal behaviors were predetermined. In all cases, the confederate was made to appear quite successful to the teacher, answering almost all questions correctly on a test of the lesson content. Moreover, we asked the teacher to use only the phrase, "Right – that's good" whenever the student answered a test item correctly. This ensured not only that the teacher's verbal behavior was well controlled, but that – because of the "students'" excellent performance – teachers had ample opportunity to praise their student. In sum, we created a situation in which all students appeared to be quite successful, and in which the teacher was providing unequivocally positive verbal praise. All that varied was the race of the student and the teacher.

To examine the teachers' nonverbal behavior, we made secret video-tapes of the teachers while they were verbally praising their student. We then took 20-second silent samples of each teacher and showed them to white and black judges, who rated how pleased teachers appeared to be with their students.

The results showed quite clearly that the race of the student influenced the teachers' facial expressions. Both the white *and* the black teachers had more pleasant, positive facial expressions when they praised a student of their own race. White teachers looked more pleased with white students, and black teachers appeared more positive with black students – even though student performance was identical in all cases. Interestingly, though, only judges who were the same race as the teachers were able to make reliable judgments. Only white judges could detect the differences in white teachers' responses to white versus black students, and only black judges could identify similar differences in positivity for black teachers. The study demonstrated, then, not only behavioral differences according to the racial composition of a teacher – student pair, but decoding differences as well.

Overall, it appeared that the hypothesis of differential nonverbal behavior according to the racial composition of a dyad was supported in this experiment, at least when looking at judgments made by raters of the same race as the teachers in question. White judges rated white teachers as being more pleased nonverbally with white than with black students; and black judges rated black teachers as showing more pleasure with black than with white students. Although neither white nor black judges in this experiment could distinguish reliably nonverbal behavioral differences in teachers of a race other than their own, it does seem that there were differential displays of affect according to the race of the teacher's student.

One drawback with the present study regarded identification of the locus of causality for our findings. Our initial hypothesis was predicated upon the notion that whites and blacks held differential attitudes towards same- versus cross-race individuals, and that it was these differential attitudes that would be reflected in the subjects' nonverbal behavior. In an indirect fashion, this notion received support. However, because we had no direct measure of subjects' attitudes, we could not draw this conclusion firmly. We therefore decided to attempt a more direct test of the hypothesis.

Racial attitudes and nonverbal behavior in tutoring dyads

In this second experiment we directly examined the attitudes of our subjects by administering the Multifactor Racial Attitude Inventory (MRAI), an instrument that was designed to identify white's attitudes towards blacks (Woodmansee & Cook, 1967). In the study, white subjects identified as high- or low-prejudiced were led to act as teachers to a successful white or black student. The spoken content of a teacher's praise once again was controlled through the use of confederates playing the role of student and by using a standard teaching plan which led to similar verbal output by all subjects. As before, samples of the nonverbal behavior of teachers were shown to a group of judges, who rated how pleased the teachers appeared to be with their student.

The results showed quite clearly that overall white teachers appeared more pleased with their white students than with their black students, even though the objective performance of the white and black students was identical. Most interesting was the finding of a significant interaction between race of student and teacher prejudice, which provided a direct test of the hypothesis that high-prejudiced teachers would show greater differentiation in their nonverbal behavior according to the race of their student than would low-prejudiced teachers. The means involved in the interaction are displayed in Figure 5.1. The findings indicate that the difference in ratings accorded low-prejudiced teachers interacting with white versus a black student was in fact significantly smaller than the ratings accorded high-prejudiced teachers interacting with a white versus black student.

However, post hoc analyses showed that both high- *and* low-prejudiced teachers appear significantly more pleased with a white student than with a black student. Furthermore, the mean ratings of the low-prejudiced teachers interacting with black students are significantly higher than the ratings of a high-prejudiced teacher interacting with black students; that is, low-prejudiced teachers appeared to be significantly more pleased with their black students than high-prejudiced teachers did with their black students.

It is clear, then, that the hypothesis tested in this study was confirmed. Untrained, naive observers were able to discern that the high-prejudiced teachers were more pleased with their white students than with their black students, even though the objective performance of the white and black students was identical. High-prejudiced teachers also were significantly less pleased with black students than were low-prejudiced teachers, as predicted. These results quite directly support the hypothesis that prejudicial attitudes are related to an individual's nonverbal behavior. The high-prejudiced stimulus teachers, selected on the basis of their expression of relatively negative attitudes towards blacks on a written measure, displayed nonverbal behavior that was congruent with their negative attitudes.

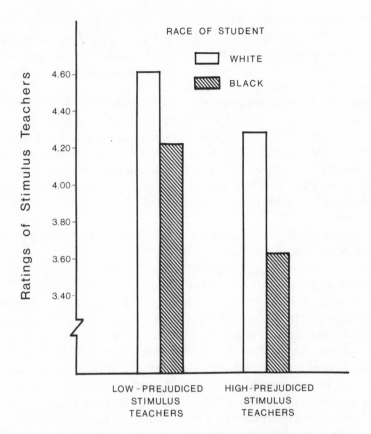

Figure 5.1. Ratings of how pleased teachers appear with their students.

Effects of student performance on teacher nonverbal behavior

In our earlier studies we were concerned with the effect of student race on teacher nonverbal behavior in instances in which the student's behavior was unequivocally successful. However, these results do not provide information regarding the nonverbal behavior of teachers whose students are unsuccessful.

We could expect that the success of student performance, per se, would be reflected in the teacher's nonverbal behavior. It has been established that generally teachers display different verbal behavior according to the success of their students. For instances, deGroat & Thompson (1949) showed that successful students received more verbal praise than nonsuccessful students, and that poorly performing students received greater disapproval than successful students. Similar findings were reported by Morrison & McIntyre (1969). We could predict that because nonverbal facial behavior tends to reflect an individual's affective state, teachers would also display more positive nonverbal behavior toward successful than unsuccessful students.

To examine this hypothesis, we experimentally controlled both the race of the student and the student's performance (Feldman & Orchowsky, 1979). White subjects played the role of teacher to a white or black student in a one-session lesson. To maintain control over the race and the performance of the student, once again confederates were used. In one condition, the confederate performed very well, answering almost every question correctly, while in the other condition, the confederate answered almost every question erroneously. It was hypothesized that the nonverbal facial behavior of subjects would be affected both by the race and the performance of the student.

We were particularly concerned with identifying whether the effects of race and performance would combine additively or if they would interact with one another. If the latter case were true, for instance, it is possible that the magnitude of the *differences* in nonverbal behavior accorded successful versus unsuccessful students would vary according to the race of the student. Thus, it is conceivable that differences in nonverbal behavior toward successful compared with unsuccessful black students would be less pronounced than the difference in nonverbal behavior toward successful compared with unsuccessful white students.

We found strong effects due to both race of student and performance of student. Teachers of whites acted more positively than those of black students, and teachers of successful students acted more positively than those with unsuccessful students.

The most interesting results concerned the relative magnitude of difference between successful and unsuccessful performance within race. Analysis of the difference in ratings between whites who were successful versus unsuccessful showed that the difference was significantly greater when looking at teachers of white students than teachers of black students. Conceptually, this implies that the degree of nonverbal differentiation of reinforcement is greater for white students than for black students. Not only did blacks generally receive less favorable nonverbal behavior from their teacher, then, but the clarity and distinctiveness of the nonverbal behavior was less dependent upon situational factors (such as success or failure) than it was for white students.

General discussion and implications for theory and practice

The results of the research we have discussed suggest a number of conclusions. First, it appears that both white and black teachers behave nonverbally more positively toward members of their own race than toward members of other racial groups, independent of what is being said verbally. Second, the nonverbal behavior of teachers seem to be related to their racial attitudes. These results suggest that the mere presence of a white or black student may be sufficient to evoke the nonverbal behaviors that are associated with particular attitudes. These nonverbal behaviors may be representative of the teacher's generalized feeling toward the student's race, relatively independent of the particular student or circumstances, or the behaviors may be a function of a teacher's more specific attitude toward the particular student or circumstances. In either case, the results of these experiments suggest that both the white and black teachers held attitudes favoring students of their own race and that their nonverbal behavior revealed these underlying attitudes.

Finally, the results of the third experiment suggest that regardless of whether a student was successful or unsuccessful, blacks still received less positive nonverbal behavior from their teachers than did white students. Moreover, it appeared that blacks received less differentiated nonverbal behavior than did whites.

It is especially notable that the subjects in the first two experiments were responding quite positively on a verbal level towards their students while at the same time they were responding relatively negatively on a nonverbal level. The fact that the negativity of the teacher's nonverbal behavior was easy to detect, even in the short 20-second samples that the judges were given, suggests that many incongruent messages probably were occurring during these interactions. In actual classrooms, if there were such incongruities between the teacher's verbal and nonverbal behavior during interracial interactions, the exchanges might be quite unpleasant or at least confusing for both teacher and student. Both participants might come away from the interaction with any existing prejudices confirmed. Thus there could be a cycle of negative attitudes leading to negative nonverbal behavior that supports and maintains the original attitudes.

On the other hand, there is evidence from our first study that only same-race judges were capable of discerning reliably the nonverbal behavior of the teacher. Does this suggest that we should not be concerned if teachers are more positive towards students of their own race? For example, if a black student is not aware that his white teacher is more nonverbally positive to white students than to black students, it is possible that the black student will not be affected directly by the teacher's display of negative nonverbal behavior. However, this argument disregards the effect of the observation of the teacher's nonverbal behavior by those students of the same race as the teacher, who *are* quite capable of decoding the teacher's meaning. If, for instance, white students are aware that their teacher displays differential nonverbal behavior to white and black students, a great deal of research on modeling suggests that the students may learn to behave nonverbally negatively towards blacks. Moreover, white students may infer (quite correctly) that the teacher holds more positive attitudes towards white students than towards black students, thus providing a mechanism for the spread of racial prejudice.

Implications for teaching practice

We have seen evidence that there are differences in the ways whites and blacks nonverbally indicate such responses as respect or understanding as well as differences in the ways the two groups decode nonverbal messages. In addition, the nonverbal responses of both white and black teachers appear to vary based on the race of the students involved in the interactions. Even though these conclusions are based on a few studies conducted in laboratories, the evidence is sufficiently consistent and robust – not to mention congruent with common sense – to underscore the importance of the issue.

What implications do these results have for teaching practice? It is tempting to suggest that we simply inform teachers of the problems involved when nonverbal behavior indicative of negative attitudes are displayed, identify those behaviors for them, and then tell them to eliminate these actions. However, there are at least two problems with asking teachers to "police" their own nonverbal signals to students. The fact that nonverbal behaviors frequently occur without an individual's awareness (which makes them good unobtrusive indices of affect to begin with) belies attempts to master them totally. As long as teachers of any race have negative or unfavorable attitudes toward students of other races, it is likely that some "leakage" of these feelings will inevitably occur. Second, it is possible that an emphasis on attending to nonverbal cues, and the effort involved in manipulating them, may result in teachers becoming overly conscious of their behavior. In turn, they may become less effective as instructors as they attend less to what they are saying and more to what they are doing.

However, some conscious control over one's nonverbal behavior is possible, and probably desirable. Certain teaching behaviors can be made habitual. For example, the distance teachers sit from their students can probably be controlled fairly easily. Other nonverbal behaviors that might be manipulated include the nature of body and head orientation toward the student, tone of voice, avoidance of cues related to anxiety and nervousness (such as postural shifts and excessive grooming behaviors), and maintenance of eye contact.

Some theorists also suggest that teachers can be trained to better decode the nonverbal behavior of their students. Although there is relatively little supportive research, one promising technique involves asking people to make judgments about the meaning of samples of others' nonverbal behavior that have been captured on videotape. After the observer makes a judgment, he or she receives immediate feedback either in the form of positive reinforcement for a correct answer or a correction if the response is incorrect. This has produced significant improvements in accuracy (Rosenthal et al., 1979), although it has not yet been used to teach decoding of nonverbal behaviors relevant to interracial interaction. One could imagine, though, making videotapes of white and black students and training teachers to learn the meaning of the nonverbal behaviors on the tapes.

Perhaps the most reasonable route to follow – at this point in our understanding of black and white nonverbal behavior – is to ensure that teachers are sensitive to the fact that students of different races may possess differing communicative codes and to inform teachers of the likely nature of such differences. Furthermore, teachers should be aware of their own attitudes and behavior and those situations in which they are likely to display negative behaviors. Such awareness is at least a first step in mitigating problems in black and white nonverbal communication.

References

Allport, G. W. (1954). *The nature of prejudice*. Reading, MA: Addison-Wesley.

Billig, M., & Tajfel, H. (1973). Social categorization and similarity in intergroup behavior. *European Journal of Social Psychology, 3*, 27–52.

Byers, P., & Byers, H. (1972). Nonverbal communication and the education of children. In C. B. Cazden, V. P. John, & D. Hymes (Eds.), *Functions of language in the classroom*. New York: Academic Press.

Campbell, A., & Schuman, H. (1968). *Racial attitudes in fifteen American cities*. Ann Arbor: Institute for Social Research, University of Michigan.

130   R. S. FELDMAN AND R. D. SALETSKY

Clark, K., & Clark, M. (1947). Racial identification and preference in Negro children. In T. Newcomb and E. Hartley (Eds.), *Readings in social psychology* (pp. 169–178). New York: Holt, Rinehart and Winston.

Crosby, F., Bromley, S., & Saxe, L. (1980). Recent unobtrusive studies of black and white discrimination and prejudice: A literature review. *Psychological Bulletin, 87,* 546–563.

deGroat, A., & Thompson, G. (1949). A study of the distribution of teacher approval and disapproval among sixth-grade pupils. *Journal of Experimental Education, 18,* 57–75.

Ekman, P. (1982). *Emotion in the human face,* (2nd ed.). Cambridge, MA: Cambridge University Press.

Erikson, F. (1979). Talking down: Some cultural sources of miscommunication in interracial interviews. In A. Wolfgang (Ed.), *Nonverbal behavior applications and cultural implications.* New York: Academic Press. Pp. 99–126.

Evans, N. J., & Dovido, J. F. (1983, April). Evaluative processing of racial stereotypes. Paper presented at the 54th annual meeting of the Eastern Psychological Association, Philadelphia, PA.

Feldman, R. S., & Donahoe, L. F. (1978). Nonverbal communication of affect in interracial dyads. *Journal of Education Psychology, 70,* 979–987.

Feldman, R. S., & Orchowsky, S. (1979). Race and performance of student as determinants of teacher nonverbal behavior. *Contemporary Educational Psychology, 4,* 324–333.

Feldman, R. S., & White, J. B. (1980). Detecting deception in children. *Journal of Communication, 30,* 121–128.

Fugita, S., Wexley, K. N., & Hillery, J. M. (1974). Black–white differences in nonverbal behavior in an interview setting. *Journal of Applied Social Psychology, 4,* 343–350.

Gallup Poll (1981, February). *The Gallup Opinion Index.* Vol. 185. Princeton, NJ: Gallup Poll.

Goldberg, G., & Mayerberg, C. K. (1973). Emotional reaction of students to nonverbal teacher behavior. *Journal of Experimental Education, 42,* 29–32.

Harris Survey. (1971, October 4). Race stereotypes continue in U.S. *The Washington Post.*

Hastings, E. H., & Hastings, P. K. (1984). *Index to International Public Opinion, 1982–1983.* Westport, CT: Greenwood Press.

Hendricks, M. & Bootzin, R. (1976). Race and sex as stimuli for negative affect and physical avoidance. *Journal of Social Psychology, 98,* 111–120.

Hraba, J., & Grant, G. (1970). Black is beautiful: A re-examination of racial preference and identification. *Journal of Personality and Social Psychology, 16,* 398–402.

Katz, P. A. (1976). *Towards the elimination of racism.* Elmsford, NY: Pergamon.

LaFrance, M., & Mayo, C. (1976). Racial differences in gaze behavior during conversation. *Journal of Personality and Social Psychology, 33,* 547–552.

Lott, A. J., & Lott, B. E. (1968). A learning theory approach to interpersonal attitudes. In A. G. Greenwald, T. C. Brock, and T. M. Ostrum (Eds.), *Psychological foundations of attitudes* (pp. 67–68). New York: Academic Press.

Lott, A. J., & Lott, B. E. (1969). Liked and disliked persons as reinforcing stimuli. *Journal of Personality and Social Psychology, 11,* 129–137.

Morrison, A., & McIntyre, D. (1969). *Teachers and teaching.* Baltimore, Penguin.

Rosenthal, R., Hall, J. A., Archer, D., DiMatteo, M. R., & Rogers, P. L. (1979). Measuring sensitivity to nonverbal communication: The PONS test. In A. Wolfgang (Ed.), *Nonverbal behavior.* New York: Academic Press.

Ross, J. M., Vanneman, R. D., & Pettigrew, T. F. (1976). Patterns of support for George Wallace: Implications for racial change. *Journal of Social Issues, 32,* 69–91.

Simpson, A. W. & Erickson, M. T. (1983). Teachers' verbal and nonverbal communication patterns as a function of teacher race, student gender, and student race. *American Educational Research Journal, 20,* 183–198.

Simpson, G. E., & Yinger, M. J. (1975). *Racial and cultural minorities: An analysis of prejudice and discrimination.* (4th ed.). New York: Harper and Row.

Weitz, S. (1972). Attitude, voice and behavior: A repressed affect model of interracial interaction. *Journal of Personality and Social Psychology, 24,* 14–21.

Willis, F. N., Jr. (1966). Initial speaking distance as a function of the speaker's relationship. *Psychonomic Science, 5,* 221–222.

Woodmansee, J., & Cook, S. (1967). Dimensions of verbal racial attitudes: Their identification and measurement. *Journal of Personality and Social Psychology, 7,* 240–250.

Word, C. O., Zanna, M. P., & Cooper, J. (1974). The nonverbal mediation of self-fulfilling prophecies in interracial interaction. *Journal of Experimental Social Psychology, 10,* 109–120.

Zuckerman, M., DePaulo, B. M., & Rosenthal, R. (1981). Verbal and nonverbal communication of deception. In L. Berkowtiz (Ed.), *Advances in experimental social psychology,* Vol. 14 (pp. 163–171). New York: Academic Press.

6   Social psychological analysis of classroom interaction

Yaffa Bar-Tal and Daniel Bar-Tal

When two or more individuals communicate with each other via verbal and/or nonverbal behavior we say that they are in interaction. An interaction, in addition to the participants' behavioral transaction, also involves cognitive and affective reactions. Interacting individuals often plan their behavior in advance, process information during the exchange and decide how to behave during the interaction itself. In addition, the exchanged behaviors are often accompanied with affect. Individuals attribute meaning to their own and participants' behaviors which in turn arouses affective reactions.

Interactions take place in every social system as long as at least two individuals participate in it. It is a basic social process which does not require being face to face. Individuals may exchange communications with each other from a distance as well. Without an interaction it is impossible to imagine any social functioning. Through interactions, other social processes such as social relations, social influences, or social coordination take place. Being that interaction is a basic social process, it is not surprising that the study of human interactions has become one of the central focuses of behavioral sciences (e.g., Argyle, 1969; Blau, 1964; Goffman, 1959, 1967, 1969; Harvey, 1963; Homans, 1974; Kelley & Thibaut, 1978; Simmel, 1950).

Most of the teaching and learning in the classroom take place by means of interaction. The teacher exchanges communication with a pupil or pupils and a pupil or pupils exchange communications with a teacher or with other pupils. The interaction in the classroom not only serves to attain educational objectives but also functions as a mechanism through which a teacher and pupils realize their personal and social goals. Interaction is the main type of social activity in the classroom and it takes up most of the available time.

Classroom interaction can be analysed from various perspectives (see Withall & Lewis, 1963). Sociology, anthropology, or eductional psychology provide knowledge which enables such analysis. But, each discipline is based on assumptions which greatly affect the level, the content, the focus, and the method of the analysis. Social psychology as a discipline which deals with interpersonal and group behavior provides a unique perspective for the understanding of education in general and classroom interaction specifically (e.g., Backman & Secord, 1968; Bar-Tal & Saxe, 1978, 1981; Guskin & Guskin, 1970; Johnson, 1970).

Social psychology by definition focuses on human behavior as influenced by others (e.g., Asch, 1952; Jones & Gerard, 1967; Raven & Rubin, 1976). It studies social behaviors, of which interaction is one of them, taking place in various situations. On the basis of accumulated knowledge in social psychology, it is possible to infer assumptions regarding human social behavior. These assumptions greatly affect the way we analyze interactions in any social system, including the classroom.

The present chapter will analyse classroom interaction using the social psychological perspective. In the first part, we will describe the nature of interaction in general and focus specifically on classroom interaction. In the second part, we will analyze classroom interaction on the basis of social psychological assumptions regarding human social behavior.

Nature of interaction

Classroom interaction, as all the interactions, can be described by a number of characteristics outlined below.

It requires participants

Interaction by definition involves participants (Argyle, 1969). At least two individuals are required to take part in an interaction, even though an interaction may take place with more than two individuals. Moreover, interaction is not only an interpersonal phenomenon, but also, may occur in an intergroup framework. Two groups or more may interact with each other (Sherif, 1966). It is also possible for one person to interact with a group as a whole and a group may interact with one individual.

In a classroom all types of interactions take place (Delamont, 1976). A teacher may interact with a single pupil, with a group of pupils or with the whole class. A pupil may interact with another pupil, with a group of pupils or may stand in front of a class and interact with all the pupils in the classroom. Also, a class may be broken into groups which may interact with each other (Sharan & Sharan, 1976). These possibilities are important for the analysis of classroom interaction. They indicate that an interaction between a teacher and a pupil or a class is only one type of interaction, though it is the most frequently observed one. Other types of interaction also take place. Pupils interact with each other all the time during class and break. Pupils are unable to sit in a classroom and ignore each other. They interact openly when a teacher asks and covertly when a teacher does not allow it.

Also, a class as a social system, may be broken into subgroups. This may be done formally by a teacher who practices group teaching or informally through the dynamics of social relationships. In both cases, however, the groups of pupils interact with each other in various situations.

It is dynamic and changeable

Interaction is not static – it is a dynamic process which changes with the passage of time. Though it consists of communications and exchanges, it cannot be described analogously to a Ping-Pong game, since it changes all the time in its quantity and quality (Argyle, 1969). The exchanges of communication are unequal in its sequences and their characteristics vary. For example, an interaction may change with regard to the number of participants, its intensity, types of behavior involved or in its contents.

A classroom interaction undergoes change though it is divided into more or less equal parts – interaction during the lessons and interaction during the breaks. At the end of the school day it ends and resumes the next morning except during holidays (Jackson, 1968). During the school day an interaction takes place in a continuous fashion but in various forms (Hargreaves, 1975). Rarely is there a complete cessation of it. Usually it starts with a teacher's appeal to the whole class. Later, a teacher may interact with a single pupil or with a group. Through the interaction the teacher may change its subject several times referring to different academic subject matters; specific personal problems of a pupil or social problems of a whole class. Sometimes a teacher does much of the talking, while pupils answer and sometimes a pupil may talk for a long time or a number of pupils may participate in a discussion. Sometimes the interaction may be quiet and controlled while occasionally it may be loud, chaotic, and aggressive.

It involves behaviors

Interaction involves behaviors. Individuals or groups interact one with another by exhibiting behaviors. Through the behaviors, the communication takes place. The behaviors can be verbal and/or nonverbal. That is, an interaction involves verbal exchanges, nonverbal exchanges or both of them. The verbal exchanges consist of sequences of speeches that express the language; of intonation, which includes pitches, stresses and junctures; and of paralinguistics, which consist of vocalizations such as coughs, splutters, giggles, cryings, laughings or yawnings. The nonverbal exchanges include kinetics which consist of body and facial movements that accompany verbal behavior and motor movements which include voluntary and involuntary acts. (For more details see Belinger, 1975; Laver & Hutcheson, 1972.) All of the above described behaviors are part of an interaction, providing it with meaning. Not only do spoken words have meanings, but other aspects of communication as well are understood by the participants' information. Each of them adds to the understanding of the intended communication.

A classroom interaction is variegated and involves all the described behaviors. The dominant pattern of exchanges is verbal (Bellack & Davitz, 1972). A teacher and pupils interact mostly via speaking to each other. Their speeches, however, are not monotonic. A teacher may laugh, yell, or whisper during the interaction with pupils. He changes the intonation by, for example, stressing certain words and using his body and face while speaking. Intonation, paralinguistics, and kinesics add special meaning to speech and, by means of them, pupils and teachers communicate messages such as agreements, encouragements, threats, anger, attentiveness, or approval (Jecker, Maccoby, & Breitrose, 1965). The described elements of behavior are culturally determined. Pupils and a teacher share them and understand their meaning.

It involves mutual influence

In interaction, the participants influence each other. It is impossible for an interaction to take place without such influence. Individuals react to each other, attend to the behaviors of others, and respond to the performed behaviors of other participants. An interaction involves communication and exchange. Both processes imply mutual influence, at least in a way which requires reaction towards others' communication or acts. In most cases, the interacting individuals leave the interaction in a different situation than that existing before entering it. Through inter-action, new information is usually provided and new knowledge is formed by the participants.

Classroom interaction in its explicit objective is carried out to add knowledge to pupils. The teacher who is a source of knowledge tries, via interaction, to transfer knowledge to pupils. As a leader of the class, the teacher exerts much influence on pupils' behavior. Through the inter-action, the teacher directs and controls pupils' behavior. He tells them what to do, evaluates their performance, and provides feedback on their behavior.

Though it is most commonly believed that the influence in the classroom is in one direction – from the teacher to pupils – we would like to suggest that the influence is mutual (e.g., Fiedler, 1975). During the interaction pupils exert influence on the teacher as well (e.g., Noble & Nolan, 1976). First of all, in the exchanges, the teacher must take into consideration the communications of the pupils in deciding how to behave. He may ignore the communication of pupils. Even in such disregard, however, he makes a decision how to react. In many cases, though, pupils play an important part in the interaction with the teacher. They also provide feedback on the teacher's behavior, evaluate it and initiate behaviors to which the teacher must respond. Thus, the pupil – teacher's interaction should be viewed as bidirectional, reciprocal, and mutual.

It has rules

Interactions have rules. They usually do not occur in chaos, but are governed by norms. The norms may be unique to a specific interpersonal interaction, to a specific group, to a specific social institution. On the other hand, they may be common to a society or even accepted by a number of societies. They may also vary from situation to situation. The norms determine such rules as who opens an interaction, when and how others participate, what kind of behaviors it involves, how many participants may participate, the length of interaction, etc.

Classroom interaction is also organized in accordance to rules (Jackson, 1968). Part of the rules of classroom interaction are shared by all the members of the society and they depend on such variables as teacher's status, children's rights, or importance of education. In cen-tralized school systems, some rules for classroom interaction may be decided by the state department of education or by a comparable institution. But, in any event, much of the interaction's rules develop within the specific school and the specific classroom, though they most always must be compatible to the norms of the society from which the pupils come. On the school level, the principal, the board, or the teacher's council determine rules of pupils' and teachers' behavior which affect classroom interaction. In the classroom environment, the teacher sets many of the rules and many others develop between the specific teacher and pupils during their interaction. Both learn what is desired, what is allowed, or what is forbidden. A teacher and pupils learn to follow the rules of classroom interaction which indicate, for example, when to speak, what can be said, how long to speak, or what kind of nonverbal behavior can accompany speaking. Thus, each class develops its own set of rules which together, with other given rules, govern classroom interaction.

It is affected by various factors

Interactions do not take place in a vacuum but in physical and social environments. The environment in which an interaction takes place influences it. Factors such as size of the room, available furniture, the intensity of the light or presence of observers may affect the nature of the interaction (Altman, 1975). Any analysis of an interaction must take the environment in which it takes place into consideration.

Classroom interaction takes place in a school. The room in which it occurs contains a blackboard and desks. Between 20 to 40 pupils either witness an interaction or participate in it. All these features affect the process and the outcome of classroom interaction. But, classrooms differ from one another in such characteristics as size of the room, the arrangement of desks, the seating position of pupils, the number of pupils, or the wall's decoration. These characteristics and others can be considered as factors which affect classroom interaction (Weinstein, 1979).

It is measurable

Interactions can be characterized on the basis of the previously outlined features. They may be described on the basis of the number and characteristics of the participants, the behaviors involved, the guiding rules, amount of influence exerted by each participant, or environmental factors affecting the interaction (e.g., Bales, 1970). In addition, interactions may be characterized and measured according to such variables as the contents of the interaction, amount and scope of behaviors used, or parts of the participants.

Classroom interaction, like all the other interactions, can be measured and characterized. Over the years, different instruments have been developed to measure various aspects of classroom interaction and numerous studies have been performed to characterize it. In early years, researchers focused mostly on the characterization of teachers' verbal behavior, assuming that the nature of classroom interaction is determined by teachers. Thus, for example, Anderson (1939) developed an instrument which classifies 24 categories of teachers' behavior and Withall (1949) offered an instrument of seven categories to analyze teachers' verbal behavior. Even an instrument developed by Flanders (1970) has seven categories to describe teachers' behavior and only two categories to describe pupils' behavior. These lists include only a limited number of possible categories. For example, classroom interaction, as was previously suggested, is reciprocal and bidirectional. Therefore, characterization of pupils' behavior is necessary for a description of classroom interaction. In any event, a measurement and characterization of classroom interaction can focus on various aspects of exchanges between pupils and a teacher and may include different categories which may be of interest for educators.

Social psychological analysis of classroom interaction

In the second part of the chapter we will analyze classroom interaction using social psychological assumptions as a guiding framework. Specifically, our point of departure will be those social psychological assumptions which are relevant for classroom social behavior and, from this basis, we shall turn to the discussion of their implications for the classroom interaction.

People are active beings

Human beings are not passive and reactive, but active and initiative. They act upon their environment and initiate much of their behavior. Individuals actively absorb information and process it in their mind, they formulate impressions and crystallize attitudes, they form expectations and act to realize them, and they decide on intentions and behave in accordance with them (see Eiser, 1980; Fishbein & Ajzen, 1975; Harvey & Smith, 1977; Heider, 1958; Krech & Crutchfield, 1948).

This assumption has implications for the analysis of every social system, including the classroom. It implies that neither a teacher nor pupils are passive beings who react only to the stimulations of the environment. This view is especially important for the description of pupils' behaviors since for years it was accepted that pupils in the classroom are mostly reacting to the teacher's behavior and the requirement of the school. The present assumption portrays a different picture. It suggests that pupils are as active and initiating as are their teachers. The school environment provides much information and stimulation which the pupils attentively absorb and process. Their behavior is not a mechanistic reaction to the stimulation, but often a calculated and considered response which may also include initiative. They may ask, comment, criticize, suggest, or tell a story, starting an interaction and they may also terminate an interaction. They may initiate much of their nonverbal behavior during the interaction as well.

Any classroom interaction must take into account the acts of the interacting individuals. Pupils and teachers interact while considering each other's behaviors. Some parts of behavior they may ignore, to some they may pay special attention and to others they may selectively attend. Many of these decisions are done deliberately in the process of encoding and weighing the information coming from the other person. We do recognize that the power balance between pupils and a teacher is asymmetrical in most cases. Teachers have more power to initiate their own behaviors and control pupils' behavior in a classroom interaction. But, a disregard for pupils' active nature may greatly distort the description of the interaction. This assumption implies that many of the behaviors involved in a classroom interaction should be viewed as intentional, weighed, and planned. They are performed in a reciprocal and bidirectional transaction in which a teacher and pupils influence and are influenced by the exchanges. That is, all the participants of classroom interaction are active as well as reactive.

Cognition is an important determinant of behavior

Social psychology greatly emphasizes the functions of cognition as a determinant of human behavior (e.g., Ajzen & Fishbein, 1980; Eiser, 1980; Schank & Abelson, 1977). This assumption focuses not only on the importance of information processing or belief formation as described in the previous assumption, but also focuses on the influence of cognition (or as we prefer to call it knowledge) on behavior. Knowledge consists of beliefs in the form of attitudes, expectations, goals or intentions, which individuals have (see Bar-Tal & Bar-Tal, in press). Individuals react to the world they believe to exist – this is an important premise that is widely accepted by social psychologists (e.g., Asch, 1952; Brunswick, 1956; Heider, 1958).

If one wants to understand the classroom interaction, she/he has to take into account the present assumption. Any analysis of classroom interaction must consider the cognition (knowledge) of the interacting individuals, pupils' or teachers'. Pupils and teachers interact on the basis of knowledge they have regarding the surrounding world (e.g., Bar-Tal, 1979; Good & Brophy, 1972).

This knowledge is the reality of the individuals involved and they behave in accordance with it. Understanding of classroom interaction, therefore, requires an understanding of pupils' and teachers' beliefs regarding the school world which is especially relevant for classroom interaction (Delamont, 1976; Hargreaves, 1975; Jackson, 1968). These beliefs concern such topics as educational objectives, pupils' role, teachers' role, school liking or educational ideology of a teacher. This analysis allows for an understanding of what pupils and a teacher had in mind when they performed their behavior in classroom interaction (e.g., Bar-Tal, 1979; Brophy & Good, 1974; Hargreaves, 1975; Rosenthal & Jacobson, 1968). Without such an analysis, we are likely to misinterpret the real intention of the actors, since each behavior may be based on different beliefs.

A specific example of this line of reasoning is an attributional model of classroom interaction proposed by Bar-Tal (1979, 1982) on the basis of Weiner's attributional model of achievement-related behavior (Weiner, 1974, 1979). According to Bar-Tal's model, pupils' causal beliefs of their academic success and failure affects their achievement-related behaviors. Specifically, pupils who tend to attribute their failure to unstable-controllable causes, such as effort, tend to persist for a long time even in a failure situation, since this attribution enables them to believe that there is a possibility of modifying the outcome in the future. Conversely, attribution of a failure to stable-uncontrollable causes does not leave the possibility of changing the outcome in the future and, therefore, there is no reason to persist. The belief in unstable-controllable causes such as effort causes the person to assume that the outcome depends on will. Therefore, these pupils perform with great intensity on achievement tasks. On the other hand, the belief in stable or uncontrollable causes, such as ability or mood, does not motivate the pupil to perform with intensity, because there is no belief in having control over the causes of success or failure. Finally, it was found that pupils tend to prefer to perform tasks that are compatible with their causal beliefs. For example, pupils who generally attribute their achievement outcome to ability are likely to choose tasks in which competence is requisite to outcome. Conversely, pupils who tend to attribute their success to luck prefer tasks which depend on chance and avoid tasks requiring competence. Similarly, Bar-Tal suggested that teachers' causal beliefs regarding pupils' academic achievement are important determinants of their behavior toward their pupils. The relationship between teachers' causal beliefs and their behavior toward pupils can be explained through the mediating process of teachers' expectations regarding pupils' future outcomes. It is suggested that teachers decide whether the same outcome will be repeated in the future on the basis of the classification of the causes on the dimensions of stability and controllability. If the teachers believe that the success or failure of their pupils is caused by stable causes, they might expect the same outcome to be repeated, because people believe that stable causes do not change over time. If the success or failure is attributed to unstable, but controllable, causes, the teachers might believe that the pupils will experience success in the future, on the assumption that pupils want to succeed. However, if the success or failure is attributed to unstable and uncontrollable causes, the teachers cannot predict the future achievement outcome of the pupils. In turn, it is proposed that teachers' expectations regarding pupils' future achievement affect their behavior toward the pupils. This proposal has been supported by numerous studies that have shown that teachers' differential behavior toward pupils is determined by their expectations regarding future outcomes (see reviews by Braun, 1976; Brophy & Good, 1975; Dusek, 1975). Finally, the model suggests that pupils' achievement behavior influences teachers' causal beliefs of pupils' success or failure and that teachers' behavior toward pupils determines pupils' causal beliefs of their success or failure. The former link is supported by evidence reviewed by West and Anderson (1976) which indicates that teachers' expectations seem to be formed on the basis of observed pupils' behavior and not on the basis of irrelevant cues. The latter link is based on evidence which suggests that teachers' provide, through verbal and nonverbal communication, information regarding pupils' causes of success and failure which is adopted by pupils (e.g., Andrews & Debus, 1978; Chapin & Dyck, 1976; Dweck, 1975; Dweck et al., 1978).

The described model has served as a basis for a number of empirical studies investigating pupils' and teachers' causal beliefs, as well as their relationships with evaluations and behavior (e.g., Bar-Tal, Goldberg & Knaani, 1984; Bar-Tal & Guttmann, 1981; Bar-Tal et al., 1982; Bar-Tal et al., 1981; Guttmann, 1984; Guttmann & Bar-Tal, 1982).

In addition to the Bar-Tal model, a number of other studies attempted to investigate pupils' beliefs (e.g., Gustafsson, 1979; Kineton, 1969; Sharples, 1969) and teachers' beliefs (e.g., Callis, 1953; Kremer, 1978; Oliver and Butcher, 1962; Shavelson & Stern, 1981; Wheeling & Charters, 1969). But the focus of all these studies was mostly on the common beliefs rather than on the unique beliefs of specific individuals in a specific class. Nevertheless, these studies provide an important glimpse into the pupils' and teachers' world and towards understanding their behavior. It cannot be assumed, however, that all the pupils shared the same beliefs about school. Pupils had different experiences and, therefore, differed in their beliefs. At the same time, because many of the experiences in school are common and the teacher and peers exert much influence on the individual pupil, many of the beliefs may be common to all the pupils in the classroom. In this vein, of special interest are those studies which took a more particularistic perspective and focused on the investigation of beliefs of a specific class (e.g., Lancy, 1976; Stebbins, 1975). These studies illustrate the unique belief system of the participants in classroom interaction and allow for an understanding not only of pupils' or a teacher's world but also of the meaning of their behaviors.

Human beings are unique

Social psychology recognizes individual differences. No two individuals are exactly alike. Individuals differ in their knowledge, personality, needs, motivations or repertoire of behaviors (e.g., Cantor & Kihlstrom, 1981; Mischel, 1968; Zanna, Herman & Higgins, 1982). The differences are a consequence of unique experiences that each individual goes through. No person can go through exactly the same experiences as another person. This assumption does not say that individuals may not be similar, but only emphasizes that any analysis of any social system must consider the uniqueness of each individual. An important implication of this assumption is recognition of the subjective nature of human beings. Each individual has her or his own view of the world which is her or his reality. An understanding of individual reality greatly contributes to the explanation of individuals' behavior.

Every one of the individuals participating in classroom interaction – pupils and a teacher – is unique. Each carries his or her own "personal bag" of unique personality, motivations, knowledge, needs, or behaviors. This bag influences the way the person interacts. No two pupils interact in the same way. Although pupils in the same classroom are sometimes dressed alike and look similar, they differ in the personal bag they carry. Therefore, though the classroom interaction may be the same with regard to the concerned subject, they are different in their content, accompanied behaviors, length, scope or in other characteristics (e.g., Brophy & Good, 1974; Brophy & Evertson, 1981). Sometimes the difference may be small and sometimes large, depending on the similarity between the individuals. But, neither the teacher nor the researcher can assume that all the pupils are alike and the classroom interaction is the same for the interacting individuals.

A group is more than the sum of its members

A group is not a mere sum of its members. A group has characteristics as a whole which are lost when the group disintegrates. Social psychology has contributed much to our knowledge of group structure and group behavior (e.g., Cartwright & Zander, 1968; McGrath & Altman, 1966; Shaw, 1976). Since much of human behavior takes place in a group, it is important to understand a group's characteristics. These characteristics differ from group to group. Each group consists of unique members and therefore, as a whole, they form a unique group. Thus, beyond the characterization of the group's members, it may characterize a group by such measures as goals, norms of behavior, cohesiveness, patterns of communication, type of leadership, differentiation of rules, or power structure. These and other characteristics determine the nature of interaction among the group members and with other groups.

A class is not only a combination of pupils and a teacher but is also a group. A teacher is an appointed leader of the group holding considerable power. Formally, all the pupils, as members of the group, have the same status, role, and power. But, in reality, the group is differentiated. Pupils come to the group with different personal bags and therefore cannot be the same as group members (e.g., Zeichner, 1978). Although each of them fulfills the role of a pupil, they differ with regard to other roles that they take upon themselves in the group. Some may be leaders, some may be organizers, some may be knowledge sources, etc. Any class as a group, therefore, has its own unique features. These features are not only a function of group members, but also of the goals and norms of the system of which the class is a part.

The class acts as a group and over time it develops characteristics which greatly influence classroom interaction (e.g., Bany & Johnson, 1964; Schmuck & Schmuck, 1983). Thus, any analysis of classroom interaction must also consider the class as a group. An understanding of classroom interaction requires a knowledge of such characteristics as the group's goals, norms, level of cohesiveness, or level of differentiation. That is, this knowledge explains why the class behaves as it does in classroom interactions.

In addition, teachers often divide the class into groups for group instruction. There are various goals and ways in dividing the class into groups (see Sharan, 1980; Slavin, this volume; Webb, 1982). For our purposes, however, we are only interested in the interaction which occurs within the group and among the groups. This interaction is also affected by the characteristics of the groups.

Finally, it should be remembered that the group exerts an influence on an individual's behavior. Thus, an interaction between a pupil and a teacher is not only affected by the personal bag of each of them, but also by the group of which they are members. A teacher, and especially pupils, follow the norms of the class group in their interpersonal interaction. Such conformity influences the nature of classroom interaction and, therefore, its analysis also requires a knowledge of the group's norms.

Social behavior is influenced by environment

Social psychology attaches great weight to environmental influences (see Altman, 1975; Baum & Valins, 1977; Sommer, 1969). An individual's behavior is greatly determined by the conditions of the environment. The environment influences what is perceived, what can be done, and how one can behave. The environment consists of the physical setting in which the behavior takes place and of other individuals who are present in the situation. The physical environment provides limitations as well as possibilities for different behavior and the presence of other people influences an individual's behavior.

The classroom as a physical and social environment influences an interaction. Pupils and teachers interact according to the available layout and decor of the classroom (e.g. Deletes & Jackson, 1972; Gump, 1974; Zifferblatt, 1972). The shape of the room, the furniture, the size and location of the windows, and the arrangement of the desks are characteristics of the physical environment that shape the classroom interaction (see Weinstein, 1979). Thus, any analysis of the classroom interaction should take into consideration the characteristics of the environment and the way it influences pupils' and teachers' behavior.

Conclusions

Most of the attempts to analyze classroom interaction have focused on the examination of the teachers' and pupils' behavior performed during interaction. These examinations have concentrated on such variables as contents of the interaction, its scope, duration, or nonverbal behavior involved. This direction of analysis allows for examination of only limited aspects of classroom interaction. Using the social psychological perspective, we suggest that an understanding of the classroom interaction requires an analysis that takes into consideration the previously outlined premises. Such an analysis must focus not only on the behavior of pupils and teachers but also on pupils' and teachers' knowledge, class structure, and the environmental characteristics of the classroom.

Any comprehensive analysis should not only focus on behavior but also try to determine the meaning of the behaviors and the factors that influence the course of the interaction. The meaning of pupils' and teachers' behaviors can be determined on the basis of their knowledge regarding the school world and the assessment of the factors influencing classroom interaction can be carried out by studying the group's characteristics and the physical setting's features. Such analysis provides a holistic and meaningful picture of the classroom interaction.

Finally, it should be noted that the social psychological assumptions we have discussed not only affect pupils' interactions and understanding, but also have explicit implications for teachers' practices in classrooms. One of the most important implications is that teachers should treat their pupils as partners. Treating pupils as partners indicates a recognition that they are active, intuitive and thoughtful actors who influence teachers' behavior and are influenced by them. This view suggests that pupils are not mindless, but their behavior is based on their previous knowledge and information they collect. Teachers should exert efforts to understand the basis of pupils behavior by trying to map pupils' goals, expectations, attitudes, or grievances. Also, teachers have to realize that pupils, though they are often dressed similarly, look similar, and come from similar backgrounds, are unique individuals. They can't all be treated alike. Each of the pupils has his or her own set of attitudes, expectations, or motivations. Thus, if teachers want to understand their pupils and know how to approach them, they should try to collect information about each of them. At the same time, teachers should recognize that pupils in the classroom form a group. A group has a structure and special characteristics that greatly affect pupils' behavior. Therefore, teachers should try to know their classroom group if they want successfully to manage their classes. In addition, teachers should realize that the physical environment of the classroom and the school affect pupils' beliefs and behaviors. They should structure it in such a way that on the one hand, it will produce positive pupil attitudes and, on the other, it will facilitate instruction, learning and interaction.

References

Ajzen, I., & Fishbein, M. (1980). *Understanding attitudes and predicting social behavior.* Englewood Cliffs, NJ: Prentice-Hall.

Altman, I. (1975). *The environment and social behavior*. Monterey, CA: Brooks/Cole.

Anderson, H. H. (1939). The measurement of domination and of socially disintegrative behavior in teachers' contacts with children. *Child Development, 10*, 73–89.

Andrews, G. R. & Debus, R. L. (1978). Persistence and the causal perception of failure: Modifying cognitive attributions. *Journal of Educational Psychology, 70*, 154–166.

Argyle, M. (1969). *Social interaction*. Chicago: Aldine.

Asch, S. E. (1952). *Social psychology*. Englewood Cliffs, NJ: Prentice-Hall.

Backman, C. W. & Secord, P. F. (1968). *A social psychological view of education*. New York: Harcourt, Brace and World.

Bales, R. F. (1970). *Personality and interpersonal behavior*. New York: Holt, Rinehart and Winston.

Bany, M. A. & Johnson, L. V. (1964). *Classroom group behavior: Group dynamics in education*. New York: Macmillan.

Bar-Tal, D. (1979). Interactions of teachers and pupils. In I. Frieze, D. Bar-Tal & J. S. Carroll (Eds.) *New approaches to social problems: Applications of attribution theory* (pp. 337–358). San Francisco: Jossey-Bass.

Bar-Tal, D. (1982). The effect of teachers' behavior on pupils' attributions: A review. In C. Antaki & C. Breisin (Eds.), *Attributions and psychological change.* (pp. 177–194). London: Academic Press.

Bar-Tal, D. & Bar-Tal, Y. (in press). Epistemological view of social psychology. In D. Bar-Tal & A. Kruglanski (Eds.) *Social psychology of knowledge*. Cambridge: Cambridge University Press.

Bar-Tal, D., Goldberg, M., & Knaani, A. (1984). Causes of success and failure and their dimensions as a function of sex and gender: Phenomenological analysis. *British Journal of Educational Psychology, 54*, 51–61.

Bar-Tal, D., & Guttmann, J. (1981). A comparison of pupils', teachers', and parents' attributions regarding pupils' achievement. *British Journal of Educational Psychology, 51*, 301–311.

Bar-Tal, D., Raviv, A., Raviv, A., & Bar-Tal, Y. (1982). Consistency of pupils' attributions regarding success and failure. *Journal of Educational Psychology, 74*, 104–110.

Bar-Tal, D., Raviv, A., Raviv, A., & Levit, R. (1981). Teachers' reaction to attributions of ability and effort and their predictions of students' reactions. *Educational Psychology, 1*, 231–240.

Bar-Tal, D., & Saxe, L. (Ed.). (1978). *Social psychology of education: Theory and research*. New York: Halsted.

Bar-Tal, D. & Saxe, L. (1981). Social psychology of education – What? *Representative Research in Social Psychology, 12*, 5–19.

Baum, A., & Valins, S. (1977). *Architecture and social behavior*. Hillsdale, NJ: Erlbaum.

Belinger, D. (1975). *Aspects of language* (2nd ed.) New York: Harcourt, Brace, Jovanovich.

Bellack, A. A., & Davitz, J. R. (1972). The language of the classroom. In A. Morrison & D. McIntyre (Eds.) *Social psychology of teaching* (pp. 99–114). Harmondsworth: Penguin.

Blau, P. M. (1964). *Exchange and power in social life*. New York: Wiley.

Braun, C. (1976). Teachers' expectations: Sociopsychological dynamics. *Review of Educational Research, 46*, 185–214.

Brophy, J. E., & Evertson, C. M. (1981). *Student characteristics and teaching*. New York: Longman.

Brophy, J. E. & Good, T. L. (1974). *Teacher–student relationships: Causes and consequences*. New York: Holt, Rinehart and Winston.

Brunswick, E. (1956). *Perception and the representative design of experiments*. (2nd ed.) Berkeley: University of California Press.

Callis, R. (1953). The efficiency of the Minnesota Teacher Attitude Inventory for predicting interpersonal relations in the classroom. *Journal of Applied Psychology, 37*, 82–85.

Cantor, N., & Kihlstrom, J. F. (Eds.) (1981). *Personality, cognition and social interaction.* Hillsdale, NJ: Erlbaum.

Cartwright, D., & Zander, A. (Eds.) (1968). *Group dynamics* (3rd ed.) New York: Harper and Row.

Chapin, M., & Dyck, D. G. (1976). Persistence of children's reading behavior as a function of N length and attribution retraining. *Journal of Abnormal Psychology, 85,* 511–515.

Delamont, S. (1976). *Interaction in the classroom.* London: Methuen.

Deletes, P., & Jackson, B. (1972). Teacher–pupil interaction as a function of location in the classroom. *Psychology in the Schools, 9* (2), 119–123.

Dusek, J. B. (1975). Do teachers bias children's learning? *Review of Educational Research, 45,* 661–684.

Dweck, C. S. (1975). The role of expectations and attributions in the alleviation of learned helplessness. *Journal of Personality and Social Psychology, 31,* 674–685.

Dweck, C. S., Davidson, W., Nelson, S., & Enna, B. (1978). Sex differences in learned helplessness: (II) The contingencies of evaluative feedback in the classroom. An experimental analysis. *Developmental Psychology, 14,* 268–276.

Eiser, J. R. (1980). *Cognitive social psychology.* London: McGraw-Hill.

Fiedler, M. L. (1975). Bidirectionality of influence in classroom interaction. *Journal of Educational Psychology, 67,* 735–744.

Fishbein, M., & Ajzen, I. (1975). *Belief, attitude, intention and behavior.* Reading, MA: Addison-Wesley.

Flanders, N. A. (1970). *Analyzing teaching behavior.* Reading, MA: Addison-Wesley.

Goffman, E. (1959). *The presentation of self in everyday life.* Garden City, NY: Doubleday Anchor.

Goffman, E. (1967). *Interaction ritual.* Chicago: Aldine.

Goffman, E. (1969). *Strategic interaction.* Philadelphia: University of Pennsylvania Press.

Good, T. L., & Brophy, J. E. (1972). Behavioral expression of teacher attitudes. *Journal of Educational Psychology, 63,* 617–624.

Gump, P. (1974). Operating environments in schools of open and traditional design. *School Review, 82,* 575–593.

Guskin, A. E., & Guskin, S. L. (1970). *A social psychology of education.* Reading, MA: Addison-Wesley.

Gustafsson, J. E. (1979). Attitudes towards the school, the teacher, and classmates at the class and individual level. *British Journal of Educational Psychology, 49,* 124–131.

Guttmann, J. (1984). The relative importance of ethnic origin and study characteristics in the formation of teachers' evaluation. *Research in Education,* No. 31, 1–10.

Guttmann, J., & Bar-Tal, D. (1982). Stereotypic perception of teachers. *American Educational Research Journal, 19,* 519–528.

Hargreaves, D. H. (1975). *Interpersonal relations and education.* London: Routledge & Kegan Paul.

Harvey, J. H. & Smith, N. P. (1977). *Social psychology: An additional approach.* St. Louis, MO: C.V. Mosby.

Harvey, O. J. (Ed.) (1963). *Motivation and social interaction.* New York: Ronald Press.

Heider, F. (1958). *The psychology of interpersonal relations.* New York: Wiley.

Homans, G. C. (1974). *Social behavior: Its elementary forms.* (2nd ed.) New York: Harcourt, Brace, Jovanovich.

Jackson, P. W. (1968). *Life in classrooms.* New York: Holt, Rinehart and Winston.

Jecker, J. D., Maccoby, N. & Breitrose, H. S. (1965). Improving accuracy in interpreting non-verbal cues at comprehension. *Psychology in the Schools, 2,* 239–244.

Johnson, D. W. (1970). *The social psychology of education.* New York: Holt, Rinehart and Winston.

Jones, E. E., & Gerard, H. B. (1967). *Foundations of social psychology,* New York: Wiley.

Kelley, H. H. & Thibaut, J. W. (1978). *Interpersonal relations: A theory of interdependence.* New York: Wiley.

Kinveton, B. H. (1969). An investigation of the attitudes of adolescents to aspects of their schooling. *British Journal of Educational Psychology, 39,* 78–81.

Krech, D. & Crutchfield, R. S. (1948). *Theory and problems of social psychology.* New York: McGraw-Hill.

Kremer, L. (1978). Teachers' attitudes toward educational goals as reflected in classroom behavior. *Journal of Educational Psychology, 80,* 993–997.

Lancy, D. F. (1976). *The beliefs and behaviors of pupils in an experimental school: School settings.* Pittsburgh: University of Pittsburgh, Learning and Research and Development Center (LRDC Publications, 1976/21).

Laver, J. & Hutcheson, S. (Eds.) (1972). *Communication in face-to-face interaction.* Harmondsworth: Penguin.

McGrath, J. E. & Altman, I. (1966). *Small group research.* New York: Holt, Rinehart and Winston.

Mischel, W. (1968). *Personality and assessment.* New York: Wiley.

Noble, C. G., & Nolan, J. D. (1976). Effect of student verbal behavior on classroom teacher behavior. *Journal of Educational Psychology, 68,* 342–346.

Oliver, R. A. C., & Butcher, H. L. (1962). Teachers' attitudes to education. *British Journal of Social and Clinical Psychology, 1,* 56–69.

Raven, B. H. & Rubin, J. Z. (1976). *Social psychology: People in groups.* New York: Wiley.

Rosenthal, R. and Jacobson, L. (1968). *Pygmalion in the classroom.* New York: Holt, Rinehart and Winston.

Schank, R., & Abelson, R. P. (1977). *Scripts, plans, goals and understanding: An inquiry into human knowledge structures.* Hillsdale, NJ: Erlbaum.

Schmuck, R., & Schmuck, O. (1983). *Group processes in the classroom.* (4th ed.) Dubuque, IA: Wm. C. Brown.

Sharan, S. (1980). Cooperative learning in small groups: Recent methods and effects on achievement, attitudes and ethnic relations. *Review of Educational Research, 50,* 241–271.

Sharan, S. & Sharan, Y. (1976). *Small-group teaching.* Englewood Cliffs, NJ: Educational Technology Publications.

Sharples, D. (1969). Children's attitude towards junior school activities. *British Journal of Educational Psychology, 39,* 72–77.

Shavelson, R. J. & Stern, P. (1981). Research on teachers' pedagogical thoughts, judgments, decisions and behavior. *Review of Educational Research, 51,* 455–488.

Shaw, M. E. (1976). *Group dynamics: The psychology of small group behavior.* (2nd ed.) New York: McGraw-Hill.

Simmel, G. (1950). *The sociology of Georg Simmel.* Glencoe, IL: Free Press.

Slavin, R. E. (1980). Cooperative learning. *Review of Educational Research, 50,* 315–342.

Sommer, R. (1969). *Personal space.* Englewood Cliffs, NJ: Prentice-Hall.

Stebbins, R. A. (1975). *Teachers and meaning: Definitions of classroom situation.* Leiden: Brill.

Webb, N. M. (1982). Student interaction and learning in small groups. *Review of Educational Research, 52,* 421–445.

Weiner, B. (1974). *Achievement motivation and attribution theory.* Morristown, NJ: General Learning Press.

Weiner, B. (1979). A theory of motivation for some classroom experiences. *Journal of Educational Psychology, 71,* 3–25.

Weinstein, C. S. (1979). The physical environment of the school: A review of the research.

Review of Educational Research, 49, 577–610.

West, C. H. & Anderson, T. H. (1976). The question of preponderant causation in teacher expectancy research. *Review of Educational Research, 46*, 613–630.

Wheeling, L. J. & Charters, W. W. (1969). Dimensions of teachers' beliefs about the teaching process. *American Educational Research Journal, 6*, 7–30.

Withall, J. (1949). The development of a technique for the measurement of social–emotional climate in classrooms. *Journal of Experimental Education, 17*, 347–361.

Withall, J., & Lewis, W. W. (1963). Social interaction in the classroom. In N. L. Gage (Ed.), *Handbook of research on teaching* (pp. 683–714). Chicago: Rand McNally.

Zanna, M. P., Herman, C. P. & Higgins, E. T. (Eds.) (1982). *Consistency in social behavior: The Ontario Symposium (Vol. 2)*. Hillsdale, NJ: Erlbaum.

Zeichner, K. M. (1978). Group membership in the elementary school classroom. *Journal of Educational Psychology, 70*, 554–564.

Zifferblatt, S. M. (1972). Architecture and human behavior: Toward increased understanding of a functional relationship. *Educational Technology, 12* (8), 54–57.

Part III

Cooperation and conflict in the classroom

7   Cooperative learning: engineering social psychology in the classroom

Robert E. Slavin

The study of cooperation and competition is one of the oldest traditions in social psychology. In 1897 Triplett found that bicycle riders would ride faster if they were in a competition than if they were riding without a competitor. In 1929 Maller published an extensive book correlating the preference for cooperation or competition with an impressive array of variables, including the quality of children's teeth, grooming, and body odor. Numerous studies investigated the question of whether two or more individuals could solve problems cooperatively better than one working alone, and by 1938 Thorndike concluded that the superiority of "two heads" to one was so well established that further research on this topic was pointless. The positive effects of cooperation on social behavior, particularly cohesiveness, were also well documented early on (see, for example, Stendler, Damrin, and Haines, 1951).

In 1949 Deutsch set forth a series of propositions concerning the likely effects of cooperative versus competitive goal structures on performance as well as affective outcomes. Deutsch's comprehensive theory has guided much social psychological research on cooperation and competition for the past thirty-six years. His perspective is represented in this volume by the work of David Johnson, who studied with Deutsch.

However, as hoary and well-established as principles of cooperative and competitive goal structures are, the *application* of these principles has come far more slowly. Despite the fact that much of the research on cooperation and competition has taken place in school settings and has involved learning and problem-solving tasks obviously adaptable to

Preparation of this chapter was supported in part by grant NIE–G–83–0002 from the National Institute of Education, U.S. Department of Education. However, the opinions expressed are those of the author alone, and do not represent Department of Education policy.

153

education, systematic applications of principles of cooperation and competition to educational settings have only come to the fore in the last decade. This chapter discusses the application of principles of cooperation to the practice of instruction, with an emphasis on the process by which these principles had to be "engineered" to the realities of the classroom and to solve problems created by the use of cooperative activities themselves.

"Pure" cooperation

The shortest route from the laboratory to the classroom was to use essentially the same cooperative tasks used in the social psychological studies. Perhaps the simplest and "purest" form of cooperative learning evaluated in classroom settings requires students to work in four- to five-member heterogeneous groups to complete worksheets together, where all students must agree on a consensus answer to each worksheet item. The groups are then praised or, occasionally, graded on the basis of the group product.

Brief studies of this type of cooperative learning, all lasting less than 6 hours, found that students who worked cooperatively produced better worksheets or problem solutions than those who worked competitively (students competed to do the best worksheet) or individually (Johnson, Johnson, & Skon, 1979; Johnson & Johnson, 1979; Laughlin, Branch, & Johnson, 1969). However, this result was probably due in part to the fact that if any one student in the cooperative condition knew the worksheet answer, all students were credited with a correct answer (Hill, 1982; Slavin, 1983a, 1983b). In contrast, students in the competitive and individualistic conditions were forbidden to interact with their classmates. These brief experiments also found higher *individual* performance on problem-solving tasks in cooperative than in competitive or individualistic conditions (Johnson & Johnson, 1981). Again, however, this result could well have been caused by more able students telling answers to less able students, since the students were tested on the same problems. For example, several studies (Johnson, Skon, & Johnson, 1980; Johnson et al., 1979) involved the solution of a Rasmussen triangle, a triangle with several smaller triangles inscribed in it. The students are asked to find all the triangles. The answer is that there are 27 triangles. In the cooperative conditions, the first student to discover this would of course tell his or her group mates, and show them the triangles. They needed only to remember the number 27. In the competitive or individualistic conditions, though, students who never arrived at the correct solution would never see it, and would fail the test. However, would the cooperative students be better able to solve *different* problems of the same type, or would a teacher have been able to teach the problem-solving task more effectively than the cooperative groups interaction? This is the critical question for the ecological validity of the studies for classroom application, but these studies do not ask it.

Several lengthier and more ecologically valid studies of "pure" cooperation strategies that lasted for 2 to 10 weeks (Johnson et al., 1976; Johnson, Johnson, & Scott, 1978; Peterson & Janicki, 1979; Wheeler & Ryan, 1973) found no achievement benefits for cooperation as compared with individualistic or control (traditionally taught) treatments. Other studies in which students in cooperative conditions worked together but received no group rewards at all produced similarly disappointing results (Huber, Bogatzki, & Winter, 1981; Peterson, Janicki, & Swing, 1981; Starr & Schuerman, 1974).

One explanation for the disappointing results of bringing "pure" cooperation directly from the laboratory to the classroom is what might be called the "free rider" problem. When all students complete a single worksheet, it may be most efficient to let one or two able group mates do all the work. There is certainly no incentive for more able students to give detailed explanations of how to do the problems to their group mates who are having difficulty understanding the worksheet problems. Webb (1982) found that the exchange of extended explanations is critical for the achievement of students in cooperative learning groups.

It is important to note that these "pure" cooperation methods did often have significantly positive effects on such affective variables as race relations (Johnson & Johnson, 1981) and attitudes toward mainstreamed academically handicapped students (Cooper, et al., 1980). However, the failure to find positive effects of these strategies on achievement suggests that, at least for this variable, a different form of cooperative learning might be needed.

Task specialization

One way to avoid the "free rider" problem in cooperative learning is to give each group member a unique task in the group activity. In this way, it is impossible for any group member to rely on another's effort or knowledge. A classic instance of task specialization is Jigsaw Teaching (Aronson et al., 1978). In this program, each of five or six group members is given a unique piece of information on a topic the whole group is studying. Students from each group meet with members of other groups who had the same piece of information in "expert groups" to discuss their information. Then all students return to their groups and teach them what they have learned, and all students take a test on all the information.

Research on the achievement effects of Jigsaw has generally been disappointing. Lucker et al. (1976) found positive effects on the achievement of minorities (blacks & Chicanos) but not of whites. Subsequent evaluations (Lazarowitz et al., 1985; Moskowitz et. al., 1983; Gonzales, 1979) failed to find any achievement effects of Jigsaw Teaching, although positive effects on student self-esteem and other social variables have been found (Blaney et al., 1977).

While Jigsaw should not (in theory) suffer from the "free rider" problem, the use of task specialization creates another problem. Students spend most of their time in Jigsaw studying their own information. They only hear about each group member's information once, during the presentations made to each team by the team's "expert" on a given topic. Because there is no group score or group reward, there is no particular reason for students to care how well their group mates are learning what they are teaching. Thus, there is a danger in Jigsaw that while students may learn about their own topics, they may not learn enough about their teammates' topics.

An interesting contrast to Jigsaw is Jigsaw II (Slavin, 1980b). Jigsaw II adds only two features to the original Jigsaw model. First, all students read the same information but focus on different topics, which they discuss in their "expert groups." For example, all students might read a chapter on South America, but one student in each team would focus on the geography of South America, another on politics, a third on natural resources, and a fourth on the peoples of South America.

Second, in Jigsaw II students are rewarded as a group based on the achievement of all group members on a final quiz on all the topics. This gives students an incentive to make certain that their group mates have learned the material they are presenting.

In a study of Jigsaw II, Ziegler (1981) found substantial positive effects of this program on student achievement, as well as on cross-ethnic attitudes and behaviors. Both of these effects continued 5 months after the end of the study.

Apparently, relatively small changes in the Jigsaw procedures make a substantial difference in achievement outcomes. It is a clear illustration of the fundamental point of this chapter: that in making the transition from the laboratory to the classroom, cooperative learning programs must be "engineered" to solve problems inherent to cooperative learning itself. In this case, task specialization, a common means of organizing cooperative activities, was not found to be beneficial for individual student achievement until two problems were solved: that students were only exposed to their own information and had to rely completely on their group mates' presentations, and that students had little incentive to make sure that their group mates were learning. These are not general problems of task specialization, but are problems of great importance in the application of cooperation with task specialization to the narrow and atypical (but highly important) case of individual student learning.

Another interesting example of task specialization is Group Investigation (Sharan & Sharan, 1976), a cooperative learning method in which students take on various tasks in preparing group reports or group projects. Students are evaluated on the basis of their group product (as in the Johnsons' "pure" cooperation method), but the task specialization diminishes the chance that any one student can do all the work while others get a "free ride." This method has been successful in increasing student achievement, particularly in "higher order" skills in social studies (Sharan, Hertz-Lazarowitz, & Ackerman, 1980) and in listening comprehension in English as a second language in Israel (Sharan et al., 1984). It is interesting to note that the overall achievement brought about by Group Investigation is relatively independent of the specific materials being taught. This method has rarely been found to make a difference in basic skills or factual knowledge. Group Investigation, like most cooperative learning models, has been consistently found to improve such social variables as intergroup relations and preference for cooperation (Sharan et al., 1984).

Group rewards for individual learning

A third major category of cooperative learning method involves students working in small groups to master a common set of information or skills initially presented by the teacher. Following a lesson presented to the entire class and a group study time, students are individually quizzed or otherwise assessed, and the results of these individual assessments are summed to form team scores. Successful teams may be recognized in newsletters, or receive certificates or other rewards. Examples of these methods include Student Team Achievement Divisions, or STAD (Slavin, 1978, 1980b) and Teams-Games-Tournament, or TGT (DeVries & Slavin, 1978; Slavin, 1980b). These methods avoid the "free rider" problem by having group success depend on the sum of individual learning performances, so that group members must be concerned about the achievement of each of their group mates. The group reward serves as an incentive to students to help one another learn and to encourage one another's learning efforts. These methods have had consistently positive effects on student achievement; statistically significant effects were found in 21 of 24 randomized field experiments in a wide variety of subjects and grade levels (Slavin, 1983a, 1983b). In direct contrast to the task specialization models, cooperative learning methods that use group rewards for individual learning have been most successfully applied to such basic skills as mathematics and language mechanics. However, their effects on such social outcomes as race relations (Slavin, 1983a; Slavin & Hansell, 1983) and attitudes toward mainstreamed students (Madden & Slavin, 1983) have been similar to those of other cooperative learning models.

The success of cooperative learning methods that use group rewards for individual learning led to a conclusion that two elements were needed to make cooperative learning methods effective for academic achievement: group rewards and *individual accountability* (Slavin, 1983b). Component analyses and comparisons of similar methods further bear out the same conclusion. Slavin (1980a) varied rewards (team vs. individual) and tasks (group vs. individual) in a study of STAD. The results of this study indicated that providing recognition based on team scores (the mean of the members' scores) increased student achievement regardless of whether or not the students were allowed to study together. The students who could study in groups but received no group rewards learned *less* than all other students, including those who studied individually and received only individual rewards. This study also found that when students in interacting groups were working toward a team reward, they helped each other substantially more than when they could work together but received no team rewards.

Huber et al. (1981) also compared STAD to group study without group rewards and to individual study. They found that STAD students learned more than the individuals working alone, but there were no differences between the group study conditions and individual study conditions. Finally, a study of TGT (Hulten & DeVries, 1976) found that providing recognition based on team scores improved achievement whether or not students were permitted to study together. Group study itself had no effects on student achievement.

In these component analyses as well as in the "pure" cooperation studies, providing an opportunity for group study without providing further structure in the form of individual assessment and group reward has not been found (among methodologically adequate studies of at least two weeks' duration) to increase student achievement more than having them work separately. In two cases (Johnson et al., 1978; Slavin, 1980a), allowing students to work together without giving them a group goal or making them dependent on one another's achievement in some other way resulted in *lower* achievement than was seen in conditions in which students worked alone. On the other hand, studies in which cooperative learning students could earn group rewards based on group members' individual academic performance were relatively consistent in showing the superiority of these methods to control methods.

Combining cooperative learning and individualized instruction

The use of group rewards based on individual achievement as a means of implementing cooperative learning solved the "free rider" problem without resorting to task specialization. However, another important problem remained to be solved. In all cooperative learning methods discussed up to this point, all students learned the same material at the same rate. The only accommodation to individual differences in level of preparation or learning rate was the help provided by group mates to students having difficulties learning the material. This may be adequate in most subjects when student heterogeneity is not excessive, but is more problematic in such hierarchically organized subjects as mathematics, where failure to master prerequisite skills makes later learning difficult or impossible. For example, a student who never learned to subtract cannot possibly do long division, and it is too much to expect teammates to do quick remediation of such major skill deficits. Of course, the problem of student heterogeneity is by no means limited to cooperative learning; the situation is no better in any form of whole-class instruction. Yet decades of research on individualized instruction has generally failed to show achievement benefits for this strategy (Schoen, 1976; Slavin, 1984).

Team Assisted Individualization, or TAI (Slavin, Leavey, & Madden, 1984; Slavin, Madden & Leavey, 1984b; Slavin, 1985), was developed as a means of solving the problem of student heterogeneity in the context of cooperative learning in mathematics. In TAI, students work in four- or five-member heterogeneous teams on self-instructional mathematics units appropriate to their level of achievement. Students within the teams check each other's work, help one another with problems, and take care of almost all clerical activities, freeing the teacher to work with homogeneous teaching groups drawn from the different teams. Teams receive certificates based on the number of units successfully completed by the team members.

TAI is by far the most successful of the cooperative learning methods for increasing student achievement. In six field experiments, the median difference in grade equivalent gains in computations between TAI and control classes has been at a ratio of 2:1; if the control group gained one grade equivalent, the TAI students gained two (Slavin et al., 1984; Slavin, Madden, & Leavey, 1984b; Slavin & Karweit, 1985). TAI has also had positive effects on student self-esteem, race relations, and attitudes toward mainstreamed students (Slavin, 1985). The specific features of the TAI program and the research on this method will now be described.

Team Assisted Individualization

The TAI program was first implemented in a single class, extensively revised, and then studied in two full-scale but brief (8 and 10 weeks, respectively) field experiments (Slavin et al., 1984), revised again, and studied in a large-scale 24-week field experiment in a suburban school district (Slavin, Madden, & Leavey, 1984b) and two smaller scale experiments in inner-city Baltimore, Maryland (Oishi, 1983; Oishi, Slavin, & Madden, 1983). It was then completely revised and then evaluated in two final field experiments of durations of 16 and 18 weeks, respectively (Slavin & Karweit, 1985). The TAI program as applied in the field experiments consisted of the following components (adapted from Slavin, 1985):

1. *Teams*. Students were assigned to four- to five-member teams. As in the Student Teams Achievement Divisions and Teams-Games-Tournament programs, each team consisted of a proportional mix of sexes and ethnic groups, high, average, and low achievers (as determined by a placement test). Students in need of resource help for a learning problem were evenly distributed among the teams. Every 8 weeks, students were reassigned to new teams by their teachers according to the same procedures.
2. *Placement test*. The students were pretested at the beginning of the project on mathematics operations. Students were placed at the appropriate level in the program based on their individual performances on this test.
3. *Curriculum materials*. During the individualized portion of the TAI process, students worked on self-instructional curriculum materials covering addition, subtraction, multiplication, division, numeration, decimals, fractions, word problems, and introduction to algebra. These materials had the following subparts:

- an Instruction Sheet explaining the skill to be mastered and providing a step-by-step method of solving problems
- several Skillsheets, each consisting of twenty problems and introducing a subskill that led to final mastery of the entire skill
- Checkouts A and B – two parallel sets of ten items assessing the skill
- a Final Test
- Answer Sheets for Skillsheets, Checkouts, and Final Test

4. *Team study method.* Following the placement test, students were given a starting point in the individualized mathematics units. They worked on their units in their teams, following these steps:

- Students formed into pairs or triads within their teams. Students located the unit they were working on and brought it to the team area. Each unit consisted of the Instruction Sheet, Skillsheets, and Checkout stapled together, and the Skillsheet Answer Sheets and Checkout Answer Sheets stapled together.
- Students exchanged Answer Sheets with partners within their teams.
- Each student read his or her Instruction Sheet, asking teammates or the teacher for help if necessary, and then began with the first Skillsheet in his or her unit.
- Each student worked on the first four problems on his or her own Skillsheet and then had his or her partner check the answers against the Answer Sheet. If all four problems were correct, the student could immediately go on to the next Skillsheet. If any were wrong, the student had to try the next four problems, and so on until he or she got one block of four problems correct (asking teammates or the teacher for help if needed).
- When students answered four in a row correctly on the last Skillsheet, they could take Checkout A, a ten-item quiz that resembled the last Skillsheet. On the Checkout, students worked alone until they were finished. When students were finished, a teammate scored the Checkout. If students answered eight or more items correctly, the teammate signed the Checkout to indicate that the students were certified by the team to take the Final Test. If students did *not* get eight items

correct, the teacher was called in to help solve any problems the students were having. The teacher would then ask the students to work again on certain Skillsheet items. The students then took Checkout B, a second ten-item test comparable in content and difficulty to Checkout A. Students then repeated the procedure with Checkout B, attempting to be certified by a teammate for the Final Test. Students would not take the Final Test until they had been passed by a teammate on a Checkout. When students "checked out," they took the Checkout to a student monitor from a different team to get the appropriate Final Test. The students then completed the Final Test, and the monitor scored it. Two or three students served as monitors each day, rotating responsibility among the class every day.

5. *Team scores and team recognition.* At the end of each week, the teacher computed a team score. This score was based on the average number of units covered by each team member, with extra points for perfect or near-perfect papers. Criteria were established for team performance. A high criterion was set for a team to be a "SUPERTEAM," a moderate criterion was established for a team to be a "GREATTEAM," and a minimum criterion was set for a team to be a "GOODTEAM." The teams meeting the "SUPERTEAM" and "GREATTEAM" criterion received attractive certificates.

6. *Teaching groups.* Every day, the teacher worked with groups of students who were at about the same point in the curriculum for 5- to 15-minute sessions. The purpose of these sessions was to prepare students for major concepts in upcoming units and to go over any points with which students were having trouble. Teachers were instructed to emphasize concepts rather than algorithms in their instruction because the individualized materials were considered adequate for teaching algorithms but not concepts. Teaching groups were recommended in the first five studies of TAI but were much more strongly emphasized in the sixth and seventh studies.

Research on TAI

Seven field experiments have been conducted to evaluate the effects of TAI on student achievement, attitudes, and behavior. The principal features and results of these studies are summarized in Table 7.1 (from Slavin, 1985) and discussed in more detail in the following sections. To avoid confusion, the studies will be referred to as "Experiment 1," "Experiment 2," and so on; the actual references for the studies appear in Table 7.1.

Research strategies. All of the TAI studies used either random assignment of classes (Experiments 4, 5, 6, and 7) or schools (Experiment 1), or matched experimental and control classes (Experiments 2 and 3). In all cases, teachers who had volunteered to use TAI were then assigned either to use TAI immediately or to serve as a control group and use TAI later. Analyses of covariance or equivalent multiple regression procedures were used to control for any initial differences between students and to increase statistical power. In three of the studies (Experiments 3, 6, and 7), the numbers of teachers involved were large enough to allow for nested analyses of covariance, which are essentially equivalent to conservative class-level analyses. In Experiment 6 the "control group" was the Missouri Mathematics Program, or MMP (Good, Grouws, & Ebmeier, 1983), a whole-class instructional method that emphasizes a high ratio of active teaching to seat work and other principles derived from direct instruction research. Experiment 7 compared TAI both to the MMP and to an untreated control group. All other studies compared TAI and untreated control groups only. Teacher training for each experiment involved a 3-hour workshop, followed by classroom visits to ensure faithful implementation. The settings for the studies ranged from inner-city Baltimore and Wilmington, Delaware, to suburban and rural Maryland. The studies involved students from grade levels three to six. Implementation periods varied from 8 to 24 weeks, with the median time being 16 weeks.

Academic achievement. Academic achievement outcomes were assessed in six of the seven studies. In Experiment 5, the original intention was to assess achievement outcomes, but the dropping out of a teacher upset the comparability of the experimental and control groups in terms of prior achievement, so achievement was not assessed. The posttest achievement data were district-administered California Achievement Tests (CAT) in Experiment 4, but in all other studies, the Comprehensive Test of Basic Skills (CTBS) was used. CTBS scores were also used as covariates to control for initial performance level in Experiments 1 and 2, and district-administered CAT scores served this purpose in Experiments 3, 4, 6, and

Table 7.1. *Summary of research on team-assisted individualization*

Study and major reports	Setting and design characteristics					Measures and results[a]		
	No. of students	Grade levels	Duration (weeks)	Kinds of schools	Experimental design	Mathematics achievement	Attitudes	Behavior ratings
Experiment 1: Full sample (Slavin, Leavey, & Madden, 1984)	506	3–5	8	Suburban	Randomly assigned schools	CTBS computations +	Liking of math class + Self-concept in math +	Classroom behavior + Self-confidence + Friendships + Neg. peer behavior +
Experiment 1: Academically handicapped students (Slavin, Madden, & Leavey, 1984a)	117	3–5	8	Suburban	Randomly assigned schools	CTBS computations 0	Liking of math class (+) Self-concept in math 0 "Best friend" choices + "Rejection" choices +	Classroom behavior + Self-confidence 0 Friendships + Neg. peer behavior +
Experiment 2 (Slavin, Leavey, & Madden, 1984)	320	4–6	10	Suburban	Matched schools	CTBS computations +	Liking of math class 0 Self-concept in math 0	Classroom behavior 0 Self-confidence 0 Friendships + Neg. peer behavior 0

Study	N	Grades	Duration	Location	Assignment	Outcomes
Experiment 3: Full sample (Slavin, Madden, & Leavey, 1984b)	1371	3–5	24	Suburban	Matched schools	CTBS computations + CTBS concepts & applications +
Experiment 3: Academically handicapped students (Slavin, Madden, & Leavey, 1984b)	113	3–5	24	Suburban	Matched schools	CTBS computations + CTBS concepts & applications +
Experiment 4 (Oishi, Slavin, & Madden, 1983)	160	4–6	16	Urban	Randomly assigned classes	CAT computations 0 CAT concepts & applications 0 Cross-Race: 0 Friends + Rejects + Nice 0 Not Nice + Smart 0 Not Smart (+)
Experiment 5 (Oishi, 1983)	120	4–6	16	Urban	Randomly assigned classes	Cross-Race: friends 0 playmates + nice 0 not nice + smart + not smart 0

(continued)

Table 7.1 (*continued*)

Study and major reports	Setting and design characteristics					Measures and results[a]		
	No. of students	Grade levels	Duration (weeks)	Kinds of schools	Experimental design	Mathematics achievement	Attitudes	Behavior ratings
Experiment 6 (Slavin & Karweit, 1985)	354	4-6	18	Urban	Randomly assigned classes	CTBS computations + CTBS concepts & applications	Liking of math + class + Self-concept + in math	
Experiment 7 (Slavin & Karweit, 1985)	480	3-5	16	Rural	Randomly assigned classes	CTBS computations + CTBS concepts & applications	Liking of math + class 0 Self-concept 0 in math	

Notes: [a] + = TAI students scored significantly higher than control students on the indicated measure, $p < .05$ or better.
(+) = Same as above, but $p < .10$.
0 = No statistically significant differences.
Source: Adapted from Slavin, 1985.

7. The Mathematics Computations scale was used in all studies, and in all but the first two, Mathematics Concepts and Applications scales were also administered.

In five of the six achievement studies, TAI students significantly exceeded control students in Computations. Similar effects were found for Concepts and Applications in only one of the four studies in which this variable was assessed (Experiment 3), but in all four studies, means for Concepts and Applications favored the TAI group. The one study in which statistically significant effects on neither achievement measures were found was Experiment 4 (Oishi et al., 1983), which took place in a Baltimore city public school. Poor implementation (particularly failure to use teaching groups) may account for this anomalous finding. In the five studies in which the treatment effects for Computations were statistically significant, they were also quite large. Even in the relatively brief Experiments 1 and 2, the TAI classes gained twice as many grade equivalents as did control students. The TAI-control differences were 42% of a grade equivalent in Experiment 3, and in Experiment 6, TAI exceeded the Missouri Mathematics Program (MMP) by 93% of a grade equivalent. In Experiment 7, TAI exceeded MMP by 30% of a grade equivalent and exceeded the untreated control group by 75% of a grade equivalent. The remarkable effects found in Experiments 6 and 7 (in only 18 and 16 weeks, respectively) may be due in part to a complete revision of the curriculum materials just before Experiments 6 and 7, and perhaps more importantly to an increased emphasis on regular use of teaching groups for concept instruction in these studies.

Searches for interactions between treatment and various student attributes failed to find any consistent patterns. Experiments 1 and 3 failed to find any interactions between academically handicapped/nonhandicapped status and treatment effect. There was an interaction between ability (pretest) and treatment in Experiment 1 favoring TAI effects for low achievers, but this was almost certainly due to a ceiling effect on the tests used; no such interactions were found in Experiments 2, 3, 6, or 7. An exhaustive search for interactions was conducted in Experiments 6 and 7; no significant interactions were found between treatment and absolute prior performance level, prior performance relative to class means, sex, or (in Experiment 7) race.

Attitudes. Two general attitude scales were used in Experiments 1, 2, 6, and 7. These were eight-item experimenter-made scales assessing Liking of Math Class and Self-Concept in Math. Statistically significant effects favoring TAI were found for "liking of math class" in Experiments 1, 6, and 7, but not in Experiment 2. For "self-concept in math," positive effects were found in Experiments 1 and 6 but not Experiments 2 or 7. However, in no case did means for these variables favor a control treatment.

The primary purpose of Experiments 4 and 5 was to assess the effects of TAI on race relations. In Experiment 4, positive effects of TAI were found on cross-racial nominations on two sociometric scales, "Who are your friends in this class?" and "Who would you rather *not* sit at a table with?" TAI students also made significantly fewer cross-racial ratings as "not nice" and "not smart." In Experiment 5, no effects were found on cross-racial "friends" nominations, but TAI students named significantly more students of another race as playmates at recess than did control students. Positive effects were also found on cross-racial ratings as "smart" and on reductions in ratings as "not nice." Interestingly, the effect on "smart" ratings was due primarily to increases in whites' ratings of black classmates.

One principal impetus for the development of TAI was to develop a means of meeting the instructional needs of academically handicapped students in the context of the regular class while providing these students with the cooperative experiences found in earlier research to improve the acceptance of academically handicapped students by their nonhandicapped classmates. Effects of TAI on academically handicapped students have been positive on several dimensions. In Experiment 1 (Slavin, Madden, & Leavey, 1984a), academically handicapped students in TAI gained more than control students in sociometric choices as "best friends" received from their nonhandicapped classmates, and they were less often checked as neither "best friends" nor as "o.k." They were also rated much more positively than control students on four behavior rating scales. In Experiment 3, academically handicapped students in TAI classes also achieved significantly more than did their counterparts in control classes.

The research on TAI shows that this method has considerably stronger effects on student achievement than have the earlier cooperative learning methods, and effects on attitudes similar to those of the previously developed methods. It is important to note that TAI is the most "engineered" of the cooperative learning methods. It incorporates the group rewards and individual accountability of STAD with individualization of instruction. Unlike other cooperative learning methods, TAI prescribes a specific set of learning materials and a structured way of using them to strike a balance between direct instruction from the teacher, individualization, mastery learning, and cooperative activities.

From theory to classroom practice: lessons learned

The principle of jet propulsion was known for two centuries before the first practical jet airplane was built. Elevators existed long before Otis made possible the high-rise city by inventing a simple antireverse device to stop an elevator if its cable broke. Scientific principles are necessary, but not sufficient bases for technological change.

Similarly, when principles of psychology are applied to the practice of education, additional development and experimentation is required in order to achieve the desired result. Research on cooperative learning illustrates this point clearly. For achievement outcomes, the most successful cooperative learning methods are those that least resemble the cooperative conditions investigated in the laboratory and in brief, artificial field studies. These methods have been developed and modified over time to solve problems inherent to the use of cooperative strategies to enhance individual learning, and to adapt these strategies to the realities of classroom life. At this stage we have reliable, effective methods capable of being used in a wide variety of instructional settings. However, development and refining of cooperative learning methods must continue if the long-established principles of cooperation are to have an important impact on the practice of education.

References

Aronson, E., Blaney, N., Stephan, C., Sikes, J., & Snapp, M. (1978). *The Jigsaw classroom*. Beverly Hills, CA: Sage.

Blaney, N. T., Stephan, S., Rosenfield, D., Aronson, E., & Sikes, J. (1977). Interdependence in the classroom: A field study. *Journal of Educational Psychology, 69*, 121–128.

Cooper, L., Johnson, D. W., Johnson, R., & Wilderson, F. (1980). Effects of cooperative, competitive, and individualistic experiences on interpersonal attraction among heterogeneous peers. *Journal of Social Psychology, 111*, 243–252.

Deutsch, M. (1949). A theory of cooperation and competition. *Human Relations, 2*, 129–152.

DeVries, D. L., & Slavin, R. E. (1978). Teams-Games-Tournament: Review of ten classroom experiments. *Journal of Research and Development in Education, 12*, 28–38.

Gonzales, A. (1979, August). Classroom cooperation and ethnic balance. Paper presented at the annual convention of the American Psychological Association, New York.

Good, T. L., Grouws, D., & Ebmeier, H. (1983). *Active mathematics teaching*. New York: Longman.

Hill, G. (1982). Group versus individual performance: Are N+1 heads better than one? *Psychological Bulletin, 91*, 517–539.

Huber, G., Bogatzki, W., & Winter, M. (1981). *Cooperation: Condition and goal of teaching and learning in classrooms*. Unpublished manuscript, University of Tübingen, West Germany.

Hulten, B. H. & DeVries, D. L. (1976). *Team competition and group practice: Effects on student achievement and attitudes.* Report No. 212. Baltimore, MD: Johns Hopkins University, Center for Social Organization of Schools.

Johnson, D. W. & Johnson, R. T. (1981). Effects of cooperative and individualistic learning experiences on interethnic interaction. *Journal of Educational Psychology, 73,* 444–449.

Johnson, D. W., & Johnson, R. T., Johnson, J., & Anderson, D. (1976). The effects of cooperative vs. individualized instruction on student prosocial behavior, attitudes toward learning, and achievement. *Journal of Educational Psychology, 68,* 446–452.

Johnson, D. W., Johnson, R. T., & Scott, L. (1978). The effects of cooperative and individualized instruction on student attitudes and achievement. *Journal of Social Psychology, 104,* 207–216.

Johnson, D. W., Johnson, R. T. & Skon, L. (1979). Student achievement on different types of tasks under cooperative, competitive, and individualistic conditions. *Contemporary Educational Psychology, 4,* 99–106.

Johnson, D. W., Skon, L., & Johnson, R. T. (1980). The effects of cooperative, competitive, and individualistic goal structures on student achievement on different types of tasks. *American Educational Research Journal, 17,* 83–93.

Johnson, R. T. & Johnson, D. W. (1979). Type of task and student achievement and attitudes in interpersonal cooperation, competition, and individualization. *Journal of Social Psychology, 108,* 37–48.

Laughlin, P., Branch, L. & Johnson, H. (1969). Individual versus triadic performance on a unidimensional complementary task as a function of initial ability level. *Journal of Personality and Social Psychology, 12,* 144–150.

Lazarowitz, R., Baird, J. H., Hertz-Lazarowitz, R., & Jenkins, J. (1985). The effects of modified Jigsaw on achievement, classroom social climate, and self-esteem in high school science classes. In R. E. Slavin, S. Sharan, S. Kagan, R. Hertz-Lazarowitz, C. Webb, & R. Schmuck (Eds.), *Learning to cooperate, cooperating to learn* (pp. 231–253). New York: Plenum.

Lucker, G. W., Rosenfield, D., Sikes, J., and Aronson, E. (1976). Performance in the interdependent classroom: A field study. *American Educational Research Journal, 13,* 115, 123.

Madden, N. A., & Slavin, R. E. (1983). Mainstreaming students with mild academic handicaps: Academic and social outcomes. *Review of Educational Research, 84,* 131–138.

Maller, J. B. (1929). *Cooperation and competition.* New York: Teachers College, Columbia University.

Moskowitz, J. M., Malvin, J. H., Schaeffer, G. A., & Schaps, E. (1983). Evaluation of a cooperative learning strategy. *American Educational Research Journal, 20,* 687–696.

Oishi, S. (1983). Effects of Team-Assisted Individualization in mathematics on cross-race and cross-sex interactions of elementary school children. Unpublished doctoral dissertation, University of Maryland.

Oishi, S., Slavin, R. E., & Madden, N. A. (1983, April). Effects of student teams and individualized instruction on cross-race and cross-sex friendships. Paper presented at the Annual Convention of the American Educational Research Association, Montreal.

Peterson, P. L., & Janicki, T. C. (1979). Individual characteristics and children's learning in large-group and small-group approaches. *Journal of Educational Psychology, 71,* 677–687.

Peterson, P. L., Janicki, T. C., & Swing, S. (1981). Ability x treatment interaction effects on children's learning in large-group and small-group approaches. *American Educational Research Journal, 18,* 453–473.

Schoen, H. L. (1976). Self-paced mathematics instruction: How effective has it been? *Arithmetic Teacher, 23,* 90–96.

Sharan, S. Hertz-Lazarowitz, R., & Ackerman, Z. (1980). Academic achievement of elementary school children in small-group vs. whole class instruction. *Journal of Experimental Education, 48,* 125–129.

Sharan, S., Kussell, P., Hertz-Lazarowitz, R., Bejarano, Y., Raviv, S., & Sharan, Y. (1984). *Cooperative learning in the classroom: Research in desegregated schools.* Hillsdale, NJ: Erlbaum.

Sharan, S., & Sharan, Y. (1976). *Small-group teaching.* Englewood Cliffs, NJ: Educational Technology Publications.

Slavin, R. E. (1978). Student teams and achievement divisions. *Journal of Research and Development in Education, 12,* 39–49.

Slavin, R. E. (1980a). Effects of student teams and peer tutoring on academic achievement and time on-task. *Journal of Experimental Education, 48,* 252–257.

Slavin, R. E. (1980b). *Using Student Team Learning. Rev. Ed.* Baltimore, MD: Johns Hopkins University, Center for Social Organization of Schools.

Slavin, R. E. (1983a). *Cooperative learning.* New York: Longman.

Slavin, R. E. (1983b). When does cooperative learning increase student achievement? *Psychological Bulletin, 94,* 429–445.

Slavin, R. E. (1984). Component building: A strategy for research-based instructional improvement. *Elementary School Journal, 84,* 255–269.

Slavin, R. E. (1985). Team Assisted Individualization: A cooperative solution for adaptive instruction in mathematics. In M. C. Wang & H. J. Walberg (Eds.), *Adapting instruction to individual differences* (pp. 236–253). Berkeley, CA: McCutchan.

Slavin, R. E., & Hansell, S. (1983). Cooperative learning and intergroup relations: Contact theory in the classroom. In J. L. Epstein & N. L. Karweit (Eds.), *Friends in school* (pp. 93–114). New York: Academic Press.

Slavin, R. E., & Karweit, N. L. (1985). Effects of whole class, ability grouped, and individualized instruction on mathematics achievement. *American Educational Research Journal, 22,* 351–367.

Slavin, R. E., Leavey, M., & Madden, N. A. (1984). Combining cooperative learning and individualized instruction: Effects on student mathematics achievement, attitudes, and behaviors. *Elementary School Journal, 84,* 409–422.

Slavin, R. E., Madden, N. A., & Leavey, M. (1984a). Effects of cooperative learning and individualization on mainstreamed students. *Exceptional Children, 50,* 434–443.

Slavin, R. E., Madden, N. A., & Leavey, M. (1984b). Effects of Team Assisted Individualization on the mathematics achievement of academically handicapped and non-handicapped students. *Journal of Educational Psychology, 76,* 813–819.

Starr, R., & Schuerman, C., (1974, March). An experiment in small-group learning. *The American Biology Teacher,* 173–175.

Stendler, C., Damrin, D., & Haines, A. C. (1951). Studies in cooperation and competition: I. The effects of working for group and individual rewards on the social climate of children's groups. *Journal of Genetic Psychology, 79,* 173–197.

Thorndike, R. L. (1938). On what type of task will a group do well? *Journal of Abnormal and Social Psychology, 33,* 409–413.

Triplett, N. (1897). The dynamogenic factors in pace-making and competition. *American Journal of Psychology, 9,* 507–533.

Webb, N. (1982). Student interaction and learning in small groups. *Review of Research in Education, 52,* 421–445.

Wheeler, R., & Ryan, F. L. (1973). Effects of cooperative and competitive classroom environments on the attitudes and achievement of elementary school students engaged in social studies inquiry activities. *Journal of Educational Psychology, 65,* 402–407.

Ziegler, S. (1981). The effectiveness of cooperative learning teams for increasing cross-ethnic friendship: Additional evidence. *Human Organization, 40,* 264–268.

8   Social categorization theory and team learning procedures

Norman Miller and Marilynn B. Brewer

Although in recent years educational emphasis in the United States has shifted toward the mastery of the fundamental content areas of the academic curriculum, there is no doubt that whatever the particular emphasis urged by the pulse of the times, schools will continue to exert broad, pervasive influences on the children who attend them - influences that extend well beyond specific courses and the information presented in them. In any society composed of diverse racial - ethnic groups, schools contribute to the pattern and quality of intergroup interaction. They do so not only when they contain members of the diverse groups, but also when they are racially homogeneous.

Berry (1984) has discussed the various patterns that characterize the relations among racial - ethnic groups that comprise a society. They range from integration to separatism and from assimilation to deculturation, and reflect two orthogonal dimensions: whether or not cultural identity and customs are to be retained and whether or not positive relations with the larger society (or other group) are sought. Regardless of where any particular instance falls within these dimensions, groups will have numerous points of contact within the various institutions of a culture. Moreover, the attitudes, perceptions, and behavior that adults bring to these settings will have been profoundly influenced by their own prior experiences during their schooling. This inevitable truth has been and continues to be acknowledged both by those who favor and those

Preparation of this chapter was supported in part by a grant to the first author from the Graduate School of the University of Southern California, and by Fulbright and Guggenheim research fellowships. We also wish to acknowledge the excellent secretarial help received from the psychology department of Bar-Ilan University.

172

who oppose school desegregation as a social policy for increasing intergroup acceptance.

Although in the United States national impetus for desegregation of schools has waned in recent years, in a pluralistic society there will always be neighborhoods of transition where children of diverse backgrounds attend a common school. In such multiethnic schools the administrative problems of maintaining day-to-day accord among the existing groups must be added to those caused by the normal incidence of friction among students. In schools where the students are racially homogeneous, though the problem of day-to-day intergroup friction is avoided, the issue of intergroup relations is not. It sometimes arises in interschool sports events, between teachers and students when the former are not of the same racial – ethnic group as the latter, and in the minds of children when they notice and contemplate why their school is homogeneous when their society is not. Effective school leaders will try to be proactive rather than reactive to these issues. In multiethnic schools they will initiate programs to improve intergroup relations. And even schools that are homogeneous with respect to racial – ethnic composition may recognize their broader social responsibilities and initiate programs designed to decrease intergroup prejudice.

Prominent among the various types of interventions designed to increase intergroup acceptance is the use of cooperative learning procedures in which racially heterogeneous teams of four to six children work together to master aspects of the academic curriculum (Aronson et al. 1978; DeVries et al. 1980; Johnson & Johnson, 1975; Slavin, 1983; Sharan & Hertz-Lazarowitz, 1980). Advocates claim that the use of cooperative teams not only increases cross-racial acceptance within the team, but also results in wider friendship networks throughout the class. The use of cooperative team activity has even been extended to the play yard as a means of combating prejudice and ethnic encapsulation (Rogers, Miller, & Hennigan, 1981).

Because cooperative learning procedures have received so much attention as an antidote for effectively combating prejudice within schools, and because they have been so widely disseminated with the last few years, it is constructive to examine them from a theoretical standpoint. This chapter will do so by presenting four well-accepted social psychological models of prejudice. It will then present data relevant to two of the models. Finally, social categorization theory – the theoretical position supported by the new data – will be discussed in greater detail and its specific implications for cooperative team learning interventions in schools will be examined.

Four theoretical models of the effects of structured intergroup cooperation

Given our focus on the concept of cooperative team learning, the presentation of each of the models starts with structured cooperative interaction (Figure 8.1; adapted from Brewer & Miller, 1984). The first model views structural features of the environment as most critical. Its underlying assumption is that prejudice is the consequence of intergroup competition. Thus, it argues that the way to eliminate prejudice is to eliminate competition and replace it with cooperation, which, in turn, promotes acceptance. In this model the cognitive, perceptual, affective, and behavioral dimensions of prejudice function as equivalent, interchangeable aspects, all of which are simultaneously altered by the externally engineered change in the structure of intergroup relations. This functionalist interpretation of prejudice can be traced back to Sumner (1906) and his discussion of the role of competition in intergroup relations. It is functional because successful restructuring of group relations makes cooperative intergroup interaction instrumental to the attainment of selfish individual or ingroup goals. This model appears to reflect the view implicit in most of the cooperative team learning procedures that have been developed for classroom settings.

The second model builds on Freudian thought and from the early work of Dollard et al. (1939) and later Adorno et al. (1950). In its original form it emphasized personality and the psychological history of the individual. Persons who have led particularly frustrating lives and who from early childhood experienced a harsh, punitive socialization are viewed as particularly prone to prejudiced behavior. Though this model views prejudice as rooted in the unique history of the individual, it does not preclude intercultural or internation differences in outgroup hostility. Culture operates to homogenize the socialization practices within a society. Thus, the modal character of the socialization process within some societies will evolve as harsher or, alternatively, as more lenient than that found in others. The authoritarian parent, who is the product of a harsh socialization, recapitulates in his or her own parenting the rigid, dogmatic, exacting standards, and physically punitive response to failures to meet them. The level of performance that is demanded, being one that the child can never adequately meet, leaves the child impaired in self-concept, and lacking self-esteem. This parentally generated self-hatred further feeds the stored reservoir of hostility that develops as the child matures. As the cycle is repeated from generation to generation it maintains within the culture or nation a modal personality that is authoritarian and inclined toward out-group hostility.

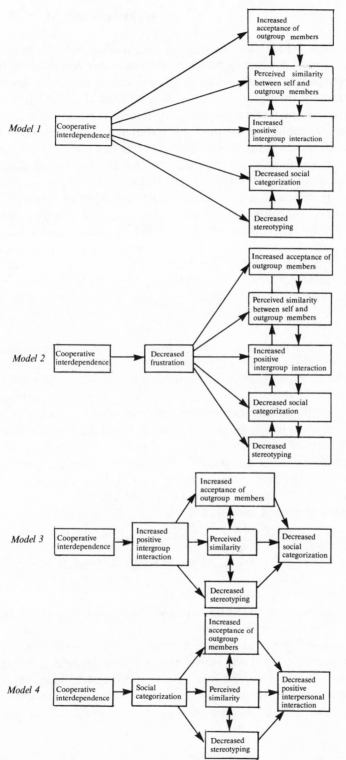

Figure 8.1. Alternative models of the process of intergroup contact effects.

In this view, which relies heavily on the Freudian defense mechanism of displacement, the strong parental strictures that preclude retaliation against the parents' harshness cause the child to repress anger toward the direct source of frustration and instead come to idealize the parents. This idealization of the nuclear in-group, the family, is readily generalized to the larger in-group, as defined by national or cultural boundaries, whereas the stored residues of childhood hostility are readily displaced onto out-group targets. To this basic model Dollard (1938) added the important ingredient of "triggering" or "legitimizing" events – actions by outgroup members that are used to justify the ingroup members' overt expression of hostility toward the out-group. The in-group member exaggerates the evil nature of these triggering actions and reinterprets them to make his or her own hostile act appear merely as retaliation that is well justified by the out-group member's breech. Thus, in the crowded bus, the accidental shove by an out-group member as the bus rounds a corner is interpreted as an intentional push that deserves not merely a response in kind, but instead, a response of even greater hostile intensity.

Although this model is rooted in personality as it emerges from the developmental process that takes the child from infancy into adulthood, the model can be recast into a social psychological framework that functions more situationally, and within a smaller frame of time. The relevant situational ingredients are an experience of frustration or failure and the presence of an out-group target. Thus, in the second model, the critical feature of cooperative interaction is that it reduces the likelihood of frustration by making it possible for everyone to succeed, whereas in competitive interaction one of the two competing groups inevitably experiences the frustration inherent in losing.

The third and fourth models differ from the first two in that they do not view intergroup acceptance as a single underlying conceptual variable in which the perceptual, cognitive, attitudinal, and behavioral components are interchangeable parts of the larger whole. Instead, they view one or another of these components as causally antecedent or causally mediating changes in the other components.

The third model is based on cognitive dissonance (Festinger, 1957) or self-perception theory (Bem, 1967). Changes in attitudinal, perceptual, and cognitive aspects of prejudice emerge as the consequence of the positive interaction that necessarily emerges from structuring cooperative interaction. In this model the final result – the decreased tendency to view out-group members in terms of their social category membership and instead view them as unique individuals – is the result of the prior changes in affective and cognitive variables. From the perspective of dissonance theory, structured cooperation requires or elicits positive or prosocial behavior toward the out-group persons on one's own cooperative learning team. This positive behavior, being inconsistent with one's prior affect and cognitions toward out-group persons, creates a state of dissonance or unpleasant psychological tension. The dissonant state can be eliminated by altering either one's behavior or one's cognitions and affect. The behavior, however, has already occurred – it cannot be easily denied; furthermore, the requirement of future cooperative team interaction guarantees more of the same behavior on one's part. Therefore, the easiest way to reduce the dissonance is to change one's affect and cognitions.

The opposite causal sequence is represented in the fourth model. There, a change in the degree to which the individual actor engages in social categorization is viewed as prior to changes in affect and cognition and this, in turn, leads to increases in positive interpersonal social interactions. In this model, persons must first abandon social-category identity as the primary basis for organizing information about others and replace it with more individuated and personalized information processing before other changes in intergroup acceptance will emerge.

Field studies of two groups of boys in a summer camp, conducted by Sherif et al. (1961) provide a useful example for illustrating how the four models interpret a single situation and its outcome and for drawing further distinctions among them. In his theoretical orientation Sherif adopted the first model, namely, the functionalist position that intergroup competition must be replaced by intergroup cooperation toward superordinate goals in order to reduce prejudice. He tried to demonstrate that when two groups have come to view one another as respective outgroups, simply placing them together to mutually participate in activities they might ordinarily find unusually pleasurable does not reduce their antagonism toward one another. Indeed, overt manifestation of their hostility was increased, if not simply maintained at existing levels as a consequence of the increased contact. Only after the successful arrangement of several contact situations in which the external environment had been manipulated to require the participation of both groups in joint action toward the achievement of superordinate goals did any reduction in intergroup conflict and stereotyping appear (e.g., after a vigorous morning swim at adjacent water holes the two groups of boys discovered that only by jointly tugging on ropes could they move a stalled truck to a sufficiently steep and lengthy incline to permit a rolling start despite its dead battery and thereby enable the counselors of the two groups to go off for food for the boys' lunch). Thus, Sherif viewed the outcome as confirming the functionalist position.

The second model interprets the reduced prejudice found after structured intergroup competition as not due to the cooperation per se, but rather as due to a reduction in the amount of frustration, threat, status insecurity, and failure experienced by each group as a result of its interaction with the other. According to this model, had the groups failed to move the truck over the crest of the incline to thereby enable a rolling start, their prejudice would not have decreased, despite the fact of their joint cooperative interaction to achieve a superordinate goal. Instead, following their failure, each group would have pointed accusingly at the other and berated them for the inability to exert sufficient effort, for their stupidity in not being able to coordinate their rope-pulling with that of the in-group. Repeated occasions of cooperative behavior to achieve a superordinate goal would only further intensify intergroup hostility if each such interaction resulted in repeated failures. According to this model, even if the groups did succeed, had the counselors evaluated one team as inferior in its efforts, disapproved of their approach to the task, challenged the existing structure of the group and recommended a change in its leadership, and finally, suggested that the group change its name from Eagles to Ostriches or Armadillos, their hostility and prejudice toward the other group would have increased despite the successful outcome of the intergroup cooperation.

Although external structuring of intergroup cooperation can often be engineered so as to minimize the likelihood of individual failure that is coordinated with group membership, the arguments developed above point to an important distinction between the first and second models. Whereas intergroup cooperation can be the starting point for improved intergroup relations in both models, in the second model the outcome of the cooperative activity assumes a critical role, whereas in the first model it does not.

Parenthetically, in his research design Sherif had sought to preclude any bearing of the personality version of this model on his results. He imposed selection standards for acceptance of boys into the two camps that were designed to eliminate children who were likely to be mal-adjusted or insecure, or who had led disruptive, frustrating lives.

In the third model, as was true for the first, the social engineer might start with attempts to restructure the environment so as to require cooperative interaction. But here, the emphasis is more upon the nature and quality of the interaction between members of the two groups than on the means used to achieve it. Indeed, from the standpoint of this model it is relatively unimportant how the positive interaction is induced. Rather than relying on the creation of cooperative interdependence for the pursuit of some superordinate goal, positive interaction might be induced instead via the observation of high-status social models who behave cooperatively with out-group members, by the presence and/or increased salience of social norms relevant to positive interaction with outgroup members, by structuring dependence of an out-group member's survival upon help from an in-group member, and so forth.

In any case, as previously indicated, according to this model, once positive behavior toward out-group members is elicited, it impacts perceptual, affective, and cognitive systems. Thus, it does not view Sherif's failure to reduce hostility between the two groups of camp boys in his initial approach (namely, by arranging for their spatial adjacency while they engaged in highly enjoyable activity such as watching an exciting movie or lighting firecrackers) as disconfirmation of the model. Adherents to the third model can legitimately claim that the model was not even tested because the experimental treatment, spatial adjacency of the out-group during pleasureable activity, failed to induce positive social interaction between members of the two groups.

Similarly, from the standpoint of the third model, Sherif's successful manipulation – jointly pulling on ropes to move the truck to the crest of the incline – worked not specifically because of the presence of a superordinate goal, but instead, because it induced the boys of the two groups to engage in positive interaction with one another. After the second episode in which the truck had failed to start, instead of maintaining their clear group boundaries by pulling on separate ropes, group boundaries became diffused and boys from each of the two groups pulled on each of the ropes. Had the counselors induced them to retain their group boundaries and thereby avoid opportunity for positive interaction, either by pulling on separate ropes or by having one group push the truck from the back while the other pulled, the third model would predict little reduction in in-group favoritism and out-group stereotyping despite the fact that these procedures also constitute joint action toward a superordinate goal. Instead, adherents of this model would expect continued bickering and hostile derogation of the other group's contribution to the success of the effort.

Thus, as was the case for the first two models, the external structuring of cooperative behavior can be the starting point for putting the third model into action as well. As indicated above, however, and as was true for the second model, there is an important implicit theoretical distinction between the third model and the first with respect to cooperation.

The first model places emphasis on the nature of the reward structure – a joint goal is achieved only via cooperative interaction. In contrast, the third places emphasis on the qualitative nature of the social interaction that transpires between members of the two groups; it only requires that an observer watching the interaction between in-group and out-group persons could appropriately describe it as positive or prosocial, though in some instances it might also appropriately be described as cooperative, too.

As previously indicated, the fourth model argues that in order to reduce prejudice persons must first be induced to adopt a more individuated, personalized approach to processing information about others before changes in their habits of intergroup rejection can occur. Whereas the major assumption of the functional theory of intergroup behavior is that in-group bias and favoritism are the result of intergroup competition and, hence, the way to eliminate them is to restructure intergroup relations into cooperative interdependence, proponents of social identity theory maintain that functional competitive interdependence is not a necessary antecedent for such bias (Tajfel, 1978; Turner, 1978.) Instead, in-group favoritism and out-group hostility are seen as consequences of the unit formation between self and other in-group members and the linking of one's identity to them. Experiments on the minimal group situation show that the establishment of category membership per se in the presence of those of another social category can be a sufficient basis for such bias (Doise, 1978; Tajfel, 1970).

In terms of the fourth model, Sherif's structuring of cooperative interdependence for the achievement of a superordinate goal was successful primarily because it succeeded in breaking down perceptions of group boundaries. Had the boys been induced to maintain their group identity, little or no positive benefit would ensue. Imagine that the counselors said to the boys, "What we need is some team spirit in order to get this heavy truck moving," and then encouraged the two groups of boys to don respectively their Eagles and Rattlers T-shirts (their self-adopted names), positioned a group flag bearer at the front of each line with the rope wrapped around his waist, gave each group a rope that matched their flag color(s), and preceded the rope-pulling with brief pep rallies in which the groups simultaneously shouted out their individual group chants.

Once again, the first model predicts reduced prejudice because there is cooperative intergroup behavior toward a superordinate goal. Without coordinated pulling, the truck will not move. The fourth model requires the dissolution of sharp group boundaries and interaction with out-group members that is personalized and attentive to the unique aspects of that person. In contrast to the third model, which argues that the valence of the interaction be positive for benefit to occur, the fourth model predicts positive effects from negatively valenced interaction as well, as long as the basis for it is not category-linked.

In other words, in the fourth model the critical ingredient is the processing of information that serves to personalize the other individuals and thereby reduce the tendency to view them as merely representatives of a particular social category. In the face of the convergent symptoms of group identity and intergroup separation described previously, however, the fourth model argues that even had the counselors succeeded in getting members of each group to shout encouragements to those on the other rope – a procedure that according to the second model should effectively reduce prejudice – little positive benefit would ensue.

Models are formulated not only to help organize one's thinking about an issue, but also to draw distinctions among ways to view things. In this latter aspect they depict extreme and oversimplified positions. The models that have been presented are no exceptions in this regard. Reality may, in fact, be far better represented by a model that incorporates aspects of each of the four and that is less unidirectional in its causal assumptions than are those presented above. Nevertheless, it makes sense to try to demonstrate that there is some value in noting their distinctions.

An empirical comparison of the hostility displacement and social categorization models

Westman and Miller (1978) used correlational data to test the second and fourth models. For this purpose two subsets of children were selected from a larger longitudinal study of the effects of school desegregation (Gerard & Miller, 1975). One group was extreme in the extent to which their prejudice increased following desegregation, whereas the other was extreme in their decrease in prejudice. The larger study from which these data were drawn, implemented in Riverside, California, measured approximately 1,800 children in elementary grades prior to the implementation of a district-wide desegregation plan in which several minority ghetto schools were closed and their students distributed throughout schools in the rest of the district. Approximately half of the 1,800 children were minority students and among these, the Hispanic children were somewhat more numerous than the blacks.

The study tracked these students over the next 5 years, administering the same basic set of measures in the first, third, and fifth years after implementation of the busing plan. The larger study as a whole was noteworthy for the richness of its data on each child. Numerous measures were obtained, including intellectual functioning as determined by IQ, scholastic achievement tests, and by class grades; personality as assessed by self-description measures, observation, and reputational measures; self report measures of social relations, aspirations, and prejudice; and family background and parental attitudes as assessed by interviews in the home. With some exceptions in the latter set, most were administered on repeated occasions over the course of the study.

The second model argues that prejudice results from frustration and the subsequent displacement of hostility onto out-group targets (Berkowitz, 1962; Dollard et al., 1939; Levin, 1975). Thus, those children who exhibit increased prejudice in the contact setting relative to their predesegregation level should have experienced higher levels of frustration in the contact setting than did those who showed a decline in prejudice. Among the larger set of measures, a number of them might serve as indexes of frustration. Low socioeconomic status might indirectly reflect the likelihood of feelings of relative deprivation. Low self-esteem, lack of tolerance for deferred gratification, feelings of little fate control (viz., victimization) and high anxiety also suggest greater overall frustration. Thus, according to the second model, the two groups of children should deviate from each other on these measures, and to a greater degree than they do on other measures.

In contrast to these expectations, the fourth model argues that social categorization is the primary antecedent of prejudice. Category-based behavior toward out-group members reflects the view that they are interchangeable and undifferentiated from one another. Information processing is shallow, efficient, and unelaborated. Though in-group members are differentiated from one another somewhat more than out-group members, they, too, are seen as highly similar. Finally, the distinction between in-group and out-group members is seen as large and nonoverlapping. On the other hand, lack of prejudice is associated with personalized responding. At this opposite extreme one responds to an in-group and out-group member alike as a person who is unique, complex, and has both similarities and dissimilarities to oneself. Out-group persons are not only seen as more distinct from one another than is the case when response is category-based, but in-group members are also viewed as more differentiated from each other and from oneself. Thus, according to this model, a high level of cognitive complexity is associated with a lack of prejudice.

Translating these perceptual and information-processing differences to the personality and other individual-difference data available in the Riverside School Study, we might expect to find that the children whose prejudice declines as opposed to increases in the contact setting are those who are higher in measures of intellectual competence, in that such measures are most likely to reflect a differentiated, complex style of information processing. (Though scholastic achievement tests and grades are typically correlated positively with IQ, they seem less relevant because they often reflect variables such as frustration and low motivation instead of a lack of ability.) Additionally, this model might also expect field independence to be related to decreased prejudice insofar as it reflects analytical ability and shows a positive relation to intelligence. Finally, teacher ratings of intellectual ability (as opposed to classroom compliance) should be higher for those children in whom contact decreases prejudice.

Method. The subset of 180 children selected for the study contained equal numbers of white, Mexican-American, and black students who exhibited the most extreme increases and decreases in prejudice between the pre- and postdesegregation period. The number of increasers, decreasers, males, and females was equated within each racial–ethnic group.

Prejudice was conceptualized as a generalized tendency to reject out-group persons. It was measured by an Ethnic Pictures Test (Green & Gerard, 1974) which consisted of two sets of six color photos of faces of elementary school children, the first being the same sex as the respondent. Each set contained two children from each of the three racial–ethnic categories in the contact setting. The child's first task was to rank the pictures on five aspects selected from previous work on the semantic differential (Osgood, Suci, & Tannenbaum, 1957): kindest, happiest, strongest, fastest, and best grades. Following this step, as a measure of ethnic awareness, the same-sex set was presented again for choices of "most like me," "most like to be," and "like for a friend." Given their uniformly strong positive loadings on a first general factor the five aspects of the first task were combined into two single evaluative summary scores by adding the unweighted out-group rankings for the five aspects separately for the predesegregation year and for the sum of year 1 and year 3 postdesegregation data. Pre- and postdesegregation scores were then standardized separately within each racial–ethnic group.

The second task, the ethnic awareness items, was treated separately, but analogously. The items were scored dichotomously for in-group versus out-group choices, separately within the pre- and 2 postdesegregation years and converted into two sets of standardized scores within each racial–ethnic group. These sets of scores were computed for the entire sample of children in the Riverside School Study.

Change in out-group prejudice following desegregation was assessed separately for children within each of the three racial–ethnic groups by means of the residual gain score method (Cronbach & Furby, 1970) which reflects the discrepancy between the child's obtained postdesegregation level of prejudice and that predicted by regression effects. Data from the children who showed the most extreme positive and negative departures of their postdesegregation level of prejudice from that predicted on the basis of their predesegregation prejudice score, ethnic awareness score, and grade level, were selected for further study.[1]

The correlates of an increase or decrease in prejudice following interracial contact were then assessed by a $2 \times 3 \times 2 \times 2$ analysis of variance factorial design in which prejudice (increase or decrease), ethnicity (white, Mexican-American, or black), and sex were between-groups factors and duration of contact (1 year vs. 3 years) was a within-groups factor. Twenty-nine dependent measures that included family social standing, intellectual competence and performance, personality, scholastic satisfaction and aspirations, and social acceptance were each analyzed separately within this design.

More specifically, these 29 measures correspond to those presented sequentially in Figure 8.2. Family socioeconomic status was assessed by the *Duncan* scale (1) and the *Educational* attainment of the head of household (2). Intellectual measures included *IQ* – a combination of Wechsler's Intelligence Scale for Children (WISC), Peabody, and Raven scores (3); *Verbal* (4) and *Total* (5) scholastic achievement, as measured by state-mandated tests; and *Math* grades (6) and *Verbal grades* (7).

Personality measures included five 15-item self-report scales that assessed *General anxiety* (8) and *School anxiety* (9) – adopted from Sarason et al. (1960); Self-esteem, as measured by estimates of *Others' attitude* toward self (10) and *Own attitude* toward self (11); and *Need for scholastic achievement* (12). Other personality measures included *Conformity* (13), patterned after Asch (1951); a rod and frame measure of *Field dependence* (Witkin et al., 1954) (14); a ring toss game which provided measures of level of *Aspiration* (15), *Goal discrepancy* (16) – the disparity between expectancy and actual performance, and *Unusual shifts* (17) – increased expectations following failure and decreased expectations after success; modified versions of Crandall, Katkovsky, and Preston's (1962) Intellec-

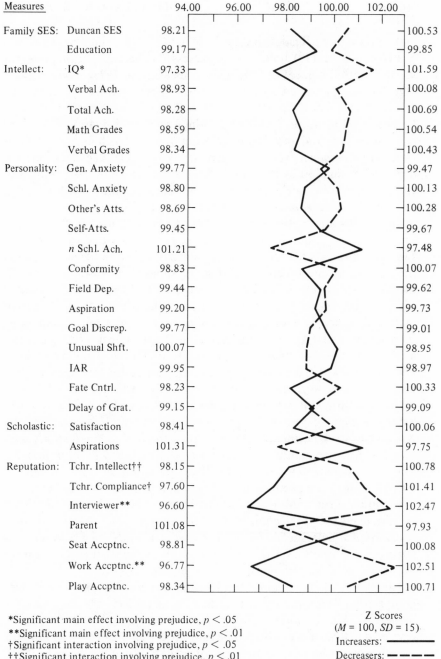

Measures			94.00	96.00	98.00	100.00	102.00	
Family SES:	Duncan SES	98.21						100.53
	Education	99.17						99.85
Intellect:	IQ*	97.33						101.59
	Verbal Ach.	98.93						100.08
	Total Ach.	98.28						100.69
	Math Grades	98.59						100.54
	Verbal Grades	98.34						100.43
Personality:	Gen. Anxiety	99.77						99.47
	Schl. Anxiety	98.80						100.13
	Other's Atts.	98.69						100.28
	Self-Atts.	99.45						99.67
	n Schl. Ach.	101.21						97.48
	Conformity	98.83						100.07
	Field Dep.	99.44						99.62
	Aspiration	99.20						99.73
	Goal Discrep.	99.77						99.01
	Unusual Shft.	100.07						98.95
	IAR	99.95						98.97
	Fate Cntrl.	98.23						100.33
	Delay of Grat.	99.15						99.09
Scholastic:	Satisfaction	98.41						100.06
	Aspirations	101.31						97.75
Reputation:	Tchr. Intellect††	98.15						100.78
	Tchr. Compliance†	97.60						101.41
	Interviewer**	96.60						102.47
	Parent	101.08						97.93
	Seat Accptnc.	98.81						100.08
	Work Accptnc.**	96.77						102.51
	Play Accptnc.	98.34						100.71

*Significant main effect involving prejudice, $p < .05$
**Significant main effect involving prejudice, $p < .01$
†Significant interaction involving prejudice, $p < .05$
††Significant interaction involving prejudice, $p < .01$

Z Scores
($M = 100$, $SD = 15$)
Increasers: ——————
Decreasers: ― ― ― ―

Figure 8.2. Profile comparing marginal mean scores for prejudice increase and decrease groups.

tual Achievement Responsibility Scale, or *IAR* (18), and Bialer's (1961) *Fate Control* Scale (19), both of which assessed beliefs concerning internal versus external control of outcomes; a measure of *Delay of gratification* (20) that was patterned after Mischel (1958); and scholastic *Satisfaction* (21) and *Aspirations* (22) that were assessed by pairs of interview items. Reputational measures included a 13-item teacher evaluation of *Intellectual competence* and motivation (23); an 18-item teacher evaluation of classroom *Compliance* (24); a five-item *Interviewer* general evaluation (25); a general evaluation by the child's *Parents* containing over 20 items (26). Finally, there were sociometric peer popularity nominations for *Seating partner* (27), *Work partner* (28) and *Play partner* (29).

The results are relatively simple and can be presented in the form of profiles for the children whose prejudice either increased or decreased. Figure 8.2 presents the results for measures obtained in the spring of the first year following desegregation. The outcomes obtained in the spring of the third year largely parallel those of Figure 2 and need not be presented here. The dependent measures are listed in the column to the left, with main effects for prejudice increasers and decreasers and interactions indicated by asterisks whenever they were obtained. Inspection shows an attenuated range of mean scores (96.60–102.47), with no mean even approaching a departure of one standard deviation. Intelligence measurements and work partner choices clearly exhibit main effects of prejudice, with children whose prejudice declined following contact having higher scores. Although one could attempt to interpret the outcome of work partner choices as supporting frustration–displacement theory – peer rejection being associated with an increase in prejudice – this interpretation does not seem likely given the absence of parallel effects for the other two measures of peer acceptance: seating choice and play choice. If frustration–displacement theory is valid, why wouldn't the more general social rejection implied by seating choice and play choice rejection also be associated with increased prejudice? The restriction of effects to popularity as a school work partner suggests that the measure be viewed as a reputational index of intellectual ability.

The statistical interaction found in the teachers' ratings of the three groups of children on the intellectual factor reflects the fact that the higher competence found among those whose prejudice declined was restricted to the white children. The same direction of effect was found for the other ethnic groups, but the constricted variance of the teacher ratings of their intellectual competence scores probably accounts for the interaction. The interaction found for the compliance factor of the teacher ratings reflects the fact that the difference seen in the first postdesegregation measurement disappeared in the second wave of measurement. The interviewer evaluation effect seen in the first wave also exhibits similar temporal instability.

These results provide no support for the frustration–displacement model, but fairly consistent support for the cognitive complexity or the social categorization model. It is not the intent here to argue that one model is correct and the other wrong. With respect to the obtained outcome in these correlational data, the theorist intent on "saving" the frustration–displacement model might point to the fact that across almost all of the dimensions, the differences between the children whose prejudice increased and those whose prejudice decreased following contact, although not large, are (from the standpoint of culturally valued traits) very uniformly in the more favorable direction for the latter group. This suggests that the latter group experienced less frustration. Were these measures independent, thereby making a simple sign test of the number of instances in which the difference is in the same direction appropriate, the consistency with which the prejudice increasers are characterized by unfavorable scores (implying greater frustration) is striking.

One curiosity that stands in strong contradiction to the expectations of this model, however, is the parent ratings. The model argues that negative parental evaluations in particular should be strongly associated with tendencies to engage in the hostility displacement mechanism, yet this is the one dimension that shows a striking reversal of the general pattern described in the preceding discussion, a reversal that is consistent across measurement waves and significant in the second wave.

At any rate, the strong statistical support favoring the social categorization–cognitive complexity model suggested that it warrants further elaboration and test. The specific form of the support, however, poses an important issue for the social engineer. IQ is supposedly a relatively stable personality trait, reflecting in the view of most psychologists at least some significant genetic component. To this degree, then, the outcome seems to contain an inherent pessimism. To argue otherwise, one must translate the findings into situational manipulations that correspond to cognitive complexity. Although it may well be the case that one cannot easily train a person to be cognitively complex, it does seem feasible to structure the environment so that it elicits among most persons the kind of information-processing behavior that the cognitively complex person might ordinarily engage in more automatically when interacting with others.

Determinants of category-based interaction

As indicated earlier, category-based interaction is the opposite of interaction that is personalized or cognitively complex. This section discusses features of social situations that promote category-based interaction (Brewer & Miller, 1984).

Categories are more likely to be generally salient if they are characterized by what Brewer and Campbell (1976) call *convergent boundaries*, in which group identities based on many different distinctions – for example, religious, economic, political – all coincide. When social category membership is so multiply determined, the probability is high that at least one cue to category identity will be relevant in almost any social situation. To some extent, the coincidence of category boundaries may arise from natural covariation among various dimensions of social differentiation. Language differences, for instance, create barriers to social exchange that may lead to concomitant differences in life-style, education, and related social distinctions. Distinctive physical features may be easily linked to cultural differences, so that one automatically cues the other. Convergent categories may also be imposed by artificial constraints within a social system. Constraints on geographical or economic mobility, for instance, may lead to ethnic specialization of occupational roles and a correspondence between social categorization based on ethnic origin and those based on socioeconomic indicators (LeVine & Campbell, 1972, chap. 10).

Convergent category boundaries may also be situation-specific. Schwarzwald and Amir (1984), for instance, describe the situation in Israeli religious schools as one in which cultural distinctions between children from Western and Middle-Eastern backgrounds are compounded in that setting by distinctions in economic advantage, residential neighborhood, and religious identity. Similarly, in the United States, when school desegregation is achieved by busing, distinctions based on preexisting ethnic and racial identity become correlated with other situationally specific differences, such as distance and mode of transportation to school, which contribute to additional distinctions between groups.

Even social categories based on single, arbitrary distinctions can coalesce into salient social identities if members of different categories are subjected to differential treatment by outside agents. Results of laboratory studies (Rabbie & Horowitz, 1969) indicate that, although mere assignment of individuals to different group labels is not sufficient to create in-group–out-group distinctions, differential treatment of groups by the experimenter does produce disjunction in perceptions of own- versus other-group members.

Experiments with the minimal intergroup situation (Brewer, 1979; Tajfel, 1970) attest to the powerful impact that perception by external authorities can have on the formation of subjective group identity on the part of those who are lumped together as a category. This effect can lead to a type of self-fulfilling prophecy. The perception that an aggregate of individuals constitutes a social category leads to common treatment of members of that category. This, in turn, produces a correlation between similarity (on some arbitrary dimension) and "common fate" that enhances group identification (Campbell, 1958). This process highlights the important role that political factors and social policies that officially recognize certain group distinctions can play in determining the salience of category membership for situations in which those policies are relevant (Sears & Allen, 1984).

Tajfel (1978) gives particular emphasis to the structure of intergroup relations at the societal level as a critical determinant of category salience. Of great relevance is the presence of intense conflict of interest between groups (as in the relation between rival football teams) or the existence of a fairly rigid system of social stratification within the society that is paralleled by established differences in the status accorded to the social categories. For those who belong to categories with superior status, the importance of category distinctions to positive identity will depend on the security of the established status differential.

When high status is secure, category identity will not be salient in most social situations, but if status differentials are perceived to be insecure or threatened, the need to preserve category distinctiveness may be high and category identity commensurately salient. For the member of inferior-status groups, category salience will depend on the extent to which category membership creates barriers to individual achievement of positive social identity. If status mobility is possible on an individual level, members of low-status groups will tend to minimize category identity and avoid category-based social behavior. But if category membership is perceived as unchangeable and a deterrent to status mobility, high category salience may be functional to group-based efforts to achieve a change in the basis of evaluation that determines relative status.

Group structure within a specific setting is also an important factor in category salience, particularly the relative proportion of members of different social categories represented in the group composition. In general, in fairly large social groupings, a relatively equal representation of two social categories will make category distinctions less salient, whereas the presence of a clear minority will enhance category salience. Findings from Hamilton, Carpenter, and Bishop's research (1984) on neighborhood desegregation illustrate the so-called solo effect, that is, the salience of category identity of a single member of a distinctive social group in an otherwise homogeneous social environment.

The effects of minority–majority representation tend to interact with differences in group status to determine the extent to which category differentiation is important or salient to members of the respective groups. Majority groups with insecure or negative self-image and minority groups with positive self-image have been found to display the greatest degree of discrimination against out-groups, whereas majority groups with secure positive self-image and minority groups with negative self-image show relatively little discrimination (Moscovici & Paicheler, 1978).

Effects of category size and group composition are more complex in situations in which more than two distinguishable social categories are represented. Based on perceptual factors alone, the salience of particular category distinctions will vary as a function of the ratio of category size to total group size. If a fairly large group is divided into several categories of relatively equal size, those categories will provide a useful way of "chunking" the social environment and category differentiation will be highly salient (each category is treated, in effect, as a distinctive minority). When several different social categories are equally represented in a much smaller total group, however, category salience should be low. When the representation of any one social category is small relative to other categories in the setting, differentiation of that category may be highly salient whereas distinctions among the other categories present are less salient.

As indicated previously, the conditions that characterize desegregation in a wide variety of settings have a number of features that predict a high likelihood of category-based social interaction. First of all, the groups involved are usually social categories that are differentiated by convergent boundaries, including distinctions in cultural, economic, linguistic, and physical features. In addition, these objective group differences tend to be confounded with status level within a larger social system – often under conditions in which the existing status structure is under threat – and that increases the salience of group distinctiveness and promotes intergroup social comparison on the part of members of both the high- and low-status categories. Moreover, desegregation frequently occurs within a context of explicit political policies that affect groups differentially and bring individuals into the situation as representatives of their respective social categories. Finally, the immediate social structure tends to be one of disproportional (majority–minority) representation of the different groups that makes category identity perceptually salient as well as emotionally significant.

Reduction of category-based interaction

Having already specified the essential features of personalized social situation, we must ask what conditions will promote such forms of social interaction? In general, the factors that promote personalization may be seen as the obverse of those that enhance the salience and relevance of category boundaries in particular settings. Social-identity theorists have emphasized the presence of multiple cross-cutting category distinctions as an important factor in reducing in-group biases (Deschamps & Doise, 1978), and anthropologists have identified the existence of cross-cutting group loyalties as a critical factor in social integration (LeVine & Campbell, 1972, chap. 4; Murphy, 1957). When category boundaries are not convergent, competing bases for in-group–out-group categorization reduce the importance of any one category identity and force the perceiver to classify other individuals on multiple dimensions at the same time.

Cross-cutting categorization may be encouraged by enhancing the relevance in the immediate social setting of multiple existing un-correlated systems of categorization, or by creating new social categories that are deliberately constructed to cross-cut existing category memberships. The danger with these approaches is that a basis for category-based perceptions and interaction remains intact. Even if multiple categorizations are available, one category distinction may become dominant and form the primary basis for social identity in that setting. In situations involving large social groups, individuals may differentiate themselves into subcategories, based on shared cross-category identities (e.g., all Polish barbers), that then become the basis of intergroup distinctions and social competition. Only situations involving extended interactions that force continual realignments among individuals on the basis of different category identities at different points in time can reduce category-based responses.

Another approach is for authorities in the contact situation to treat each individual differentially on the basis of multidimensional characteristics. Policies can be designed to reduce as much as possible the experience of common fate among members of a social category.

Attempts to compose groups of equally large numbers of members of the relevant social categories should also be effective. Probably the single, most critical aspect of the contact situation with respect to social identity is the reduction of status differences that are correlated with category membership. Cohen (1982) has reviewed the bases for interventions designed to equalize or offset category-based status difference in desegregated classrooms.

In the most general sense the effects of categorization on social interaction will be reduced most successfully (a) when the nature of the interaction in the contact situation promotes an interpersonal orientation rather than a task orientation toward fellow participants, and (b) when the basis for assignment of roles, status, social functions, and subgroup composition in the situation is perceived to be category-independent rather than category-related. These two hypotheses subsume a large number of specific structural and psychological features of the contact situation that have been proposed as important determinants of inter-group acceptance. When translated into their implications for the cooperative learning procedures now in widespread use, a number of specific recommendations emerge. Some of these recommendations have now been tested and confirmed in a program of laboratory research that has emerged out of our earlier work and is designed to explore the implications of the social categorization model for the optimal structuring of cooperative team interaction (Brewer & Miller, 1984; Miller, Rogers, & Hennigan, 1983).

Specific implications of the social categorization model for the implementation of cooperative learning procedures

The two major theoretical variables emphasized previously in this chapter for their crucial importance in reducing category-based responses can be translated into a number of specific recommendations. These recommendations regard the implementation of cooperative team learning in particular, but address other educational practices as well.

Competition. Competition promotes a task focus. Some cooperative learning procedures, although they organize students into heterogeneous groups that engage in intrateam cooperation, also include interteam competition. The widely known Teams-Games-Tournament procedure, developed at Johns Hopkins by DeVries and Edwards and widely disseminated under Robert Slavin's aegis, exemplifies this feature. As argued by Johnson, Johnson, and Maruyama (1984) in their meta-analysis of the effects of various group goal structures on intergroup acceptance, interteam competition detracts from the beneficial effects of cooperation. In Brewer and Miller (1984) we present data from a University of Southern California dissertation by Marian Rogers that uses an experimental laboratory paradigm that structurally parallels the cooperative team learning intervention in desegregated classrooms. The results show that, although competition increases intrateam cohesiveness, thereby increasing out-group acceptance within the team, these effects are not generalized to other out-group persons. Indeed, in comparison to interteam cooperation, interteam competition decreases generalization of the positive effects of intrateam cooperation on out-group acceptance.

Task versus interpersonal focus. Some cooperative learning procedures focus more manifestly and exclusively on mastery of the curriculum materials than do others. The Teams-Games-Tournament procedure and Slavin's (1983) Student Team Achievement Divisions seem to focus children's attention primarily on curriculum mastery, whereas Aronson (1978) in his Jigsaw procedure, and Johnson and Johnson (1975) in their procedures for training teachers to use cooperative learning, specifically direct children's attention to the within-team processes events that transpire and help them develop skills to deal with difficulties that arise in within-team interactions. To this degree, the children do not exclusively take a task focus, but are attentive to the unique, personal, idiosyncratic aspects of each other, thereby reducing category-based responding toward the out-group members of their team. In Rogers's dissertation, previously mentioned, an experimental manipulation of a task versus an interpersonal focus was crossed with the experimental manipulation of interteam cooperation and competition and shown to affect generalization of the beneficial effects of intrateam cooperation in a manner consistent with these theoretical expectations.

Basis for assignment to teams. In virtually all cooperative team learning interventions, the teacher assigns children to teams in a ratio that corresponds as closely as possible to their overall ratio within the class. Teachers who have used cooperative team learning procedures report that the children are quite aware of this basis of assignment. Social categorization theory argues that to the extent that they are, it will promote category-based responding among the children. The teachers' behavior instructs them that social category membership is salient to a high-status figure – the teacher – and that he or she uses this information as a basis for his or her own decisions. A more constructive procedure would make some unique attribute of each child the basis of assignment. Though either procedure can be used to produce racially heterogeneous teams, the latter reduces the salience of category membership whereas the former increases it.

In another dissertation recently completed at the University of Southern California, that employed the same laboratory paradigm used by Rogers, Keith Edwards (1984) compared the effects of category-based assignment to those obtained when assignment of team members was based instead on the distinctiveness of their beliefs about which attitude dimensions from among a large array were the most important ones. In comparison to the latter basis of assignment, category-based assignment produced greater bias against out-group persons with whom team members had had no prior interaction. In other words, category-based assignment disrupted generalization of the positive effects of intrateam cooperation on attitudes toward the outgroup persons on one's team.

Other relevant variables. Although we have not examined them yet in laboratory experimentation, theoretical analysis suggests that a number of other variables will importantly modify the effectiveness of intrateam cooperative activity. As suggested in the more general discussion that immediately precedes this one, organizational factors within the team are likely to be important. If the two white students on the team are given the subgroup task of writing the essay and their two black teammates given the task of reproducing, collating, and assembling copies for the rest of the class (or vice versa), such role specialization, coordinated as it is with category membership, is likely to enhance category salience. Similar effects are likely if decision making and other forms of power within the team are correlated with category membership. In cases where the team task requires division of labor or where decision making by team consensus is for one reason or another infeasible or inappropriate, the teacher should make sure that subgroup formation cuts across category membership boundaries.

Experiences of failure that are linked to the team as a whole or to a subgroup on the team, in contrast to those by individuals within a team that are not linked by category, are also likely to compromise the ordinary benefits of cooperation. Newsletters and other public displays of team standings, as employed in TGT and STAD, tend to emphasize team failures; in contrast, the Jigsaw procedure, which employs testing on an individual basis, lessens the salience of the team as a unit of evaluation.

Though threat is often conceptually linked to failure, a distinction can be drawn between a group outcome as defined by some external agent (e.g., the teacher) and the events that transpire prior to that outcome. The latter can be conceptualized as threat. Events or circumstances that threaten the team are also likely to have mixed effects, producing increased intrateam cohesion when the team can adequately meet the threat, but sharpening perceptual differentiation and within-team in-group and out-group categorization when things go poorly for the team in its attempt to cope with the threat.

Finally, as discussed earlier, the numerical distinctiveness of one or another category within a team is likely to enhance category distinctiveness. Supportive evidence for this view is found in the field studies of Cohen (1984) and Rogers, Hennigan, Bowman, and Miller (1984), as well as in experimental laboratory studies by Duval and Duval (1983) and Edwards (1984).

As indicated, the implications of these principles extend beyond their specific applications to cooperative learning procedures for heterogeneous teams. A number of such extrapolations can be enumerated. For instance, when one is designing a school desegregation program, the implications of numerical distinctiveness have bearing on the optimal configuration of the relative size of groups within a school. Second, given the well-established correlation between academic performance and racial–ethnic identity, homogeneous ability grouping is likely to exacerbate category-based responding. Third, the preceding discussion of the implications of role assignments that are correlated with category membership as opposed to assignments that cross-cut it is obviously relevant to much classroom activity other than cooperative team learning. Also relevant are the groupings of power configurations. Are the pairs of classroom monitors or street-crossing supervisors racially homogeneous or heterogeneous? A fourth application concerns activities outside the classroom. Elsewhere (Rogers et al., 1981), it has been found that the girls in desegregated elementary schools are particularly prone to resegregate themselves in their playground activity. Thus, the development of programs for girls consisting of cooperative games may be particularly valuable in such situations. In high school, however, where team sports seem to naturally evolve into racially homogeneous groupings (e.g., basketball team – black; swimming team – white; defensive unit of the football team – black; debate team – white; track team – black, etc.), it may not be feasible to restructure greater heterogeneity within teams. Here, the most fruitful approach appears to be one that focuses on enhancing loyalties to the larger grouping, that is, the particular high school.

Note

1 Before presenting the results that bear on an evaluation of the two theoretical models, the subject selection procedure warrants further comment. As previously indicated, it was designed to guard against a regression (statistical artifact) interpretation of pre – post-desegregation change in out-group prejudice. Had simple gain scores served as the criterion for selection, statistical regression requires that those children who showed the greatest increase in prejudice would have been those whose initial prejudice was lowest, whereas the opposite would have been true of those showing the greatest decrease in prejudice (Campbell & Clayton, 1961; Campbell & Stanley, 1963). By contrast, analysis of variance showed initial comparability in the predesegregation prejudice levels of those indexed by our selection procedure as increasers and decreasers, respectively ($F < 1$). Other analyses reported in Westman and Miller (1978) provide evidence of some minor differences between ethnic and sex groups in postdesegregation prejudice, and change in prejudice, but do not qualify the basic soundness of the selection procedures.

References

Adorno, T. W., Frenkel-Brunswik, E., Levinson, D. J., & Sanford, R. N. (1950). *The authoritarian personality*. New York: Harper and Row.

Aronson, E., Blaney, N., Stephan, C., Sikes, J., & Snapp, M. (1978). *The jigsaw classroom*. Beverly Hills, CA: Sage.

Asch, S. E. (1951). Effects of group pressure upon the modification and distortion of judgments. In H. Guetzkow (Ed.), *Groups, leadership, and men*. Pittsburgh, PA: Carnegie Press.

Bem, D. J. (1967). Self-perception: An alternative interpretation of cognitive dissonance phenomena. *Psychological Review, 74*, 183–200.

Berkowitz, L. (1962). *Aggression: A social psychological analysis*. New York: McGraw-Hill.

Berry, J. W. (1984). Cultural relations in plural societies: Alternatives to segregation and their sociopsychological implications. In N. Miller & M. B. Brewer (Eds.), *Groups in contact: The psychology of desegregation* (pp. 11–26). Orlando, FL: Academic Press.

Bialer, I. (1961). Conceptualization of success and failure in mentally retarded and normal children. *Journal of Personality, 29*, 303–320.

Brewer, M. B. (1979). Ingroup bias in the minimal intergroup situation: A cognitive-motivational analysis. *Psychological Bulletin, 86*, 307–324.

Brewer, M. B., & Campbell, D. T. (1976). *Ethnocentrism and intergroup attitudes: East African evidence*. New York: Halsted Press (Sage).

Brewer, M. B., & Miller, N. (1984). Beyond the contact hypothesis: Theoretical perspectives on desegregation. In N. Miller & M. B. Brewer (Eds.), *Groups in contact: The psychology of desegregation* (pp. 281–300). Orlando, FL: Academic Press.

Campbell, D. T. (1958). Common fate, similarity, and other indices of the stress of aggregates of persons as social entities. *Behavioral Science, 3*, 14–25.

Campbell, D. T., & Clayton, K. N. (1961). Avoiding regression artifacts in panel studies of communication impact. *Studies in Public Communication, 3*, 99–118.

Campbell, D. T., & Stanley, J. C. (1963). *Experimental and quasi-experimental designs for research*. Chicago: Rand McNally.

Cohen, E. G. (1982). Expectation states and interracial interaction in school settings. *Annual Review of Sociology, 8*, 209–235.

Cohen, E. G. (1984). The desegregated school: Problems in status, power, and interethnic climate. In N. Miller & M. B. Brewer (Eds.), *Groups in contact: The psychology of desegregation* (pp. 77–95). Orlando, FL: Academic Press.

Crandall, V. J., Katkovsky, W., & Preston, A. (1962). Motivational and ability determinants of young children's intellectual achievements behavior. *Child Development, 33*, 643–661.

Cronbach, L. J. & Furby, L. (1970). How should we measure "change" – or should we? *Psychological Bulletin, 74*, 68–80.

Deschamps, J. C., & Doise, W. (1978). Crossed category memberships in intergroup relations. In H. Taijfel (Ed.), *Differentiation between social groups* (pp. 141–158). London: Academic Press.

DeVries, D. L., Slavin, R. E., Fennessey, G. M., Edwards, K. J., & Lombardo, M. M. (1980). *Teams-games-tournament: The Team learning approach*. Englewood Cliffs, NJ: Educational Technology Publications.

Dollard, J. (1938). Hostility and fear in social life. *Social Forces, 17*, 15–25.

Dollard, J., Doob, L. W., Miller, N. E., Mowrer, O. H., & Sears, R. R. (1939). *Frustration and aggression*. New Haven: Yale University Press.

Doise, W. (1978). *Groups and individuals: Explanations in social psychology*. Cambridge: Cambridge University Press.

Duval, S., & Duval, V. H. (1983). *Consistency and cognition: A theory of causal attribution*. Hillsdale, NJ: Erlbaum.

Edwards, K. J. (1984). The effect of category salience and status on intergroup and intragroup perceptions and evaluative attitudes. Unpublished doctoral dissertation, University of Southern California.

Festinger, L. (1957). *A theory of cognitive dissonance*. New York: Harper and Row.

Gerard, H. B., & Miller, N. (1975). *School desegregation*. New York: Plenum Press.

Green, J. A., & Gerard, H. B. (1974). School desegregation and ethnic attitudes. In H. Fromkin & J. Sherwood (Eds.), *Integrating the organization*. Glencoe, IL: Free Press.

Hamilton, D. L., Carpenter, S., & Bishop, G. D. (1984). The desegregation of suburban neighborhoods. In N. Miller & M. B. Brewer (Eds.), *Groups in contact: The psychology of desegregation* (pp. 97–119). Orlando, FL: Academic Press.

Johnson, D. W., & Johnson, R. (1975). *Learning together and alone: Cooperation, competition, and individualization*. Englewood Cliffs, NJ: Prentice-Hall.

Johnson, D. W., Johnson, R., & Maruyama, G. (1984). Goal interdependence and interpersonal attraction in heterogeneous classrooms: A metanalysis. In N. Miller & M. B. Brewer (Eds.), *Groups in contact: The psychology of desegregation* (pp. 187–203). Orlando, FL: Academic Press.

Levin, J. (1975). *The functions of prejudice*. New York: Harper and Row.

LeVine, R. A., & Campbell, D. T. (1972). *Ethnocentrism: Theories of conflict, ethnic attitudes and group behavior*. New York: Wiley.

Miller, N., Rogers, M., & Hennigan, K. (1983). Increasing interracial acceptance: Using cooperative games in desegregated elementary schools. In L. Bickman (Ed.), *Applied Social Psychology Annual: 4* (pp. 119–159). Beverly Hills, CA: Sage.

Mischel, W. (1958). Preference for delayed reinforcement: An experimental study of a cultural observation. *Journal of Abnormal and Social Psychology, 56*, 57–61.

Moscovici, S., & Paicheler, G. (1978). Social comparison and social recognition: Two complementary processes of identification. In H. Tajfel (Ed.), *Differentiation between social groups* (pp. 251–266). London: Academic Press.

Murphy, R. F. (1957). Intergroup hostility and social cohesion. *American Anthropologist, 59*, 1018–1035.

Osgood, C. E., Suci, G. J., & Tannenbaum, P. H. (1957). *The measurement of meaning*. Urbana: University of Illinois Press.

Rabbie, J. M., & Horowitz, M. (1969). Arousal of ingroup-outgroup bias by a chance win or loss. *Journal of Personality & Social Psychology, 13*, 269–277.

Rogers, M., Miller, N., & Hennigan, K. (1981). Cooperative games as an intervention to promote cross-racial acceptance. *American Educational Research Journal, 18*, 513–518.

Rogers, M., Hennigan, K., Bowman, C., & Miller, N. (1984). Promoting voluntary interethnic interaction on the playground. In N. Miller & M. B. Brewer (Eds.), *Groups in contact: The psychology of desegregation*. Orlando, FL: Academic Press.

Sarason, S. B., Davidson, K. S., Lighthall, F. F., Waite, R. R., & Ruebush, B. K. (1960). *Anxiety in elementary school children*. New York: Wiley.

Schwarzwald, J., & Amir, Y. (1984). Interethnic relations and education: An Israeli perspective. In N. Miller & M. B. Brewer (Eds.), *Groups in contact: The psychology of desegregation* (pp. 53–72). Orlando, FL: Academic Press.

Sears, D. O., & Allen, H. M., Jr. (1984). The trajectory of local desegregation controversies and whites' opposition to busing. In N. Miller & M. B. Brewer (Eds.), *Groups in contact: The psychology of desegregation*. Orlando, FL: Academic Press.

Sharan, S., & Hertz-Lazarowitz, R. (1980). Enhancing prosocial behavior through cooperative learning in the classroom. In E. Staub, D. Bar-Tal, J. Karylowski, & J. Reylowski (Eds.), *Development and maintenance of prosocial behavior* (pp. 423–441). New York: Plenum Press.

Sharan, S., & Sharan, Y. (1976). *Small-group teaching*. Englewood Cliffs, NJ: Educational Testing Publications.

Sherif, M., Harvey, O. J., White, B. J., Hood, W. R., & Sherif, C. W. (1961). *Intergroup conflict and cooperation: The Robber's Cave experiment*. Norman: University of Oklahoma Press.

Slavin, R. E. (1983). *Cooperative learning*. New York: Longman.

Sumner, W. G. (1906). *Folkways*. Boston: Ginn.

Tajfel, H. (1970). Experiments in intergroup discrimination. *Scientific American, 223*(2), 96–102.

Tajfel, H. (Ed.) (1978). *Differentiation between social groups: Studies in the social psychology of intergroup relations*. London: Academic Press.

Tajfel, H. (1978). Social categorization, social, identity and social comparison. In H. Tajfel (Ed.), *Differentiation between social groups* (pp. 61–76). London: Academic Press.

Turner, J. C. (1978). Social categorization and social discrimination in the minimal group paradigm. In H. Tajfel (Ed.), *Differentiation between social groups* (pp. 101–140). London: Academic Press.

Westman, G., & Miller, N. (1978). Concomitants of outgroup prejudice in desegregated elementary school children. *SSRI Technical Report*. No. 78-10.

Witkin, H., Lewis, H., Machover, K., Meisner, P., & Wapner, S. (1954). *Personality through perception*. New York: Harper and Row.

9 Academic conflict among students: controversy and learning

David W. Johnson, Roger T. Johnson, and Karl A. Smith

Introduction

Since the general or prevailing opinion on any subject is rarely or never the whole truth, it is only by the collision of adverse opinion that the remainder of the truth has any chance of being supplied.

—John Stuart Mill

A group of students working on a cooperative project are arguing about what the results of a survey they have just conducted within their class means. Several alternative ways of interpreting the results are suggested. Some members of the group believe that one interpretation is the best explanation; other members favor another interpretation. The two factions argue back and forth, each trying to convince the other to agree with the interpretation they think is correct. Such conflicts as this are inevitable within classrooms. They will occur no matter what teachers and students do. The question is not whether such conflicts can be prevented but rather how they are managed. Controversy among students is a moment of truth, a test of the health of the relationships among group members. They are critical events that may bring increased learning, creative insight, high-quality problem solving, and closer relationships. Or they may elicit lasting resentment, smoldering hostility, psychological scars, closed minds, and a refusal to perform role responsibilities. Conflicts have the potential for producing both highly constructive and highly destructive consequences, depending upon how they are managed. Being able to promote conflicts and capitalize on their constructive outcomes is an essential teaching strategy.

When students are asked to interact with other students while they learn, conflicts among their ideas, conclusions, theories, information, perspectives, opinions, and preferences are inevitable. Yet there is evidence that in many classrooms conflicts are avoided and suppressed (DeCecco & Richards, 1974). Conflicts are commonly viewed as divisive,

199

creating dislike and resentment, and alienating students from each other, with the less capable individuals being intellectually beaten and humiliated (Collins, 1970). There are social scientists, however, who insist that conflict has potentially constructive outcomes and can result in positive relationships among students as well as increased motivation to learn, enjoyment of the instructional experience, and perceptions of encouragement and support among students (Deutsch, 1973; Johnson, 1979, 1980; Johnson & Johnson, 1982). The purpose of this chapter is to present a systematic program of research aimed at demonstrating the constructive impact of academic conflicts on instructional outcomes.

We shall first define the various types of academic conflicts, note the basic questions we investigated, and briefly describe our research procedures. We then describe the basic processes of academic conflicts, the conditions determining their constructiveness, and the application of the theory and research to the classroom.

Definitions

Within instructional situations students can engage in controversy, debate, concurrence seeking, or individualistic learning. The type of conflict most important for learning and intellectual development is *controversy*, the situation that exists when one student's ideas, information, conclusions, theories, and opinions are incompatible with those of another, and the two seek to reach an agreement. An example of controversy is when a learning group is given the assignment of deciding whether or not wolves should be a protected species. Two members of the group are given the position that wolves should be a protected species and the other two members are given the position that farmers, ranchers, and hunters should be allowed to kill wolves. Within such a learning situation there are both positive goal interdependence (a consensus on the fate of the wolf must be determined) and resource interdependence (different students have different information).

Debate exists when two or more students argue positions that are incompatible with one another and a winner is declared on the basis of who presented his or her position the best. In a debate students compete to see who is best in presenting his or her position. An example of debate is when each member of a learning group is assigned a position as to whether or not wolves should be a protected species and the teacher declares as the winner the student who makes the best presentation of his or her position to the group. A cooperative element (resource interdependence) is added to the debate when students are also given the assignment of mastering the information each group member presents in support of his or her position.

Concurrence seeking occurs when members of a learning group inhibit discussion to avoid any disagreement or arguments, emphasize agreement, and avoid realistic appraisal of alternative ideas and courses of action. An example of concurrence seeking is when a learning group is assigned to decide whether or not the wolf should be a protected species, with the stipulation that group members are not to argue but rather to compromise quickly whenever opposing opinions are expressed. Most classrooms in the United States seem to be dominated more by concurrence seeking than by controversy or debate (DeCecco & Richards, 1974; Deutsch, 1973; Johnson, 1979).

Individualistic learning exists when students work alone without interacting with each other, in a learning situation in which their learning goals are unrelated and independent from each other.

A key to the effectiveness of conflict procedures is the mixture of cooperative and competitive elements within the procedure. The greater the cooperative elements and the less the competitive elements, the more constructive the conflict (Deutsch, 1973). Cooperative elements alone, however, do not ensure maximal productivity from a learning group. There has to be both cooperation and conflict.

	Controversy	Debate	Concurrence seeking	Individualistic
Positive goal interdependence	Yes	No	Yes	No
Resource interdependence	Yes	Yes	No	No
Negative goal interdependence	No	Yes	No	No
Conflict	Yes	Yes	No	No

Basic questions

The questions addressed by the theory and research reported in this chapter have been the center of the work by our students and ourselves for many years at the University of Minnesota. Students who have worked with us on the issue of how to utilize constructive conflict, in a temporal ordering, include: Dean Tjosvold, Patricia Noonan-Wagner,

Dennis Falk, Antoine Garibaldi, Karl Smith, Nancy Lowry, Susan Lund, Virginia Lyons, Patricia Roy, Margaret Tiffany, Todd Pierson, Renee Peterson, and several others. We list them because they have been important contributors to the work described.

For a number of years the question that guided our research was, "What is the impact of perspective taking on conflict resolution?" (Johnson, 1971). In collaboration with Dean Tjosvold that question was rephrased to be, "What is the impact of conflict on perspective taking?" In the past it was assumed that conflicts inevitably resulted in a fixation of one's own perspective and a rejection and derogation of the perspectives of others (Rapoport, 1960). In our early research on controversy, however, we demonstrated that conflict among positions and reasoning could in fact increase the accuracy of perspective taking (Tjosvold & Johnson, 1977, 1978). From that question we evolved to the investigation of the inquiry, "What are the conditions under which academic conflicts become constructive or destructive?" From our evolving clarification of controversy we asked, "What is the process by which controversy positively affects academic motivation, learning, and other instructional outcomes?" and, "Can conflict be deliberatively structured by educators to promote desired educational outcomes?" From these queries have come a systematic program of theorizing, research, and application.

Basic research procedures

Our activities have included:

1. Developing a theory concerning the process by which controversy promotes positive outcomes.
2. Conducting a series of laboratory and field experimental studies to validate the theory.
3. Developing the procedures necessary for applying the validated theory in instructional situations.
4. Working with elementary schools, secondary schools, and colleges throughout North America to field test and implement controversy into academic learning situations.

The following section briefly describes the procedures we used in our laboratory and field experiments.

Laboratory experiments

Our typical laboratory experimental study compared presence of controversy with absence of controversy – no-controversy – and used college students as subjects. Students discussed a moral dilemma with a trained confederate taking the opposite position from the student (in the controversy condition) or the same position (in the no-controversy condition). The experiments typically were conducted in four phases:

1. Individually deciding what course of action should be taken in a moral dilemma
2. Working with a partner to prepare for a discussion about the moral dilemma with a member of another pair
3. Discussing the moral dilemma with a student from another group and then writing a joint statement
4. Debriefing

Two research subjects and two confederates (posing as subjects) were scheduled at each session. The experimenter stated that the study investigated how different groups of people discuss moral issues. Subjects were asked to indicate what course of action should be taken by a person caught in the dilemma. One participant and one confederate were then escorted into a room where they were informed they had the same opinion on the issue. They were instructed to prepare each other to represent their position in discussion with a member of the opposing pair who had a different opinion. Each subject was then paired with a confederate who followed a script (different for each condition) in discussing the moral issue. Subjects were led to believe that they would report back to their original partner as to the nature of the agreement reached in the discussion. Subjects then filled out a questionnaire and were debriefed.

Field experiments

We chose to conduct highly controlled experimental field studies in actual classrooms. These studies lasted from 2 to 10 weeks, compared cooperative controversy with concurrence seeking and/or debate and/or individualistic learning situations, and involved students from different ability levels. Three classroom teachers typically assisted in conducting the study. In order to ensure that there were no differences among students in each condition, students were randomly assigned to conditions, stratifying for sex and ability level. To ensure that high-quality teaching occurred in each condition, teachers received a minimum of 90 hours of training on how to implement controversy, concurrence seeking, debate, and individualistic learning and were given a daily script to follow. In order to make sure that any differences found among

204

conditions were not due to differences in teaching ability, teachers were
rotated across conditions, so that each teacher taught each condition an
equal amount of time. To make sure that the study did in fact test the
theory, the ways in which the conditions were implemented were
carefully structured to be unambiguous. To make sure that any differences found among conditions were not due to differences in curriculum
materials, the students studied the identical curriculum. To verify that the
teachers were teaching the conditions appropriately, they were observed
daily. Finally, how students interacted with each other was observed. We
were determined to conduct our research in as highly controlled and
careful a way as possible so we could be confident about the results. What
follows is a summary of our theory and the validating research.

Processes of controversy, debate, and concurrence-seeking

> Have you learned lessons only of
> those who admired you, and were tender
> with you, and stood aside for you?
>
> Have you not learned great lessons
> from those who braced themselves
> against you, and disputed the passage
> with you?

—Walt Whitman, 1860

The posited consequences of controversy, debate, concurrence seeking,
and individualistic learning are listed in Figure 9.1. When controversy,
debate, concurrence seeking, or individualistic learning occurs there are
certain consequences that may be hypothesized to result (Berlyne, 1966;
Hunt, 1964; Johnson, 1979, 1980; Johnson & Johnson, 1979; Piaget, 1948,
1950). All four types of learning begin with students categorizing and
organizing their present information and experiences so that a conclusion is derived (see Figure 9.1).

In controversy, the students realize that others have a different
conclusion and that the students' conclusions are being challenged and
contested. The students then become uncertain about the correctness of
their conclusion and an internal state of conceptual conflict or disequilibrium is aroused. In hopes of resolving their uncertainty, students
actively search for more information, new experiences, improved reasoning, and a more adequate cognitive perspective. They listen to and
attempt to understand their opponents' conclusions and rationale. They
actively represent their position and reasoning to the opposition, thereby
engaging in considerable cognitive rehearsal of their position and its
rationale.

The cognitive rehearsal of their own position and the attempts to understand their opponents' position result in a reconceptualization of their position, characterized by accurate understanding of the opposing perspective, incorporation of the opponents' information and reasoning, attitude and position change, and the use of higher level reasoning strategies. This process is repeated until the differences in conclusions among students have been resolved, an agreement is reached, and the controversy has ended. The whole process results in high productivity, including high mastery and retention of the material being learned, high-quality decision making and problem solving, high creativity, and high continuing motivation to learn about the issue (as the uncertainty does not fully end when a joint conclusion is reached). The process of arguing and coming to a joint conclusion creates a positive cathexis among participating students toward each other, themselves, the subject matter being learned, and the controversy procedures.

Within debate, students realize that others have a different conclusion and that the students' conclusions are being challenged and contested. The students then become uncertain about the correctness of their conclusion and an internal state of conceptual conflict or disequilibrium is created. Due to the competitiveness inherent in the situation, students tend to defensively fixate on their original position and, consequently, there is only a moderate search for new information. Students listen to opposing positions, but derogate and reject them. Students actively represent their position and its rationale to the opposition. The mixture of cooperative and competitive elements results in only a partial reconceptualization of the issue characterized by a failure to understand different cognitive perspectives, and moderate incorporation of opponents' information, attitude change, and use of higher level reasoning. Productivity tends to be moderate. Continuing motivation to learn about the issue is mild. Opposing students are moderately rejected, the subject area is moderately disliked, and arguing and disagreeing are viewed as moderately destructive activities.

Within concurrence seeking, there is a suppression of different conclusions, an emphasis on quick compromise, and a lack of disagreement. Students become fixated on their own positions and little uncertainty arises as to the correctness of their conclusions. New information that may challenge their conclusions is avoided. The students restate the accepted conclusions without elaboration or exploration of the reasoning and rationale underlying the position. Opposing views are derogated and rejected. A failure to reconceptualize or understand different cognitive perspectives results. There is a lack of attitude change and lower level reasoning strategies tend to be used. The low information search and the lack of attempt to find a more adequate cognitive perspective and rationale result in low mastery and retention of the material being learned, low quality decisions, and a lack of creativity. Continuing motivation to learn more about the issue is mild. Opposing students are rejected, the subject area is disliked, and arguing and disagreeing are viewed as destructive activities.

In an individualistic learning situation there is the presence of only the student's conclusions. The student becomes fixated and satisfied with the information he or she has. There is no felt need to restate or elaborate on one's position and rationale. Students are unaware of different perspectives being learned. Mastery and retention of the material being learned is low. They have a sense of closure on the material and, therefore, continuing motivation to learn is low. They are neutral toward other students and the subject area. Arguing and disagreeing are viewed as destructive activities.

The process by which controversy sparks greater learning than do debate, concurrence seeking, and individualistic efforts is outlined in Figure 9.2. It consists of six steps leading to increased educational productivity and more positive student attitudes. The steps and their validating research are discussed in detail in the following sections.

Step 1: Organization of information and derivation of conclusions

Learning begins with students categorizing and organizing their present information and experiences so that a conclusion is derived. Students' interaction with the world always involves categorization or conceptualization, the forming or being aware of concepts. Concepts are then systematized into coding systems or conceptual structures that organize related concepts from the very specific to the generic. Conceptual structures promote retention of information and the transfer and application of learning. Conceptual structures are used to organize information. Conclusions are then derived based on the principles of scientific inquiry and deductive and inductive logic.

Step 2: Challenge by students with opposing views

In controversy (and debate), students' conclusions are challenged by other students who present an opposing position.

Controversy	Debate	Concurrence Seeking	Individualistic
DERIVING CONCLUSIONS BY CATEGORIZING AND ORGANIZING INFORMATION AND EXPERIENCES	DERIVING CONCLUSIONS BY CATEGORIZING AND ORGANIZING INFORMATION AND EXPERIENCES	DERIVING CONCLUSIONS BY CATEGORIZING AND ORGANIZING INFORMATION AND EXPERIENCES	DERIVING CONCLUSIONS BY CATEGORIZING AND ORGANIZING INFORMATION AND EXPERIENCES
BEING CHALLENGED BY OPPOSING VIEWS	BEING CHALLENGED BY OPPOSING VIEWS	QUICK COMPROMISE TO ONE VIEW	PRESENCE OF ONLY ONE VIEW
UNCERTAINTY ABOUT THE CORRECTNESS OF OWN VIEW, COGNITIVE CONFLICT	UNCERTAINTY ABOUT THE CORRECTNESS OF OWN VIEW, COGNITIVE CONFLICT	HIGH CERTAINTY	HIGH CERTAINTY
HIGH EPISTEMIC CURIOSITY	MODERATE EPISTEMIC CURIOSITY	ABSENCE OF EPISTEMIC CURIOSITY	NO EPISTEMIC CURIOSITY
ACTIVE REPRESENTATION AND ELABORATION OF POSITION AND RATIONALE	ACTIVE REPRESENTATION AND ELABORATION OF POSITION AND RATIONALE	ACTIVE RESTATEMENT OF ORIGINAL POSITION	NO ORAL STATEMENT OF POSITION
HIGH RECONCEPTUALIZATION	MODERATE RECONCEPTUALIZATION	NO RECONCEPTUALIZATION	NO RECONCEPTUALIZATION
HIGH PRODUCTIVITY	MODERATE PRODUCTIVITY	LOW PRODUCTIVITY	LOW PRODUCTIVITY
HIGH POSITIVE CATHEXIS	MODERATE POSITIVE CATHEXIS	LOW POSITIVE CATHEXIS	LOW POSITIVE CATHEXIS

Figure 9.1. Processes of controversy, debate, concurrence seeking, and individualistic learning.

Step 3: Conceptual conflict and uncertainty

When students are challenged by information that is incompatible with and does not fit with their conclusions, conceptual conflict can result. The greater the disagreement among students or between the teacher and the students, the more frequently the disagreement occurs, the greater the number of people disagreeing with a student's position, the more competitive the context of the controversy, and the more affronted the student feels, the greater the conceptual conflict and uncertainty the student will experience (Asch, 1952; Burdick & Burnes, 1958; Festinger & Maccoby, 1964; Gerard & Greenbaum, 1962; Inagaki & Hatano, 1968, 1977; Lowry & Johnson, 1981; Tjosvold & Johnson, 1977, 1978; Tjosvold, Johnson, & Fabrey, 1980; Worchel & McCormick, 1963).

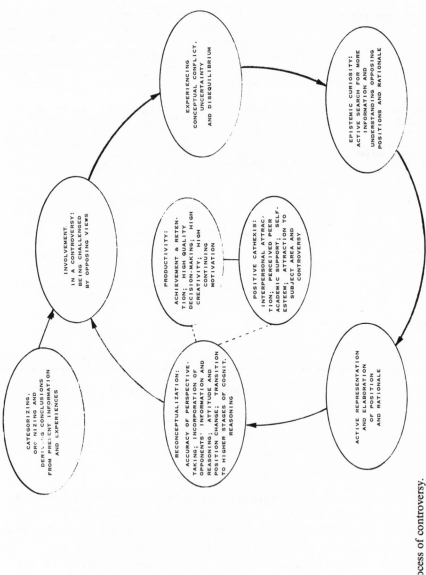

Figure 9.2. Process of controversy.

Step 4: Epistemic curiosity

Epistemic curiosity is reflected in students' active search for more information and seeking to understand the position and its supporting rationale of the opposing students.

Active search for more information. Conceptual conflict motivates an active search for more information (often called epistemic curiosity) in hopes of resolving the uncertainty. Lowry and Johnson (1981) found that students involved in controversy, compared with students involved in concurrence seeking, read more library materials, reviewed more classroom materials, more frequently watched an optional movie shown during recess, and more frequently requested information from others. Smith, Johnson, and Johnson (1981) found that controversy, compared with both concurrence seeking and individualistic study, promoted greater use of library materials and more frequent viewing of an optional film. Also interesting to note is that concurrence seeking promoted greater use of library materials and more frequent viewing of an optional film than did individualistic study.

Johnson and Johnson (1985) and Johnson, Johnson, and Tiffany (1984) found that controversy, compared with debate and individualistic study, promotes greater search for more information outside of class. Johnson, Brooker, Stutzman, Hultman, and Johnson (1985) found that students engaged in controversy have greater interest in learning more about the subject being studied than do students engaged in concurrence seeking or individualistic study. Students engaged in controversy have been found to be motivated to know others' positions and to develop understanding and appreciation of them (Tjosvold & Johnson, 1977, 1978; Tjosvold et al., 1980; Tjosvold, Johnson, & Lerner, 1981).

Understanding of the positions of others. A number of studies have found that students involved in a controversy developed a more accurate understanding of other positions than did students involved in non-controversial discussions, concurrence-seeking discussions, and individualistic efforts (Smith, Johnson, & Johnson, 1981; Tjosvold & Johnson, 1977, 1978; Tjosvold et al., 1980).

Step 5: Active representation of and elaboration on position

Within controversy, students advocate their position and defend it against refutation. Students actively represent their position and reasoning to the opposition, thereby engaging in considerable cognitive rehearsal and elaboration of their position and its rationale. A number of research studies have found that students engaged in controversy, compared with students engaged in debate, concurrence seeking, and individualistic study, contribute more information to the discussion, more frequently repeat information, share new information, elaborate the material being learned, present more ideas, present more rationales, make more higher level processing statements, make more comments aimed at managing their efforts to learn, make fewer intermediate level cognitive-processing statements, and make more statements managing the group's learning (Johnson & Johnson, 1985; Johnson, Johnson, & Tiffany, 1984; Johnson, Johnson, Pierson, & Lyons, in press; Lowry & Johnson, 1981; Smith et al., 1981; Smith, Johnson, & Johnson, 1984).

Nijhof and Kommers (1982) found that the presence of controversy in cooperative groups increases the oral participation of group members. Disagreements within a group have been found to provide a greater amount of information and variety of facts as well as changes in the salience of known information (Anderson & Graesser, 1976; Kaplan, 1977; Kaplan & Miller, 1977; Vinokur & Burnstein, 1974).

A central aspect of controversy is having students advocate their position to an opposing pair of peers. Students are instructed to teach their position and its rationale to the other members of their group. There is evidence that people learn things better if they learn it in order to teach someone else (Allen, 1976; Benware's study, cited in Deci, 1975; Gartner, Kohler, & Reissman, 1971). Higher level conceptual understanding and reasoning are promoted when participants have to teach each other a common way to think about problem situations (Johnson & Johnson, 1979, 1983; Murray, 1983).

The way people conceptualize material and organize it cognitively is markedly different when they are learning material for their own benefit from when they are learning material to teach to others (Annis, 1983; Bargh & Schul, 1980; Murray, 1983). Material learned to be taught is learned at a higher conceptual level than is material learned for one's own use. Peers are frequently able to teach their classmates more effectively than specially trained experts (Fisher, 1969; Sarbin, 1976). Finally, people are particularly prone to increase their commitment to a cause that they have attempted to persuade another to adopt (Nel, Helmreich, & Aronson, 1969).

Step 6: Reconceptualization

The quality of students' reconceptualization of their position depends on the accuracy of their perspective taking, their incorporation of opponents' information and reasoning into their own position, their attitude and position change, and their transition to higher stages of cognitive reasoning.

Accuracy of perspective taking. In resolving controversies, students need to be able to both comprehend the information being presented by their opposition and to understand the cognitive perspective their opposition is using to organize and interpret the information. A cognitive perspective consists of the cognitive organization being used to give meaning to a person's knowledge, and the structure of a person's reasoning. Tjosvold and Johnson (1977, 1978) and Tjosvold et al. (1980) conducted three experiments in which they found that the presence of controversy promotes greater understanding of another person's cognitive perspective than does the absence of controversy.

Students engaging in a controversy were better able to subsequently predict what line of reasoning their opponent would use in solving a future problem than were students who interacted without any controversy. Kurdek (in press) found that high cognitive perspective-taking skill is related to arguing with peers. Smith et al. (1981) noted that students engaged in a controversy are better able to understand their opponents' perspective than are students involved in concurrence-seeking discussions or individualistic efforts. Johnson, Johnson, Pierson, and Lyons (in press) found that low, medium, and high ability students in the controversy condition are better able to take the opposing perspective than are students participating in concurrence-seeking discussions.

Perspective taking skills are of great importance for exchanging information and opinions within a controversy. More information, both personal and impersonal, is disclosed when one is interacting with a person engaging in perspective-taking behaviors (Colson, 1968; Noonan-Wagner, 1975; Sermet & Smyth, 1973; Taylor, Altman, & Sorrentino, 1969). Perspective-taking ability increases people's ability to phrase messages so that they are easily understood by others and to accurately comprehend other people's messages (Feffer & Suchotliff, 1966; Flavell, 1968; Hogan & Henley, 1970). Engaging in perspective-taking behaviors in conflicts results in increased understanding and retention of the opponent's information and perspective (Johnson, 1971). During controversies, perspective-taking behaviors (compared with egocentrically emphasizing one's own information and perspective) results in more creative and higher quality solutions (Falk & Johnson, 1977) and in greater gains in accuracy of problem solving (Johnson, 1977). Finally, perspective-taking behaviors promote more positive perceptions of information-exchange process, fellow problem-solvers, and the problem-solving experience (Falk & Johnson, 1977; Johnson, 1971, 1977; Noonan-Wagner, 1975).

Incorporation of opponents' information and reasoning. A more accurate understanding of the opponents' position, reasoning, and perspective has been posited to result in greater incorporation of the opponents' reasoning into one's own position. There is evidence that participation in a controversy, compared with participating in noncontroversial or concurrence-seeking discussions or individualistic efforts, results in greater incorporation of opponents' arguments and information (Johnson & Johnson, 1985; Johnson, Johnson & Tiffany, 1984; Tjosvold, et al., 1981). These findings, however, are limited to conditions where the overall context is cooperative and students have the skill of disagreeing while confirming their opponents' competence.

Tjosvold and Johnson (1978) found that when the context is cooperative there is more open-minded listening to the opposing position. When controversy occurs within a competitive context, a closed-minded orientation is created in which students comparatively feel unwilling to make concessions to the opponent's viewpoint, and refuse to incorporate any of it into their own position.

Within a competitive context the increased understanding resulting from controversy tends to be ignored for a defensive adherence to one's own position. Lowin (1969) and Kleinhesselink and Edwards (1975) found that when individuals are unsure of the correctness of their position, they select to be exposed to disconfirming information when it could easily be refuted, presumably because such refutation could affirm their own beliefs. Van Blerkom and Tjosvold (1981) found that students select to discuss an issue with a peer with an opposing position more frequently when the context is cooperative rather than competitive, and that students in a competitive situation more often select a less competent peer with whom to discuss an issue. Tjosvold (1982) and Tjosvold and Deemer (1980) found that when the context is competitive, participants in a controversy understand but do not use others' information and ideas. When the context is cooperative, the information and ideas provided by opponents are used. Tjosvold et al. (1980) and Tjosvold et al. (1981) found that when students involved in a controversy have their personal competence disconfirmed by their opponents, a closed-minded rejection of the opponents' position, information, and reasoning results. The amount of defensiveness generated influences the degree to which students will incorporate the opponents' information and reasoning into their position, even when they accurately understand their opponents' position.

Attitude and position change. Disagreements within a group have been found to provide a greater amount of information and variety of facts, and a change in the salience of known information which, in turn, results in shifts of judgment (Anderson & Graesser, 1976; Kaplan, 1977; Kaplan & Miller, 1977; Nijhof & Kommers, 1982; Vinokur & Burnstein, 1974).

A number of studies have found that controversy promotes greater attitude change than does concurrence seeking, no-controversy, and individualistic efforts (Johnson & Johnson, 1985; Johnson, Brooker, Stutzman, Hultman, & Johnson, 1985).

Transition to higher stages of cognitive reasoning.

> *In the course of his contacts (and especially, his conflicts and arguments) with other children, the child increasingly finds himself forced to reexamine his own percepts and concepts in the light of those of others, and by so doing, gradually rids himself of cognitive egocentrism.*

—John Flavell, 1963

Cognitive development theorists (Flavell 1963; Kohlberg, 1969; Piaget, 1948, 1950) have posited that repeated interpersonal controversies in which students are forced to take cognizance of the perspective of others' promote cognitive and moral development, the ability to think logically, and the reduction of egocentric reasoning. Such interpersonal conflicts are posited to create disequilibrium within students' cognitive structures, which motivate a search for a more adequate and mature process of reasoning. There are several studies that demonstrate that pairing a conserver with a nonconserver, and giving the pair conservation problems to solve, results in the conserver's answer prevailing on the great majority of conservation trials and in the nonconserver learning how to conserve (Ames & Murray, 1982; Botvin & Murray, 1975; Doise & Mugny, 1979; Doise, Mugny, & Perret-Clermont, 1976; Knight-Arest & Reid, 1978; Perret-Clermont, 1980; Miller & Brownell, 1975; Mugny & Doise, 1978; Murray, 1972; Murray, Ames, & Botvin, 1977; Silverman & Geiringer, 1973; Silverman & Stone, 1972; Smedslund, 1961a).

These results have been found in groups of one-on-one, two-on-one, and three-on-two; in kindergarten, first, second, third, and fifth grades; and with normal and learning-disabled, black and white, and middle and low-SES children. Inagaki (1981) and Inagaki and Hatano (1968, 1977) found that fourth-graders (2/3 of whom were nonconservers) who were placed in small groups and given a conservation task and who argued among themselves, could give more adequate and higher level explanations than could the control subjects who did not argue with one another. Experimental subjects showed greater progress in generalizing the principle of conservation to a variety of situations and tended to resist extinction more often when they were shown an apparently nonconserving event. The discussion of the task per se did not produce the effects. There had to be conflict among students' explanations for the effects to appear.

There are a number of studies that demonstrate that when students are placed in a group with peers who use a higher stage of moral reasoning, and the group is required to make a decision as to how a moral dilemma should be resolved, advances in the students' level of moral reasoning result (Blatt, 1969; Blatt & Kohlberg, 1973; Crockenberg & Nicolayev, 1977; Keasey, 1973; Kuhn et al., 1977; LeFurgy & Woloshin, 1969; Maitland & Goldman, 1974; Rest, Turiel, & Kohlberg, 1969; Turiel, 1966). Taken together, these studies provide evidence that controversies among students can promote transitions to higher stages of cognitive and moral reasoning. Such findings are important as there is little doubt that higher levels of cognitive and moral reasoning cannot be directly taught (Inhelder & Sinclair, 1969; Sigel & Hooper, 1968; Sinclair, 1969; Smedslund, 1961a, 1961b; Turiel, 1973; Wallach & Sprott, 1964; Wallach, Wall, & Anderson, 1967; Wohlwill & Lowe, 1962).

Results of the controversy process

Productivity

The six steps previously outlined in the controversy process promote higher achievement and retention, higher quality decision making, higher creativity, and greater continuing motivation as will now be further described.

Achievement and retention. Controversy results in greater mastery and retention of the subject matter being learned (Johnson, Johnson, Pierson, & Lyons, in press; Johnson, Brooker, Stutzman, Hultman, & Johnson, 1985; Lowry & Johnson, 1981; Pellegrini, 1984; Smith et al., 1981). Furthermore, students who experience conceptual conflict resulting from controversy are better able to generalize and apply the principles they learn to a wider variety of situations than are students who do not experience such conceptual conflict (Inagaki & Hatano, 1968, 1977).

Quality of problem solving. The purpose of controversy within a group is to arrive at the highest quality problem solution or decision that is possible. There is evidence that the occurrence of controversy within a group results in a higher quality problem solution (Boulding, 1964; Glidewell, 1953; Hall & Williams, 1966, 1970; Hoffman, Harburg, & Maier, 1962; Hoffman & Maier, 1961; Maier & Hoffman, 1964; Maier & Solem, 1952).

Creativity. Controversy promotes creative insight by influencing students to view a problem from different perspectives and reformulate a problem in ways that allow the emergence of new orientations to a solution. There is evidence that controversy increases the number of ideas, quality of ideas, feelings of stimulation and enjoyment, and originality of expression in creative problem solving (Bahn, 1964; Bolen & Torrance, 1976; Dunnette, Campbell & Jaastad, 1963; Falk & Johnson, 1977; Peters & Torrance, 1972; Torrance, 1970, 1971, 1973; Triandis et al., 1963).

There is also evidence that controversy results in more creative problem solutions, with more member satisfaction, compared to group efforts that do not include controversy (Glidewell, 1953; Hall & Williams, 1966, 1970; Hoffman et al., 1962; Maier & Hoffman, 1964; Rogers, 1970). These studies further demonstrated that controversy encourages group members to dig into a problem, raise issues, and settle them in ways that show the benefits of a wide range of ideas being used. Controversy also promotes a high degree of emotional involvement in and commitment to solving the problems the group is working on.

Positive cathexis

The six steps of the controversy process and the resulting productivity also result in a positive cathexis that generalizes to the other students, oneself, the subject being studied, and the controversy process.

Interpersonal attraction among students. It is often assumed that the presence of controversy within a group will lead to difficulties in establishing good interpersonal relations and will promote negative attitudes toward fellow group members (Collins, 1970). Within controversy and debate there are elements of disagreement, argumentation, and rebuttal that could result in students disliking each other and could further create difficulties in the establishing of good relationships between students. It is often assumed that arguing leads to rejection, divisiveness, and hostility among peers.

However, conflicts have been hypothesized to potentially create positive relationships among participants (Deutsch, 1962; Johnson & Johnson, 1982), although in the past there has been little evidence to validate such a hypothesis. It may be posited that when conflict takes place within a cooperative context and facilitates the achievement of one's goals, a positive cathexis results that generalizes to one's attitudes toward the other individuals in the situation, oneself, the subject area, and the process of controversy (Deutsch, 1962; Johnson & Johnson, 1979).

Within the research on controversy there is consistent evidence that controversy promotes greater liking among participants than does debate, concurrence seeking, no-controversy, or individualistic efforts Lowry & Johnson, 1981; Smith et al., 1981; Tjosvold, 1982; Tjosvold & Deemer, 1980; Tjosvold & Johnson, 1978; Tjosvold et al., 1980; Tjosvold et al., 1981). Concurrence seeking and debate promote greater interpersonal attraction among participants than does individualistic study. The more cooperative the context, the greater the cooperative elements in the situation; the greater the confirmation of each other's competence, the greater the interpersonal attraction.

Perceived peer academic support. While there is considerable evidence that cooperative learning experiences promote greater perceptions of peer academic support than do competitive or individualistic learning situations (Johnson & Johnson, 1983), there has been some doubt that such perceptions would exist while students are engaging in academic arguments (Collins, 1970). There is consistent evidence, however, that controversy promotes greater perceived peer academic support than does individualistic learning (Johnson & Johnson, 1985).

Self-esteem. Many educators assume that low ability students' academic self-esteem will be damaged by participating in controversies with more capable peers. Not being as persuasive in presenting arguments and in rebutting the opposing position has been assumed to result in lowered academic self-esteem. There is considerable evidence, however, that the academic self-esteem of low, medium, and high ability students is higher in cooperative than competitive or individualistic learning situations (Johnson & Johnson, 1983). Since controversy is basically a cooperative activity, it may be hypothesized that the experience of disagreeing with other students and deriving a joint position that reflects the best reasoning of all students results in higher self-esteem. Johnson and Johnson (1985) did in fact find that controversy promoted higher academic self-esteem than did debate or individualistic learning, and debate promoted higher academic self-esteem than did individualistic learning. Johnson, Johnson, Pierson, and Lyons (in press) found that controversy promoted higher academic self-esteem than did concurrence seeking. Smith, Johnson, and Johnson (1982) found that controversy promoted greater academic self-esteem than did individualistic learning.

Attitudes toward subject area. Students who engaged in controversies tend to like the subject area better than did students who engaged in concurrence-seeking discussions or individualistic learning (Johnson, Johnson, Pierson, & Lyons, in press; Lowry & Johnson, 1981; Smith et al., 1981).

Attitudes toward controversy. There is considerable evidence that conflict is perceived negatively within our schools and generally avoided (Johnson & Johnson, 1982). Yet students involved in controversy (and to a lesser extent, debate) like their instructional procedures better than do students learning individualistically (Johnson & Johnson, 1985) and participating in a controversy consistently promotes positive attitudes toward the experience (Johnson, Johnson, Pierson, & Lyons, in press; Johnson, Johnson & Tiffany, 1984; Johnson, Brooker, Stutzman, Hultman, & Johnson, 1985; Lowry & Johnson, 1981; Smith et al., 1981, 1984).

The presence of controversy does not always mean that high productivity and positive attitudes will result. There are a number of necessary conditions that must be present if controversy is to have beneficial effects.

Conditions determining the constructiveness of controversy

Although academic controversies can operate in a beneficial way, they will not do so under all conditions. As with all types of conflicts, the potential for either constructive or destructive outcomes is present in a controversy. Whether there are positive or negative consequences depends on the conditions under which controversy occurs and the way in which it is managed. These conditions and procedures include:

1. The goal structure within which the controversy occurs.
2. The heterogeneity of students.
3. The amount of relevant information distributed among students.
4. The ability of students to disagree with each other without creating defensiveness.
5. The ability of students to engage in rational argument.

Cooperative goal structure

Deutsch (1973) emphasizes that the context in which conflicts occur has important effects on whether the conflict turns out to be constructive or destructive. There are two possible contexts for controversy: cooperative and competitive. A cooperative context facilitates constructive controversy and a competitive context promotes destructive controversy in several ways (Johnson & Johnson, 1978, 1986). The following describes prerequisites for constructive controversy:

1. In order for controversy to be constructive, information must be accurately communicated. Communication of information is far more complete, accurate, encouraged, and utilized in a cooperative context than in a competitive context.
2. Constructive controversy requires a supportive climate in which group members feel safe enough to challenge each other's ideas. Cooperation provides a far more supportive climate than competition.
3. In order for controversy to be constructive, it must be valued. Cooperative experiences promote stronger beliefs that controversy is valid and valuable (Johnson, Johnson, & Scott, 1978; Lowry & Johnson, 1981; Smith et al., 1981).
4. Constructive controversy requires dealing with feelings as well as with ideas and information. There is evidence that cooperativeness is positively related and competitiveness is negatively related to the ability to understand what others are feeling and why they are feeling that way.
5. How controversies are defined has a great impact on how constructively they are managed. Within a competitive context, controversies tend to be defined as "win–lose" situations.
6. Constructive controversy requires a recognition of similarities as well as of differences between positions. Group members participating in a controversy within a cooperative context identify more of the similarities between their positions than do members participating in a controversy within a competitive context (Judd, 1978).

Evidence supports the argument that a cooperative context aids constructive controversy. Tjosvold and Johnson (1978) found that a cooperative context promotes more open-minded reception to the opponent's position as well as greater liking for the opponent and the opponent's ideas and arguments than does a competitive context. Van

Blerkom and Tjosvold (1981) found that participants in a controversy within a cooperative context seek out individuals with opposing opinons to test the validity of their ideas and reap the benefits of controversy, while participants in a controversy within a competitive context attempt to strengthen their opinions either by choosing a more competent partner with the same opinion or a less competent discussant with an opposing view.

Tjosvold and Deemer (1980) and Tjosvold (1982) found that controversy within a cooperative context induces (a) feelings of comfort, pleasure, and helpfulness in discussing opposing opinions; (b) expectations of the opponent being helpful; (c) feelings of trust and generosity toward the opponent; (d) uncertainty about the validity of the opponent's position; (e) motivation to hear more about the opponent's arguments; (f) more accurate understanding of the opponent's position; and (g) the reaching of more integrated positions where both one's own and the opponent's conclusions and reasoning are synthesized into a final position. The experimenters also found that controversy within a competitive context promotes closed-minded disinterest and rejection of the opponent's ideas and information. Avoidance of controversy results in little interest in or actual knowledge of opposing ideas and information and the making of a decision that reflects one's own views only.

The results of these experiments indicate that the context within which the controversy takes place should be cooperative, not competitive. There should be no winner and no loser, only a successful, creative, and productive solution to a problem. The emphasis should be on achieving the group's goals, not on dominating the group. Members should not argue over who is "right" and who is "wrong." The issue is not to establish who has the best answer but to make the best group decision possible by exploring different perspectives and synthesizing different information. All members should benefit equally from a constructive controversy. Statements such as "We are all in this together" and "Let's make the best possible decision" should dominate the group, not statements like "I am right and you are wrong." If members begin to compete, the nature of the group's goals, the feeling of mutuality shared by members and the complementary use of members' resources to ensure a collaborative and productive group should be highlighted.

Heterogeneity among members

Differences among students in personality, sex, attitudes, background, social class, reasoning strategies, cognitive perspectives, information, ability levels, and skills lead to diverse organization and processing of information and experiences, which, in turn, begin the cycle of controversy. Such differences have been found to promote learning (Fiedler, Meuwese, & Oonk, 1961; Johnson, 1977; Torrance, 1961; Webb, 1977). Heterogeneity among students leads to potential controversy, and to more diverse interaction patterns and resources for learning. Therefore, the greater the heterogeneity among students, the greater the amount of time spent in argumentation (Nijhof & Kommers, 1982).

Distribution of information

If controversy is to lead to achievement, students must possess information that is relevant to the completion of the tasks on which they are working. The more information students have about an issue, the greater their learning tends to be. Having relevant information available, however, does not mean that it will be utilized. Students need the interpersonal and group skills necessary to ensure that all individuals involved contribute their relevant information and that the information is synthesized effectively.

Skilled disagreement

In order for controversies to be managed constructively, students need a number of collaborative and conflict management skills (Johnson, 1981; Johnson & Johnson, 1982; Johnson, Johnson, Holubec, & Roy, 1984). One of the most important skills is to be able to disagree with each other's ideas while confirming each other's personal competence. Disagreeing with others, and at the same time imputing that they are incompetent, tends to increase their commitment to their own ideas and their rejection of any opposing information and reasoning (Tjosvold, 1974). Disagreeing with others while simultaneously confirming their personal competence, however, results in an individual being better liked and in opponents being less critical of opposing ideas, more interested in learning more about the opposing ideas, and more willing to incorporate opposing information and reasoning into their own analysis of the problem (Tjosvold, Johnson, & Fabrey, 1980; Tjosvold, Johnson, & Lerner, 1981).

Another important set of skills for exchanging information and opinions within a controvresy is perspective taking. More information, both personal and impersonal, is disclosed when one is interacting with a person engaging in perspective-taking behaviors such as paraphrasing to demonstrate understanding and communicating the desire to understand accurately. Perspective-taking ability increases one's capacity to phrase messages so that they are easily understood by others and to accurately comprehend the messages of others. Engaging in perspective taking in conflict results in increased understanding and retention of the opponent's information and perspective (Johnson, 1971). Perspective taking facilitates the achievement of creative, high quality problem solving (Falk & Johnson, 1977; Johnson, 1977). Finally, perspective taking promotes more positive perceptions of the information-exchange process, fellow group members, and the group's work. To obtain a creative synthesis of all positions in a controversy, group members must obtain a clear understanding of all sides of the issues and an accurate assessment of their validity and relative merits. In order to do this fully, they must accurately perceive the frame of reference from which a classmate is viewing and analyzing the situation and problem.

A third set of skills involves the cycle of *differentiation* of positions and their *integration*. Students should ensure that there are several cycles of differentiation (bringing out differences in positions) and integration (combining several positions into one new, creative position). Differentiation must be set in motion before integration is attempted. Differentiation involves seeking out and clarifying differences among members' ideas, information, conclusions, theories, and opinions. It involves highlighting the differences among members' reasoning and seeking to fully understand what the different positions and perspectives are. All different points of view must be presented and explored thoroughly before new, creative solutions are sought.

Integration involves combining the information, reasoning, theories, and conclusions of the various group members so that all of them are satisfied. After it has differentiated positions, the group needs to seek a new, creative position that synthesizes the thinking of all the members. The group should never try to integrate members' positions before adequate differentiation has taken place. The potential for integration is never greater than the adequacy of the differentiation already achieved. Most controversies go through a series of differentiations and integrations.

Rational argument

During a controversy students have to follow the canons of rational argumentation. They should generate ideas, collect and organize relevant information, reason logically, and make tentative conclusions based on current understanding. Members should present their perspective and the rationale for their position as well as their conclusions. At the same time, they should ask other members for proof that their analyses and conclusions are accurate. Members should keep an open mind, changing their conclusions and positions when other members are persuasive and convincing in their presentation of rationale, proof, and logical reasoning. The abilities to gather, organize, and present information, to challenge and disagree, and to engage in rational argument are essential for the constructive management of controversies.

Given the strong empirical validation of the efficacy of the process of controversy, the next step is to operationalize it in ways that teachers can readily use in their classrooms. In the next section we briefly describe our efforts in operationalizing the controversy process and in training teachers to use it in their classrooms.

Applications

For the past several years we have been training teachers within a number of school districts throughout the United States and Canada to use structured controversies. It is now being used in a wide variety of grade levels and subject areas. At the University of Minnesota we are using structured controversies in several courses for engineering students and for undergraduate and graduate education students. We have written a number of curriculum units structured for controversies on issues such as energy production, hazardous waste regulations, acid rain, preservation of wolves, national parks, and other energy and environmental issues. Such structured controversies have been found to be extremely interesting and stimulating for students.

The basic format teachers are trained in using to structure controversies consists of choosing the discussion topic, preparing the instructional materials, preparing students for structured controversy, and conducting the structured controversy. Each of these steps is discussed briefly in the following section.

Choose discussion topic

The choice of a topic for a structured controversy depends on the interest of the instructor and the focus of the course. Criteria for the selection include that at least two well-documented positions can be prepared and that the content be manageable by the students. Most environmental, energy, public policy, social studies, literature, and scientific issues are appropriate.

Prepare instructional materials

The following materials are typically prepared for each position:

1. A clear description of the group's task.
2. A description of the phases of the controversy procedure and the collaborative skills to be utilized during each phase.
3. A definition of the position to be advocated with a summary of the key arguments supporting the position.
4. A set of resource materials (including a bibliography) that support and elaborate upon the arguments for the position to be advocated.

Structure the controversy

The principal prerequisites for a successful structured controversy are a cooperative context, skillful group members, and heterogeneity of group membership. The cooperative context is established by (a) assigning students to groups of four, (b) dividing each group into two pairs who are assigned opposing positions on the topic to be discussed, and (c) requiring each group to reach a consensus on the issue and turn in a group report on which all members will be evaluated. Students will need to be taught the necessary collaborative skills. The skills may be taught simultaneously as students participate in structured controversies. Heterogenity among group members adds to the resources and the perspectives that may be contributed to spirited and constructive argumentation and increases the quality of the structured controversy experience.

Conduct the controversy

The procedure used consists of five basic phases. The specific instructions given to students are as follows:

1. *Plan positions.* Meet with your partner and plan how to argue effectively for your position. Read the materials supporting your position and plan an effective presentation. Make sure you and your partner have mastered the information supporting your

assigned position and ensure that the opposing pair masters the information you will present.

2. *Present positions.* Present your position as a pair. Be forceful and persuasive in presenting your position. Then listen carefully to the opposing position. Take notes so you can clarify anything you do not understand.

3. *Argue the issue.* Argue forcefully and persuasively for your position, presenting as many facts as you can to support your point of view. Critically listen to the opposing pair's position, asking them for the facts that support their point of view. Try to think of opposing arguments. Remember, this is a complex issue and you need to know both sides to write a good report. Work together as a total group to learn all the facts. Make sure you understand the facts that support both points of view.

4. *Practice perspective reversal.* Working as a pair, present the opposing pair's position as if you were they. Be as forceful and persuasive as you can. Add any new facts you know of. Elaborate upon their position.

5. *Reach a decision.* Drop the advocacy of your assigned position. Summarize the best arguments for both points of view. Reach a consensus on a position that is supported by facts. Change your mind only when the facts and rationale clearly indicate that you should do so. Write out the supporting evidence and rationale for the synthesis your group has agreed on.

The discussion rules the students are instructed to follow during the controversy are:

1. I am critical of ideas, not people.
2. I focus on making the best decision possible, not on "winning."
3. I encourage everyone to participate and master all the relevant information.
4. I listen to everyone's ideas, even if I do not agree.
5. I restate what someone has said if it is not clear.
6. I first consider *all* the ideas and facts supporting both sides, and then I try to put them together in a way that makes sense.
7. I try to understand both sides of the issue.
8. I change my mind when the evidence clearly indicates that I should do so.

Some time is spent after the structured controversy is completed in assessing how well the group functioned and how its performance may be enhanced during the next controversy. The specific collaborative skills students need to master are highlighted and discussed.

Summary

If teachers wish to maximize achievement, creativity and continuing motivation to learn, they will be well advised to carefully structure controversies among students. Controversy exists when one student's ideas, information, conclusions, theories, and opinions are incompatible with those of another, and the two seek to reach an agreement. Controversy sparks conceptual conflict within students, creates epistemic curiosity, promotes active representation and elaboration of students' positions and rationales, and results in students reorganizing and reconceptualizing what they know about the issue being studied. Teachers can encourage constructive controversies by structuring learning activities cooperatively, ensuring that the cooperative learning groups are heterogeneous, structuring and conducting the controversy, teaching students the collaborative skills they need to disagree productively, and ensuring that the canons of rational argumentation are followed.

References

Allen, V. (1976). *Children as teachers: Theory and research on tutoring.* New York: Academic Press.
Ames, G., & Murray, F. (1982). When two wrongs make a right: Promoting cognitive change by social conflict. *Developmental Psychology, 18*(6), 894–897.
Anderson, N., & Graesser, C. (1976). An information integration analysis of attitude change in group discussion. *Journal of Personality and Social Psychology, 34*, 210–222.
Annis, L. (1983). The processes and effects of peer tutoring. *Human Learning, 2*, 39–47.
Asch, S. (1952). *Social psychology.* Englewood Cliffs, NJ: Prentice-Hall.
Bahn, C. (1964). The interaction of creativity and social facilitation in creative problem solving. Doctoral dissertation, Columbia University (Ann Arbor, MI: University Microfilms No. 65-7499).
Bargh, J., & Schul, Y. (1980). On the cognitive benefits of teaching. *Journal of Educational Psychology, 72*, 593–604.
Berlyne, D. (1966). Notes on intrinsic motivation and intrinsic reward in relation to instruction. In J. Bruner (Ed.), *Learning about learning* (Cooperative Research Monograph No. 15). Washington, DC: U.S. Department of Health, Education, and Welfare, Office of Education.
Blatt, M. (1969). The effects of classroom discussion upon children's level of moral judgment. Unpublished doctoral dissertation, University of Chicago.
Blatt, M., & Kohlberg, L. (1973). The effects of classroom moral discussion upon children's level of moral judgment. In L. Kohlberg (Ed.), *Collected papers on moral development and moral education.* Harvard University: Moral Education and Research Foundation.

Bolen, L., & Torrance, E. (1976, April). An experimental study of the influence of locus of control, dyadic interaction, and sex on creative thinking. Paper presented at the American Educational Research Association, San Francisco.

Botvin, G., & Murray, F. (1975). The efficacy of peer modeling and social conflict in the acquisition of conservation. *Child Development, 45,* 796–799.

Boulding, E. (1964). Further reflections on conflict management. In R. Kahn & E. Boulding (Eds.), *Power and conflict in organizations* (pp. 146–150). New York: Basic Books.

Burdick, H., & Burnes, A. (1958). A test of "strain toward symmetry" theories. *Journal of Abnormal and Social Psychology, 57,* 367–369.

Collins, B. (1970). *Social psychology.* Reading, MA: Addison-Wesley.

Colson, W. (1968). Self-disclosure as a function of social approval. Unpublished masters thesis, Howard University, Washington, DC.

Crockenberg, S., & Nicolayev, J. (1977, March). Stage transition in moral reasoning as related to conflict experienced in naturalistic settings. Paper presented at the Society for Research in Child Development, New Orleans.

DeCecco, J., & Richards, A. (1974). *Growing pains: Uses of school conflict.* New York: Aberdeen Press.

Deci, E. L. (1975). *Intrinsic motivation.* New York: Plenum Press.

Deutsch, M. (1962). Cooperation and trust: Some theoretical notes. In M. Jones (Ed.), *Nebraska symposium on motivation* (pp. 275–319). Lincoln: University of Nebraska Press.

Deutsch, M. (1973). *The resolution of conflict.* New Haven, CT: Yale University Press.

Doise, W., & Mugny, G. (1979). Individual and collective conflicts of centrations in cognitive development. *European Journal of Social Psychology, 9,* 105–108.

Doise, W., & Mugny, G., & Perret-Clermont, A. (1976). Social interaction and cognitive development: Further evidence. *European Journal of Social Psychology, 6,* 245–247.

Dunnette, M., Campbell, J., & Jaastad, K. (1963). The effect of group participation on brainstorming effectiveness of two industrial samples. *Journal of Applied Psychology, 47,* 30–37.

Falk, D., & Johnson, D. W. (1977). The effects of perspective-taking and ego-centrism on problem solving in heterogeneous and homogeneous groups. *Journal of Social Psychology, 102,* 63–72.

Feffer, M., & Suchotliff, L. (1966). Decentering implications of social interaction. *Journal of Personality and Social Psychology, 4,* 415–422.

Festinger, L., & Maccoby, N. (1964). On resistance to persuasive communications. *Journal of Abnormal and Social Psychology, 68,* 359–366.

Fisher, R. (1969). An each one teach one approach to music notation. *Grade Teacher, 86,* 120.

Flavell, J. (1963). *The developmental psychology of Jean Piaget.* Princeton, NJ: Van Nostrand.

Flavell, J. (1968). *The development of role-taking and communication skills in children.* New York: Wiley.

Gartner, A., Kohler, M., & Reissman, F. (1971). *Children teach children: Learning by teaching.* New York: Harper & Row.

Gerard, H., & Greenbaum, C. (1962). Attitudes toward an agent of uncertainty reduction. *Journal of Personality, 30,* 485–495.

Glidewell, J. (1953). Group emotionality and production. Unpublished doctoral dissertation, University of Chicago.

Hall, J., & Williams, M. (1966). A comparison of decision-making performance in established and ad hoc groups. *Journal of Personality and Social Psychology, 3,* 214–222.

Hall, J., & Williams, M. (1970). Group dynamics training and improved decision making. *Journal of Applied Behavioral Science, 6,* 39–68.

Hoffman, L., Harburg, E., & Maier, N. (1962). Differences and disagreements as factors in creative problem solving. *Journal of Abnormal and Social Psychology, 64,* 206–214.

Hoffman, L., & Maier, N. (1961). Sex differences, sex composition, and group problem solving. *Journal of Abnormal and Social Psychology, 63,* 453–456.

Hogan, R., & Henley, N. (1970). *A test of the empathy-effective communication hypothesis.* (Report No. 84). Baltimore, MD: Johns Hopkins University, Center for Social Organization of Schools.

Hunt, J. (1964). Introduction: Revisiting Montessori. In M. Montessori (Ed.), *The Montessori method.* New York: Schocken Books.

Inagaki, K. (1981). Facilitation of knowledge integration through classroom discussion. *Quarterly Newsletter of the Laboratory of Comparative Human Cognition, 3,* 26–28.

Inagaki, K., & Hatano, G. (1968). Motivational influences on epistemic observation. *Japanese Journal of Educational Psychology, 16,* 221–228.

Inagaki, K., & Hatano, G. (1977). Application of cognitive motivation and its effects on epistemic observation. *American Educational Research Journal, 14,* 485–491.

Inhelder, B., & Sinclair, H. (1969). Learning cognitive structures. In P. H. Mussen, J. Langer, & M. Covington (Eds.), *Trends and issues in development psychology* (pp. 2–21). New York: Holt, Rinehart & Winston.

Johnson, D. W. (1971). Students against the school establishment: Crisis intervention in school conflicts and organization change. *Journal of School Psychology, 9,* 84–92.

Johnson, D. W. (1977). Distribution and exchange of information in problem-solving dyads. *Communication Research, 4,* 283–298.

Johnson, D. W. (1979). *Educational psychology.* Englewood Cliffs, NJ: Prentice-Hall.

Johnson, D. W. (1980). Group processes: Influences of student–student interaction on school outcomes. In J. McMillan (Ed.), *The social psychology of school learning* (pp. 123–168). New York: Academic Press.

Johnson, D. W. (1981). *Reaching out: Interpersonal effectiveness and self-actualization* (2nd ed.). Englewood Cliffs, NJ: Prentice-Hall.

Johnson, D. W., & Johnson, R. (1978). Cooperative, competitive, and individualistic learning. *Journal of Research and Development in Education, 12,* 3–15.

Johnson, D. W., & Johnson, R. (1979). Conflict in the classroom: Controversy and learning. *Review of Educational Research, 49,* 51–61.

Johnson, D. W., & Johnson, R. (1982). *Joining together: Group theory and group skills* (2nd ed.). Englewood Cliffs, NJ: Prentice-Hall.

Johnson, D. W., & Johnson, R. (1983). The socialization and achievement crises: Are cooperative learning experiences the solution? In L. Bickman (Ed.), *Applied Social Psychology Annual 4.* (Pp. 119–164) Beverly Hills, CA: Sage.

Johnson, D. W., & Johnson, R. (1985). Classroom conflict: Controversy vs. debate in learning groups. *American Educational Research Journal, 22,* 237–256.

Johnson, D. W., & Johnson, R. (1986). *Learning together and alone: Cooperation, competition, and individualization,* (2nd ed.). Englewood Cliffs, NJ: Prentice-Hall.

Johnson, D. W., Johnson, R. T., Holubec, E., & Roy, P. (1984). *Circles of learning: Cooperation in the classroom.* Alexandria, VA: Association for Supervision and Curriculum Development.

Johnson, D. W., Johnson R., Pierson, W., & Lyons, V. (In press). Controversy versus concurrence seeking in multi-grade and single-grade learning groups. *Journal of Research in Science Teaching.*

Johnson, D. W., Johnson, R., & Scott, L. (1978). The effects of cooperative and indi-

228   D. W. JOHNSON, R. T. JOHNSON, AND K. A. SMITH

vidualized instruction on student attitudes and achievement. *Journal of Social Psychology, 104*, 207–216.

Johnson, D. W., Johnson, R., & Tiffany, M. (1984). Structuring academic conflicts between majority and minority students: Hindrance or help to integration. *Contemporary Educational Psychology, 9*, 61–73.

Johnson, R., Brooker, C., Stutzman, J., Hultman, D., & Johnson, D. W. (1985). The effects of controversy, concurrence seeking, and individualistic learning on achievement and attitude change. *Journal of Research in Science Teaching, 22*, 197–205.

Judd, C. (1978). Cognitive effects of attitude conflict resolution.*Conflict Resolution, 22*, 483–498.

Kaplan, M. (1977). Discussion polarization effects in a modern jury decision paradigm: Informational influences. *Sociometry, 40*, 262–271.

Kaplan, M. & Miller, C. (1977). Judgments and group discussion: Effect of presentation and memory factors on polarization. *Sociometry, 40*, 337–343.

Keasey, C. (1973). Experimentally induced changes in moral opinions and reasoning. *Journal of Personality and Social Psychology, 26*, 30–38.

Kleinhesselink, R., & Edwards, R. (1975). Seeking and avoiding belief-discrepant information as a function of its perceived refutability. *Journal of Personality and Social Psychology, 31*, 787–790.

Knight-Arest, I., & Reid, D. (1978, May). Peer interaction as a catalyst for conservation acquisition in normal and learning-disabled children. Paper presented at the Eighth Annual Symposium of the Jean Piaget Society, Philadelphia.

Kohlberg, L. (1969). Stage and sequence: The cognitive-developmental approach to socialization. In D. A. Goslin (Ed.), *Handbook of socialization theory and research* (pp. 347–480). Chicago: Rand McNally.

Kuhn, D., Langer, J., Kohlberg, L., & Haan, N. S. (1977). The development of formal operations in logical and moral judgment. *Genetic Psychological Monographs, 55*, 97–188.

Kurdek, L. (In press). Relationship between cognitive perspective-taking and teachers' rating of children's classroom behavior in grades one through four. *Journal of Genetic Psychology*.

LeFurgy, W., & Woloshin, G. (1969) Immediate and long-term effects of experimentally induced social influence in the modification of adolescents' moral judgments. *Journal of Personality and Social Psychology, 12*, 104–110.

Lowin, A. (1969). Further evidence for an approach-avoidance interpretation of selective exposure. *Journal of Experimental Social Psychology, 5*, 265–271.

Lowry, N., & Johnson, D. W. (1981). Effects of controversy on epistemic curiosity, achievement, and attitudes. *Journal of Social Psychology, 115*, 31–43.

Maier, N., & Hoffman, L. (1964). Financial incentives and group decision in motivating change. *Journal of Social Psychology, 64*, 369–378.

Maier, N., & Solem, A. (1952). The contributions of a discussion leader to the quality of group thinking: The effective use of minority opinions. *Human Relations, 5*, 277–288.

Maitland, D., & Goldman, J. (1974). Moral judgment as a function of peer group interaction. *Journal of Personality and Social Psychology, 30*, 699–704.

Miller, S. A., & Brownell, C. A. (1975). Peers, persuasion, and Piaget: Dyadic interaction between conservers and nonconservers. *Child Development, 46*, 992–997.

Mugny, G., & Doise, W. (1978). Socio-cognitive conflict and structure of individual and collective performances. *European Journal of Social Psychology, 8*, 181–192.

Murray, F. (1972). Acquisition of conservation through social interaction. *Development of Psychology, 6*, 1–6

Murray, F. (1983). Cognitive benefits of teaching on the teacher. Paper presented at American Educational Research Association Annual Meeting, Montreal, Quebec.

Murray, F., Ames, G., & Botvin, G. (1977). Acquisition of conservation through cognitive dissonance. *Journal of Educational Psychology, 69*, 519–527.

Nel, E., Helmreich, R., & Aronson, E. (1969). Opinion change in the advocate as a function of the persuasibility of his audience: A clarification of the meaning of dissonance. *Journal of Personality and Social Psychology, 12*, 117–124.

Nijhof, W., & Kommers, P. (1982, July). Analysis of cooperation in relation to cognitive controversy. Paper presented at Second International Conference on Cooperation in Education, Provo, UT.

Noonan-Wagner, M. P. (1975). Intimacy of self-disclosure and response processes as factors affecting the development of interpersonal relationships. Unpublished doctoral dissertation. University of Minnesota.

Pellegrini, A. (1984). Identifying causal elements in the thematic-fantasy play paradigm. *American Educational Research Journal, 21*, 691–701.

Perret-Clermont, A. (1980). *Social interaction and cognitive development in children*. London: Academic Press.

Peters, R., & Torrance, E. (1972). Dyadic interaction of preschool children and performance on a construction task. *Psychological Reports, 30*, 747–750.

Piaget, J. (1948). *The moral judgment of the child* (2nd Ed.). Glencoe, IL: Free Press.

Piaget, J. (1950). *The psychology of intelligence*. New York: Harcourt.

Rapoport, A. (1960). *Fights, games and debates*. Ann Arbor: University of Michigan Press.

Rest, J., Turiel, E., & Kohlberg, L. (1969). Relations between level of moral judgment and preference and comprehension of the moral judgment of others. *Journal of Personality, 37*, 225–252.

Rogers, C. (1970). Towards a theory of creativity. In P. Vernon (Ed.), *Readings in creativity*. London: Penguin.

Sarbin, T. (1976). Cross-age tutoring and social identity. In V. Allen (Ed.), *Children as teachers: Theory and research on tutoring*. New York: Academic Press.

Sermet, V., & Smyth, M. (1973). Content analysis of verbal communication in the development of a relationship: Conditions influencing self-disclosure. *Journal of Personality and Social Psychology, 26*, 332–346.

Sigel, I. E., & Hooper, F. H. (Eds.) (1968). *Logical thinking in children: Research based on Piaget's theory*. New York: Holt, Rinehart and Winston.

Silverman, I. W., & Geiringer, E. (1973). Dyadic interaction and conservation induction: A test of Piaget's equilibration model. *Child Development, 44*, 815–820.

Silverman, I. W., & Stone, J. M. (1972). Modifying cognitive functioning through participation in a problem-solving group. *Journal of Educational Psychology, 63*, 603–608.

Sinclair, H. (1969). Developmental psycho-linguistics. In D. Elkind & J. H. Flavell (Eds.), *Studies in cognitive development: Essays in honor of Jean Piaget* (pp. 315–336). New York: Oxford University Press.

Smedslund, J. (1961a). The acquisition of conservation of substance and weight in children: II. External reinforcement of conservation and weight and of the operations of addition and subtraction. *Scandinavian Journal of Psychology, 2*, 71–84.

Smedslund, J. (1961b). The acquisition of conservation of substance and weight in children: III. Extinction of conservation of weight acquired 'normally' and by means of empirical controls on a balance. *Scandinavian Journal of Psychology, 2*, 85–87.

Smith, K., Johnson, D. W., & Johnson, R. (1981). Can conflict be constructive? Controversy versus concurrence seeking in learning groups. *Journal of Educational Psychology, 73*, 651–663.

Smith, K., Johnson, D. W., & Johnson, R. (1982). Effects of cooperative and individualistic instruction on the achievement of handicapped, regular, and gifted students. *Journal of Social Psychology, 116*, 277–283.

Smith, K. A., Johnson, D. W., & Johnson, R. (1984). Effects of controversy on learning in cooperative groups. *Journal of Social Psychology, 122*, 199–209.

Taylor, D. A., Altman, I., & Sorrentino, R. (1969). Interpersonal exchange as a function of rewards and costs and situational factors: Expectancy confirmation-disconfirmation. *Journal of Experimental Social Psychology, 5*, 324–339.

Tjosvold, D. (1974). Threat as a low-power person's strategy in bargaining: Social face and tangible outcomes. *International Journal of Group Tensions, 4*, 494–510.

Tjosvold, D. (1982). Effects on approach to controversy on superiors' incorporation of subordinates' information in decision-making. *Journal of Applied Psychology, 67*, 189–193.

Tjosvold, D., & Deemer, D. (1980). Effects of controversy within a cooperative or competitive context on organizational decision-making. *Journal of Applied Psychology, 65*, 590–595.

Tjosvold, D., & Johnson, D. W. (1977). The effects of controversy on cognitive perspective-taking. *Journal of Educational Psychology, 69*, 679–685.

Tjosvold, D., & Johnson, D. W. (1978). Controversy within a cooperative or competitive context and cognitive perspective-taking. *Contemporary Educational Psychology, 3*, 376–386.

Tjosvold, D., Johnson, D. W., & Fabrey, L. (1980). The effects of controversy and defensiveness on cognitive perspective-taking. *Psychological Reports, 47*, 1043–1053.

Tjosvold, D., Johnson, D. W., & Lerner, J. (1981). Effects of affirmation of one's competence, personal acceptance, and disconfirmation of one's competence on incorporation of opposing information on problem-solving situations. *Journal of Social Psychology, 114*, 103–110.

Torrance, E. (1961). Can grouping control social stress in creative activity? *Elementary School Journal, 62*, 139–145.

Torrance, E. (1970). Influence of dyadic interaction on creative functioning. *Psychological Reports, 26*, 391–394.

Torrance, E. (1971). Stimulation, enjoyment, and originality in dyadic creativity. *Journal of Educational Psychology, 62*, 45–48.

Torrance, E. (1973, February). Dyadic interaction in creative thinking and problem solving. Paper presented at American Educational Research Association annual meeting, New Orleans.

Triandis, H., Bass, A., Ewen, R., & Midesele, E. (1963). Teaching creativity as a function of the creativity of the members. *Journal of Applied Psychology, 47*, 104–110.

Turiel, E. (1966). An experimental test of the sequentiality of development stages in the child's moral judgment. *Journal of Personality and Social Psychology, 3*, 611–618.

Turiel, E. (1973). Stage transition in moral development. In R. Travers (Ed.), *Second handbook of research on teaching* (pp. 732–758). Chicago: Rand McNally.

Van Blerkom, M., & Tjosvold, D. (1981). The effects of social context on engaging in controversy. *Journal of Psychology, 107*, 141–145.

Vinokur, A., & Burnstein, E. (1974). Effects of partially shared persuasive arguments on group-induced shifts. *Journal of Personality and Social Psychology, 29*, 305–315.

Wallach, L., & Sprott, R. (1964). Inducing number conservation in children. *Child Development, 35*, 1057–1071.

Wallach, L., Wall, A. J., & Anderson, L. (1967). Number conservation: The roles of reversibility, addition-subtraction, and misleading perceptual cues. *Child Development, 38*, 425–442.

Webb, N. (1977). Learning in individual and small group settings. (Tech. Rep. No. 7). Stanford, CA: Stanford University, School of Education, Aptitude Research Project.

Wohlwill, J. F., & Lowe, R. C. (1962). Experimental analysis of the development of the conservation of number. *Child Development, 33*, 153–167.

Worchel, P., & McCormick, B. (1963). Self-concept and dissonance reduction. *Journal of Personality, 31*, 589–599.

Part IV

The social aspects of motivation

10   Effective motivation: the contribution of the learning environment

Carole Ames

Recent research on student motivation has focused on a wide variety of cognitive-based processes, including, for example, attributions, personal efficacy, metacognitive processes, and self-evaluations. This research is distinguished from alternative conceptions of motivation such as general personality traits or dispositions, arousal level, or engaged time, by its emphasis on the specific cognitive processes in achievement motivation. These cognitive–motivational processes are not only affected by certain learning experiences, but they also influence subsequent achievement-directed behavior. The purpose of this chapter is to examine how some of these motivational processes are influenced by the context of one's learning experience. Context here refers to the structure of the learning situation. Traditionally, the structure has referred to the type of goal or reward structure (e.g., competitive, cooperative, or individualistic), but other dimensions, some broader by definition (e.g., extent of social comparison) and some more focused (e.g., student autonomy), have also emerged as ways to conceptualize the context or structure of classroom learning experiences.

While there is a long tradition of research on the effects of classroom structure, much of this research has focused exclusively on achievement outcomes (Johnson et al., 1981). Only recently has the research literature begun to seriously address the development of motivational processes within different achievement contexts. This research literature indicates that certain cognitive–motivational processes are affected, and perhaps socialized, by the structure of classroom learning experiences. In this chapter, I will first present a framework for conceptualizing motivational processes and then examine the influence of the classroom learning environment on these processes, identifying some problems in the learning environment research, and suggesting a framework for future inquiry. Throughout this discussion, certain author biases may be noted, and these should be shared with the reader at the outset as follows: (a)

235

motivational processes are one of the central concerns in discussions of important educational outcomes or products, (b) when motivation is construed as a set of dispositions, the impact of specific educational experiences is likely to be underestimated, (c) students experience success and failure in the context of certain learning goals, evaluational systems, and so forth, and these contextual factors serve to shape students' motivation and opportunities to become involved in their own learning, and (d) it is time to move away from using achievement as the singular measure for evaluating everything that happens in the classroom.

A concept of effective motivation

Motivation can be viewed as *goal-directed activity* that involves different ways of thinking. As described by Corno and Mandinach (1983), two students may be equally motivated to learn but may differ in how they think about themselves, how they think about the task, and how they think about the goal. Within this perspective, motivation can be conceptualized as a qualitative, rather than quantitative, construct (Ames & Ames, 1984). As a quantitative variable, motivation is equated with a conceptualization of *activity* that involves energy and persistence. From a qualitative perspective, however, activity involves specific cognitive–mediational processes, for example, information processing, metacognitive processes, and attributions. Thus, positive motivation is more than the demonstration of effortful activity or even time spent on a task: It is reflected in how students think about themselves, the task, and their performance.

The *goal* of one's activity can also be qualitatively conceived in that goals have different meanings for different individuals. For example, Nicholls (1981) has theorized that students have different reasons for learning: to gain ability versus to demonstrate ability. The difference here is that learning for some students is valued in itself, that is, the process is valued; for other students, learning may be valued only as a means to show one's capabilities or to achieve some extrinsic goal. Further, the meaning of a goal can differ as a function of the context or setting. Clinkenbeard (1983), for example, found that students reported different reasons for being satisfied with their success in competitive and individualistic settings. Competitors derived satisfaction from having done the best project, but for the students in the individualistic setting, feelings of satisfaction were more related to "learning about the topic." Thus, within a quantitative perspective, goal-directed activity is easily translated into time-on-task (academic engaged time), resulting in the depiction of students being "highly motivated" versus "not motivated." Within a qualitative perspective, however, goal-directed activity refers to the content of students' thoughts. Tasks, as well as situations, can be described according to the thought processes that are elicited. Here we do not ask how we can get students *more* motivated, instead we ask questions such as, why students process or attend to different sources of information, why certain goals are valued over others, what metacognitive processes are used, and how students evaluate and attribute their performance in different achievement contexts.

Effectiveness is a term that is currently being used to label excellent schools, excellent teachers, excellent instructional practices, and excellence or effectiveness is typically demonstrated by looking at student achievement test scores as the outcome. Declines or increases in student achievement are taken as evidence for the effectiveness of the educational system. The "condition" of schooling is inferred from local, state, and national norms on standardized achievement tests. Effectiveness, however, is more than what is assessed on standardized tests. In light of other important educational outcomes, effectiveness can also be evidenced by the *quality* of task engagement, including those cognitive motivational processes that are characteristic of autonomous, self-directed learners. A study by Pascarella et al. (1981) shows that these motivational processes cannot always be inferred from successful achievement. The study found that although teacher control (or decreased student choice) was positively related to science achievement in secondary school, it was also negatively related to behavioral indicators of continuing motivation. In other words, some factors that contribute to higher achievement may not contribute to motivational processes that are necessary for outcomes such as continuing motivation, positive self-worth, and self-regulated learning.

Elsewhere, an effective learner has been described as one who has certain cognitive skills (Corno & Mandinach, 1983; Marx, 1984). This learner not only is equipped with more information and knowledge but also has better acquisition skills and processing strategies. It is proposed here that an effective learner also has certain cognitive–motivational skills, related to the learner's efficacy, attributions, and self-regulatory processes. To suggest that these cognitive processes are skills, rather than dispositions, orientations, or traits is consistent with research that has shown that these cognitions can be acquired and modified through training (Dweck, 1975; Schunk, 1983; Andrews & Debus, 1978) just as other cognitive and social skills. The effective learner, thus, needs certain cognitive–motivational skills in the learning situation. Perhaps when we begin to think of these processes as skills, the motivation of the learner will come to be viewed as a shared responsibility (between teacher and learner), rather than as a responsibility (or fault) of the learner. Effectiveness of the learner must be examined in relation to those beliefs, perceptions, interpretations, and expectations that enable learners to become involved, independent, and confident in their own learning. Effectiveness of classrooms must be examined in relation to those practices which serve to develop, enhance, and elicit these specific cognitive–motivational processes.

The context of motivation

Let me now turn to examining the context of motivation, that is, the context in which learning occurs, namely, the classroom. Classrooms depict academic work settings where the tasks are cognitive and compulsory. These academic tasks are embedded within an organizational structure that conveys explicit information about what goals are to be achieved and the evaluative system defining successful goal accomplishment, as well as implicit information about what are valued student characteristics and how students are to relate to each other and to the task. For example, in a competitive structure, rewards are scarce or few and reserved for only the best or highest performers. The goal is to be a winner, to outperform other students, and students are evaluated using social comparative criteria. Ability is a valued characteristic (Covington & Beery, 1976; Ames & Ames, 1984); the capable students are more assured of success, and failure is certain for those who lack it. In competitive situations, students tend to be more concerned about their own ability than about how to do the task (Ames, 1984), and they engage in considerable "besting" behaviors (Pepitone, 1980) as well as other negative social behaviors. The organizational structure of the classroom, therefore, impacts a range of teacher–student, student–task, and student–student relations.

Research on the classroom learning environment has had a long and active history, involved a variety of foci (e.g., type of goal structures, grouping practices, and source of control), and has involved both observational and experimental (or quasi-experimental) approaches. The observational approach has studied the classroom as it appears to the external observer. Through coding and tabulating the incidence of specific instructional practices or events by observers, classrooms have been characterized as involving more teacher talk than student talk, or as being more management oriented than instruction oriented, or as more teacher centered than student centered.

Recent research on classroom processes, however, points to several problems that are indigenous to an observational approach. First, although external observers are viewed by many as providing an objective and accurate description of the classroom, only the student can provide a perspective of the classroom as it is experienced by him or her (Moos, 1980). Student perceptions give us a phenomenological perspective of the day-to-day events of the classroom. There is now substantial research that shows that observers and students do differ in their perceptions of classroom events (Weinstein et al., 1982; Weinstein & Middlestat, 1979), and it is the student perceptions which appear to correlate more with student achievement (Stayrook, Corno, & Winne, 1978).

Also imbedded in observational approaches is the implicit assumption that frequent behaviors are significant behaviors. Taking teacher praise as an example, Brophy (1981), has argued that it is not the frequency of teacher praise that is important, but instead, it is the context of the feedback and how it is interpreted by the student. Praise can be perceived as providing different information, depending upon the recipient, the behavior, and the context. Brophy further suggests that the frequency of praise per se is probably less important than the specificity and contingency of its use in the classroom (Brophy, 1981, p. 21). Thus, observational approaches tend to overlook the critical role of perceptual and interpretive processes that mediate instruction and learning outcomes.

More experimental-based approaches to studying classroom learning environments have followed the general paradigm of manipulating the organizational structure of the classroom and then measuring changes in student achievement or general psychosocial outcomes such as self-esteem. For example, some classrooms may use a team or cooperative approach when others use a traditional or alternative individual approach, and differences in resulting student achievement and attitudes are the outcome measures (see Johnson & Johnson, this volume; and Slavin, this volume, for reviews). Unfortunately, this approach has almost uniformly followed a process–product paradigm (Winne, 1984). Because student achievement is typically the sole dependent measure, it tells us little about the "why" or the reason for the effects. Attempts to provide reasons have typically resulted in discussions of hypothetical mediating processes. This approach has led to an advocacy of certain types of structures, particularly cooperative goal structures. Cooperative structures have been related to higher achievement and more positive attitudes toward oneself, toward the school, and toward peers (e.g., Johnson et al.,

1981; Johnson & Johnson, 1974; Slavin, 1977). The missing link is an understanding of the cognitive processes that mediate these outcomes: what kinds of operations are students engaged in, what is the direction or form of student thinking as well as their beliefs about the causes of success and failure. Thus, in spite of the hundreds of research studies on classroom learning environments, we still have little understanding of why learning does or does not occur, why students are or are not involved, or what students are thinking in different types of classroom environments.

To a great extent, research on classroom learning environments has also focused on group effects, that is, the average performance of the group is taken as the criterion measure. Yet, the effects of classroom experiences are mediated by student perceptions and interpretations, and these cognitive processes may also differ according to the student's sex (Dweck et al., 1978), achievement history (Corno & Mandinach, 1983; Peterson et al., 1982), personality attributes (Ames, 1978), and age (Eccles, Midgley, & Adler, 1984). Similarly, when student reports have been used to measure classroom environment, the group average is used to depict the perceived environment. Moos and Moos (1978) provide the following rationale: "the consensus of individuals characterizing an environment constitutes a measure of the social climate of that environment" (p. 265). However, as argued by Weinstein and Marshall (1984) and others (Peterson et al., 1982), the effects of school experiences cannot be determined solely by looking at the students within a classroom as a group. Students are active participants and the effects of classroom environments as well as their perceptions of these environments depend on the individual student's history. To understand the meaning of different learning environments, we need to ask questions about students' perceptions and thought processes. How do children learn about their own ability in the context of different learning environments? How do they evaluate their performance? How can we describe the form of student task engagement?

The classroom learning environment

Children's cognitive–motivational processes have been shown to differ as a function of development (Nicholls & Jagacinski, 1983), aptitude (Corno & Mandinach, 1983), individual dispositions (Dweck, 1975), and, more recently, classroom environment. It is the influence of the classroom learning environment on these processes that is the focus of the remainder of this chapter. Unlike research which has studied linkages between classroom processes and student achievement, the focus here is on that research that has studied teacher and student perceptions, attributions, and self-regulating processes. The next sections highlight some of the recent research which has looked at the relationship between classroom learning environment and motivated cognitions.

Teacher perceptions and beliefs

Before we turn to the relevant research on students, let us first briefly look at how the classroom structure influences teacher beliefs and behavior. There are two reciprocal linkages that should be noted: (a) teacher values and beliefs influence the type of structure he or she creates in the classroom and (b) the structure itself influences teacher perceptions. An example adopted from Doyle (1984) may serve to illustrate this reciprocal process. A teacher who values work and efficiency may create an environment organized around familiar tasks, work patterns, and routines; and such an organization may, in turn, cause the teacher to proceed in a regimental type of instruction with high surveillance of student activity and low expectations for student performance.

There is research evidence supporting both of these linkages. Swann and Snyder (1980), for example, found that teacher beliefs about the nature of ability influenced their selection of teaching strategies. Teachers who held an extrinsic theory on the development of student ability (i.e., ability depends on external teaching actions) utilized a more competitive structure involving strategies that would confirm their low expectation of low ability students. On the other hand, teachers who had a more intrinsic view (i.e., ability develops through personal understanding) tended to use strategies that were aimed at enhancing the performance of low ability students. Evidence for the second linkage comes from a study by Ames and McKelvie (1982) in which teachers were given vignettes describing hypothetical students in competitively or cooperatively structured classrooms. They were then asked to evaluate the performance of certain high and low achieving students in each structure. Evaluations of the high and low achievers were significantly more discrepant for the competitive rather than the cooperative situation. That is, the difference between the positive evaluation of the high performer and the negative evaluation of the lower performer was greater in the competitive situation. Teacher perceptions, therefore, were influenced by the context of the students' performances.

The findings of these two studies taken together show how easily a negative motivational cycle can develop in a competitive environment. Differential expectations are likely to be held by the teacher, communicated to students, and then internalized by students. Thus, through the teachers' eyes, a competitive structure can serve to reinforce an ability stratification system in the classroom. That teachers differentially value student achievement is well documented (Harari & Covington, 1981; Weiner & Kukla, 1970), but finding that the valuation of student achievement is related to teacher beliefs and classroom structure suggests that the classroom learning environment may serve to minimize or maximize teacher expectation effects in the classroom.

Student perceptions of teacher behavior

Recent studies on teacher expectancy have shown that the potential effects of differential teacher treatment are mediated by student perceptions. When Weinstein et al. (1982) asked elementary school children to rate how often specific teacher behaviors were accorded to high and low achieving students, teacher treatment as it was perceived by students was different for high and low achievers. High achievers were seen as receiving more opportunities and higher expectations than low achievers; whereas, low achievers were seen as targets of more teacher direction and vigilance. What was particularly interesting and relevant here was their analysis across different types of classrooms.

Based on principal and teacher reports, they had initially classified the classrooms as either open or traditional; however, differential treatment to high and low achievers was reported equally in both types of classrooms. Nevertheless, there was substantial variation in the extent of perceived differential treatment across classrooms; and through a post hoc analysis of student interviews, they found that students in those classrooms with high differential treatment reported the occurrence of more public communication about ability differences. Public social comparison proved to be a factor that effectively distinguished classrooms with high versus low differential treatment. When social comparison was public, students perceived differential expectations. Thus, there is evidence that the classroom environment influences how students perceive teachers as well as how teachers perceive students; and competition or social comparison appears to be a factor that makes differences among students salient to both the teacher and students themselves.

Student self-perceptions of ability

Within the American culture, ability is a highly valued commodity and one need only look at the extent of competition to realize the emphasis placed on differentiating the more able from the less able. According to the self-worth theory of achievement motivation (Covington & Beery, 1976), student achievement behavior is directed toward maintaining a positive self-concept of ability, and one's self-worth is dependent upon the circumstances of success and failure. To succeed without trying is certain evidence of one's ability, but to have tried and then to have failed negatively impacts one's self-concept of ability. Thus, students often engage in a variety of tactics (e.g., not trying, procrastinating) to avoid the negative implications of failure.

In the self-worth theory, self-perceptions of one's ability are the primary ingredient in achievement-motivated behavior (Covington & Omelich, 1981). Self-efficacy theory also underscores the importance of ability in student achievement behaviors (Schunk, 1984). Self-efficacy refers to a student's belief that he or she has the ability to perform and this belief influences effort expenditure, persistence, and actual performance. Self-efficacy refers to the student's belief about his or her ability rather than some objective evidence of ability. From both self-worth and self-efficacy perspectives, a student's self-concept of ability influences achievement behavior; thus, the formation of a positive self-concept of ability should be of central concern to educators.

There are two trends in the research literature that concern the relationship between classroom structure and ability perceptions: first, the degree to which ability perceptions become shared and solidified, and second, the degree to which ability perceptions of high and low achievers become dichotomized. Related to the first trend is the work of Rosenholtz and her colleagues. In one study, Rosenholtz and Wilson (1980) showed that classroom structure was related to perceptions of ability differentiation in the classroom, that is, the degree to which self-perceptions of ability are shared by others. In this study, they first identified a cluster of characteristics that differentiated what they labeled as high versus low resolution classrooms. (In later work, uni- versus multidimensional replaced the labels of high versus low resolution, respectively.) Compared to low resolution classrooms, teachers in high resolution classrooms were found to use more whole-class instruction, provide fewer opportunities for students to make choices and decisions regarding their academic work, and to make more frequent evaluations based on social comparative criteria. What they found was a higher degree of general agreement about an individual's academic ranking in the high than in the low resolution classrooms. There emerged a general consensus as to who were the bright students and not-so-bright students. Not only did students agree on the ranking of others, they agreed with others about their own ranking. Similarly, Filby and Barnett (1982) have found greater agreement about who are the better readers in unidimensional, than multidimensional-type classrooms.

Social comparison information has also proved to be a salient factor influencing students' thoughts when they are in achievement settings (Ames, Ames, & Felker, 1977; Ames, 1984). In one study (Ames, 1984), elementary school-age children were placed in competitive and individualistic performance situations and were asked to report what they were thinking after a particular task performance on which they were either successful (or won) or unsuccessful (or lost). The students were given a questionnaire that contained a variety of statements and asked to identify which statements reflected what they were thinking. Children who were competing selected more ability-related statements (e.g., "I was smart"; "I was not smart.") than did children who were not competing. Children in the individualistic setting reported more effort ("I tried hard"; "I need to work harder.") and strategy-related ("I need to make a plan....") thoughts. Thus, when social comparison was made salient, children became focused on their ability and engaged in substantial self-evaluations of their own ability. That social comparison makes ability a salient factor for evaluation has been discussed extensively elsewhere (Ames & Ames, 1984; Blumenfeld et al. 1982). The unfortunate circumstance that one's own ability is the target of evaluation in competitive situations is compounded by the likelihood that these perceptions are likely to become stable over time (Nicholls, 1979b) as well as shared by both peers and teachers (Nicholls, 1979a; Stipek & Hoffman, 1980; Stipek, 1984).

The structure of the classroom can also contribute to a perception of differences among students. In a subsequent analysis of the data reported in Rosenholtz and Wilson (1980), Rosenholtz and Rosenholtz (1981) also found that students' views of their own and their classmates' ability were more dichotomized in unidimensional than multidimensional classrooms. Oren (1983) has similarly found that internal attributions (which include the ability factor) of high and low achievers are more polarized in classrooms that emphasize comparative achievement in contrast to classrooms where the evaluation system is individualized (i.e., related to past performance, student effort, and progress). In one of our studies

(Ames & Felker, 1979), we asked children in grades one through six to make certain evaluations of hypothetical children described in brief vignettes. In each vignette, two hypothetical children were described as performing in a competitive, cooperative, or individualistic setting, one as a high achiever and one as a low achiever. The findings showed that children's evaluations of the high and low achievers' ability were more discrepant in competitive and individualistic settings than in the cooperative setting. Here, both the competitive and individualistic situations involved comparative criteria: social comparison in the competitive condition and normative comparison (external norms) in the individualistic condition.

In another study (Ames et al., 1977), children actually performed in a competitive or noncompetitive performance setting. Competing children were admonished to try to win, to see who could solve more puzzles. In the noncompetitive condition, children performed alongside a partner and were rewarded for trying rather than outperforming their partner. The actual performance of the children was manipulated so that each situation involved a high performing child and a low performing child. When children were asked to evaluate themselves and their partner on a number of dimensions, the findings showed that self–other perceptions were more discrepant in the competitive setting. Using a similar paradigm in a subsequent study (Ames, 1981) comparing competitive and cooperative settings, perceptions of self–other ability differences were again greater in the competitive setting. Although there were real differences in the performance level of the high and low achievers in each condition of both studies, a perception of ability differences emerged only in the competitive conditions.

Explicit social and normative comparisons convey much information about children's ability such that performance and ability evaluations become more correlated than in classrooms where students are focused on evaluating their own and others' ability. Thus, in classrooms where social comparison is emphasized, the perceived distribution of ability is likely to become hierarchical. Nicholls (1979b) suggests that a perceived ability differentiation produces an inequality of motivation in that the motivation of the high performers derives from the presence of low performers. Nicholls further suggests (Nicholls & Jagacinski, 1983) that a high self-concept of ability may be necessary for optimal achievement in competitively structured situations. In other words, differential self-perceptions of ability lead to effective and ineffective achievement behaviors, establishing and maintaining an hierarchical stratification of achievement. The implication here is that self-perceptions of ability are probably more variable among students in competitive structures. Because these beliefs are important mediators of achievement behavior, differential achievement is the probable result.

Classroom structure and attributions

The study of achievement-related attributions tells us how students (or teachers) assess or interpret the causes of success and failure. Some achievement outcomes require attributional explanation more than others and some are more difficult to explain than others. Nevertheless, attributional explanation is a rational attempt to understand what has happened and has significant consequences for one's subsequent achievement behavior and emotional well-being. Achievement outcomes can be attributed to a wide range of factors (e.g., ability, effort, task, help from others), although the differentiation of ability and effort has received the most attention and perhaps has the greatest implication for one's self-evaluation and academic performance. Both ability and effort describe characteristics of the person (i.e., they are internal as opposed to externally located factors), but they differ in perceived stability and controllability. Ability is generally perceived (except by very young children) as an innate factor that cannot be enhanced. Effort, however, is generally perceived as more subject to one's volition. If this differentiation is important, we can ask what difference it makes that some students believe they failed because they lack ability while others believe they didn't try hard enough. Students who have a tendency to attribute failure to lack of effort have been labeled as success or mastery oriented while those who ascribe failure to lack of ability have been labeled failure-avoiding or helpless (Covington & Beery, 1976; Diener & Dweck, 1978). There is now a substantial empirical basis for expecting different patterns of coping within the academic environment from these students. Research findings show that it is the mastery-oriented children – those who believe that achievement is related to one's effort – who are more likely to persist in difficult situations (Diener & Dweck, 1978). Additionally, they tend to become strategy focused when they encounter failure, that is, they think about how to plan, direct and execute their actions. By contrast, the helpless children tend to focus on the inadequacy of their ability following failure and desist in their achievement attempts. The importance of attributional beliefs to achievement behavior is well documented (Weiner & Kukla, 1970; Graham, this volume;

Forsyth, this volume).

Unfortunately, however, research examining the learning environment as a contextual factor influencing student attributions is very limited. In part, this apparent void can be explained by the differing trends in the attribution and classroom environment literature. In the study of causal attributions, there has been over a decade of intense research on the antecedents, processes, and consequences of attribution. And, although the learning environment can surely be conceived as an antecedent variable, attribution research has typically looked at patterns of performance, variance of outcome, and other specific performance cues as antecedents. With some exceptions, much of this research has occurred in experimental settings far removed from the classroom. On the other hand, much of the literature on classroom environment has evolved from attempts to measure parameters of the classroom climate (Moos & Moos, 1978; Trickett, 1978; Trickett & Moos, 1973; Walberg, 1974). In this tradition, outcomes such as grades, absenteeism, self-esteem, and satisfaction, are correlated with various dimensions (e.g., control, involvement) of classroom climate. Not only does the direction of causality remain uncertain, but the mediating or moderating processes are left to hypothetical conjecture at best. Thus, while the research on attribution has been guided by a clear conceptual framework, the research on learning environments has been guided more by an empirical focus and continues to lack a unified conceptual scheme. Nevertheless, research linking learning environment to student attributions is now beginning to emerge and some of these studies will now be reviewed.

Two studies (Ames & Ames, 1981; Covington, 1984) are described here in some detail because although they used different methodologies and age groups, they nicely converge in their findings. First, the Ames and Ames study involved a simulated laboratory setting in which elementary school-age children worked on a novel task over a series of trials on which they either experienced considerable success or failure. Each child was then paired with another child and placed in either a competitive or individualistic condition and again experienced either a high (winning) or low (losing) level of success on the task. Student attributions assessed after the final manipulation showed that achievement outcomes were attributed more to effort in the individualistic than in the competitive setting and more to luck in the competitive than in the individualistic setting.

In a field-based study using college-age students, Covington similarly found that an individualistic mastery-based reward system increased the perceived role of effort in student success. Students in the mastery system were graded according to a criterion-referenced system of evaluation and were given multiple test options as compared to students in a conventional system who were graded on a curve (norm-referenced system) and given a single exam to determine their grade. The combination of absolute standards and multiple trys on the exams in the mastery system was shown to contribute to perceptions of personal control through effort expenditure.

In both of these studies, a noncompetitive (nonreliance on social comparison for evaluation) system of evaluation and the opportunity for self-improvement elicited effort attributions as a mediator of one's outcome. Other field-based investigations that have linked individualized programs of learning to effort-related attributions have been reported by Heckhausen and Krug (1982) and Wang (1976). The opportunity for self-improvement which involves an element of individual choice appears to be a central feature of these programs.

deCharms's work probably represents the most extensive field-based approach to studying the relationship between the classroom environment and different achievement–motive patterns. The underlying assumption of deCharms's research is that motivation can be enhanced by specific learning experiences. Further, it is the work of the teacher to create learning experiences that enhance student "personal causation," a belief that one can cause desired outcomes. These educational experiences are described as "origin-enhancing." deCharms characterizes an origin classroom as one which encourages realistic goal-setting by students, gives students choice in determining their goals, and encourages students to take personal responsibility for their actions. The recent findings of deCharms's Carnegie project (deCharms, 1984) provide support for the relationship between "origin" classroom and "origin" behavior. More specifically, children in the origin classroom began to take personal responsibility (feel in control) for their behavior, and there was some evidence to suggest that these experiences had effects beyond the immediate school year. deCharms's work shows us that classrooms that emphasize a more individualized or mastery-based structure influence students' beliefs about personal control.

In addition to the self-percept that effort and outcome convey, other achievement cognitions have become associated with an individualistic goal structure, as evidenced by Ames's study (1984), described earlier. In this study, elementary-age students were asked to report what they were thinking after completing a set of tasks in competitive and individualistic performance conditions. Using this modified "think aloud" approach, children performing in an individualistic structure reported significantly more effort-related thoughts than did children in a competitive structure. Moreover, these children reported significantly more self-instructional and self-monitoring types of thoughts (e.g., "I will make a plan ... I will work carefully ... "). Thus, while the children were indeed focused on their effort, their reports also reflected a mastery orientation (Diener & Dweck, 1978) in that they were actively searching for ways to maintain or enhance their performance. By contrast, children in the competitive structure reported ability-related attributions as the focus of their thoughts. The contrast between the two performance conditions of this study can be exemplified by differentiating two types of questions. The children who were competing seemed to be asking themselves, "Was I smart?" but children in the individualistic setting were more focused on "Did I try hard enough?" and "How can I do this?" types of questions.

Although there is currently much interest in involving children in more cooperative efforts in school situations, there is very little research that has examined children's attributions and achievement cognitions in cooperative situations. Thus, a discussion of how cooperative structures influence these cognitions is necessarily speculative. Cooperative structures differ from competitive and individualistic structures in that there is a group orientation and norms for helping one another are present (Ames, 1984; Ames & Ames, 1984). Thus, in addition to concepts of ability and effort, concepts such as cooperation and helpfulness may be salient. However, as we examine the research literature, we find that attribution questions, particularly as they are related to these latter concepts, have not been asked. Further, whether feelings of efficacy remain high and whether children engage in task cognitions such as self-planning is uncertain. Corno and Mandinach (1983) have suggested that "resource management" thoughts may figure prominently in cooperative group work. Resource management involves thinking about how individuals can pool their resources for the purpose of accomplishing the task. Concepts such as resource sharing, coordination of effort, and division of labor are intrinsic to many models of cooperative learning and children may be focused on thoughts related to these management efforts. Thus, in contrast to the task-mastery cognitions – "How can I do this?" – in individualistic structures, cognitions related to resource management concerns – "How can we do this?" – may be more apparent in cooperative structures. The bottom line here is that although there is abundant research on cooperative learning structures and student achievement, there is now need for research on the motivated cognitions that mediate achievement and other outcomes.

In sum, the classroom environment or structure is shown to affect student perceptions and attributions. Although, as earlier noted, this work is not extensive at this time, the findings are, by and large, convergent rather than contradictory. When the learning environment is characterized by social comparative and competitive, as opposed to individualized or mastery-oriented practices, students tend to be focused inward on their own ability to perform and are likely to not feel in control. In these classrooms, self-perceptions of ability are likely to mediate achievement behavior. In classrooms where goal setting, self-improvement, and/or individual choice is the norm, self-concept of ability should not be the primary mediator of achievement behavior. Effective achievement behaviors are more likely to depend on one's willingness to expend effort and engage in the necessary strategies and to one's belief that the outcome is realistic, achieveable, and controllable. Thus, in a competitive classroom, student achievement behavior may be a matter of whether the student is convinced of his/her ability to perform. In alternative noncompetitive classrooms, achievement behavior may be more a matter of whether the student believes the goal is achievable and desirable.

A framework for studying the context of student motivation

This section is, in part, a summary of the chapter but also an attempt to suggest a set of guidelines for further research. Perhaps the main point of the chapter has been to suggest that we need to begin asking questions such as how the classroom environment or structure affects forms of cognitive engagement, the value of achievement outcomes, beliefs about the reasons for learning, self-concept of ability, and beliefs about the causes of success and failure. Although these cognitive–motivational processes have been linked to a wide range of student achievement behaviors, they have not received sufficient scrutiny in the research on classroom learning environments. Some related points require elaboration:

1. Much of the literature on classroom structures has begged the question of why one structure is or is not more effective than others. For example, cooperative structures have been highly touted by many for some time for producing higher achievement and better peer relations, yet we are just beginning to examine some of the processes (see Webb, 1980) involved in cooperative learning and we still know little about how it affects student motivational thought processes. Other people have suggested that all types of structures have their place in the classroom

and that we just need to increase the use of some and decrease the use of others. Yet we have little data to tell us why, for example, cooperation is effective or what desirable effects competition may have in small doses.

2. We need to examine when and how certain classroom structures can enhance motivational skills in students. In doing so, we need to sort out two approaches to motivation change – one that focuses on the structure of the classroom and another that focuses on the individual. Are they complementary or can the structure of the classroom (when inappropriate) serve to undermine the effects of individual change programs. Since individual change programs have shown to be effective, can change programs aimed at the classroom environment also change how the student thinks and have longer lasting effects? Is the choice between individual and classroom intervention affected by the age or grade level of the students? In other words, developmental issues related to student conceptions of ability may mediate the effectiveness of specific programs.

3. We also need to look at individuals within the classroom. Recognizing that students have different experiences in the same classroom, we need to move away from studying the students in the classroom as a group. It is important to attend to the interaction of student history, cultural expectations, and developmental characteristics with the classroom environment. The examination of such high order interactions are central to understanding the classroom experience of the student.

4. Finally, as we study motivational processes in the context of the classroom, we need to define motivation qualitatively as representing a set of cognitions that students have about themselves, the task, their performance, and others. This definition goes beyond looking at quantitative concepts such as time on task or achievement and involves more specificity in the cognitive structure than certain personality characterizations (e.g., locus of control, self-esteem) allow. Further, if motivation can be conceived as a set of skills, training procedures that have demonstrated long-term effects in other areas such as social skills training (Oden & Asher, 1977) may prove effective when also applied to academic motivation training.

Conclusions

Acknowledging that many questions remain concerning the effects of classroom learning environments on student motivation, what can we tell practitioners about what they can do about the classroom environment to enhance motivation?

1. The structure of the classroom is a potential socializer of children's thinking. How the situation is structured influences children's self-perceptions, attribution patterns, and ways of thinking. There is substantial evidence to show that learning environments that emphasize social comparison focus children on evaluating their own and others' ability. For most students, other than perhaps the most capable, such an ability focus can negatively influence achievement behavior and peer relations. Learning environments that emphasize goal setting, self-improvement, and student choice (de-emphasizing social comparison) have been linked to those thought processes associated with effective motivation.

2. Students who have a history of failure or those who are characterized by a preponderant belief that inadequate ability prevents their achieving success may benefit from specific intervention programs. One such program is attribution retraining. Through cueing and reinforcement, this program helps students focus on the role of effort in their performance. Two caveats to such an approach are that the task must be realistic and the classroom structure must support a belief in the value of effort. First, task-related goals must be obtainable from the students' perspective such that reasonable effort will lead to success. Further, the classroom structure must be such that effort is salient and reinforced. Clearly a competitive structure or one where student–student comparisons are made may exacerbate the original problem and undermine efforts to change individual thought processes. The classroom structure then can serve to facilitate or impede efforts directed at individual change.

3. Recent research suggests that effort attributions may be linked to other cognitive activities that are directed toward monitoring and regulating one's learning. This strategy orientation has been linked to learning structures that utilize a noncompetitive (mastery) form of evaluation, emphasizing self-improvement. This is not to say that a sense of personal responsibility is a sufficient condition for the occurrence of a strategy orientation, but the occurrence of effort attributions and performance-linked strategies may be facilitated by the same classroom conditions. Those conditions which contribute an ability focus may obstruct students' engagement in these strategies.

4. Perhaps the most basic and important recommendation is to remove explicit and implicit social comparison in the classroom. Competition and social comparison not only affect student thinking but also affect teachers' perceptions and evaluations of students, having negative consequences for teachers' instructionally related behaviors. Giving

students choices, autonomy, rewards for self-improvement, and differentiated tasks should be secondary to how the classroom is structured. That is, when a competitive structure exists, students do not have these opportunities; thus, the first step is eliminating social comparisons in the classroom.

Before concluding the following should be noted. The benefits versus the detriments of different types of goal structures may not be evident by focusing on short-term achievement outcomes. The decision as to how to structure the classroom must be weighed in relation to motivation outcomes. The context of the classroom may socialize children into a predominant mode of motivation that has long-range consequences for achievement, goals, and reasons for learning.

References

Ames, C. (1978). Children's achievement attributions and self reinforcement: Effects of self-concept and competitive reward structure. *Journal of Educational Psychology, 70,* 345–355.

Ames, C. (1981). Competitive versus cooperative reward structures: The influence of individual and group performance factors on achievement attributions and affect. *American Educational Research Journal, 18,* 273–287.

Ames, C. (1984). Achievement attributions and self-instructions under competitive and individualistic goal structures. *Journal of Educational Psychology, 76,* 478–487.

Ames, C. & Ames, R. (1981). Competitive versus individualistic goal structures: The salience of past performance information for causal attributions and affect. *Journal of Educational Psychology, 73,* 411–418.

Ames, C., & Ames, R. (1984). Systems of student and teacher motivation: Toward a qualitative definition. *Journal of Educational Psychology, 76,* 535–536.

Ames, C., Ames, R., & Felker, D. (1977). Effects of competitive reward structure and valence of outcome on children's achievement attributions. *Journal of Educational Psychology, 69,* 1–8.

Ames, C., & Felker, D. (1979). An examination of children's attributions and achievement-related evaluations in competitive, cooperative, and individualistic reward structures. *Journal of Educational Psychology, 71,* 413–420.

Ames, C., & McKelvie, S. (1982). Evaluation of student achievement behavior within cooperative and competitive reward structures. Paper presented at annual meeting of the American Educational Research Association, March, New York.

Andrews, G. & Debus, R. (1978). Persistence and the causal perception of failure: Modifying cognitive attribution. *Journal of Educational Psychology, 70,* 154–166.

Blumenfeld, P. C., Pintvich, P. R., Meece, J., & Wessels, K. (1982). The formation and role of self perceptions of ability in elementary classrooms. *Elementary School Journal, 82,* 401–420.

Brophy, J. (1981). Teacher praise: A functional analysis. *Review of Educational Research, 51,* 5–32.

Clinkenbeard, P. (1983). Winners or losers: Negative aspects of success in competition. Paper presented at the American Educational Research Association annual meeting.

Corno, L., & Mandinach, E. (1983). The role of cognitive engagement in classroom learning and motivation. *Educational Psychologist, 18,* 88–108.

Covington, M. (1984). The motive for self-worth. In R. Ames & C. Ames (Eds.), *Research on motivation in education: Student motivation* (pp. 17–113). New York: Academic Press.

Covington, M., & Beery, R. (1976). *Self worth and school learning.* New York: Holt, Rinehart and Winston.

Covington, M., & Omelich, C. (1981). As failures mount: Affective and cognitive consequences of ability demotion in the classroom. *Journal of Educational Psychology, 73,* 796–808.

deCharms, R. (1984). Motivation enhancement in educational settings. In R. Ames & C. Ames (Eds.), *Research on motivation in education: Student motivation* (pp. 275–310). New York: Academic Press.

Diener, C., & Dweck, C. (1978). An analysis of learned helplessness: Continuous changes in performance, strategy, and achievement cognitions following failure. *Journal of Personality and Social Psychology, 36,* 451–462.

Doyle, W. (1984). Patterns of academic work in junior high school science, English and mathematics classes. Paper presented at American Educational Research Association annual meeting, New Orleans.

Dweck, C. (1975). The role of expectations and attributions in the alleviation of learned helplessness. *Journal of Personality and Social Psychology, 31,* 674–685.

Dweck, C., Davidson, W., Nelson, S., & Enna, B. (1978). Sex differences in learned helplessness: II. The contingencies of evaluative feedback in the classroom, and III. An experimental analysis. *Developmental Psychology, 14,* 268–276.

Eccles, J., Midgley, C., & Adler, T. (1984). Grade-related changes in the school environment: Effects on achievement motivation. In J. G. Nicholls (Ed.), *The development of achievement motivation.* Greenwich, CT: JAI Press.

Filby, N., & Barnett, B. (1982). Student perceptions of better readers in elementary school classrooms. *Elementary School Journal, 5,* 435–449.

Harari, O., & Covington, M. (1981). Reactions to achievement behavior from a teacher and student perspective: A developmental analysis. *American Educational Research Association, 18,* 15–28.

Heckhausen, H., & Krug, S. (1982). Motive modification. In A. Stewart (Ed.), *Motivation and society* (pp. 274–318). San Francisco: Jossey Bass.

Johnson, D., & Johnson, R. (1974). Instructional goal structure: Cooperative, competitive, or individualistic. *Review of Educational Research, 44,* 213–240.

Johnson, D., Maruyama, G., Johnson, R., Nelson, D., & Skon, L. (1981). Effects of cooperative, competitive, and individualistic goal structures on achievement: A meta-analysis. *Psychological Bulletin, 89,* 46–62.

Marx, R. W. (1984, April). Self regulation of cognitive strategies during classroom learning. Paper presented at the American Educational Research Association annual meeting, New Orleans.

Moos, R. (1980). Toward a typology of classroom social environments. *American Educational Research Journal, 15,* 53–60.

Moos, R. H., & Moos, B. S. (1978). Classroom social climate and student absences and grades. *Journal of Educational Psychology, 70,* 263–269.

Nelson, L. L., & Kagan, S. (1972). Competition: The star spangled scramble. *Psychology Today, 6,* 53–56.

Nicholls, J. G. (1979a). Development of perception of own attainment and causal attributions for success and failure in reading. *Journal of Educational Psychology, 71,* 94–99.

Nicholls, J. G. (1979b). Quality and equality in intellectual development: The role of motivation in education. *American Psychologist, 34*, 1071–1084.

Nicholls, J. G. (1981). Striving to demonstrate and develop ability: A theory of achievement motivation. Unpublished manuscript. W. Lafayette, IN: Purdue University.

Nicholls, J. G. (1984). Conceptions of ability and achievement motivation. In R. Ames & C. Ames (Eds.), *Research on motivation in education: Student motivation* (pp. 39–73). New York: Academic Press.

Nicholls, J. G., & Jagacinski, C. (1983, July). Conceptions of ability in children and adults. Paper presented at the International Conference on Anxiety and Self-Related Cognitions, West Berlin, Germany.

Oden, S., & Asher, S. R. (1977). Coaching children in social skills for friendship making. *Child Development, 48*, 495–506.

Pascarella, E. T., Walberg, H. J., Junker, L. K., & Haertel, G. D. (1981). Continuing motivation in science for early and late adolescents. *American Educational Research Journal, 18*, 439–452.

Pepitone, E. (1980). *Children in cooperation and competition: Toward a developmental social psychology*. Lexington, MA: Heath.

Peterson, P. L., Swing, S. R., Braverman, M. T., & Buss, R. (1982). Students' aptitudes and their reports of cognitive processes during direct instruction. *Journal of Educational Psychology, 74*, 535–547.

Rosenholtz, S. J., & Rosenholtz, S. H. (1981). Classroom organization and the perception of ability. *Sociology of Education, 54*, 132–140.

Rosenholtz, S. J., & Wilson, B. (1980). The effect of classroom structure on shared perceptions of ability. *American Educational Research Journal, 17*, 75–82.

Schunk, D. H. (1983). Effects of effort attributional feedback on children's perceived self-efficacy and achievement. *Journal of Educational Psychology, 75*, 848–856.

Schunk, D. H. (1984). Self-efficacy perspective on achievement behavior. *Educational Psychologist, 19*, 48–58.

Slavin, R. (1977). Classroom reward structure: Analytical and practical review. *Review of Educational Research, 47*, 633–650.

Stayrook, N. G., Corno, L., & Winne, P. H. (1978). Path analyses relating student perceptions of teacher behavior to student achievement. *Journal of Teacher Education, 24*, 51–56.

Stipek, D. J. (1984). The development of achievement motivation. In R. Ames & C. Ames (Eds.), *Research on motivation in education: student motivation* (pp. 145–174). New York: Academic Press.

Stipek, D. J., & Hoffman, J. M. (1980). Development of children's performance-related judgments. *Child Development, 51*, 912–914.

Swann, W. B., & Snyder, M. (1980). On translating beliefs into action: Theories of ability and their application in an instructional setting. *Journal of Personality and Social Psychology, 38*, 879–888.

Trickett, E. J. (1978). Toward a social-ecological conception of adolescent socialization: Normative data on contrasting types of public school classrooms. *Child Development, 49*, 408–414.

Trickett, E., & Moos, E. (1973). The social environment of junior high and high school classrooms. *Journal of Educational Psychology, 65*, 93–102.

Trickett, E., & Moss, R. (1974). Personal correlates of contrasting environments: Student satisfaction in high school classrooms. *American Journal of Community Psychology, 2*, 1–12.

Walberg, H. J. (Ed.). (1974). *Evaluating educational performance*. Berkeley, CA: McCutchan.

Wang, M. C. (1976). *The self-schedule system for instruction-learning management and adaptive school learning environments*. Pittsburgh, PA: Learning Research and Development Center, University of Pittsburgh.

Webb, N. (1980). A process-outcome analysis of learning in group and individual settings. *Educational Psychologist, 15*, 69-83.

Weiner, B., & Kukla, A. (1970). An attributional analysis of achievement motivation. *Journal of Personality and Social Psychology, 15*, 1-20.

Weinstein, R. & Marshall, H. (1984). *Ecology of students' achievement expectations*. Final report: National Institute of Education, Washington, DC.

Weinstein, R., Marshall, H., Brattesani, K., & Middlestat, S. (1982). Student perceptions of differential teacher treatment in open and traditional classrooms. *Journal of Educational Psychology, 74*, 678-692.

Weinstein, R., & Middlestat, S. (1979). Student perceptions of teacher interactions with male high and low achievers. *Journal of Educational Psychology, 71*, 421-431.

Winne, P. H. (1984). *Methodology for theoretical research about teaching, student cognition, and achievement*. (Occasional Paper No. 84-01). Simon Fraser University, Burnaby, BC, Canada.

11 Teacher socialization as a mechanism for developing student motivation to learn

Jere Brophy and Neelam Kher

Student motivation has been an enduring and popular topic in the psychology of education, and an impressive body of theory and research has accumulated on it. Much of this work has treated motivation as a predictor variable within the context of a focus on individual differences. That is, measures of inferred mediating variables such as achievement motivation, self-efficacy perceptions, or attributional tendencies are gathered and used to predict individual differences in achievement-related behaviors such as task choice, persistence, goal setting, or degree of mastery achieved. Such research typically shows that variance in achievement-related behaviors is partly predictable from variance in preexisting motivational patterns.

But where did these preexisting motivational patterns come from? How can desirable motivational patterns be developed? Can teachers socialize students in ways that will enhance the motivational patterns that the students bring into the classroom? These questions, which imply consideration of student motivation as a dependent variable, are of central concern in this chapter. Theory and research will now be reviewed bearing on the question of how a particular kind of motivation – student motivation to learn – can be developed by teachers through modeling, communication of expectations, and other socialization mechanisms.

Publication of this work is sponsored by the Institute for Research on Teaching, College of Education, Michigan State University. The Institute for Research on Teaching is funded primarily by the Program for Teaching and Instruction of the national Institute of Education, United States Department of Education. The opinions expressed in this publication do not necessarily reflect the position, policy, or endorsement of the National Institute of Education, Contract No. 400-81-0014. The authors wish to thank Tom Good and Mary Rohrkemper for their comments on earlier drafts, and June Smith for her assistance in manuscript preparation.

257

Definition of motivation to learn

The focus on student motivation to learn, rather than on motivation considered more generally, implies a restriction of purview in at least two senses. First, this chapter will concentrate on learning within the typical classroom setting, with all that this implies (in particular, that most student time will be spent on tasks imposed by the teacher rather than chosen by the students, and will involve working in a public setting in which one's performance will often be witnessed by peers, and will be monitored and graded by the teacher). Second, the focus here is on student motivation to learn the knowledge and skills included in the formal curriculum and specifically adopts the definition of student motivation to learn offered by Brophy (1983):

We may conceptualize "student motivation to learn" as both a general trait and a situation-specific state. As a general trait, motivation to learn refers to an enduring disposition to value learning for its own sake – to enjoy the process and take pride in the outcomes of experiences involving knowledge acquisition or skill development. In specific situations, a state of motivation to learn exists when students engage themselves purposefully in classroom tasks by trying to master the concepts or skills involved. Students who are motivated to learn will not necessarily find classroom tasks intensely pleasurable or exciting, but they will take them seriously, find them meaningful and worthwhile, and try to get the intended benefit from them. (p. 200).

Implied in this definition is a distinction between learning and performance, with learning referring to the information processing – sense making, and comprehension or mastery advances that occur during the acquisition of knowledge or skill – and performance referring to the demonstration of such knowledge or skill after it has been acquired. Many approaches to the study of relationships between motivation and behavior have ignored this distinction or have been content to deal only with performance. Such approaches are inappropriate for studying student motivation to learn because of the heavily cognitive nature of classroom learning. With a few exceptions such as penmanship or zoology dissection skills, school learning is primarily covert and conceptual rather than overt and behavioral. It is true that overt behaviors (verbal responses to questions, written responses to assignments) must be elicited in order to provide practice and application opportunities to students and to supply diagnosis and evaluation data to teachers, but such behaviors mostly involve performance (reproduction or application) based on learning that has occurred previously. Obviously, both learning and performance are important, but the focus here is on learning, and in particular on how student motivation to learn affects student cognition and information processing during activities designed to promote knowledge and skill acquisition.

This chapter's approach fits within general social learning theory, and in particular, within Expectancy x Value theory, which posits that people's effort expenditure on a particular task will be a product of (a) the value that they place on doing the task or reaping the benefits that it offers and (b) the degree to which they expect to be able to succeed if they apply themselves. This is the same general orientation shared by such approaches to motivation as those based on the concepts of achievement motivation, efficacy perceptions, and causal attributions. However, these formulations are concerned with the expectancy term of the Expectancy x Value equation. This chapter's approach complements (rather than opposes) these approaches by concentrating on the value term of that equation (Parsons & Goff, 1980). Thus, the focus here is not so much concerned with students' desire to achieve in the sense of competing with standards of excellence as it is concerned with students' desire to learn content and master skills. Similarly, it is not so much concerned with perceptions of efficacy (focused on the self) as with perceptions of comprehension (focused on the content), and not so much concerned with students' attributions about the causes of success or failure as with their attributions concerning their reasons for participating in academic activities.

The approach employed here also has much in common with those of Lepper (1983) and others who have written about intrinsic motivation. These approaches apply primarily to free choice or play settings, however, and concentrate on factors that make tasks attractive or unattractive to people. Their findings suggest that students' intrinsic motivation to engage in school tasks can be enhanced by developing more interesting and enjoyable tasks or by allowing students more free choice concerning what to do and how to do it. In addition, Lepper and Gilovich (1982) have shown that even imposed tasks can be presented in ways that generate interest and minimize concern about external evaluation and awareness of the fact that the tasks are not freely chosen. These notions are acceptable, but with two qualifications. First, teachers' opportunities for allowing genuine choices by students are limited. If they are to teach the formal curriculum, teachers will have to require attention to lessons and hold students accountable for completing assignments and mastering the content. Thus, a major challenge for educators is to find ways to stimulate intrinsic motivation in students who must participate in compulsory activities in the work setting of the school. Second, approaches to motivation that focus on intrinsic interest in tasks are concerned primarily with the affective aspects of motivation – how much students enjoy tasks. Although student enjoyment of tasks (within what is reasonable to expect) should be one of the teacher's goals, it is important to focus more on the cognitive aspects of motivation – students' perceptions of why they are engaged in the task and what they are supposed to get out of it.

Among recent contributions to the psychology of motivation in the classroom, this chapter's approach is closest to (and has been most directly informed by) the work of Berlyne (1967) on curiosity (c.f. Keller, 1983 on classroom applications), Maehr (1976) on continuing motivation, Condry and Chambers (1978) on qualitative aspects of task engagement as they relate to instrinsic motivation, Kruglanski (1978) on endogenous versus exogenous attribution of task engagement as it relates to performance, and Corno and Mandinach (1983) on qualitative aspects of students' cognitive engagement in classroom activities. The key concepts are illustrated in Table 11.1.

As shown in the table, students' attitudes toward classroom tasks can be construed as following a continuum from negative through neutral to positive. They also can be classified as concerned with factors endogenous to the task (the processes involved in engaging in the task and the learning that it engenders) versus exogenous to the task (focused on the self rather than the task, or on anticipated consequences of task performance). Finally, students' attitudes can be classified as concerned either with the value that the students place on the task or with the expectations they have for succeeding on the task or being rewarded for performance. This chapter's focus is on developing ways for teachers to stimulate student motivation that is positive in direction of attitude (described in the bottom sections of Table 11.1), especially motivation that can be described as task endogenous (described in the two bottom sections in the left half of Table 11.1).

Optimizing student motivation to learn

The top sections of Table 11.1 describe negative attitudes and other undesirable aspects of student motivation. One takes it as given that negative motivation of this sort, along with the factors that cause it, must be eliminated because one cannot reasonably expect to develop positive motivation in students who are burdened by negative attitudes, anxiety, or fear of failure. Thus, one assumes that necessary (but not sufficient) conditions for the development of positive task-endogenous motivation to learn will include: (a) a patient, encouraging teacher who supports students' learning efforts and does not engender anxiety through hypercritical or punitive treatment; (b) an appropriate match between student ability and task difficulty, so that students can expect to succeed if they put forth reasonable effort (thus maximizing success experiences and efficacy perceptions, and minimizing tendencies toward learned helplessness and attribution of failure to lack of ability); (c) sufficient task quality and appropriateness (the tasks make sense as effective means for accomplishing worthwhile academic objectives); (d) sufficient task variety and interest value to minimize boredom due to sheer satiation; and (e) a generalized teacher tendency to present academic tasks as learning opportunities assisted by a helpful instructor rather than as ordeals to be endured or hurdles to be cleared merely in order to please a demanding authority figure.

These conditions should be sufficient to set the stage for development of positive task-endogenous motivation in most students, although there will be individual differences in attitudes toward different subject matter and types of task, and although a few alienated or deeply discouraged students will need intensive and individualized remedial treatment. Even if totally successful, however, elimination of negative motivation will merely create a state of neutrality (see the middle sections of Table 11.1). Given the realities of classroom life, a neutral stance toward classroom tasks is in effect a slightly negative motivational posture. That is, if students simply do not care about the processes or outcomes involved in academic tasks, there is no positive motivation to counteract the probable negative motivation associated with the facts that school tasks involve effort (they are work, not play), are done under accountability pressure, and will be graded. Thus, if teachers want more than a minimal level and quality of task engagement, they will have to take actions designed to motivate their students.

Teachers are often advised to use strategies intended to foster task-exogenous motivation (see the two lower right hand sections of Table 11.1) for this purpose. Task-exogenous strategies that focus on task value involve attempts to develop enthusiasm for the task by making it meaningful or important to the students or by showing them that they will need the knowledge or skills that the task develops in order to succeed in life. Task-exogenous approaches that focus on performance outcome involve offering rewards for success. These task-exogenous approaches can be effective in improving student task performance, although they will not develop task-endogenous motivation to learn

Table 11.1. *Qualitative aspects of students' motivation related to specific academic tasks*

Direction of attitude	Task-endogenous motivation		Task-exogenous motivation	
	Task value focus	Performance outcome focus	Task value focus	Performance outcome focus
Negative	Affect: Anger or dread. Student dislikes the task, which is in effect a punishment. Cognition: Task focus is "invaded" by resentment, awareness of being coerced into unpleasant or pointless activity.	Affect: Anxiety, embarrassment, fear of failure. Cognition: Task focus is "invaded" by perception of confusion, failure, helplessness. Attribution of (poor) performance to insufficient ability.	Affect: Alienation, resistance. Student doesn't want to acquire this knowledge or skill. Cognition: Perceptions of conflict between what this task represents and one's self concept, sex role identification, etc. Anticipation of undesirable consequences to involvement in such tasks.	Affect: Apathy, resignation, resentment. Cognition: Perceptions that one cannot "win," that one has no realistic chance to earn desired rewards, satisfactory grades, etc.
Neutral	Neutral attitude toward task; open minded (if new) or indifferent (if familiar).	No particular expectations; neither success nor failure are salient concerns.	Neutral: The knowledge or skills developed by the task elicit neither avoidance nor excitement.	No extrinsic consequences are expected; performance will neither be rewarded nor punished.

Positive	Affect: Enjoyment, pleasure. Engagement in this task is a reward in its own right.	Affect: Satisfaction (perhaps occasional excitement) as skills or insights develop. Pride in craftsmanship, successful performance.	Affect: Energized, eager to learn this knowledge or skill (for its instrumental value).	Affect: Excitement, happy anticipation of reward.
Positive	Cognition: Relaxed concentration on the processes involved in doing this task. "Flow." Metacognitive awareness of what the task requires and how one is responding to it. Focus on the academic content when learning, and on the quality of the product when performing.	Cognition: Perception of progress toward goals, achieved with relative ease. Attribution of (successful) performance to (sufficient) ability plus (reasonable) effort. Focus on one's developing knowledge and skills.	Cognition: Recognition that the task is a sub-goal related to attainment of important future goals (often as a "ticket" to social advancement). Focus on the "relevant" aspects of the learning.	Cognition: Recognition that one can attain desired rewards with relative ease. Focus on meeting stated performance criteria.

(except perhaps indirectly, if they induce self-efficacy perceptions and these perceptions lead to increased interest in similar tasks). Furthermore, if used inappropriately, task-exogenous approaches can undermine intrinsic motivation and produce a suboptimal quality of performance in which students are more concerned about maximizing rewards while expending minimal effort than about mastering the knowledge or skills being taught (Condry & Chambers, 1978). Fortunately, research has shown that these undesirable effects of rewards can be minimized by tying reward delivery to quality rather than mere quantity of performance and by seeing that the task itself, and not just the expected reward, is salient to the students. Guidelines for emphasizing this are given in Table 11.2 (these guidelines are phrased with respect to delivery of verbal praise, but the same principles would apply to delivery of other types of reward, as well).

Student motivation to learn is optimized when it has the qualities associated with positive task-endogenous motivation (described in Table 11.1). That is, students value (enjoy, or at least find meaningful and worthwhile) the processes involved in learning content, value mastery of the content itself, and exhibit pride in craftsmanship while performing practice or application tasks. During such performance, their focus is on the processes involved in working with the content or performing the skill, and not on themselves, their abilities, how their progress will be perceived by others, or issues of success or failure or reward or punishment (although such concerns may surface before or after performance). In short, they will be absorbed in the task to the extent of experiencing a state of "flow" as described by Csikszentmihalyi (1975). During "flow" experiences, people experience direct, immediate rewards from engaging in the processes involved in activities: a sense of control, clear perception of feedback, merging of thought and awareness, loss of self consciousness, and a feeling of enjoyment. These experiences usually occur during self-chosen recreational activities, but Graef, Csikszentmihalyi, and Giannino (1981) have shown that many people experience them at work or in other settings in which they are engaged in compulsory activities. Furthermore, they report that the explanation for "flow" experiences lies less in the attributes of tasks than in the tendencies of individuals to generate such experiences for themselves in various tasks and situations. In other words, the tendency to experience "flow" appears to act as a trait variable, developed to different degrees in different individuals through experience (and presumably, socialization).

Effective praise	Ineffective praise
1. is delivered contingently.	1. is delivered randomly or unsystematically.
2. specifies the particulars of the accomplishment.	2. is restricted to global positive reactions.
3. shows spontaneity, variety, and other signs of credibility; suggests clear attention to the student's accomplishment.	3. shows a bland uniformity that suggests a conditioned response made with minimal individual attention to the student's accomplishment.
4. rewards attainment of specified performance criteria (which can include effort criteria, however).	4. rewards mere participation, without consideration of performance processes or outcomes.
5. provides information to students about their competence or the value of their accomplishments.	5. provides no information at all or gives students information about their status.
6. orients students toward better appreciation of their own task-related behavior and thinking about problem solving.	6. orients students toward comparing themselves with others and thinking about competing.
7. uses students' own prior accomplishments as the context for describing present accomplishments.	7. uses the accomplishments of peers as the context for describing students' present accomplishments.
8. is given in recognition of noteworthy effort or success at difficult (for *this* student) tasks.	8. is given without regard to the effort expended or the meaning of the accomplishment.
9. attributes success to effort and ability, implying that similar successes can be expected in the future.	9. attributes success to ability alone or to external factors such as luck or (easy) task difficulty.
10. fosters endogenous attributions (students believe that they expend effort on the task because they enjoy the task and/or want to develop task-relevant skills).	10. fosters exogenous attributions (students believe that they expend effort on the task for external reasons—to please the teacher, win a competition or reward, etc.).
11. focuses students' attention on their own task-relevant behavior.	11. focuses students' attention on the teacher as an external authority figure who is manipulating them.
12. fosters appreciation of, and desirable attributions about, task-relevant behavior after the process is completed.	12. intrudes into the ongoing process, distracting attention from task-relevant behavior.

urce:* J. Brophy (1981). "Teacher Praise: A Functional Analysis," *Review of Educational Research, 51*, pp. 5–32. Copyright 1981 by American Educational Research Association, Washington, D.C. Reprinted with permission.

Diener and Dweck's (1978) studies of "mastery-oriented" and "help-less" students provide another glimpse of this optimal level of task-endogenous motivation to learn. Helpless students gave up easily when they encountered frustration, attributing their problems to lack of ability. Their task persistence was impaired by distracting thoughts of hopeless-ness, despair, and negative self-evaluation, as well as negative affect (anxiety, anticipation of failure). In contrast, mastery-oriented students concentrated on the problem rather than on themselves or the quality of their performance. When they encountered difficulties they intensified their efforts and sought to diagnose the source of their confusion, but did not become upset or conclude that the task was too hard. When things were progressing smoothly, they concentrated on just doing the task. Thus, they neither told themselves that they were stupid or that the task was too hard when they had problems, nor told themselves that they were bright or that the task was easy when they learned without difficulty. This suggests that although attribution retraining programs may be needed as remedial treatment for the helpless students, such training will not by itself engender task-endogenous student motivation to learn. Presumably, development of the latter will require modeling and specific instruction in task-endogenous attitudes and related cognitive skills (learning sets, information processing, and problem solving skills; self-monitoring of comprehension and other metacognitive awareness skills). That is, one must have not only the intention to learn, but the skills for doing so effectively. Thus, the task-endogenous aspects of student motivation to learn lie at the juncture of motivation and learning/instruction.

Student motivation to learn in the classroom

If task-endogenous student motivation to learn is optimal, what is the incidence of such motivation in typical classrooms? This question has not been investigated systematically, but what data do exist are not encouraging.

Anderson and her colleagues (Anderson, 1981; Anderson et al., 1984) observed first-grade students working on seat-work assignments and then interviewed them about what they had done, why they did it, and how they did it. Their data indicated that many students (especially low achievers) did not understand how to do their assignments. Rather than ask the teacher or get help in other ways, however, they were content to respond randomly or to rely on response sets that had nothing to do with the content supposedly being learned (alternating or geometrical patterns for circling multiple choice answers; picking one word from a list of new words to fill the blank in a sentence, without reading the sentence itself). Low achievers tended to be more concerned about completing assignments than about understanding the content. As one student said softly as he finished a work sheet, "I don't know what it means, but I did it." (Anderson et al., 1984, p. 20).

High achievers completed most assignments successfully and showed less concern about getting finished on time, but even they gave little evidence of understanding the content-related purposes of the assignments. No student consistently explained assignments in terms of their specific content. Most responses were vague generalities ("It's just our work." or "We learn to read."). In general, seat-work assignments were virtually meaningless rituals for many of the low achievers in these first-grade classes, and even many of the high achievers seemed only dimly aware of the purposes of assignments or the skills they were practicing as they carried them out.

Analysis of the teachers' presentations of assignments to the students suggested that a major reason for the students' low quality of engagement in assignments was teacher failure to call attention to their purposes and meanings. Most presentations included procedural directions or special hints (e.g., pay attention to the underlined words), but only 5% explicitly described the purpose of the assignment in terms of the content being taught, and only 1.5% included explicit descriptions of the cognitive strategies to be used when doing the assignment.

Rohrkemper and Bershon (1984) interviewed elementary grade students about what was on their minds when they worked on assignments. They found that, of 49 students who gave codable responses, two were concerned only about getting finished, 45 were concerned about getting correct answers, but only two mentioned trying to understand what was being taught. Corno and Mandinach (1983) and Blumenfeld et al. (1983) have also expressed concern about the low quality of students' engagement in classroom tasks. Doyle (1983) suggests that most students are preoccupied with maximizing their ability to predict, and if possible control, the relationship between their academic performance and the grades that they will receive. In particular, he suggests, students will seek to avoid tasks that involve ambiguity (about precisely what will be needed to earn high grades) or risk (high difficulty level or strict grading standards), and thus will avoid asking questions or seeking to probe more deeply into the content because they want to stick with safe, familiar routines.

In summary, available data concerning students' thinking about classroom tasks reveal little evidence of motivation to learn. Also, it appears that neither teachers nor students typically reveal much awareness of the purposes of activities, and that concern about grades may suppress whatever motivation students may have to learn about the subject matter.

Developing student motivation to learn

These conclusions from classroom research are supported by research on intrinsic motivation that also indicates that such motivation is diminished when task performance is monitored by authority figures, evaluated, or followed by reward or punishment (Lepper, 1983). Thus, the prospects for stimulating motivation to learn in the work setting of the classroom appear dim. However, even if the grading system and the teacher's role as an authority figure do counteract efforts to develop student motivation to learn, such effects should be a matter of degree. Motivation to learn might not be in evidence in the classes of authoritarian teachers who make tests salient and threatening, but considerable evidence of such motivation might appear in the classes of supportive teachers who attempt to develop it and who follow the guidelines summarized in Table 11.2.

It appears also that most teachers could do a great deal more than they do now to develop student motivation to learn. The findings of Anderson et al. (1984) on teachers' failure to call students' attention to the purposes of activities certainly suggest this. So do similar findings by Roehler, Duffy, and Meloth (in press), who studied reading instruction at the fifth-grade level. Here again, teachers typically failed to call attention to the purposes of assignments, and students failed to mention learning of specific content when asked what they were doing and why. Following up on these findings, Roehler et al. trained teachers to provide more detailed explanations of content, and in particular to make sure that they called their students' attention to the purposes of academic activities. Data from this follow-up study revealed that the students of the trained teachers showed significant increases in awareness of the purposes of activities, and more generally, in metacognitive awareness of their own information processing and learning progress when working on assignments.

Such data provide cause for optimisim. Perhaps there is not much motivation to learn in the classrooms because teachers typically fail to do much to develop such motivation. A series of studies designed to explore this possibility will now be discussed.

Teachers' task introductions and students' task engagement

The first study involved motivational application of recent theorizing about the self-fulfilling prophecy effects of teachers' expectations. Although the teacher expectation literature has concentrated on student achievement as the outcome of interest, it is theoretically possible for teachers' expectations to have self-fulfilling prophecy effects on a great range of outcomes. As Good and Brophy (1984) have pointed out, the success of teachers' classroom management efforts is probably determined in part by expectations communicated about student conduct. Classroom atmosphere probably depends in part on expectations communicated about student cooperation and interpersonal relationships. Student responsiveness to academic activities probably depends in part on expectations communicated about the meaningfulness, interest potential, or practical value of those activities. Following up on the latter hypothesis, the first study (Brophy et al., 1983) was designed to test for predictable relationships between the comments that teachers make about classroom tasks in the process of introducing those tasks to their students and the subsequent motivation displayed by the students as they worked on the tasks (as inferred from task engagement ratings made by classroom observers). Data were collected in 6 intermediate grade (4–6) classrooms that were observed 8–15 times each during reading and mathematics periods. The classes were all taught by experienced teachers working in a school serving a racially mixed working class population in a small Midwestern city.

Each reading or mathematics period involved one or more (usually two to four) different tasks. Observers noted verbatim records of what the teachers said about each task when introducing it, and then rated apparent student task engagement 5 minutes after the task began and again 10 minutes later (if the task was still going on). These were purely naturalistic data: Teachers knew that we were interested in student motivation but did not know what data were being recorded, and the only instructions they received were to teach as they normally would.

The relative frequencies of various task presentation statements made by the teachers are shown in Table 11.3, classified according to the concepts illustrated in Table 11.1. The data in Table 11.3 indicate that teachers' task introductions were spread across many different categories, rather than concentrated in just one or two. The most frequently coded category was "None" (the bottom row in Table 11.3), indicating that the teacher launched directly into the task without taking time to make

Table 11.3. *Classifications of 317 task presentation statements made by six elementary school teachers*

	N	%
Task-endogenous value-focused statements		
Apology (teacher apologizes to the students for foisting this task on them).	1	<1
Cues negative expectation (teacher indicates directly that the students are not expected to like the task or to do well on the task).	25	8
Cues positive expectation (teacher states directly that the students are expected to enjoy the task or to do well on it).	52	16
Self-actualization value (teacher suggests that students can develop knowledge or skill that will bring pleasure or personal satisfaction).	0	0
Teacher enthusiasm (teacher directly expresses his or her own liking for this type of task).	8	3
Task-endogenous, performance expectation-focused statements		
Positive challenge/goal setting (teacher sets some goal or challenges the class to try to attain a certain standard of excellence).	18	6
Task-exogenous, value-focused statements		
Embarrassment (teacher tries to show the importance of the task to the students, but does this in a negative way, indicating that they are likely to be embarrassed at some time in the future if they do not learn the skills involved).	1	<1
Survival value (teacher points out that students will need to learn these skills to get along in life or in our society as it is constructed presently).	13	4
Personal relevance–other (teacher makes some other kind of statement that tries to tie the task to the personal lives or interests of the students).	10	3
Teacher personalizes (teacher expresses personal beliefs or attitudes directly or tells the students about personal experiences that illustrate the importance of this task).	3	1
Task-exogenous, performance expectation-focused statements		
Threats/punishment (teacher threatens negative consequences for poor performance).	12	4
Accountability (teacher reminds students that the work will be carefully checked or that they will be tested on the material soon).	18	6
Recognition (teacher promises that students who do well on the task will be recognized with symbolic rewards, hanging up of good papers in the classroom, etc.).	7	2
Extrinsic reward (teacher promises reward for good performance).	2	1
Other (unclassified) statements		
Time reminder (teacher reminds students that they only have limited time to get the assignment done so they had better concentrate).	19	6
Cues effort (teacher urges students to work hard).	31	10
Continuity (teacher notes relationship between this task and previous work students have done, especially recently).	29	9
None (teacher launches directly into the task with no introduction).	68	21

Note: Based on data presented in Brophy (1982).

general comments about it or to try to develop student motivation to engage in it. When the teachers did make such general task descriptions or motivational attempts, their comments were coded into one or more of the other 17 categories (multiple coding occurred when teachers' task introductions included concepts that fit two or more categories). The motivationally relevant task introductions observed most frequently were "Cues positive expectations" (stating that the students probably would enjoy the task or do well on it), "Cues effort" (urging the students to work hard), noting the continuity between this task and previous tasks, and "Cues negative expectations" (stating that the students would probably not enjoy the task or not do well on it). The only category never used even once was the category for task-endogenous, value-focused motivation: None of the six teachers ever mentioned that a task might have self-actualization value or present opportunities for students to experience pleasure or personal satisfaction through development of knowledge or skills.

Brophy et al. (1983) further analyzed data from the 165 tasks that had been coded both for teachers' introductory statements and students' task engagement. These data indicate that teachers made no introductory statement at all for 49 (30%) of the 165 tasks. Their presentation statements for the remaining 116 tasks yielded 206 codes, or almost two per task. Thus, although teachers jumped directly into tasks without giving a general introduction or motivational attempt 30% of the time, the introductions that they gave the other 70% of the time were lengthy and substantial enough to include, on the average, mention of two separate considerations likely to affect student motivation.

There was considerable individual variation across the six teachers. One launched directly into tasks without giving any introduction only 5% of the time, while two others did this 46% and 40% of the time respectively. One teacher was responsible for most of the "Time reminder" and "Positive challenge/goal setting" codes, and several other codes were used primarily with just two or three teachers. Task introductions were primarily positive (offering reward or recognition opportunities, expressing enthusiasm, or trying to develop positive expectations) for two teachers; neutral (using time-reminder, continuity, or effort-cuing statements) for three others; and negative (using accountability reminders, cuing negative expectations) for the sixth.

Within each of the six data sets (one for each teacher), scores based on the teacher's introductions to tasks (presence/absence scores for the categories shown in Table 11.3) were correlated with scores representing the level of student engagement in those tasks (recorded by the classroom observer). As expected, student engagement was relatively poor on tasks that had been introduced in ways that were classified as likely to have negative effects on student motivation (threatening punishment for poor performance, cuing negative expectations about the task). However, there was no parallel tendency for student engagement to be relatively high following task introductions expected to have positive effects on motivation (offering reward or recognition opportunities, cuing positive expectations about the task). Instead, student engagement tended to be highest on tasks that the teachers launched into directly without making introductory statements codable in any of our categories. Thus, although negative task introductions were associated with low task engagement, positive task introductions were not associated with high task engagement.

In general, there was little support for the notion that teachers' task introductions might have positive effects on student engagement. The correlations for the "none" category (launching directly into the task) showed positive relationships with engagement in three classes, no significant relationship for two classes, and a negative relationship in one class. Thus, for only one class was it true that task engagement was higher when the teacher said something intended to motivate the students than when the teacher said nothing at all. Furthermore, only 14 of a possible 52 relationships reached statistical significance for the other 17 task introduction categories, and 12 of these 14 were negative relationships. Thus, most relationships indicated lower student engagement when teachers made some codable introductory statement than when they did not.

Many of these negative relationships were expected, because they occurred for task introduction categories that had been classified as likely to have negative effects on student motivation (threatening punishment, reminding the students of accountability pressures, and cuing negative expectations about the task). Also, the "personal relevance – other" category, which had been classified as likely to have positive effects on student motivation, did show one positive correlation with student engagement (and no negative correlations). However, negative correlations were sometimes observed (and positive correlations were never observed) for task introductions that had been classified as likely to have positive effects on student motivation ("survival value," "teacher enthusiasm"), as well as for one of the categories that had been classified as neutral ("positive challenge/goal setting").

In thinking about follow-ups to these findings, the experimenters have concentrated on two aspects. First, it is possible that some of the classifications of task introductions – positive, neutral, or negative with respect to their probable effects on student motivation – were incorrect. For example, teachers' communication of their own enthusiasm about tasks were classified as likely to have positive effects, on the assumption that students will generally take their teachers' statements at face value. However, it may be that such communications of teacher enthusiasm should be classified as neutral (if students tend not to identify with their teachers and thus are not likely to infer that they will enjoy tasks merely because the teacher does) or even as negative (if students are alienated from their teachers or predisposed to believe that teachers' preferences are contradictory to, rather than merely different from their own preferences). Time reminders provide another example. These task introductions were classified as neutral, reasoning that they carry no information about the nature of the task itself or about possible consequences of task performance. However, it is possible that students regard such time reminders either positively (because they perceive them as well intended attempts to provide helpful information) or negatively (because they are perceived as nagging or criticism, or merely because they remind the students that the task is imposed externally and their performance will be evaluated). Such ambiguities, combined with the surprising correlational findings for some of the categories, pointed to the need for information from students themselves on their reactions to teachers' task introductions.

A second focus for follow-up was the lack of much support for the expectation that positive task introductions would maximize student engagement. Among several possible explanations for this (to be discussed in a later section), one that was intriguing and seemed to call for immediate follow up was suggested by the teachers themselves during debriefing interviews. When asked why task engagement might have been higher when no introductory statements were made at all than when such statements were made, several teachers indicated that perhaps they tended to launch directly into tasks when things were going smoothly, and to take time to try to generate motivation only (or at least primarily) when they expected trouble because the class was becoming restive or because prior experiences with the task had gone poorly. If teachers do in fact have such tendencies, and if students should become aware of them, the students would have reason to discount or even react negatively to task introductions intended to stimulate motivation. A dissertation study by Kher (1984) was designed to discover whether in fact students are predisposed to discount or react negatively to teachers' motivation attempts.

Students' reported responses to teachers' task introduction statements

Kher (1984) interviewed 32 second graders, 32 fourth graders, and 32 sixth graders, mostly from the same working class school within which the data of Brophy et al. (1983) had been collected 2 years earlier. Half of the students interviewed at each grade level were male and half were female, and within sex, half were high achievers and half were low achievers. The students were interviewed individually about how they would respond to various ways in which their teachers might introduce a hypothetical seat-work assignment in mathematics (referred to as a "math assignment"). This general reference to a math assignment was used in preference to showing a specific assignment (or more probably, a different specific assignment for each grade level) because math seat-work assignments were familiar to all of the students and because we wanted to focus student attention on statements that teachers might make when intro-ducing assignments rather than on the assignments themselves.

Pilot work indicated that students had difficulty responding to open-ended questions about the general topic of teacher task introductions ("What might your teacher say about a math assignment when presenting it to you?") or about particular task introductions considered individually ("What goes through your mind when you hear the teacher say 'I like these kinds of problems and I think you will enjoy them too'?"). However, the students could respond adequately when questioned using a paired comparison format in which they were presented with two sample introduction statements and asked first to choose which statement they would prefer their teacher to make when introducing the hypothetical math assignment, and then to explain why they preferred that statement over the other. Consequently, the interviews began with a series of 17 of these paired comparison questions, using pairs of introduction state-ments selected from the set shown in Table 11.4.

The statements shown in Table 11.4 were selected for use in the Kher (1984) study because they were typical of the statements observed in the Brophy et al (1983) study, with two exceptions. First, because our primary interest was in students' responses to teachers' positive task introduction statements, 8 of the 12 statements used (the first 8 shown in Table 11.4) were selected from among those classified as positive in the previous study. Second, the statements were kept short and phrased in simple

Table 11.4. *Teacher statements used in paired comparisons*

1. It's important that you know these skills. You'll need them for math next year.
2. I like these kinds of problems and I think you will enjoy them too.
3. Page 37 should be no trouble at all but the ones on page 39 are harder. You'll have to think before you do them.
4. If you do a really good paper, I will put it up on the bulletin board.
5. It's important that you know these skills. You'll need them when you go grocery shopping or to the bank.
6. If you do a really good paper, then later on I'll let you play some games.
7. Some of these problems are really tricky. I like tricky problems because they make me think hard, but then I really feel good when I get them right.
8. I never knew how important these skills were when I was your age but I found out when I started writing checks and had to take care of my money.
9. Problems like these will be on your next test, so work carefully.
10. You have only 20 minutes to finish, so work quickly.
11. If you don't get at least ten of them right, you'll have to do another page.
12. Let's see how many of you can get them all correct.

words, in order to maximize clarity and minimize the memory demands made on the students.

The eight positive items were always paired with other positive items (using a design that ensured that each item was paired with each other item an equal number of times). The last four items in Table 11.4 had been classified as neutral or negative in the previous study. These items were paired only with one another or (in the case of the neutral items) with selected positive items. This paired-comparison format yielded data on the relative popularity of the items, but it should be kept in mind that its primary purpose was to elicit students' free-response descriptions of their thoughts and feelings following teachers' task introduction statements.

Once the students had completed the paired-comparison items and were accustomed to talking about their thoughts and feelings in regard to teachers' task presentation statements, they were asked two open-ended questions. The first was designed to elicit students' beliefs about what it means when teachers launch directly into tasks without making introductory statements ("When would your teacher say 'Do the problems on pages 37 and 39' and nothing more?"). The second question was designed to identify the task introductions that would be most motivating to the students ("What kinds of things could your teacher say when giving assignments that would make you feel like working really hard in math?").

The students' responses to all questions were tape recorded, transcribed, coded, and then analyzed for general trends as well as for main effects or interactions involving grade level, gender, or achievement status.

The data revealed no significant tendency for students to discount or negatively interpret their teachers' motivation attempts. Only one student (a low achieving sixth-grade boy) responded negatively to the hypothetical task introductions. This boy stated: "You feel like the teacher is just pressuring you and pressuring you and telling you that page 37 is easy but 39 is hard; so you feel like you want to just cry, that you have to do harder and harder work." Later, he stated: "He's acting like he's just your owner and can boss you around anywhere." All of the other students accepted the teacher statements at face value and treated them as well-intended attempts to provide useful information or to help make schooling a positive experience. Even the one disgruntled student, although he was unhappy about having to work hard and resented the teacher's position of authority over him, accepted the teacher's comments at face value in that he never suggested that the teacher might be lying or attempting to "con" him. Nor did he or any of the other 95 students ever suggest that teacher attempts to motivate students are clues that tasks will be frustrating or unpleasant. No one ever said anything such as "When she tells you you're going to like it, watch out!" or "If it really was going to be something you'd like, he wouldn't be telling you all this."

Similar findings were seen in the students' responses to questions about when teachers might fail to give task introductions. These responses made it clear that the students considered task introductions to be normal and helpful (or at least well intended). No student ever suggested that teachers would omit task introductions because certain tasks were so obviously enjoyable that they needed no "hype." Instead, the reasons commonly offered for omission of task introductions were that the assignment was a review task with which the students were already familiar, the teacher was upset because the class was noisy and inattentive, or teacher was busy or in a hurry. In general, then, the data provide no evidence that the students saw teachers as launching directly into enjoyable tasks but taking time to try to generate motivation for boring or frustrating tasks. Instead, it is encouraging to find that the students appeared to accept teachers' task introductions at face value and perceive them as intended to be informative and helpful (although some students did say that teachers do not really know what students like or that just because a teacher likes something does not mean that students will like it too).

Other data from this study are less encouraging, however. The students' preferences among the eight positive statements that were systematically paired with one another (statements 1–8 in Table 11.4) suggest mixed signals with respect to student receptivity to developing motivation to learn. Statement 1 ("It's important that you know these skills. You'll need them for math next year.") was the most popular, being selected over the alternatives 68% of the time. This result sounds promising, because it suggests student interest in skills themselves rather than merely in obtaining rewards for mastering the skills. However, the least popular alternative, selected only 38% of the time, was statement 8 ("I never knew how important these skills were when I was your age, but I found out when I started writing checks and had to take care of my money."). Furthermore, statement 5 ("It's important that you know these skills. You'll need them when you go grocery shopping or to the bank.") was preferred only 41% of the time. Thus, student preference for statement 1 cannot be attributed to student motivation to learn the skills as such. Instead, statement 1 apparently was a popular choice because it provides students with information that will help them to succeed in school. Student interest in school success is also implied by the next most popular statement, preferred 58% of the time: statement 4 ("If you do a really good paper, I will put it up on the bulletin board").

The reasons that the students offered when explaining their paired comparison preferences also seem promising at first. The most frequently mentioned reasons were that the skills to be learned would be useful in the future, that it was important to learn or do hard problems, and that the student would feel proud about doing good work. Motivation to learn the content and pride in craftsmanship were mentioned more frequently than seeking to be rewarded for success, avoiding negative consequences for failure, appreciating the advance warnings contained in reminders about tests or deadlines, getting peer recognition through good work, or hoping that mastery of the task would make math easier to do in the future. Unfortunately, however, the majority of these statements about enjoying learning or taking pride in craftsmanship appeared to have been induced by the content of the items. Mention of enjoying working on problems, for example, occurred only in explanations for choices involving Statement 2 ("I like these kinds of problems and I think you will enjoy them too."). More generally, the students' explanations of their paired comparison choices appeared to be paraphrasings of the language used in our questions rather than credible statements of the students' own thinking expressed in their own words. Thus, it was not surprising that somewhat different results were obtained in the students' responses to our open-ended question about what teachers could say or do to make them want to work hard on a math assignment.

By far the most popular element in these free response answers, mentioned by about ⅔ of the students, was the suggestion that the teacher could motivate them to work hard by offering rewards. Other popular responses were threatening punishment for poor performance or challenging the students to meet stated goals (each mentioned by about ⅓ of the students), communicating the importance of the task, making a personal appeal to the students to work hard, and giving them easy work (each mentioned by about 15% of the students). Here, the emphasis is on issues of reward and punishment or success and failure, with much less emphasis on the importance of the task and virtually no mention of motivation to learn the content or to take pride in craftsmanship.

There were few sex differences in these analyses, and those that did appear did not fall into general patterns. There also were few achievement level differences, but those that did appear bore out expectations based on previous research. High achievers responded more positively than low achievers to challenges and mention of tricky problems, and low achievers responded more positively to opportunities to gain recognition by peers, teachers, or parents. In general, high achievers were more concerned with the task itself and whether they would enjoy or learn something from it, whereas low achievers were more concerned with getting support from the teacher and with obtaining rewards or avoiding punishments for their performances.

Grade level differences were more frequent and sizeable than sex or achievement level differences. In the paired comparison data, second and fourth graders were more likely than sixth graders to prefer statements 4 and 6 (promising that good performance would be rewarded by hanging papers on the bulletin board or letting the students play games), but sixth graders were more likely to prefer statement 1 (telling the students that the skills would be needed for math next year). Thus, younger students were more concerned with the consequences of performance, and older students more concerned with the task itself. The second graders' rationales explaining their preferences were generally the most global and expressed in affective terms (liking enjoyable problems or playing games). The second graders were not especially concerned with the relevance of the content or its practical utility in the future. Their responses generally had a positive, upbeat tone, with emphasis on enjoying academic activities, taking pride in doing good work, and looking forward to being rewarded for success (but without much mention of the specific content of the work).

The fourth graders showed more concern than the second graders about the relevance and practical utility of the work, but they expressed similar enthusiasm about enjoyment of games and about being rewarded for good work. Furthermore, they differed from both the second graders and the sixth graders in being especially concerned about getting easy work. Even more than getting rewarded for success, the fourth graders were concerned about avoiding failure and its negative consequences.

The sixth graders were the most likely to mention concern about the importance of the learning and its future application, although they were more concerned about future application in school than in life outside of school (possibly because their teachers often mentioned the need to "get them ready" for junior high school). The sixth graders were also the most likely to express appreciation for warnings about the importance of learning particular material (because it will be needed next year or will appear on a test). They were the least likely to mention rewards or the opportunity to play games. In general, second graders were most likely to mention enjoying the work and anticipating being rewarded for completing it successfully, fourth graders were most likely to mention fear of failure and concern about getting easy work, and sixth graders were most likely to mention needing information about what was important to learn so that they could adjust their study strategies.

Grade-level differences in the students' free responses to the final question paralleled the trends seen in their paired comparison choices, except that the sixth graders mentioned that teachers could present the task as enjoyable or offer rewards for success in addition to pointing out the importance of learning the material.

Taken together, the data from the Kher (1984) study provide mixed messages concerning the potential of teacher socialization as a mechanism for developing student motivation to learn in classrooms. Positive indicators include the fact that students appear to accept what their teachers tell them about tasks at face value and to consider such statements as well intended and likely to be helpful. Thus, there is no reason to fear that students will discount or question the motives behind teacher socialization attempts. However, the data also indicate that students are preoccupied with enjoying themselves (particularly the younger students) or with what Becker, Geer, and Hughes (1968) call the exchange of performance for grades (especially the older students), and not with motivation to learn. Interest in learning the content and pride in mastering skills are mentioned only secondarily if at all. This is not surprising in view of the failure of the teachers studied by Brophy et al. (1983) to mention these potential outcomes of student task engagement, and it suggests that intensive and systematic intervention may be necessary to induce meaningful change.

The Kher (1984) findings also may explain why most of the "positive" task introductions observed in the Brophy et al. (1983) study appeared to be ineffectual or counterproductive. For example, in the earlier study, teachers frequently communicated positive expectations that the task would be easy or enjoyable. However, the students interviewed in the Kher study rarely mentioned enjoying academic tasks, and when they did, it was probably because they had been cued by one of our stimulus statements. Similarly, except for some of the fourth graders, informing students that a task would be easy did not appear likely to boost their motivation. In general, the students reported more enthusiasm when told that a task would be important or challenging than when told that it would be easy.

Other teacher motivation attempts commonly observed in the previous study included teachers' expressing personal enthusiasm for tasks or relating the knowledge and skills being taught to successful coping with life outside of school. However, the students interviewed in the Kher study were not enthused by such teacher statements. Thus, most of the "positive" task introduction statements observed in the earlier study were among the types that did not yield strong positive reactions from the students interviewed in the Kher study, and most of the statements that received positive response from the students in the Kher study (offering rewards for good performance or communicating the importance of the task for future school success) were rarely used by the teachers in the earlier study. Thus, it appears that there is a poor match between the incentives stressed by teachers when attempting to motivate their students and the incentives preferred by the students.

The Kher (1984) data also confirm that some of the classifications of task introduction statements as positive, neutral, or negative should be revised, although in many cases the Kher data deepen rather than resolve the mysteries raised by the earlier data. For example, accountability statements (reminding students that material is going to be graded or tested) were classified as negative and did have a negative correlation with student engagement in the earlier study, but the students interviewed in the Kher study generally responded positively to such accountability statements. Rather than perceive them as threats, the students perceived them as well intended and helpful hints about how to organize their study time. The differences in student response may be linked to differences in the actual wording. The accountability statement used in the Kher study ("Problems like these will be on your next test, so work carefully.") was neutrally worded and could easily be appreciated as a friendly tip from the teacher. However, inspection of the wording of statements coded in the accountability category in the previous study suggests that many of these were in fact threats rather than friendly reminders.

The time-reminder category produced mixed results in the previous study (one positive correlation and two negative correlations with student engagement). However, the students interviewed in the Kher study responded very negatively to the time-reminder item (statement 10 in Table 11.4). When explaining these negative reactions, the students usually said that they hated to be rushed and resented being put in a position where they might have to turn in an incomplete paper or a paper that represented something less than their best work. Inspection of the data from the earlier study cleared up the mystery here. The two teachers in whose classes were observed negative correlations between time reminders and student engagement both gave time reminders similar to the one used in the Kher study; namely, time reminders geared to the immediate present, suggesting that the students were running out of time to finish the assignment they were working on at the moment. In contrast, the teacher in whose classroom was observed a positive correlation between time reminders and student engagement used a different kind of time reminder. His time reminders were geared to the week or unit rather than the immediate present, and had the effect of being helpful information that the students could use in planning their study time. Thus, he would remind the students on Tuesday that a series of workbook assignments was due on Friday.

The data on challenge/goal setting statements by teachers continue to be confusing. Such statements had originally been classified as neutral. However, this category produced three negative correlations and no positive correlations with student engagement in the earlier study, suggesting that such challenge or goal-setting statements should be classified as likely to have negative effects on student motivation. Yet, comments on challenge statements by students in the Kher study implied that such statements are perceived positively. The paired comparison data revealed that the students preferred statement 12 of Table 11.4 ("Let's see how many of you can get them all correct."), not only in comparison with other presumably neutral statements, but also in comparison with several presumably positive statements. Furthermore, many students mentioned a teacher challenge in their free responses to the question about things that teachers could do to motivate them to work hard, and very few negative comments were made about such challenge statements.

Thus, the negative correlations seen in the earlier study remain un-explained. Inspection of the challenge statements made by the teachers in whose classrooms these negative correlations were observed suggests that these teachers tended to throw out such challenges in demanding and somewhat negative ways (e.g., "You should be able to do these problems correctly by now, unless you work carelessly."). These and other informal observations from the previous study suggest that the tone and manner with which teachers make task presentation statements may be at least as important as the content of those statements in determining students' motivational responses.

Finally, the Kher study introduces some anomalies of its own. In particular, it is not clear why students respond positively to information suggesting that the task teaches skills that are important for future school success, and yet do not respond very positively to statements indicating that the task teaches skills that are important for success in life outside of school. Most adults would probably expect students to respond at least as positively to the latter statements as to the former. The youngest students interviewed in the Kher study were the least responsive to statements about the value of skills for coping with life outside of school. Perhaps the applications that were mentioned (grocery shopping, banking) were too removed from their present life concerns to be very meaningful to them. Whatever the reasons, it was surprising to find that statements linking school tasks to life outside of school did not produce more positive student response. Looked at from another point of view, these findings are yet another indication of the degree to which students tend to be preoccupied with success and failure issues and with the exchange of performance for grades, to the point that concern about what they are learning is clearly secondary.

In responding to the Kher data, it is important to bear in mind that they are based on self-report rather than observed behavior. As noted above, we have reason to question the validity of many of the responses to the paired comparison items. Furthermore, even the data based on responses to the two open-ended questions should be considered tentative pending verification in actual classroom settings. The students' responses to the interview questions may not accurately describe their responses to teachers' actual introductions of classroom tasks.

Socializing student motivation to learn

The data in this chapter and those of others (Doyle, 1983; Harter, 1981; Lepper, 1983) all suggest that there is little evidence of student motivation to learn in the typical classroom. Apparently, students start school with enthusiasm but gradually settle into a dull routine in which interest centers on being able to meet demands. The students become attuned to and appreciative of information that clarifies and helps them to meet these demands successfully, but they do not appear to develop enthusiasm for the knowledge or skills being taught or for their applications outside of the school setting. In theory, teachers should be able to develop motivation to learn in their students by socializing the students' beliefs, attitudes, and expectations concerning academic activities, as well as the information-processing and problem-solving strategies that the students use when engaged in those activities. However, it appears that very little such socialization occurs, and what does occur seems too halfhearted or otherwise lacking in credibility (from an adult perspective, at least) to be very effective.

Recall that none of the six teachers studied by Brophy et al. (1983) ever made reference to the fact that students could derive personal satisfaction from developing their knowledge or skills, and that in general, positive task introductions were infrequent except for the statement that the work would be easy. The following examples that were observed came the closest to approaching the kinds of teacher socialization that there should be more of in the typical classroom.

- These are not elementary, high school, or college level words; these are living level words. You'll use them everyday in life. If you plan to be a writer or enjoy reading, you will need these words.
- Remember: the essential thing is to do them correctly, not to be the first to finish.
- I think you will like this book. Someone picked it out for me, and it's really good.
- This is a really strange story. It's written in the first person, so that the person talking is the one who wrote the story about his experience. It has some pretty interesting words in it. They are on the board.
- The stories in this book are more interesting than the ones in the earlier level books. They are more challenging because the stories and vocabulary are more difficult. Reading improves with practice, just like basketball. If you never shoot baskets except when you are in the game, you are not going to be very good. Same with reading. You can't do without it.

- Answer the comprehension question with complete sentences. All these stories are very interesting. You'll enjoy them.
- You girls should like this story because it is a feminist story. You boys will enjoy yours too. Your story is especially interesting. I want you to be sure to read it. It's a mystery and you'll enjoy it.
- Percent is very important. Banks use it for interest loans, and so on. So it is important that you pay attention.
- You're going to need to know fractions for math next year. You will need fractions in the world to come.

At least three things should be noted about these examples. First, these are the best examples we could find in data representing about 100 hours of classroom observation. Second, notice how minimal and essentially barren most of these remarks are. They do not go into enough detail to be very meaningful or memorable for most students, and many of them have a perfunctory, go-through-the-motions-without-much-enthusiasm-or-conviction quality to them. Third, whatever positive effect these remarks may have had was probably undercut by the facts that: (a) most of the teachers' remarks to the students concerned procedural demands and evaluations of work quality or progress rather than description of the task itself or what the students might get out of it, and (b) many of the rest included remarks such as the following:

- Today's lesson is nothing new if you've been here.
- If you get done by 10 o'clock, you can go outside.
- Your scores will tell me whether we need to stay with multiplication for another week. If you are talking, I will deduct 10 points from your scores.
- This penmanship assignment means that sometimes in life you just can't do what you want to do. The next time you have to do something you don't want to do, just think "Well, that's just part of life."
- Get your nose in the book, otherwise I'll give you a writing assignment.
- You don't expect me to give you baby work every day, do you?
- You've been working real hard today, so let's stop early.
- You'll have to work real quietly, otherwise you'll have to do more assignments.
- My talkers are going to get a third page to do during lunch.
- We don't have a huge amount to do, but it will be time consuming.
- This test is to see who the really smart ones are.

If the teachers we have been studying are typical (there is reason to believe that as a group they are, if anything, better than average), then it appears that there will continue to be little evidence of student motivation to learn in the typical classroom until teachers are trained to socialize such motivation in their students. Furthermore, it appears that nothing short of a high-powered, systematic teacher training effort is likely to succeed. The next step in this program of research will be to develop such an effort. Undoubtedly, it will have to include elements designed to change teachers' attitudes, beliefs, and expectations in addition to elements designed to train them to perform specific practices. Many teachers presently believe that it is not realistic to expect students to develop motivation to learn in classrooms, and most of the rest appear to act as if they hold this belief even if they have never articulated it consciously. Thus, part of this program's effort will be to persuade teachers to believe that the development of student motivation to learn through socialization is a realistic goal, or at least to suspend disbelief and commit themselves to this goal for the duration of the experiment.

Assuming such commitment, it will then be necessary to work with the teachers to create conditions favorable to the development of student motivation to learn and to train them in techniques designed to foster such motivation. Some of the effort will be directed toward setting the stage by eliminating undesirable elements and creating desirable conditions: ensuring an adequate match between the demands of academic activities and the abilities of students, encouraging students to ask questions and learn from their mistakes, minimizing the salience of the teacher's authority-figure role and of testing and grading, and using praise and rewards (if at all) according to the guidelines summarized in Table 11.2

Working within these established conditions, teachers would then be trained to socialize motivation to learn directly through such techniques as the following:

1. Modeling attitudes, beliefs, and expectations regarding academic activities that illustrate motivation to learn.
2. Modeling (with overt verbalization of associated self-talk) the processes involved in engagement in academic activities.
3. Instructing students directly in relevant information processing, problem solving, metacognitive awareness, and self-monitoring skills.
4. Establishing optimal learning sets for academic activities through task introductions that stress their purposes and intended outcomes.

5. Focusing attention on these knowledge and skill outcomes
through the kinds of questions asked and the kinds of feedback
given to the students.

This brief list is being expanded and elaborated upon during pilot
activities underway at present. The plan is to develop a training program
that is systematic and powerful enough to make important changes in
teacher behaviors believed to affect student motivation to learn, and yet
assimilable within traditional approaches to classroom teaching. If this
training program is successful, it will be possible to find out whether
student motivation to learn can be stimulated through teacher socialization and can coexist with the grading system, the prescribed curriculum, and all of the other features of the classroom as a work place. It
is hoped that such teacher socialization behavior can succeed, not only in
stimulating student motivation to learn particular content, but ultimately
in developing motivation to learn as a personal trait or predisposition
that students would begin to generate spontaneously as they engage in all
kinds of activities, in or out of the classroom, voluntary or involuntary.

There will be realistic limits on how far such effects can carry, of
course. For one thing, even those who are most generally motivated to
learn cannot learn everything, so that individuals' preferences for certain
topics or tasks over others can be expected to develop, and these will
deepen over time. So will their actual and perceived differences in
aptitudes for various tasks. Also, many of the tasks that students are
asked to do seem pointless or unnecessarily boring, so that in these cases,
finding better tasks is a more sensible response to low motivation than
attempting to stimulate interest in such tasks. Nevertheless, it remains
true that even otherwise optimal schooling will remain primarily a work
setting in which students are required to engage in externally imposed
tasks. They can either fight this situation all the way, making things
miserable for themselves and their teachers, or else make the best of it by
trying to enjoy it and get as much out of it as they can. The research
program described here is designed to identify strategies that teachers can
use to encourage students to follow the latter course.

References

Anderson, L. (1981). Short-term student responses to classroom instruction. *Elementary
    School Journal, 82*, 97–108.
Anderson, L., Brubaker, N., Alleman-Brooks, J., & Duffy, G. (1984). *Making seatwork work.*
    (Research Series No. 142). East Lansing: Michigan State University, Institute for
    Research on Teaching.

Becker, H. Geer, B., & Hughes, E. (1968). *Making the grade: The academic side of college life.* New York: Wiley.

Berlyne, D. (1967). Arousal and reinforcement. In D. Levine (Ed), *Nebraska symposium on motivation* (pp. 1-110). Lincoln: University of Nebraska Press.

Blumenfeld, P., Hamilton, V., Wessels, K., & Meece, J. (1983). Teacher talk and student thought: Socialization into the student role. In J. Levine and M. Wang (Eds.), *Teaching and student perceptions: Implications for learning* (pp. 143-192). Hillsdale, NJ: Erlbaum.

Brophy, J. (1983). Conceptualizing student motivation. *Educational Psychologist, 18*, 200-215.

Brophy, J., Rohrkemper, M., Rashid, H., & Goldberger, M. (1983). Relationships between teachers' presentations of classroom tasks and students' engagement in those tasks. *Journal of Educational Psychology, 75*, 544-552.

Condry, J., & Chambers, J. (1978). Intrinsic motivation and the process of learning. In M. Lepper and D. Greene (Eds.), *The hidden costs of reward: New perspectives on the psychology of human motivation* (pp. 61-84). Hillsdale, NJ: Erlbaum.

Corno, L., & Mandinach, E. (1983). The role of cognitive engagement in classroom learning and motivation. *Educational Psychologist, 18*, 88-108.

Csikszentmihalyi, M. (1975). *Beyond boredom and anxiety.* San Francisco: Jossey-Bass.

Diener, D. & Dweck, C. (1978). An analysis of learned helplessness: Continuous changes in performance, strategy, and achievement cognitions following failure. *Journal of Personality and Social Psychology, 36*, 451-462.

Doyle, W. (1983). Academic work. *Review of Educational Research, 53*, 159-199.

Good, R. & Brophy, J. (1984). *Looking in classrooms* (3rd ed.). New York: Harper and Row.

Graef, R., Csikszentmihalyi, M., & Giannino, S. (1981). Measuring intrinsic motivation in everyday life. Paper presented at the annual meeting of the American Psychological Association, Los Angeles.

Harter, S. (1981). A new self-report scale of intrinsic vs. extrinsic orientation in the classroom: Motivational and informational components. *Developmental Psychology, 17*, 300-312.

Keller, J. (1983). Motivational design of instruction. In C. Reigeluth (Ed.), *Instructional-design theories and models: An overview of their current status* (pp. 383-434). Hillsdale, NJ: Erlbaum.

Kher, N. (1984). Students' perceptions of teachers' introductions to tasks: Is there a communication gap? Unpublished doctoral dissertation, Michigan State University, College of Education.

Kruglanski, A. (1978). Endogenous attribution and intrinsic motivation. In M. Lepper and D. Greene (Eds.), *The hidden costs of reward: New perspectives on the psychology of human motivation.* Hillsdale, NJ: Erlbaum.

Lepper, M. (1983). Extrinsic reward and intrinsic motivation: Implications for the classroom. In J. Levine & M. Wang (Eds.), *Teacher and student perspectives: Implications for learning* (pp. 281-317). Hillsdale, NJ: Erlbaum.

Lepper, M. & Gilovich, T. (1982). Accentuating the positive: Eliciting generalized compliance through activity-oriented requests. *Journal of Personality and Social Psychology, 42*, 248-259.

Maehr, M. (1976). Continuing motivation: An analysis of seldom considered educational outcome. *Review of Educational Research, 46*, 443-462.

Parsons, J. & Goff, S. (1980). Achievement motivation and values: An alternative perspective. In L. Fyans (Ed.), *Achievement motivation: Recent trends in theory and research* (pp. 349-373). New York: Plenum.

Roehler, L., Duffy, G., & Meloth, M. (in press). The effect and some distinguishing
    characteristics of explicit teacher explanation during reading instruction. In J. Niles
    (Ed.), *Changing perspectives in research in reading: Language processing and instruction.*
    (Thirty-third Yearbook of the National Reading Conference). Rochester, NY: National
    Reading Conference.
Rohrkemper, M., & Bershon, B. (1984). Elementary school students' reports of the causes
    and effects of problem difficulty in mathematics. *Elementary School Journal, 85,* 127–
    147.

12 Confronting culture with culture: a perspective for designing schools for children of diverse sociocultural backgrounds

Brenda D. Baden and Martin L. Maehr

Introduction

Cultural diversity

Cultural diversity exists not only across but also *within* each society. Although certain societies may be more heterogeneous than others, there exists in nearly every society groups of individuals who, by virtue of their ethnicity, socioeconomic background, age, sex, or religion, constitute a minority or "subculture" distinguishable from the major cultural group. Such subcultures can exert a powerful influence on the behaviors, attitudes, and values of their members (Maehr, 1974a, 1974b; Maehr & Stallings, 1975). They may spawn orientations which are idiosyncratic to the cultural group of which the person is a member. Moreover, these orientations may not only be different from those held by other groups, but they may actually be in conflict with them.

In general, people tend to interact with others who share a similar cultural orientation. While this may be largely a matter of their preference, it is also true that other cultural groups and the wider society often force this pattern upon them. Thus, subcultures with their differential approaches to life tend not only to persist, but often persist in isolation and sometimes in conflict with other segments of society. Moreover, beliefs, attitudes, and behaviors characteristically associated with the subcultures may inhibit members of these groups from participating effectively in the wider society.

Cultural diversity as a problem

In viewing such cultural diversity, one might simply conclude, *vive la différence*. However, such cultural diversity poses a problem of sig-

The authors are indebted to a number of individuals, especially Carole Ames, Jennifer Archer, and Joyce Wolverton.

289

nificance for the schools. Public policy, not to mention philosophical and ethical concerns of educators, make it mandatory for public education to intervene and disrupt the existence of cultural homogeneity. Specific attempts are made to bring participants from various cultural groups into contact with each other and to confront the goals of society at large. By design, schools and classrooms often exhibit cultural diversity. It is in the classroom where, sometimes for the first time, the child must confront an alien culture. It is also in the classroom where teachers must deal with children of different cultural backgrounds. Indeed, as often as not teachers will be confronted with cultural diversity and heterogeneity. A teacher's culturally derived beliefs about the role of the school, the nature of achievement, the worth of learning, and ways of attaining success may be in direct conflict with one or more members of their class. In some cases teachers may even find themselves to be in the minority in their own classroom.

The existence of cultural diversity in and of itself poses a special pedagogical challenge. Additionally, when such diversity is associated with differential achievement, the challenge becomes a problem. It can hardly be ignored that membership in subcultural groups has been associated with differences in achievement. In spite of the best intentions and programs, large numbers of blacks, Mexican-Americans, and Native Americans, for example, have not managed to join the mainstream so far as school achievement is concerned (Coleman et al., 1966; Smith et al., 1972; St. John, 1975). Indeed, it sometimes seems that the school and its various programs have served more to confirm inequality and reinforce socioeconomic status than to change it. Often, the school has reinforced a closed system rather than creating an open path for mobility and interaction in the wider culture (Apple, 1979). Such a persistence of inequality in school achievement among various subcultural groups has stimulated a dismal view of the school's capacity to deal effectively with cultural diversity. It has presented a discouraging picture of the school's ability to create equal societal opportunity through equality of educational opportunity. Worse still is the fact that this state of affairs has provided the occasion to excuse the persistence of social inequalities by pointing to failed efforts in the schools as evidence of inherent inferiorities in the intellectual and educational potential of certain minority groups.

The problem diagnosed

As is the case with the assessment of most complex problems, it is easier to identify the symptoms than to isolate the causes and suggest the remedy. The disparity of academic outcomes among various social and cultural groups indicates a serious problem. That minority children all too often graduate from high school without being able to read, write, or do simple mathematics is cause for concern. That differences in culture are often associated with disparities in learning and achievement is troublesome. Not surprisingly, it is the school that is often blamed. But this proposition must be submitted to closer analysis: to what extent is the school in fact a cause? After all, the students are also a product of a family background and powerful peer experiences. The school only claims a limited portion of their time. But given that the school does, indeed, play a significant causal role, what can the major actors within the school – the teachers and the administrators – do to positively affect the motivation and achievement of students from so-called disadvantaged minority groups?

Effectiveness of schools

It is apparent that many factors affect school achievement besides the school. Walberg's (1981, 1983; Walberg, Harnisch & Tsai, in press; Walberg & Shanahan, 1983) extensive research on educational productivity has made this point quite clear. Yet, Walberg's research, as well as that of others, has also indicated that not only does schooling make a difference, but that schools are differentially effective. Educational quality varies among schools; some schools simply are better than others.

In an early study, for example, Bock and Wiley (1967) found that only 20 to 30% of sampling variance was attributed to differences among pupils, whereas the remaining 70 to 80% was related to schools and classrooms within schools. Because of the significant effects of schools and classrooms upon student achievement, it has become common for researchers to treat such aggregates as a single "subject" and to focus analyses upon the group level (Cronbach, Daken, & Webb, 1976). Similarly, the growing literature on school effectiveness (Brookover et al., 1979) indicates that certain schools are not only more effective than others but that they can also deal more effectively with the cultural diversity that exists within their confines. Recently, considerable attention has been given to the capacity of school leaders to create a culture or school environment that fosters the pursuit of excellence (Sergiovanni, 1984). In this regard Purkey and Smith (1982) stress particularly the importance of the expectations that are held for student behavior. It is these expectations, doubtless a part of the school culture, that are critical to school effectiveness.

Preliminary findings of our own research have provided further support and specification of this proposition. Fyans, Maehr, and Archer (1985), in a comprehensive study of randomly selected students and schools in Illinois, found that the school, as a contextual entity, has a pervasive effect on the achievement of individual students. Schools apparently have their own "personalities" and those "personalities" in turn make a difference in what happens to students. Interestingly, the school effects were greater for different subject matter areas and for different grade levels. For example, schools as a cultural entity were more effective in furthering math achievement than in promoting achievement in the language arts areas. Moreover, effectiveness of schools seemed to be greater at the elementary rather than at the secondary level.

In a parallel study, Fyans and Maehr (1985) are currently considering differences in educational goals held by schools and students relating such differences to school effectiveness. This study focuses on the direction as well as on the intensity of the beliefs that teachers and students have for the value of schooling (Nicholls, Patashnick & Nolen, 1985). There is reason to believe, for example, that valuing learning for learning's sake (rather than for the extrinsic rewards an education might bring) is especially effective in promoting continuing motivation for learning outside school walls (Maehr, 1976) and with a higher degree of intellectual growth over the long term.

In summary, then, it appears that there is something about the school as an entity – the overall learning environment it provides – that may be important (Brookover et al., 1979; Brookover et al., 1982; Rutter et al., 1979). Indeed, our review of the literature suggests a simple conclusion. Schools cannot fully determine student achievement. They are not fully responsible for disparities observed between various social groups. But the quality of the school and the nature of the learning environment it provides *do* make a difference.

Schools are effective through affecting motivation

There is evidence to support the proposition that the schools *can* be effective even when faced with cultural diversity. We will proceed now to assert further that they are effective as they affect motivation. Again, we admit that this is by no means the whole story nor the total solution. We would only stress that there is evidence to indicate that it is an important component of the solution. Moreover, we will suggest further that motivating students is not just a teacher's problem, it is the school's problem as well. What the teacher does to students in the classroom or what happens on the playground can be determined by a more pervasive school environment or culture that has an overall influence on student motivation. One is not limited to talking to teachers about how to motivate students. One can also talk to principals and instructional leaders about creating a school climate that induces motivation in all the participants (Greenblatt, Cooper, & Muth, 1984; Sergiovanni & Corbally, 1984; Sergiovanni & Starratt, 1983).

According to a number of investigators (Cooper & Tom, 1984; Maruyama, 1984) motivation appears consistently as a necessary condition for learning. Similarly, it has been pointed out that problems associated with minority group membership are more often than not motivational in nature (Maehr, 1974b). In this regard, Nicholls (1979) has argued that motivation should rightly be considered *the major focus* of the school in attempting to achieve educational equity. In any event, researchers as well as practitioners have expressed an awareness of the importance of motivation in educational achievement. They have also expressed an awareness of problems that ensue when one attempts to motivate children of culturally diverse backgrounds. In addition, these problems are often exacerbated by the heterogeneity of cultural backgrounds in the same classroom. Inevitable social comparisons, for example, often work to the detriment of the child of a different race, class, or culture. And so, motivation may well be the critical factor in affecting optimum performance of culturally diverse groups in a culturally diverse classroom or school.

How can motivation be enhanced?

Motivation, then, is an important problem in dealing with cultural diversity. It appears to be a problem in the reduced achievement of certain minority groups. Granted that it is a problem, what can be done about it?

In the last several years, considerable research has been conducted on this particular problem by Maehr and various colleagues at the University of Illinois and elsewhere (Maehr & Nicholls, 1980; Willig et al., 1983). Maehr has recently begun to summarize much of this research in a Theory of Personal Investment (1984; Maehr & Braskamp, 1986). The basic outlines of this theory are simple. First, the concept of "personal investment" is proposed as an alternative for the term motivation. This change is more than semantic in nature. The use of the term *personal investment* is designed to stress that motivation is particularly indicated by the kinds of choices that the person makes in his or her life. Therewith, it is stressed that the primary problem in the case of minority group members is not that they are lacking in motivation, but rather that they may be investing their time, talent, and energy in different places or in a different way than is expected or desired by the teacher. Thus, for example, when one considers the Mexican-American child to be "unmotivated" in the classroom, one probably is only observing that he or she is not choosing to direct attention to the particular task at hand. In another context or situation one may observe that this same child shows all the energy, activity, and output that indicates "motivation." The point is that there is not really anything "wrong" with the child: he or she is not lacking in drive, or simply being lazy. The situation or context is just not attracting his or her investment of time and energy. Thus, the teacher in such cases is well-advised to ask: What is there about this situation or this context that does not serve to elicit this child's investment of time or energy? The burden for change is placed especially on the situation. More particularly, the focus is placed on the meaning of the situation to the person. What this situation means to the person is the critical determinant of how or whether he or she will invest himself or herself in it.

In a series of studies designed to specify and operationalize the meaning of "meaning," Maehr and his colleagues (Fyans et al., 1983; Maehr, 1984; Maehr & Braskamp, 1986) have concluded that meaning is appropriately viewed as consisting of three components. First, there are certain perceived options or action possibilities available to the person in the situation. That is, the person may view a certain course of action as possible and acceptable. Another course of action may not be known or not be acceptable. Playing the violin is a possible and acceptable course of action for some, but not for others. This perception of action possibilities is a first component of meaning. Second, there are certain views of oneself in relationship to the situation, including, in particular, one's view of oneself as being able to perform competently. Third, there are perceived incentives available in the situation: reasons for or goals in performing the task. These three interactive components form what is termed the meaning of the situation to the person. And, it is this meaning that determines whether or not a person will invest himself or herself in a particular task.

Of course, there are a variety of factors that affect the meaning of the situation to the person. One cannot deny, first of all, that persons come to any situation with a certain package of meanings that bias them to respond in certain ways. But it is important to stress that the structural nature of the situation has a major effect. Recently, Maehr and Braskamp (1986) have been studying the effects of different jobs and work situations on meaning and motivation. This work has focused especially on how different ways of designing tasks lead to different goals, or to different personal incentives in performing the task. Thus, for example, if one gives the person choice in what to do and minimizes external evaluation and control, one is likely to encourage the meaning that the task is something to be done for its own sake. Therefore, one is more likely to work on the task with a minimum degree of external inducements, such as money. Conversely, the more that an external kind of control is exercised, the more one creates the meaning that the task is *not* done for its own sake. It is a *job*, something the person should be paid for, something to be done for someone else. When a task is not valued for its own sake, people are less likely to work on it on their own or to return to it on their own time and for their own reasons. In other words, such a view does not encourage what has been called "continuing motivation" (Maehr, 1976).

In addition to identifying how various features of jobs may affect meaning and, ultimately, personal investment, Maehr and Braskamp (1986) have explored how wider aspects of the task/job situation may affect these meanings. They have referred to these wider aspects of the organization as the "culture" of the organization. Further, they have indicated how certain policies and practices of the organization can influence the meanings of the participants and affect their personal investment toward the ends desired by the organization. In short, they have suggested how certain features of the organization can affect the perceptions and meanings of the participants in such a way that they will be differentially motivated to perform in the situation.

While this work was initially done in various work organizations, it is currently being applied to schools. There is, of course, considerable literature that indicates that the school or classroom *as a social and cultural entity* reflects certain meanings, which likely affect the behavior of staff and students. Research on effective schools, for example, tends to suggest this possibility, as implied earlier. Thus, the salient meanings created by the school are likely to have a major controlling effect on whether or how students invest their time and talent in this particular context.

School culture and motivation

There is, then, considerable evidence that the work environment can affect the meaning of work to the worker. This basic principle can conceivably apply to schools as well. Indirectly, at least, there is evidence that suggests that the way the school is managed and the policies it espouses might make a difference in the motivation exhibited by its staff and students. This general proposition deserves extended analysis in its own right. This chapter will examine, in detail, a more limited aspect of that general proposition; that is, that there may be certain policies, practices, and procedures utilized in managing a school that may be useful in encouraging children from culturally diverse backgrounds to achieve. The chapter will not only look at certain features of the organizational "culture" that might influence personal investment generally, but will make a special point of considering whether they are appropriate in dealing with a culturally diverse student body. The concern here is with the question of facilitating the best efforts of all students, regardless of their sociocultural origin.

The term *culture* is used as a summary term to describe the facets of an organization that seem to be especially critical in this regard. While the use of the term has precedent in the wider literature (Deal & Kennedy, 1983), a special point should be made of the fact that this concept is not being used in its broadest or most technical sense (Maehr, 1974a). Rather, it is being used to reflect the fact that within any organizational context there are shared perceptions of desired ends, goals, or outcomes worth striving to achieve. There are also perceptions of whether and how these goals may be attained. When the term culture is used in this chapter to refer to certain characteristics of the school, it is the more limited concept that we have in mind (cf. Maehr & Braskamp, 1986). We prefer this term to such other terms as *climate* or *environment* because it seems to better reflect our stress on shared perceptions of valued ends and their attainment.

Dimensions of classroom/school culture

Recently, considerable research has been conducted on motivational factors and classroom achievement (Ames & Ames, 1984; Nicholls, 1984; Paris, Olson, & Stevenson, 1983). This research has yielded a set of variables associated with classroom environments, which appear to be regularly associated with motivation and personal investment. Indeed, for the present purposes at least, this research seems to be well on its way to defining the nature and dimensions of an effective learning environment. These variables can be fitted into four categories, as they relate primarily to (a) goal/reward structures, (b) roles/power relationships, (c) evaluation/feedback systems and, what we refer to as (d) symbols of identity and purpose. These four categories or dimensions are tentatively proposed as critical dimensions of school and classroom cultures that affect personal investment in learning.

Goal/reward structures. The first dimension considered here in understanding school/classroom culture is the goal structure and system of reward distribution that predominates. These terms refer to both the pupil–pupil and the pupil–task interactions as they are expected and rewarded by the teacher. Within this dimension, three goal structures consistently appear in the research literature. They are (a) the competitive structure, (b) the cooperative structure, and (c) the individual structure (Ames, 1984; Nicholls, 1984). Rewards are distributed within these respective structures on the basis of (a) comparative performance between individuals, (b) group accomplishment of a shared task, and (c) individual gains in task performance. Although not exhaustive of possible goal/reward interactions, these three orientations are those most commonly associated with classroom structures in the research literature. These structures differentially affect both behavioral and cognitive patterns of the students. In particular, they affect personal investment and academic outcomes.

Numerous researchers have been interested in systems of goal/reward structure and the way in which they translate into children's and teachers' behavior. Their research indicates that children under varying structures of goal and reward will exhibit different attributional patterns and self-instructions (Ames, 1981; Diener & Dweck, 1978), will vary in school attachment, self-concept, interpersonal attraction across ethnic groups, and performance (Aronson et al., 1978; Johnson & Johnson, 1981), and are differentially affected by negative test motivation and anxiety (Hill, 1984).

Just what is it about these different goal/reward structures that affects attitudes and behavior so strongly? What processes are tapped by these varying systems that so effectively act to encourage or discourage personal investment in the schools? Perhaps this can be best understood by considering the nature of the various goal structures. In a competitive environment, for instance, one's performance is valued by its position in relation to others. Skill and winning or "being the best" are stressed as desirable and necessary goals. This emphasis has been found to correlate strongly with the prevalence of internal, stable attributions of ability among children in these environments (Ames, 1981; Covington & Beery, 1976; Nicholls, 1984). In these competitive situations, children are more likely to strive toward outcomes that will enhance, or at least not jeopardize, their status in the classroom on the basis of their compared performance. Thus, what Maehr and Nicholls (1980) refer to as "ego goals" emerge as another characteristic of competition (Maehr & Sjogren, 1971). Conclusions about one's competence become stable over time as repeated experiences of success or failure reinforce them. Of course, what is critical is that these cognitions (perceptions) are antecedent to certain behavior patterns that affect the subsequent direction and persistence of a child's personal investment.

When ability attributions and ego goals are salient, the resulting behavior becomes increasingly dependent on the child's sense of competence. When children draw conclusions about their own competence, these conclusions lead to specific options. In a competitive environment, these options are restricted because "success" is defined by relative terms of position, rather than task mastery. This limits the number of potential "successes" available in the classroom (i.e., only a few children can be at the top), thereby restricting the action possibilities perceived by the child. If a child feels competent, he or she may compete for the academic goals offered by the teacher. However, if the child has experienced failure and feels less than competent academically, competitive situations may become anxiety provoking and thus will be avoided. Indeed, in a competitive environment, sense of competence becomes a critical, if not *the* critical, variable in determining personal investment and, ultimately, achievement (Maehr, 1983, 1984).

Particularly when the classroom is culturally diverse, and its diversity is accompanied by significant variation in performance levels, the prevalence of ego goals and ability attributions is likely to encourage labels of unequal status and stereotypical attitudes. In many of the studies of positive contact between racially or culturally different groups, positive contact has usually occurred as a result of the contact taking place within a specific context where "equal status" existed between the groups (Allport, 1954; Amir, 1969; Miller & Maruyama, 1976). Traditionally competitive classrooms, or ones which are structured according to a tracking system, are not conducive to and, in fact, undermine the very concept of "equal status."

In contrast to the competitive structure, the cooperative classroom is based upon students working together toward interdependent group goals. This goal structure can be particularly beneficial in integrating children of diverse sociocultural backgrounds into the classroom (Johnson et al., 1981). Purkey (1978) refers to what he calls "the disinvited," students who are called on less frequently and are given less time to answer. These students are often disproportionately poor and members of minority groups. Their options are limited by their perception that their contributions are not valued by the school. In response, the feeling often becomes mutual.

Recent theory and research suggest that cooperative classrooms have a positive effect on the integration of minority students into the classroom. Thus, classrooms that employ the "Jigsaw Technique" (Aronson et al., 1978), enhance the value of the contributions of *each* child by distributing individual "pieces" of the task among members of the groups. This encourages interdependence within the group and requires each child to take responsibility for his/her piece of the task. Presumably, cooperative tasks in which success is determined by the accomplishment of the task (rather than by social comparison) and for which participation is minimally dependent upon skill level, would tend to reduce the avoidance behaviors of those who do not feel personally competent. Through their participation in a cooperative task, low-achieving children increase their chances of actually learning the skills they may be lacking.

The third system of goal/reward structure, the individual/task orientation, differs from the previous two in structure, but is similar in effect to the cooperative classroom. By focusing on the task itself and rewarding mastery on an individual basis, the individual structure avoids the emphasis on outcome and social comparison that exists in the competitive environment. Available options are regarded individually, thereby corresponding more closely to the child's own competence level than either the cooperative or the competitive structure. Children are told to do their best, rather than to do better than others: effort and individual progress toward task mastery are stressed and interpersonal comparisons of performance are minimized.

Nicholls (1984) has recently argued that individual task involvement will produce the most desirable outcomes, especially in attempting to optimize the achievement of children of culturally diverse backgrounds (Nicholls, 1979). He asserts that this goal structure is most likely to maintain equal and optimum motivation for intellectual development as it fosters challenge seeking (Maehr, 1983, 1984) and continuing motivation (Maehr, 1976). As also noted earlier, the atmosphere of ego goals and ability attributions, prevalent in competitive structures, systematically handicaps those who experience low performance or have low ability perceptions. An individual structure also encourages effort attributions (Ames, 1981) and, consequently, promotes effective cognitive, task-related self-instructions (Ames, 1981; Diener & Dweck, 1978). These cognitions tend to provide children with a broader range of options than are extant in the competitive classroom. In order to offer a learning climate that makes learning an appropriate option for all students, regardless of sociocultural background or varying goals, values, and perceptions of ability, one does well to create a goal/reward structure that enhances task involvement and task competence.

By placing minimal emphasis on external evaluation, the individual structure encourages task mastery and effort attributions. In addition, recent classroom programs developed by Hill (1984) demonstrate that when the feedback that is given is more specific and more task oriented, it can teach the child that the task is within his/her power to change; that is, sense of control will be enhanced.

All in all, then, it is clear that goal structure is a critical determinant of what happens in the classroom. Goals affect personal involvement in the learning process. Moreover, different goals have different effects in optimizing the performance of students of culturally diverse back-grounds. The strong hypothesis is that task and cooperative goals appear to be more effective than competitive goals in optimizing the perform-ance of *all* children.

Roles/power relationships. Another dimension that is readily apparent in most classrooms is the roles and power relationships that govern behavior in the designated classroom situation. Many roles establish themselves within the classroom, regardless of external inducement of any kind. What this dimension refers to, however, is the role of the teacher–pupil relationship that is established by the teacher through the learning/instructing relationship he or she chooses. Primarily, this dimension refers to elements of autonomy and self-reliance as opposed to elements of control and forced obedience.

A number of researchers (Deci, 1980; Hackman & Oldham, 1980; Maehr & Braskamp, 1986) have also been interested in this dimension. Among these, deCharms (1976) has suggested the delineation of this dimension in a most fascinating way. Briefly summarized, deCharms conceptualized environments as creating "origin" or "pawn" perspectives in persons. Origin and pawn perceptions are basically beliefs regarding one's role as initiator versus recipient in how certain behavior is chosen and pursued. The beliefs or perceptions are created by the way in which power is distributed and individual autonomy fostered. Thus, the essential hypothesis proposed is that when individuals believe they are an origin rather than a pawn, they will invest their time and effort accordingly. More specifically, when they perceive themselves to be an origin, they are not only more likely to involve themselves in the task at hand, they may also invest themselves in different ways. Thus, they are likely to take independent action, be concerned with improving their competence, and be more willing to confront challenge (Maehr, 1983, 1984).

According to deCharms (1976), pawn perspectives are likely to be present in many traditional classrooms where children are assigned tasks and expected to complete them with little or no say over the process. An origin classroom, on the other hand, occurs when children are given autonomy in task selection and certain aspects of classroom governance. The key to the origin environment is that it places maximum emphasis on choice. Encouraging participation and self-reliance in task selection can help to create a feeling of responsibility or commitment to the task.

Taking part in one's own education (as opposed to being the passive, if not the hostile, recipient of that imposed by someone else) also involves specific training in the process of setting goals and organizing one's behavior. In many classrooms, the child is given no opportunity to develop or expand his or her goal-setting skills. Instead, he or she is expected to follow the goals outlined by the teacher, which may or may not be valued by the child and his or her peers. When the classroom is composed of culturally diverse individuals, it becomes increasingly probable that there will be discrepancy between what the teacher sees as valuable and what the various groups of children value. Rather than subject the students' education to a hit or miss attempt by the teachers to discover what subject matter might be appealing to his or her diverse group, a more effective strategy might be to allow for the child's participation. Simply allowing choice between several alternatives may create more of a sense of autonomy than no choice at all.

Making choices and selecting goals is doubtless also of importance in preparing children for coping with the complex society in which they must live today. However, the point at issue here is that such self-determination has important and immediate motivational effects in the classroom. Some optimum degree of autonomy, individual initiative, and choice seems to enhance a personal investment in classroom tasks. That seems to be a conclusion of deCharms's (1968) extensive research on the enhancement of minority group children. It is a finding that receives support elsewhere in the literature (e.g., Deci, 1980).

Evaluation/feedback. A third dimension of importance in considering the culture of the classroom is the system of evaluation and feedback which is used. This refers both to the type and the amount of feedback given a child in response to his or her performance.

Since evaluation in some form inevitably pervades the instructional process, it must be viewed as an important dimension of the culture of the school or classroom. The way performance is appraised affects the definition of goal structures and reinforces power and role relationships. Self-evidently, evaluation can give rise to "winners" and "losers" or can communicate progress toward personal goals. It serves as a critical factor in establishing or reinforcing a given goal/reward structure. Evaluation can reinforce the power of the teacher and the dependency of the student to a greater or lesser degree. Thus, it can reinforce the pawn status or encourage the student to think of himself or herself as an origin.

In a series of studies (Fyans et al., 1981; Maehr & Stallings, 1972; Salili et al., 1976), it has been demonstrated that evaluation practices have an influence on motivation. In particular, they can affect the willingness of students to take responsibility for their own learning, to proceed independently, and to exhibit a continuing motivation in learning beyond the immediate context. More recently, these studies and others have been interpreted to suggest that evaluation is a crucial factor in establishing the goals that a person holds in performing a task (Maehr, 1983, 1984; Maehr & Nicholls, 1980). More broadly, the way in which evaluation is conducted determines the meaning that a student attaches to a learning or performance situation. A heavy emphasis on external (teacher-dominated) evaluation as opposed to internal (student-centered) evaluation is likely to change the meaning of the situation for the student. In the latter case, the focus is on doing the task for its own sake. That is, a task orientation is fostered and intrinsic motivation (Deci, 1975) is enhanced. In the former case, an extrinsic orientation is established, and the student is likely to perform when external evaluation is present, but not when such external evaluation is removed. That is, the learning task becomes simply a job to be done for someone else, such as the teacher.

It is especially interesting that such effects of evaluation practices have been demonstrated to be similar across widely diverse cultural groups. Thus, in a cross-cultural study conducted by Fyans et al. (1981), external and internal evaluation operated similarly in such contrasting cultures and school contexts as Iran and the United States. One might assume, then, that variation in evaluation practices, especially variation in the external control aspect, may cut through the diverse cultural orientations of individual students and create an effective learning environment – in spite of diversity in student backgrounds and in spite of the wider cultural context in which the school happens to exist. Evaluation has powerful effects in creating a culture that is special to the situation and which supersedes other sociocultural inputs.

In sum, the evaluation/feedback dimension is a critical one in creating the school or classroom culture. The evaluation/feedback dimension, of course, is not readily separable in practice from the preceding two dimensions. More generally, it is one of several factors that influence goals and perceptions of interpersonal relationships in a classroom or school. Additionally, it should be stressed that *what* is evaluated is also important. By selecting the behavior that will be responded to, the teacher and the school can reveal priorities, convey expectations, and define the purpose and meaning of schooling.

Symbols of identity and purpose. The final dimension of school and classroom culture relates to symbols of identity and purpose. Although manifest in the goals, reward systems, power relationships, and evaluation systems that are set up and conveyed by teacher and school, such symbols of identity and purpose are also important in their own right. Basically, they reflect a question of much deeper and broader significance regarding the role of the school in disseminating its values and purposes. While conceptually inherent in the other three dimensions, this fourth dimension is, in practice, distinct in terms of its implications for creating an effective school climate.

Studies of effective work organizations (Deal & Kennedy, 1983; Maehr & Braskamp, 1986; Peters & Waterman, 1982) indicate that an important part of any organizational culture is the values it holds. It is when the organizational expectations are salient that participants are likely to be the most productive. Companies with a mission make a difference. Possibly, the same holds true also for schools. Indeed, there is at least considerable anecdotal evidence that this is the case. Thus, when visiting various so-called effective schools, one of the characteristics that one notes is that school officials regularly and consistently express that the school *stands for something.* They convey expectations for student behavior (Purkey & Smith, 1982) through slogans and posters, and by focusing on certain role models. They also reinforce these symbols of what the school stands for through policies and the consistency with which these policies are implemented.

Further, it may be noted that such symbols of purpose, of the "mission" of the school, are perhaps most clearly communicated by school leaders (Purkey & Smith, 1982), who play a critical role in affecting school culture. As they manipulate goal/reward structures, roles/power relationships, and the evaluation/feedback systems they can create a summary meaning of the overriding purpose of the school and the meaning of schooling.

In considering, particularly, the case of diverse minority group children, one inevitably confronts a diversity of values, and will often note a conflict of values among the participants. Yet, one cannot avoid the fact that school itself represents a system that operates on values of its own. Therefore, as teachers and schools confront the problems of cultural diversity in the classroom, the question of values cannot be ignored. On the basis of what little research is available on this point, it should be stressed that it is important that the schools know *what* they are about and stating this explicitly to their constituency.

In their examination of what they consider to be crucial elements in creating climates for excellence, various authors (Nicholls et al., 1985; Rosenholtz, 1985; Rutter, et al., 1979) speak of the importance of clearly reflecting the goals and purpose of the school. Such goals should reflect the core values of the school. These values ought to include a central belief in the positive function of the school, as well as an acknowledgment of the importance of each individual. In addition, it is helpful for the school to focus on a single aim (e.g., academic excellence) through which they establish a sense of school identity. This identity can then be directly translated into slogans and other symbols of identity and purpose. This focus can also be exemplified in the behavior of the school leaders and in a reward system which focuses on students portraying school values. Tactics such as these are likely to be conducive to strengthening the saliency of the school culture. They should also promote overall commitment to the values of the school.

Cultural clarity is perhaps in no instance more important than when the school population is characterized by cultural diversity. Diffuse cultural norms and goals might produce uncertainty and false notions about the purpose and values of the school. When, however, the purposes, goals – the mission – of the school is stated clearly and translated into practice and policy, cultural clarity results. One might surmise that for the culture to have an effect it must be clearly articulated and salient. Moreover, there is reason to suggest that when the culture of an organization is made salient, commitment to the organization is enhanced. This is a recent and major finding of Maehr and Braskamp (1986) in a study of a variety of work organizations. Although such notions have not, as yet, been subjected to thorough empirical testing in school settings, they do have a sound basis in organizational theory. Moreover, they seem to be supported by our own preliminary observations in school settings. At the very least, it appears that the saliency of school culture is a variable worth examining more systematically.

Conclusion

The educational process is by no means a simple one. Many factors affect academic outcomes that are neither within the means nor the jurisdiction of educators to change. The school can do little about extraschool environments that the child happens to have experienced in the past or continues to experience in the present. These factors are largely beyond the school's control. Admittedly, what goes on in a classroom or school is affected to some degree by these factors. However, the argument here is that such factors do not *fully* determine educational outcomes.

Regardless of the sociocultural composition of the student body, effective action to achieve educational goals can be taken. Principals and teachers make choices – often without even realizing that choices have been made – regarding the norms and structures that will prevail in a school or classroom. These choices eventuate in contextual features that have been previously defined as the culture of the school. It was then argued further that not only can the culture of the school be identified and assessed, it also can be consciously and systematically affected by principals and teachers. Moreover, it was suggested that such school effectiveness in the case of a socially and culturally diverse student population is likely to demand a special type of school climate or culture.

The phrase "confronting culture with culture" summarizes the essential thrust of this chapter's argument. It suggests a broad perspective for designing schools that can be both practical and effective when dealing with children of diverse sociocultural backgrounds. It is drawn not only from the authors' research but also that of others. Moreover, this same research gives rise to the possibility that the differential effectiveness of schools might be a response to the culture or climate that happens to exist. Again the term "culture" is used in a very special sense in this chapter to suggest a generally shared perception of possible options and opportunities to pursue certain desired ends. Both the expression of what these desired ends are and the explication of how one attains them are critical.

Often, school leaders are confronted with a socially and culturally diverse student body. Characteristically associated therewith are problems in encouraging students to invest themselves in learning and in any enterprise that is arguably necessary for coping in their future, if not also their present world. Motivational change programs based on a clinical/counseling model often focus on reversing the faulty motivational patterns students have acquired (McClelland, 1985). Such approaches are problematic. There is neither the time, the money, nor perhaps the inclination for the intensive effort that is required by such approaches. Besides, it might be misplaced effort (Maehr, 1974a).

In any case, school leaders do well to focus on the organizational context, which to some degree they control, and to consider how they can change that context for the better. In this chapter, evidence has been presented indicating that school context makes a difference. Variables have also been suggested that can be manipulated by school leaders with predictable effects on school outcomes. One *can* change the school, its culture, its climate; the result can be an effective school. This perspective is perhaps of greatest value in facilitating an optimal learning experience for children of culturally diverse backgrounds.

References

Allport, G. W. (1954). *The nature of prejudice*. Reading, MA: Addison-Wesley.

Ames, C. (1981). Competitive versus cooperative reward structure: The influence of group performance factors on achievement attributions and affect. *American Educational Research Journal, 18*, 273–287.

Ames, C. (1984). Competitive, cooperative, and individual goal structures: A cognitive-motivational analysis. In R. Ames & C. Ames (Eds.), *Research on motivation in education: Student motivation* (pp. 177–207). New York: Academic Press.

Ames, R., & Ames, C. (Eds.). (1984). *Research on motivation in education: Student motivation*. New York: Academic Press.

Amir, Y. (1969). Contact hypothesis in ethnic relations. *Psychological Bulletin, 71*, 319–342.

Apple, M. (1979). *Ideology and curriculum*. London: Rutledge & Kegan Paul.

Aronson, E., Stephan, C., Sikes, J., Blaney, N., & Snapp, M. (1978). *The Jigsaw classroom*. Beverly Hills, CA: Sage.

Bock, R. D., & Wiley, D. E. (1967). Quasi-experimentation in educational settings: Comment. *School Review, 75*, 353–366.

Brookover, W., Beady, C., Flood, P., Schweitzer, J., & Wisenbaker, J. (1979). *School social systems and student achievement: Schools can make a difference*. New York: J. R. Bergin.

Brookover, W., Beamer, L., Efthim, H., Hathaway, D., Lezotte, L., Miller, S., Passalacqua, J., & Tornatzky, L. (1982). *Creating effective schools: An inservice program for enhancing school learning climate and achievement*. Holmes Beach, FL: Learning Publications.

Coleman, J. S., Campbell, E. Q., Hobson, C. J., McPartland, J., Mood, A. M., Weinfeld, F. D., & York, R. L. (1966). *Equality of educational opportunity*. Washington, DC: United States Department of Health, Education, and Welfare.

Cooper, H., & Tom, D. (1984). Socioeconomic status and ethnic group differences in achievement motivation. In R. Ames & C. Ames (Eds.), *Research on motivation in education: Student motivation*. New York: Academic Press.

Covington, M., & Beery, R. (1976). *Self-worth and school learning*. New York: Holt, Rinehart and Winston.

Cronbach, L., Daken, J., & Webb, N. (1976). *Research on classrooms and schools: Formulation of questions, design, and analysis*. (Evaluation Consortium Occasional Paper). Stanford, CA: Stanford University.

Deal, T. E., & Kennedy, A. A. (1983). Culture and school performance. *Educational Leadership, 40*, 14–15.

deCharms, R. (1968). *Personal causation.* New York: Academic Press.

deCharms, R. (1976). *Enhancing motivation: Change in the classroom.* New York: Irvington.

Deci, E. L. (1975). *Intrinsic motivation.* New York: Plenum Press.

Deci, E. L. (1980). *The psychology of self-determination.* Lexington, MA: Heath.

Diener, C., & Dweck, C. (1978). An analysis of learned helplessness: Continuous changes in performance strategy, and achievement cognitions following failure. *Journal of Personality and Social Psychology, 36*, 451–462.

Fyans, L. J., Jr., Kremer, B., Salili, F., & Maehr, M. L. (1981). The effects of evaluation conditions on continuing motivation: A study of the cultural, personological and sitautional antecedents of a motivational pattern. *International Journal of Intercultural Relations, 5*, 147–163.

Fyans, L. J., Jr., & Maehr, M. L. (1985). [An examination of variations in students' perceptions of the value of science across schools.] Unpublished raw data.

Fyans, L. J., Jr., Maehr, M. L., & Archer, J. (1985). [The effects of goal setting on students' academic achievement.] Unpublished raw data.

Fyans, L. J., Jr., Salili, F., Maehr, M. L. & Desai, K. (1983). A cross-cultural exploration into the meaning of achievement. *Journal of Personality and Social Psychology, 44*, 1000–1013.

Greenblatt, R. G., Cooper, B. S., & Muth, R. (1984). Managing for effective teaching. *Educational Leadership, 41*(5), 57–59.

Hackman, J. R., & Oldham, G. R. (1980). *Work redesign.* Reading, MA: Addison-Wesley.

Hill, K. T. (1984). Debilitating motivation and testing: A major educational problem-possible solutions and policy applications. In R. Ames & C. Ames (Eds). *Research in motivation in education: Student motivation* (pp. 245–274). New York: Academic Press.

Johnson, D. W., & Johnson, R. T. (1981). Effects of cooperative and individualistic experiences on interethnic interaction. *Journal of Educational Psychology, 73*, 454–459.

Johnson, D. W., Maruyama, G., Johnson, R., Nelson, D., & Skon, L. (1981). Effects of cooperative, competitive, and individualistic goal structures on achievement: A meta-analysis. *Psychological Bulletin, 89*, 47–62.

Maehr, M. L. (1974a). Culture and achievement motivation. *American Psychologist, 29*, 887–896.

Maehr, M. L. (1974b). *Sociocultural origins of achievement.* Monterey, CA: Brooks/Cole.

Maehr, M. L. (1976). Continuing motivation: An analysis of a seldom considered outcome. *Review of Educational Research, 46*, 443–462.

Maehr, M. L. (1982). *Motivational factors in school achievement.* (Commissioned paper). Washington, DC: U.S. Department of Education, National Commission on Excellence in Education.

Maehr, M. L. (1983). On doing well in science: Why Johnny no longer excels; why Sarah never did. In S. Paris, G. Olson, & H. Stevenson (Eds.), *Learning and motivation in the classroom.* Hillsdale, NJ: Erlbaum.

Maehr, M. L. (1984). Meaning and motivation. In R. Ames & C. Ames (Eds.), *Research on motivation in education: Student motivation.* New York: Academic Press.

Maehr, M. L., & Braskamp, L. A. (1986). *The motivation factor: A theory of personal investment.* Lexington, MA: Lexington Press (D.C. Heath).

Maehr, M. L., & Nicholls, J. G. (1980). Culture and achievement motivation: A second look. In N. Warren (Ed.), *Studies in cross-cultural psychology* (Vol. 3). New York: Academic Press.

Maehr, M. L., & Sjogren, D. (1971). Atkinson's theory of achievement motivation: First step toward a theory of academic motivation? *Review of Educational Research, 41*, 143–161.

Maehr, M. L. & Stallings, W. M. (1972). Freedom from external evaluation. *Child Development, 43*, 177–188.

Maehr, M. L., & Stallings, W. M. (Eds.). (1975). *Culture, child and school*. Monterey, CA: Brooks/Cole.

Maruyama, G. (1984). What causes achievement? An examination of antecedents of achievement in segregated and desegregated classrooms. In D. Bartz & M. L. Maehr (Eds.), *The effects of school desegregation in motivation and achievement*. Greenwich, CT: JAI Press.

McClelland, D. (1985). *Human motivation*. Glenview, IL: Scott, Foresman, & Co.

Miller, N. & Maruyama, G. (1979). The reexamination of normative influence processes in desegregated classrooms. *American Educational Research Journal, 16*, 273–283.

Nicholls, J. (1979). Quality and inequality in intellectual development: The role of motivation in education. *American Psychologist, 34*, 1071–1084.

Nicholls, J. (1984). Conceptions of ability and achievement motivation. In R. Ames & C. Ames (Eds.), *Research on motivation in education: Student motivation*. New York: Academic Press.

Nicholls, J., Patashnick, M., & Nolen, S. (1985). Adolescent theories of education. Unpublished manuscript.

Paris, S. G., Olson, G. M. & Stevenson, H. W. (Eds.). (1983). *Learning and motivation in the classroom*. Hillsdale, NJ: Erlbaum.

Peters, T. J., & Waterman, R. H., Jr. (1982). *In search of excellence: Lessons from America's best-run companies*. New York: Harper & Row.

Purkey, S. C. (1978). *Inviting school success*. Belmont, CA: Wadsworth.

Purkey, S. C., & Smith, M. S. (1982). Too soon to cheer? Synthesis of research on effective schools model. *Phi Delta Kappan, 64*, 689–694.

Rosenholtz, S. J. (1985). Effective schools: Interpreting the evidence. *American Journal of Education, 93*, 352–388.

Rutter, M., Maughan, B., Mortimer, P., & Ouston, J. (1979). *Fifteen thousand hours: Secondary schools and their effects on children*. Cambridge, MA: Harvard University Press.

St. John, N. H. (1975). *School desegregation: Outcomes for children*. New York: Wiley.

Salili, F., Maehr, M. L., Sorensen, L., & Fyans, L. J., Jr. (1976). A further consideration of the effects of evaluation on motivation. *American Educational Research Journal, 13*, 85–102.

Sergiovanni, T. J. (1984). Leadership and excellence in schooling. *Educational Leadership, 41*, 4–13.

Sergiovanni, T. J., & Corbally, J. E. (Eds.). (1984). *Leadership and organizational culture*. Urbana: University of Illinois Press.

Sergiovanni, T. J., & Starratt, R. J. (1983). *Supervision: Human perspectives*. New York: McGraw-Hill.

Walberg, H. J. (1981). A psychological theory of educational productivity. In F. H. Farley & N. Gordon (Eds.), *Psychology and education*. Berkeley, CA: McCutchan.

Walberg, H. J. (1983). Scientific literacy and economic productivity in international perspective. *Daedalus, 11*, 1–28.

Walberg, H. J. (1984). Improving the productivity of American schools. *Educational Leadership, 41*, 19–30.

Walberg, H. J., Harnisch, D., & Tsai, S. L. (in press). Elementary school mathematics productivity in twelve countries. *Journal of Educational Research*.

Walberg, H. J., & Shanahan, T. (1983). High school effects on individual students. *Educational Researcher, 12*, 4–9.

Willig, A. C., Harnisch, D. C., Hill, K. T., & Maehr, M. L. (1983). Sociocultural and educational correlates of SUCCESS – failure attributions and evaluation anxiety in the school setting for black, Hispanic and Anglo children. *American Educational Research Journal, 20*, 385–410.

Part V

Education, culture, and society

13   Socialization to computing in college: a look beyond the classroom

Vitaly Dubrovsky, Sara Kiesler, Lee Sproull, and David Zubrow

And the first time it's like, "Wow, a computer! I've never used one of these before. I wonder how it works?"... You didn't know what you were doing. I mean, you knew because the teacher told you what to do but you were just like, "Oh, well, I type this, then I type that, and I hope it works. Here goes...."

As computers become more significant in our work and life, more nontechnical people encounter them. Today initial encounters with computers take place in homes (Rogers, Daley, and Wu, 1982), elementary and secondary schools (Taylor, 1980), and the workplace (Zuboff, 1982; Engelberger, 1980; Rice, Johnson, & Rogers, 1982). College campuses also provide initial encounters where freshmen and nontechnical students are taking programming courses and using computers in courses in ways that only a few years ago were reserved for advanced science and engineering students. Indeed, many colleges are beginning to require all students to demonstrate some computing competence, and some colleges require students to purchase computers.

Previous investigations of initial encounters with computing have typically employed one or more of three perspectives: technical capabilities, instructional practices, and individual abilities. Analyses using a technical capabilities perspective focus on the relative ease or difficulty with which new users learn particular computer operations as a function of equipment or software variables (e.g., Black & Moran, 1982). Often the users in these studies are not new to computing itself, but rather are new to the particular operations being studied (e.g., DeYoung, Kampen, & Topolski, 1982; Schneider et al., 1982). Analyses using an instructional

This research was supported by grants from the IBM corporation to Clarkson University and Carnegie-Mellon University, and from the System Development Foundation to Carnegie-Mellon University. We are grateful to Siva Kolla, Angela Mucci, Beheruz Sethna, and Daniel Smith for their help in collecting and analyzing the data. Work on this research was shared; authorship is alphabetical.

313

perspective usually measure the accuracy with which people learn certain material, perhaps as a function of alternative instructional techniques (e.g., Taylor, 1980). Analyses of individual abilities assume that more able students will have better experiences (e.g., Arndt, Feltes & Hanak, 1983). In none of these perspectives does the investigation concern what the new person learns about such issues as:

- the context in which computing occurs
- available status positions for those who compute
- the kinds of people who compute
- the social organization of computing
- the values the institution places on computing

These are cultural lessons. In employing a cultural perspective, we assume the existence of an ongoing culture in which particular computing equipment and software are merely artifacts. What we have investigated is how novices – in this case, college students – encounter this culture within their own college and what lessons they learn about it, themselves, and their institution as a result. The lessons and experiences we are interested in are not those narrowly related to computing assignments per se or classroom exercises but rather those learned in the multipurpose social setting where computing is carried out by all members of the campus computing community.

Computing as culture

As the technology and marketing of computers has developed, a culture of computing has developed too. The computing culture is manifested most strongly in research, development, and engineering divisions within the computer industry itself and in computer science departments of major universities. These "hacker" communities are expert, cohesive, believe they represent the vanguard of social as well as technological change, reinforce in one another a sense of difference from the rest of society, and have a special language and idiosyncratic behaviors (Steele, et al., 1983; Turkle, 1984). As is true in many other professions such as law, medicine, and the arts, socialization of its own members to the computer culture is intense. But unlike the case for most other professions, which are isolated physically and organizationally from lay persons, the computer culture influences lay persons as well as professionals. In universities where these communities exist, every person may encounter the computer culture. One reason is that computers are used for many different purposes. On a college campus the same machine or machines might be used for research, administration, accounting, teaching, and text processing. This increases everyone's exposure to the culture of computing. Second, many kinds of people have direct access to computers. That is, people have their own accounts or even their own computers; there need be no expert persons intervening between them and the machine. Third, many of the people with access are young students – smart, with time and the stamina for absorbing themselves in computing and computing values. Finally, universities tend to be less bureaucratic and formal than most government, commercial or manufacturing settings. Where smart people have direct access to flexible machines in nonbureaucratic settings, the culture of computing, and the consequences of its socialization processes, are nurtured and flourish.

What are the characteristics of this culture? At the outset, the culture is not a single, monolithic entity. Hackers at Stanford University are not the same as hackers at IBM. Yet identifiable elements of a common culture exist at both places. Every culture has values and norms, language, a status hierarchy, membership signs, artifacts, and boundaries to distinguish members from nonmembers (Gamst & Horbeck, 1976). The computing culture is adolescent. Pranks, tricks, and games are benignly tolerated when not actually encouraged. People are often impolite, unconventional, adventurous, and irreverent. Mild larceny, such as faking accounts, breaking codes, stealing time, and copying proprietary software, is admired if not rewarded explicitly. The culture highly values individual achievement. Many projects need teamwork, but individual work is revered. There is competition to write the best, fastest, biggest program or to build the best, fastest, smallest hardware. The culture values idiosyncracy in both people and systems, persistence, and independence. True members of the culture may be found at a terminal or computer at all hours of the day and night. These values and norms are revealed through the status hierarchy and language of the culture, which assigns people to such categories as wizards, wheels, hackers, randoms, users, and losers. (See Steele et al., 1983, for a glimpse into the language of this culture; see Turkle, 1984, for an extended cultural description.)

Today, computing in educational and work organizations exists within a general environment of computer populism. For many individuals and most organizations, computers have positive symbolic legitimacy. Computers are depicted in advertising, popular magazine articles, and the reports of university presidents as vehicles for increasing productivity, making learning easier, and improving the quality of work life. From the perspective of society and many organizations, the computer culture and populist computing are comfortably symbiotic. Advances in microchip technology from the computer professionals make it possible to bring more machines to more people. The good reputations of computer science departments increase universities' ability to market their computer education programs and research facilities to prospective students and faculty. But from the perspective of the individual student who encounters them for the first time, the esoteric and rigorous mores of the computer culture have little to do with the "user friendly" experience they expected. Thus, despite its rapid intrusion into many areas of life, computing for these students is not just something new, but something alien.

Consider a college student encountering a computer and some of the ways in which academic computing differs from other course work. Whereas in other courses students are free to choose the time and places that suit them best to do their homework, students of computing are tied to terminals and computers. When students read history books, the pages never go blank. When students are writing papers, if their pencils break they can sharpen them. But computer tools are not under students' control. Computing also differs in speed and nature of feedback. If a student is doing a physics assignment, the first wrong digit he or she writes on the page does not generate a cascade of error messages. In other courses, students may stop after their exertions and imagine that the essay is good enough or that they have worked enough math problems. In computing, there is no stopping until the program actually runs.

In order for novices actually to use a computer system, they must make their way through a host of arbitrary conventions that are totally unrelated to the science or theory of computing. A new student is thrown into a sea of syntax, I/O devices, priority classes, programs, and system quirks with no conceptual life vest to keep him afloat. The stylized nature of person–computer interaction can be particularly alienating to this student. All new disciplines involve learning conventions, but it is humiliating to be at the mercy of so many trivial and arbitrary ones. (To exit one program, you say "bye." Others require "exit"; others, "quit"; and still others, a control character.) It's like trying to play a game whose rules you don't know. It's hard to discern the legal moves, and those who are experienced can play out more sophisticated gambits. Not only is it difficult for novices to do their work once they have gained access, but simply gaining access itself may be difficult. At many colleges computing is a scarce resource; thus, students may be forced to wait long periods of time just to gain access to the potentially frustrating machine.

As strange as these experiences may be, their strangeness is exacerbated by the fact that they occur within a social context in which other people are quite at home. This embedding of computing in the larger life of the organization distinguishes students' computing encounters from those of, say, the physics laboratory. While the physics laboratory may also lead students to feel out of control, it is a very sheltered and isolated environment apart from the real business of physics or the rest of the university. By contrast, the new computing student must compete for computing resources with administrators who are managing accounting, secretaries who are typing manuscripts, faculty members who are doing research, students who are doing assignments, and hackers.

Encountering processes

In this work we have drawn on a considerable social psychological literature on situations in which people encounter unpredictability or uncertainty. There is also a literature on the adjustment and outcomes of professional sojourners to foreign countries, such as Peace Corps workers, students, and managers. Our model of individual encountering processes is based in part on what is known about novices in alien cultures, and our hypotheses about organizational differences are taken from research on host culture characteristics, such as the development of protective enclaves which shelter novices (see Church, 1982).

One learns a culture through socialization into it. In being socialized, an individual acquires the social knowledge and skills necessary to assume a role in the culture. In the case of a computing professional, socialization transcends the particular organization in that once having acquired that role in any organization one then occupies a different status in all subsequent organizations. In the case of a computer novice, having sojourned in the culture of computing prepares the person for encounters with the culture in all subsequent organizations.

If the culture is an alien one, as we suggest for computing, then socialization will occur under conditions of strangeness. Strangeness or unfamiliarity means that the novice's habitual and efficient models for learning will not be useful and appropriate. That is, novices must learn *how* to learn as well as *what* to learn. They must develop new ways of assimilating information and a new framework for it. They must learn how to recognize and interpret cues, and whom to rely on as informants. They must learn how to organize new bits and pieces of knowledge into coherent theories of behavior. In these processes, the novice brings capabilities, prior experiences, and expectations to the new setting. Sometimes these capabilities, prior experiences, and expectations impart sufficient confidence or problem-solving skills to deal successfully with the confusing situation.

The interaction between the novice and the setting provides the occasion for socialization into the culture. The process of initial socialization has four major features: reality shock, absence of control or confusion, control attempts, and socialization outcomes, including cultural lessons. In the rest of this section, we describe these features and illustrate them using remarks made by students themselves (Sproull, Kiesler, & Zubrow, 1984). All of the remarks were made by nontechnical students (liberal arts or management majors) in two universities about their first college encounters with computers.

During the early days in a new culture, the novice experiences the perception of changes, contrasts, and surprises (Louis, 1980); we call this constellation of experiences, *reality shock*. Changes are simply objective differences from the novice's prior situation, for example, in title, workload, customs. Contrasts are differences in what is subjectively salient, for example in surroundings and language (Smalley, 1963). Surprises are unanticipated differences between expectations and reality, for example, the loss of social status that people sent abroad to work may experience (Byrnes, 1966; Higbee, 1969).

In the case of academic computing, novices encounter both technical strangeness and cultural strangeness. Technical strangeness is reflected in how unexpectedly time-consuming computing is due to scarce resources, demands of programming, machine unreliability, and machine invisibility, as the following comments indicate:

University A

It's not like another class where you can take books someplace. You can't lift a terminal up and take it anywhere.

I was almost finished with a program and it crashed. I didn't have a save. I didn't put save on. I had to start over. It was heartbreaking.

I mean, sometimes I feel like the computer is out after me. You know, everybody gets that feeling that the computer's after them sometimes.

University B

I didn't expect the programs to be so picky. If I made a minor error, I expected the program to run anyways. You have to be careful about how you type things in . . . I felt especially discouraged with this program. I can't figure out a particular error. I've checked and rechecked and I can't figure it out. I've worked on it for two days now.

Our economics teacher is making us work an "economy" by making us change certain variables – switching them up – and everything is right justified. I didn't right justify everything, so instead of making a ten it went into the wrong column and ended up as a thousand, and my economy blew up. I had to purge everything and start over. I spent three hours trying to get everything back to the starting point.

Cultural strangeness is reflected in resources that are designed for and even shared with computer experts, and course demands that express values of the computer culture, that is, to inculcate computer science principles rather than specific computing skills.

University A
I was surprised, really surprised at the people set up along the benches. There's no privacy. Where I was, in the computer science department, they had little stalls for each terminal. I thought that was a much better idea, just because I would think that working at a bench like that would be really distracting. It reminded me of a horse at a trough.

I feel like I'm in *1984* – cells right next to each other. It's like Russia. You've got to just get as many people as you can, crammed in there. [The walls] are all white. And all they have are computer information on them. Maybe they could have a Picasso picture. Anything just to break the monotony. All you see are computer geeks and computers and the Xerox machines and white on the walls.

I didn't think it was going to be something to learn how to program a computer. I thought it was going to be teaching us how to use the computer.

I did not expect I'd have to write out programs. I expected to learn here's how to use it to our advantage with economics and all sorts of fun courses like that.

University B
The books in the terminal room are strange. The professors suggest using them to look up error mesages, but I don't know where to start. They are pretty useless.

It's not what I expected. There is more concept work in COBOL. . . . there is a lot of programming. The programming is all right – that's logic, but the concept work is like memorization.

I didn't think computing would be as big a part of academic life as it is.

The strongest experience of cultural strangeness is embodied in direct encounters with members of the computer culture:

University A
I was on the computer and something happened. I didn't know what was going on. I saw a guy sitting over there who looked like a real hacker. So I asked him, and he got up, and he started doing all of this stuff with my account without telling me what he was doing. He started messing around, "You need this. Let's see. I'll give you this file." It's like, what are you doing? He wouldn't tell me.

University B
Some of the people are weird. Out and out weird. In the terminal room. They are strange. That's all there is to it.

It's tough, but I wasn't surprised at that. One thing that surprised me about the people, they aren't well-rounded at all. They are very into their work.

As these interview responses illustrate, reality shock is the product of features in the culture and the novice's perceptions of them. Reality shock is important to the novice because it signals that prior instrumental behaviors are no longer appropriate and new ones must be learned. It is also important because it colors the early lessons learned in the new culture. How demands of new culture are managed by the novice is key to the outcomes of socialization (David, 1971).

Some people experience reality shock as a problem in the environment to be solved. Some people experience reality shock as confusion and absence of control in themselves (Oberg, 1966). Novices may feel overwhelmed and may question their own competence. These feelings can express themselves in thoughts such as, "I don't know what I'm doing" and "I must look foolish" or "Maybe I'm not the person I thought I was." These feelings lead novices to question the capabilities of people they must depend upon, "Why can't these people communicate?"

University A
It's frightening when everyone else is around you just typing in as fast as they can, and you don't even know what to do.

I get the feeling from my computing teacher that he's just telling me half the story. That's all he is telling me because when I get to the computer I still don't know what I'm doing. Even after listening to him in class. He explains procedures and functions and major things but he doesn't tell us how to write a program.

University B
It was tough. . . . In high school all they had was BASIC. You just turned it on and started typing in your program. There was no "go" mode or "edit" mode and stuff like that.

I spend a lot of time moving statements around and I can't figure out why moving statements around would change the whole program.

One expression of lack of control is the attempt to regain it. In attempting control, novices try to reduce discrepancies between their expectations and the current state (e.g., Bandura, 1977; Carver and Scheier, 1982; Kanfer and Hagerman, 1981; Thompson, 1981). Control attempts can entail mental activity, such as constructing metaphors to explain what is happening:

University A
In the computation center they have little gnomes and they sit down in the basement . . . in bug hot rooms, like the devil, and mess around with students and put errors in their programs.

If you stretch it a little, you can think of the user consultant as a librarian, someone who advises you when you don't know what to do.

Control attempts can also entail talking with others and seeking help overtly:

University B
I met a lot of people in the computer room who are willing to help, if you ask.

When cultural encounters lead novices to feel out of control, negative socialization outcomes – anger or withdrawal – are likely to result (Brockner, 1979; Carver, Blaney, and Scheier, 1979). Anger leads to intransigence, active rejection of the values of the socializing agents (Goffman, 1961). The angry novice says, "These people are so crazy that only an idiot would want to act like them." Withdrawal also precludes positive socialization. The withdrawn novice might say, "I'm no good at this and there's no sense in trying."

Here, we assume that students normally have good self-esteem and every culture specifies particular abilities that are important. Difficulty or anxiety attached to learning these abilities is neither unusual nor inconsistent with successful socialization. But when the interaction of culture and individual capability leads novices to feel confused, foolish, and unable to control consequences of their behavior, and if the novices are entrapped into the continuing experience of these phenomena, then they will suffer anger and withdrawal and a continuing decrement in self-esteem. And, as well, they will learn negative cultural lessons. We illustrate these responses in University A.

Anger:

The fact that you have to fight to get on, you – the whole computer theory, everything about computing here is a fight to do it. It's something you don't want to do and you have to fight to get in there to do it. And you have to fight to sit down and do it. And you have to fight the system to stay up. And you have to fight your program to make it work. And the whole time you're fighting the clock.

Withdrawal:

Looking back, I'm really not afraid of computers. But I'm going to try to stay away from computers. I know I shouldn't because it's probably the thing of the future. But I'm really kind of leery to get into any type of computing again.

A negative cultural lesson:

Some people just live and die with computers. They sleep there. They don't get any sleep because they sleep with computers. . . . They can't relate to anything but the computer. They can't talk to a normal guy. Even when they talk, they talk computer language. It's like they've turned into a computer.

Self-confidence leads novices to feel they can solve problems; this is reinforced by actually experiencing positive outcomes and being able to help others. Positive outcomes are those in which the novice gains the skills, motivation, and positive cultural lessons needed to become further socialized or even to become a cultural recruit.

University A

My first program ... it wasn't real tough, but everybody else was having trouble with it and I thought it was pretty easy. And I got to help everybody out so that's pretty good.

One student at University A learned that she would have to do a history assignment on the computer the semester following her computer course:

I was glad that we were doing it on the computer. I don't know why. I just thought, "Oh neat, we get to use the computer again."

University B

[I was surprised] how easily learning the system and learning programming came to me. I became fairly successful at it. It's not difficult if you have the right attitude.

Completing a program correctly makes you feel good. At least you have something to show for it.

In these examples, we have seen how all novices learn cultural lessons. But successful socialization is associated especially with positive cultural lessons, as may be seen in the following remarks by proud freshmen:

University A

I would say the first time I had a program actually work on the computer [I felt proud]. It had taken some work to get through all the debugging. I call it debugging now. It's just correcting errors.

The amount of more intelligent people I've met down there ... What I did on the computer seems so amazing to me. ... Then I thought that some of the people around me were doing much more complicated things and how smart they must be.

University B

I'd advise freshmen to be investigative. Just use the system.

Most novices will ultimately come to terms with the culture of computing. At an elementary level, they will learn to avoid or to work with computers, and some will become experts. But if the above framework is meaningful novices will also learn much more in their initial encounters with computing. They will develop an image of "the computer," of the culture, and of their own relationship to it. For educating students in meanings, uses, and organizational values of computing, these understandings are probably more important than the technical details of particular hardware or software that can be conveyed to novices in an introductory encounter.

Method

The study we describe here is part of an ongoing annual investigation of students and computing which we began in 1982. We report our most recent findings; however, other years' results are similar.

Our approach is a field-based comparative questionnaire study of student encounters with computing in two universities. As described in Table 13.1, both universities emphasize technical subjects, and in both, computing is highly valued. In fact, both institutions announced in 1982 a major expansion of computing for students and faculty. But the computer culture, we assert, is much stronger at one of the universities. University A is a research university where the computer science department has a world-class reputation, and computer science is one of the most prestigious graduate programs on campus. By contrast, University B is more professionally oriented with a strong reputation for excellent undergraduate education whose computer science department was created only recently.

Freshman students at Universities A and B were surveyed toward the end of the 1984 academic year. Both technical and nontechnical majors were surveyed. Table 13.2 describes our sample. At University A the questionnaire was administered to students in one core social science course. This course is part of the required curriculum for liberal arts freshmen in the humanities and social sciences and is recommended as an elective to many technical students. At University B the survey was administered to a random sample of sections of a humanities course required of all freshmen. Our principal intention was to compare those students' experiences in their different courses, including computer science.

The questionnaire used to measure the students' experiences with their freshman courses was a 23-item version of a questionnaire that the authors had used in earlier studies (Sproull et al., 1984). Based on interitem correlations, at least one item was chosen to measure each component of the socialization process model (reality shock, confusion, control attempts) as well as positive (cultural learning, pride) and negative (anger, withdrawal) socialization outcomes. Figure 13.1 displays the questionnaire items.

The students answered questions about courses in four subject areas that they took during the semester they were enrolled in computer science. Typically, students took courses in English, social science or business, mathematics and computer science. We compared what students said about their computer science course with their responses to their other courses. This controls for general "freshman year" effects. The analyses presented here involve only a comparison between computer science and mathematics. Mathematics is a good comparison course for two reasons. First, both computer science and mathematics require

Table 13.1. *Comparing the culture of computing at two universities*

	University A	University B
Organizational description		
Total enrollment	5341	4107
Undergraduates	4027	3760
Male	2710	2899
Female	1317	861
% Female	32.7%	22.9%
Graduate students	1308	347
Male	1015	291
Female	293	56
% Female	22.4%	16.1%
% Graduates vs. all	24.5%	8.4%
Number Employees	1200	587
Number of Faculty	481	251
Major academic divisions or colleges	Science	Science
	Engineering	Engineering
	Management (grad. only)	Management
	Humanities & social sciences	Liberal studies
	Public affairs (grad. only)	Graduate school
	Fine arts	
Libraries		
Number of libraries	3	4
Number of books	650,000	700,000
Computing culture		
Presence of computing professionals		
Size of computer science (CS) department (faculty)	approx. 60	9
First degrees in computer science	1965	1982
First computers on campus	1950s	1960s
Other CS related departments? (e.g., robotics)	Yes	No
Values and norms of computing professionals in campus community		
Presence of computer network/mail linking whole campus?	Yes	No
Any faculty may have an account on the network?	Yes	No
Telephone directly includes computer user-IDs?	Yes	No
Administrators have personal computers or terminals at home linked to mainframe?	Most	No

Table 13.1. *(cont.)*

	University A	University B
Terminal room modeled after CS terminal room rather than library? reading rooms?	Yes	No
Computer education resources integrated with audiovisual and libraries?	No	Yes
Control over computer resources decentralized?	No	Yes, college controlled
Computing taught only by CS faculty?	Yes	No, also by college faculty
Popular computing values		
Full computerization of campus		
Announce goal	1982	1982
Personal computers on campus	approx. 2500	approx. 2000
Terminals on campus	approx. 2000	approx. 400
Talking about computing		
Size of description in student catalogue	102 lines	84 lines
Number of mentions of computing in the president's annual report, 1983	14 mentions	6 mentions
Top administrators with terminals or personal computers in office	All	Most
Students debated over computerization	Yes	Yes

quantitative and analytic competence and both are considered important technical skills. Second, mathematics is taken by most freshmen, which provided us with the largest usable sample of students who also took computer science.

The students rated each course on each item using the following scheme: 3 = true or mostly true, 2 = neither true nor false, and 1 = false or mostly false. We recoded these responses to a simple 0–1 scale where 1 = true or mostly true and 0 = false or neither true nor false. To carry out the analyses, students were categorized based on the college or academic division in which they were enrolled. Technical students were defined as those in engineering or science. Nontechnical students were defined as those in arts, humanities, management, or business.

Table 13.2. *Sample characteristics by university*

	University A	University B
Samples size N	181	184
Demographic distributions (%)		
Curriculum		
Technical	39.2	79.9
Nontechnical	60.8	20.1
Gender		
Male	69.1	81.5
Female	30.9	18.5
Prior computing		
Yes	66.3	75.5
No	33.7	24.5
Computer games		
Yes	61.2	78.7
No	38.8	21.3

Findings

The results of this research address four questions. Does the difference between computing and other courses we found in two earlier studies persist? Do nontechnical students have more negative encounters than technical students, controlling for experience in mathematics? Do University A students have more negative encounters than do University B students (because of the strength of the computer culture at University A)? Does our model of the socialization process account for patterns of student behavior?

Computer science versus mathematics: The alien culture persists

Data comparing students' computer science course with their mathematics course, categorized by curricula and university, are presented in Table 13.3. These data show that both technical and nontechnical students reported more negative experiences with computer science than with mathematics. More students felt angered by their computer science course than by their mathematics course. Differential responses to the withdrawal item were less pronounced. Positive outcomes present a

Personal characteristics

1. What is your class? (Freshman, Sophomore, Junior, Senior)
2. What is your college? (e.g., Science, Engineering, Management)
3. What was your high school GPA?
4. What is your most probable career?
5. Are you male or female?
6. Did you have a computing course before college?
7. Do you play computer games in arcades?
8. Do you play home video games?
9. Do you play computer games at college?
10. Describe a computer to someone who has never seen or used one.

Attitudes about each course (Answer true, false, or neither)

1. Very different from other courses
2. I feel I don't know what I am doing
3. I talk to people who know more than I do
4. This course makes me angry
5. I want to do just enough to get by
6. I am learning the language of this field
7. I feel proud of my performance

Parts of this course remind me of:
8. Visiting a mental hospital
9. Visiting the Library of Congress
10. Being in a war
11. Competing for a sports team

12. What grade did you receive or do you expect to receive in this course?

Figure 13.1. Items in the survey, 1984.

different picture. Technical students reported greater pride concerning their performance in computer science than in mathematics. Nontechnical students were more proud of their performance in mathematics than in computer science. For cultural learning all students (but more so for nontechnical students) reported learning the language of computing to a somewhat greater degree than they reported learning the language of mathematics.

Curriculum and university differential impacts

Based on our ideas about the presence of a computer culture and students' abilities to deal with its alien aspects, we developed the following hypotheses.

Table 13.3. *Percent of students responding true by curriculum, university and course for socialization model components, 1984*

Course	University A		University B	
	Computing	Mathematics	Computing	Mathematics
Items	Technical curriculum			
Process measures				
Reality shock	60.6**	12.7	55.9	11.7
	(N = 71)		(N = 145)	
Confusion	13.9**	1.4	18.2	6.8
	(N = 72)		(N = 148)	
Control attempt	47.2**	29.2	46.4	38.4
	(N = 72)		(N = 138)	
Outcomes				
Negative				
Anger	28.8**	12.3	34.2	9.6
	(N = 73)		(N = 146)	
Withdrawal	13.9*	12.5	15.6	7.5
	(N = 72)		(N = 147)	
Positive				
Pride	64.4**	43.8	49.7	40.8
	(N = 73)		(N = 147)	
Cultural learning	83.6	72.6	68.3	66.9
	(N = 73)		(N = 145)	
	Nontechnical curriculum			
Process measures				
Reality shock	72.0**	21.5	47.1	14.7
	(N = 107)		(N = 34)	
Confusion	46.3**	5.6	11.1	11.1
	(N = 108)		(N = 36)	
Control attempt	66.7**	27.8	41.4	34.5
	(N = 108)		(N = 29)	
Outcomes				
Negative				
Anger	64.2**	5.5	47.2	27.8
	(N = 109)		(N = 36)	
Withdrawal	35.5**	19.1	19.4	19.4
	(N = 110)		(N = 36)	
Positive				
Pride	30.8**	53.3	50.0	47.2
	(N = 110)		(N = 36)	
Cultural learning	47.2**	40.7	61.8	41.2
	(N = 108)		(N = 34)	

Notes: Significance is based on paired T-test of items by curriculum pooling across universities.
*p < .05. **p < .01.

1. Nontechnical students will have more negative experiences and outcomes toward computing than will technical students when they encounter computing.
2. Students from the university with the more active computer culture (University A) will have more negative experiences and outcomes than will students at the university where the computer culture is less active (University B).
3. Nontechnical students at the university with the more active computer culture will have the most negative negative encounters and outcomes as a group.

To analyze the effects of curriculum and university, a series of logit equations was estimated for each of the seven items in our questionnaire which measured socialization – three process measures and four outcome measures. The data used for these analyses are all categorical, true versus not true responses to all items. Again, we included mathematics as a comparison course; it was entered as an independent variable in the logit equations (Kennedy, 1983).

For each item a set of hierarchical equations was estimated to provide a meaningful set of goodness-of-fit statistics for comparison. All equations included terms to adjust for sampling effects. The first contained main effects for mathematics, curriculum, and university. The second equation added the curriculum x university interaction. Subsequent equations added higher-order interactions with mathematics until a fully-saturated equation was constructed. To test our hypotheses we compared the change in goodness-of-fit statistics, the component chi-square, among these equations. If a significant difference ($\alpha = .05$) is found, then the addition of the effect significantly contributes to explaining the data. The final equation selected for interpretation is the one containing the highest order effect of interest making a significant improvement in goodness-of-fit and exceeding the overall goodness-of-fit criterion ($\alpha = .1$). Once an equation is selected for interpretation, its parameter estimates for the effects of interest can be analyzed to determine the direction and magnitude of the effect upon a subject's odds of ending up in one level versus another level of the dependent variable. The results for these equations are discussed below and displayed in Table 13.4.

Logit analysis calculates the probability (expressed as the log-odds ratio) that a person will end up in one, rather than another, category of a dependent variable. The computational procedure for the logit equations used the following categories as the reference categories for each variable. For mathematics the reference category is not experiencing the stated socialization component. The reference category for curriculum is the technical curriculum. For university, University A is the reference category. The coefficients reported in Table 13.4 are applied directly to those students whose attributes fall into the reference categories. For student attributes not in a reference category, the negation of the effect coefficient applies in determining the final log-odds ratio. For instance, for reality shock the coefficient for mathematics is .359. This means that for the group of students not experiencing reality shock in mathematics, their log-odds ratio for reality shock in computing is increased .359. Therefore, the probability of not experiencing reality shock in computing also is increased. For students who did experience reality shock in mathematics, the coefficient used would be −.359. This would indicate a decrease in the log-odds ratio for reality shock in computing; the probability of not experiencing reality shock in computing given that they did experience it in mathematics decreased, and hence, the probability of experiencing reality shock increased.

Similarly, the logit coefficients reported for interactions apply to students falling into the group belonging either to both reference groups or to neither reference group. The negation of the coefficient applies to those students who belong to the reference category for only one variable of the interaction pair. This can be illustrated using the university × curriculum interaction for confusion. For both students in technical majors at University A and students in nontechnical majors at University B the coefficient, .288, is applied toward determining the final log-odds ratio for these groups of students. For nontechnical majors at University A and technical majors at University B, −.288 is used. What distinguishes the final log-odds ratios among these groups of students that receive the same coefficient for the interaction of the university x curriculum effect are the coefficients for the main effects of university and curriculum. All coefficients and effects are used toward determining the log-odds ratio for each group of students defined by the cross classification of the variables used in the analysis.

The dependent variable in all of the logit equations was the log-odds ratio for student response to the socialization component items for the computing course. The ratio was defined as the probability of not experiencing the component over the probability of experiencing the component.

For reality shock only the main effects of math, curriculum, and university were necessary to meet the fit criterion. For four of the other six items analyzed (confusion, control attempts, anger, and pride), the model selected for interpretation included main effects for math, curriculum, and university plus the curriculum x university interaction. Only for

Table 13.4. *Logit equation coefficients for socialization model components with computing as the dependent variable*

Socialization Component	Effect coefficients							
	Constant	Mathematics	Curriculum	University	University × curriculum	Mathematics × university	Mathematics × curriculum	Mathematics × university × curriculum
Reality shock	−.495	.359**	.015	−.125*				
Confusion	.480	.256*	.119	−.228**	.288**			
Control attempts	−.147	.358**	.088	−.181**	.130			
Anger	.011	.176*	.258**	−.060	.143*			
Withdrawal	.486	.351**	.066	−.050	.167*		.190*	
Cultural understanding	.332	.263**	.205**	.018	.192**	.084	.161*	
Pride	−.018	.254**	.208**	−.035	.184**			.139

Notes: *$p < .05$. **$p < .01$. The coefficients represent the contribution of each variable to the overall log-odds ratio of the percentage of students not experiencing the listed socialization component for computing over those who did. These same models were estimated with prior computing included as an additional effect. Prior computing, although significant in its own right, did not significantly alter the results; the interpretation of curriculum and university effects remains the same.

withdrawal and initial cultural learning are additional terms necessary to achieve an acceptable fit. In general, the significant parameter estimates show the effects to be in the expected direction. And, specifically for mathematics, the main effect indicates that students had a tendency to replicate their experience with mathematics in their computer science course. Therefore, the main effects of mathematics are not discussed further.

For reality shock a main effect for university ($p < .05$) was found, indicating that students in the more intense computer culture, University A, were more likely to experience reality shock when they took computer science. For confusion a main effect for university ($p < .01$) and a curriculum x university interaction ($p < .0015$) were found. The main effect shows an increased likelihood for students from University A to experience confusion about computing. Furthermore, the interaction of curriculum and university indicates that nontechnical students within University A have the greatest likelihood of experiencing confusion in their computing course. For control attempts, there is a significant main effect for university ($p < .01$) and a weak curriculum $\times$ university interaction ($p < .07$). These effects are similar to those for confusion and have the same interpretation. In sum, we find a significant negative influence of the more intense computing culture on the encountering process; the impact of computing hits hardest upon nontechnical students in the university where the computing culture is stronger. Counter to our hypothesis, no main effect for curriculum was found for any of the process measures.

There were four outcome measures: anger, withdrawal, cultural learning, and pride. For anger, a curriculum effect ($p < .00002$) and a curriculum $\times$ university interaction ($p < .025$) were significant. The effects suggest that nontechnical students are more likely to be angered by their computing course and nontechnical students at University A are most likely to be angered. For the second negative outcome, withdrawal, the only significant effect of interest is the curriculum by university interaction ($p < .05$). This effect shows a decrement in the odds that withdrawal will be experienced by technical students at University A. In addition a significant effect ($p < .03$) was also found for the math $\times$ curriculum interaction suggesting that technical students who did not experience withdrawal in math also benefited from an additional decrease in the odds ratio for experiencing withdrawal in computing beyond that associated with a favorable experience in mathematics alone.

The results for the positive socialization outcomes suggest technical students profit more in their computer science course. For pride in performance, a main curriculum main effect ($p < .0015$) and curriculum $\times$ university interaction ($p < .0032$) were found. These results favor technical students, particularly those at University A. The results for cultural learning are similar to those for pride in performance except that one higher-order effect involving math was also significant. Both the main effect for curriculum and the curriculum by university interaction were present and significant ($p < .006$ and $p < .01$, respectively). The interesting point about the higher order interaction is that it tends to increase the odds of a positive outcome for technical students: it provides an increment of the odds ratio for technical students who also acquired a cultural learning in mathematics ($p < .032$).

As a whole the results support our hypotheses regarding the differential impact of computing on technical versus nontechnical students and the difference in effect of the computing culture in the two universities. Additionally, the significant curriculum $\times$ university interactions suggest that nontechnical students have a more difficult time with computing at University A where the computing culture is stronger.

A description of the socialization process

We have demonstrated that computing does seem to be different from other courses, the experience is different for technical and nontechnical students, and the experience is different for students at the two universities where the computing culture varies in strength. We now use another approach to describe the encountering experiences of groups of students. We specify the encountering process as a tree structure with reality shock as the top node. From this, two branches emerge representing the paths of those who did and those who did not experience reality shock. Each of these leads to a confusion node and from both of the confusion nodes two more branches emerge representing students who did or did not experience confusion. This branching continues for the paths from confusion to control attempts and then from control attempts to the socialization outcomes. All in all there are eight (2^3) paths from reality shock through control attempts; each path terminates in its own set of three outcome categories.

The three outcome categories were created based on students' responses to the four socialization outcome items on the questionnaire. Two items indicated negative outcomes, anger and withdrawal, and two indicated positive outcomes, pride of academic performance and learning the language. The responses were simply added together with each negative outcome equal to -1 and each positive outcome equal to $+1$. If the resulting sum was positive then the student was coded into the positive category. If the sum equalled 0 then the student was coded into the mixed category, and those with a negative sum were placed into the negative category.

Cross tabulations can produce a process tree for the sample as a whole or for specifically defined sets of students, such as technical students only or only those from one university. Trees can also be constructed for specific courses. Many of these process trees were created and analyzed. The striking finding from this analysis is the integral role of confusion as a predictor of outcomes. Basically, across various groups of students, different courses, and for both universities, a pattern emerges that shows those who report confusion have a high probability of experiencing a negative outcome. Alternatively, those who do not report confusion are more likely to experience positive socialization. This implies that confusion is a pivotal concept in the socialization process.

This is not to say that all the trees are the same. The proportion of students following the various branches of the tree changes depending on the analysis. Figures 13.2 and 13.3 display some of these differences. For instance, at University A, 68.7% of the sample experienced reality shock in computing, whereas at University B, the figure was 50.5%. At the next level, only 44.8% of those students who experienced reality shock at University A also reported confusion. The comparable figure for University B is 25.7%. However, when the outcome total is analyzed by comparing the percentage of students at the end of each process path that fall into the negative outcome category the pattern is clear. At University A the average percentage of students who reported confusion ending up in the negative outcome category is 73.5% versus 13.2% for the students who did not report confusion. Similarly, at University B the comparable figures are 49.5% versus 15.5%. This finding illustrates the importance of confusion in the socialization process.

Discussion

We have described research on social psychological aspects of the introduction to computing and to the computing culture. The socialization model that we proposed has been supported by data from both technical and nontechnical students at two universities. Consistent with the model, students were more likely to report reality shock, confusion,

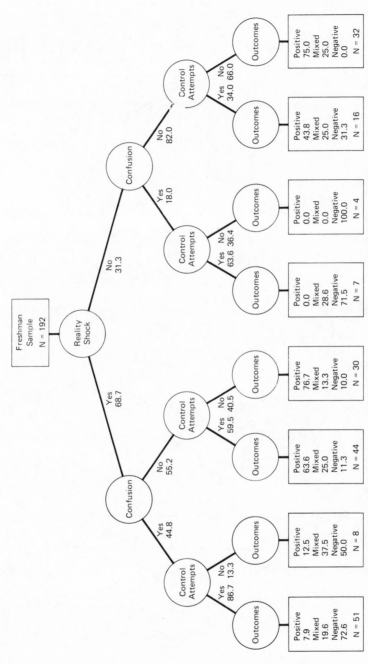

Figure 13.2. Tree diagram showing the percentage of students following different socialization paths in computing at University A.

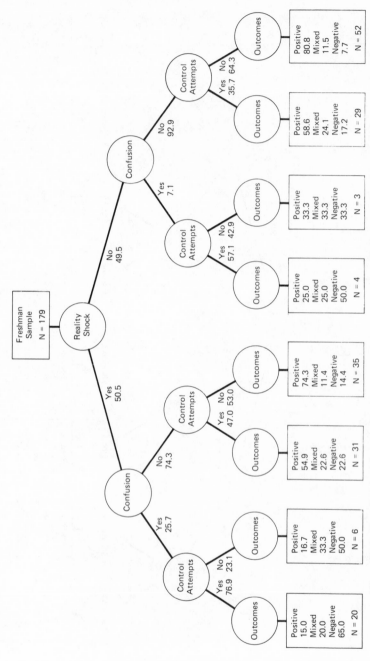

Figure 13.3. Tree diagram showing the percentage of students following different socialization paths in computing at University B.

control attempts, anger, and withdrawal in their computing courses than in their other required courses such as mathematics. This pattern was more typical of students in the research-oriented university than in the teaching-oriented university and more typical of nontechnical students than of technical students. Our findings suggest the fallacy of thinking about the introduction of computing as simply imparting technical skills. Cultural experiences and socialization processes are also important.

Why would an organization which places a high value on computing create a situation in which it is hard for novices to be enthusiastic? We have thought of three possibilities. First, a certain utopian blindness to problems may be in the nature of rapid technological change (Boguslaw, 1965). Second, most college administrators may lack personal experience with the technology. This leads them to depend on technical experts, to devote insufficient attention and resources to novices, and to neglect the need to integrate the technology with more general educational values. Third, if students are encountering an alien culture, members of that culture are encountering alien invaders. Should the computer culture have any obligation to allow anyone to join? Or should it be protective and exclusive, allowing only the "most fit" to join? At the moment, far more people seem to want (or to require) computer training than there are people willing to train them. It is a sellers' market and the sellers need not be hospitable to keep their numbers up. For programmers and computer scientists, allowing the masses of "users" into their territory will surely vitiate their competitive advantage. Thus, there may be some advantage in making the computing culture as alien as possible (W. Thorngate, personal communication, 1984).

Obviously, society is in a transitional period with respect to computing. Ten years from now it will be rare for any student to enter college with no previous computing experience. As students interact with computers at younger ages, they will be more sheltered from the computing culture. And if they develop technical mastery prior to encountering the computing culture, they will find the culture less alien, if and when they do encounter it.

Our own data show that previous experience with computing in school or at home does not turn nontechnical college students into technical college students (i.e., the gap remains with respect to their reaction to computer science). And previous experience does not change the relative influence of the university environment. On the other hand, students who entered college with previous computing experience had a more positive experience in college with their computer science course, other things equal, than did students without this experience. Their small advantage could develop into significant competence differences later.

We did not study the nature of students' precollege experiences with computing, so we must guess why earlier experience helped in college. Skills learned by most students in the lower grades are different from those learned in college, and the culture of computing is only faintly represented in schools. But skills learned in school probably include familiarity with computer keyboards and computer algorithms, each of which would tend to reduce confusion in college. And using a computer in school or at home will entail exposure to the language and conventions of computing, and even to young computer hackers. These various exposures might inoculate students against experiencing computing as alien, just as travel in childhood, learning a foreign language, and the study of cultural variation inoculates people against culture shock when they visit or live abroad.

Our research suggests several steps to increase the probability of successful socialization to computing for novices. All of these steps entail acknowledging the importance of cultural variables. For administrators and teachers, this means considering more than instructional processes. One important factor is the physical environment in which students compute. Most administrators probably worry about finding the resources to buy another disk drive or a new machine. They do not consider that novices are more likely to notice the color of paint on the walls (or lack of it) than they are the number of computer instructions executed per second.

A second important factor is characteristics of the "native guides" provided to help novices. Today these guides, at least technically proficient ones, are scarce. Universities often rely on student user consultants or teaching assistants. Elementary and high schools sometimes recruit computer teachers from local computer science departments or they depend on self-styled hackers. Those guides themselves may be members of the computer culture who share a belief that novices are inferior people. Administrators should consider the cultural beliefs (and not just the technical skills) of guides.

A third important factor is providing sheltered orientation experiences for novices before asking them to learn computing skills. Because computing is currently an activity that is performed in public, novices need to learn the ropes of the public settings. Novices may feel uncomfortable and experts may resent them for not knowing procedures concerning the use of shared equipment such as printers. Unless and until they do so, their unease will distract their attention from instructional learning. Novices also may feel reluctant to demand their share of the computer facilities. Teachers need to set up time-sharing rules, so novices don't have to fight to get a turn. Novices who cannot practice their skills in a comfortable, noncompetitive environment may abandon computing to the expert minority.

A fourth important factor is ensuring that educational organizations are a market for software that builds on all students' interests, not just those of technical students. It seems reasonable to assume that if a student interested in music can use a computer to compose, or if he or she can read a bulletin board about upcoming concerts and available records, then that student might have more interest in using the computer. Administrators should take more interest in the computer's potential for communication to encourage all students to use computers. The contents of computer network mail and bulletin board posts need have nothing to do with computers or with technical subjects. They can be about sports, rock stars, getting together after school – whatever students want to talk about.

Finally, teachers and administrators should help novices understand that they are having cultural, not just instructional, experiences. That realization can help novices sort out their confusions, gain control, and lead to positive socialization.

References

Arndt, S., Feltes, J., & Hanak, J. (1983). Secretarial attitudes towards word processors as a function of familiarity and locus of control. *Behavior and Information Technology, 2*(1), 17–22.

Bandura, A. (1977). Self-efficacy: Toward a unifying theory of behavior change. *Psychological Bulletin, 84*, 191–215.

Black, J. & Moran, T. (1982). Learning and remembering command names. In *Proceedings of the conference of human factors in computer systems* (pp. 8–11). Washington, DC: Association for Computing Machinery.

Boguslaw, R. (1965). *The new utopians: A study of system design and social change.* Englewood Cliffs, NJ: Prentice-Hall.

Brockner, J. (1979). The effects of self-esteem, success-failure, and self-consciousness on task performance. *Journal of Personality and Social Psychology, 37*, 1732–1741.

Byrnes, F. C. (1966). Role shock: An occupational hazard of American technical assistants abroad. *The Annuals, 368*, 95–108.

Carver, C. S., Blaney, P. H., & Scheier, M. F. (1979). Reassertion and giving up: The interactive role of self-directed attention and outcome expectancy. *Journal of Personality and Social Psychology, 37*, 1859–1870.

Carver, C. S., & Scheier, M. F. (1982). Control theory: A useful conceptual framework for personality-social, clinical, and health psychology. *Psychological Bulletin, 92*, 111–135.

Church, A. T. (1982). Sojourner adjustment. *Psychological Bulletin, 91*, 540–572.

David, K. H. (1971). Culture shock and the development of self-awareness. *Journal of Contemporary Psychotherapy, 4*, 44–48.

DeYoung, G., Kampen, G., & Topolski, J. (1982). Analyzer-generated and human-judged predictors of computer program readability. *Proceedings of the conference on human factors in computer systems* (pp. 223–228). Washington, DC: Association for Computing Machinery.

Engelberger, J. (1980). *Robotics in practice.* New York: Anacom.

Fienberg, S. E. (1980). *The analysis of cross-classified categorical data.* Cambridge: The MIT Press.

Goffman, E. (1961). *Asylums.* Garden City, NJ: Anchor Books.

Gamst, F., & Horbeck, E. (Eds.). (1976). *Ideas of culture: Sources and uses.* New York: Holt, Rinehart and Winston.

Higbee, H. (1969). Role shock – A new concept. *International Educational and Cultural Exchange, 4*(4), 71–81.

Kanfer, F. H., & Hagerman, S. (1981). The role of self-regulation. In L. P. Rehm (Ed.), *Behavior therapy for depression: Present status and future direction* (pp. 143–179). New York: Academic Press.

Kennedy, J. J. (1983). *Analzying qualitative data: Introductory log-linear analysis for behavioral research.* New York: Praeger.

Louis, M. (1980). Surprise and sense making: What newcomers experience in entering unfamiliar organizational settings. *Administrative Science Quarterly, 25*, 226–251.

Oberg, K. (1966). Cultural shock: Adjustment to new cultural environments. *Practical Anthropology, 7*, 177–182.

Rice, R. E., Johnson, B., & Rogers, E. (1982). The introduction of new office technology. *Proceedings of the office automation conference* (pp. 653–660). San Francisco, CA: American Federation of Information Processing Societies.

Rogers, E., Daley, H., & Wu, T. (1982). *The diffusion of home computers.* Palo Alto, CA: Stanford University, Institute for Communication Research.

Schneider, M. L., Nudelman, S., & Hirsh-Pasek, K. (1982). An analysis of line numbering strategies in text editors. In *Proceedings of human factors in computer systems* (pp. 148–151). Washington, DC: Association for Computing Machinery.

Smalley, W. A. (1963). Culture shock, language shock, and the shock of self-discovery. *Practical Anthropology, 10*, 49–56.

Sproull, L., Kiesler, S., & Zubrow, D. (1984). Encountering an alien culture. *Journal of Social Issues, 40*(3), 31–48.

Steele, G. L., Woods, D. R., Finkel, R. A., Crispin, M. R., Stallman, R. M., & Goodfellow, G. S. (1983). *The hackers dictionary.* New York: Harper and Row.

Taylor, R. P. (Ed.). (1980). *The computer in the school.* New York: Teachers College Press.

Thompson, S. C. (1981). Will it hurt less if I can control it? A complex answer to a simple question. *Psychological Bulletin, 90*, 89–101.

Turkle, S. (1984). *The second self.* New York: Simon and Schuster.

Zuboff, S. (1982). New worlds of computer-mediated work. *Harvard Business Review, 60*(5), 142–152.

14   On the social psychology of using research reviews: the case of desegregation and black achievement

Harris M. Cooper

Overview and Introduction

Investigators interested in the social psychology of education often confront a time-worn problem faced by all applied researchers: how can objective or consensual rules of data gathering and interpretation be used to study issues that are value-laden and tied in with well-entrenched attitudes? Perhaps this problem is best exemplified by the debate surrounding the effects of school desegregation. The intensity of social and political pressures, the salience of the researcher's personal beliefs, and the complexity of the problem make desegregation an especially difficult area for interpretation using social-psychological principles and techniques. This chapter presents the results of a case study examining what happened to the attitudes of six experts on the effects of desegregation when they interactively reviewed the relevant research literature. The impact of their resulting reviews on the attitudes of a less expert audience (i.e., graduate students) was also examined.

In the summer of 1982, the National Institute of Education's (NIE) Desegregation Studies Team (DST) undertook an attempt to reconcile the research literature concerning the effects of desegregation on black children's achievement. The several major reviews in this area had produced conflicting results, leading the DST to feel there was a need to clarify what was known about the effects of desegregation, what needed to be discovered, and what directions the next research should take.

The research was supported by National Institute of Education grant #NIE-G-82-0022 though the opinions expressed do not necessarily reflect those of NIE. The author wishes to thank Richard Petty, Lee Ross, and Lee Shulman for comments on an earlier draft and Spencer Ward for help throughout the research project.

341

Jeffrey Schneider (1982), the head of the DST at the time of this effort, wrote:

DST knew from the beginning of the project that much of the available research on school desegregation and its effect on black students' academic achievement suffered from design flaws. DST also knew from the beginning that much of this research raised more questions than were answered. We did not know if desegregation research suffers from this in any greater measure than other topical research areas. Nor did we know why so many reputable scholars disagreed in their interpretations of analytical results. To help answer these questions, NIE commissioned a set of papers in an effort to obtain the views of six reputable scholars who had reported opposing conclusions in this area and one research methodologist who had not been identified as a desegregation researcher. The NIE interest in this project was in finding if under similar conditions, with the same set of data, and common ground rules, similarities and differences in scholarly analysis can be identified and clarified. The participants were selected by an NIE staff analysis of previous research findings, by an informal poll of persons engaged in desegregation research, and by a request that each of the possible participants identify others having similar and divergent views from their own. The panel members were Robert Crain, Paul Wortman, David Armor, Norman Miller, Walter Stephan, and Thomas Cook, who served as methodologist.
     The seven scholars met in July 1982 at which time they discussed the state of the research literature and agreed on the use of a comprehensive criteria in selecting studies to be analyzed.... A total of 157 empirical studies were identified that looked at black student academic achievement in desegregated schools. The selection process resulted in a "core" of 19 studies. Panel members agreed, however, that individual reviewers would be allowed to add or delete studies from the "core" (pp. 6-8).

After their initial meeting, the panel members prepared first drafts of their papers. They then reconvened in December 1982 to review and evaluate each other's work.

At the same time that the DST's effort was beginning, NIE's Dissemination in Practice Program was agreeing to fund my research which proposed to study the literature review as a knowledge-synthesis process. The first objectives of this research were a naturalistic examination of how literature reviews are carried out and how they are evaluated by interested readers. Obviously, the convening of NIE's panel on desegregation and black achievement provided a rare opportunity for studying the process of research synthesis. Six expert researchers were asked to draw conclusions about a single hypothesis using a nearly common set of studies. Both the DST and the panelists agreed to take part in my research. It is the outcome of this research that will be reported in this chapter.

Because of the structure of the panel's assignment, certain aspects of the reviewing process could be examined as part of the naturalistic study. First, each panelist came to the assignment with extensive knowledge of the topic. Nearly all panel members had previously written reviews of desegregation research and had taken part in analysis of primary desegregation data. Therefore, the sources of the experts' predispositions toward the topic could be studied.

Second, the assignment of the panel included a phase in which the quality of desegregation research was to be examined. This allowed for an assessment of the experts' beliefs concerning how a study's design affected its informational utility.

A third set of questions involved attitude change. It was possible to compare the panelists' prior beliefs about desegregation with their beliefs at the assignment's conclusion. An obvious question to ask was: Did the panel experience move the participants toward more positive or negative conclusions concerning the effects of desegregation? Also, did the panel experience enhance or diminish participants' confidence in their conclusions? And perhaps most important, did the panel experience create greater consensus or dispersion among the opinions of participants?

A fourth area of research synthesis that could be examined involved the written products of panel members. The six written reviews could be read by an interested audience and their reactions to the papers assessed.

The characteristic of the panel that made asking these questions especially meaningful was that all six reviewers addressed a common question yoked to a common body of evidence: All reviewers began with an identical core of 19 studies but were then allowed to add other studies on their own. It is important to note, however, that this same characteristic precluded the asking of some other questions about research synthesis. First, differences in how the reviewers might define the notions of "desegregation" and "achievement" could not be examined. Some panelists found the need for a common definition of these terms restricted their analysis of the problem. Also, variations in literature-searching strategies could not be studied because the panel used a preexisting evidential base. Finally, the panelists all agreed that the generation of an average effect size estimate and the examination of variance in effect sizes across studies was the strategy to be used for integration of study results. Thus, while different reviewers might choose different mathematical formulas, the basic soundness of the quantitative approach was generally accepted.

The factors influencing choices of definitions, literature-search strategies and synthesis techniques are as central to the outcomes of reviews as are the factors influencing predispositions, research-quality judgments, because the panel was structured in a manner that meant these parameters of integrative research reviewing were not as free to vary as were others.

Collection of data

Data collection for the first part of this study was accomplished through two telephone interviews with each panelist. The first interview occurred after the panelists initially met but before actual work on their papers began. This phone interview included closed-ended quantitative scale questions, open-ended questions, and nondirective requests for general observations.

Each participant was asked what his predisposition was concerning the research on desegregation – did it enhance, have no effect on, or diminish black achievement, or could no conclusion be drawn? Participants were also asked how confident they were that their interpretation was correct and, in the event that they believed there was a desegregation effect, participants described its magnitude on a scale from "very small" to "very large." The panelists next listed those variables they felt might mediate the effect of desegregation. For instance, among the mediators offered were the child's age at desegregation, curriculum factors, and staff attitudes, to name a few.

In the final part of the structured interview, participants rank-ordered six aspects of experimental design with regard to their impact on the "informational utility" of a desegregation study. The six aspects of experimental design included (a) the definition of desegregation employed in the study, (b) the adequacy of the control group, (c) the validity of the achievement measure, (d) the representativeness of the sample, (e) the representativeness of the environmental conditions surrounding the test, and (f) the statistical analysis. So, for instance, if a participant ranked the adequacy of the control group first, it meant he felt this aspect of the research design had the greatest impact, either positive or negative, on the value of a study's results.

In the second telephone interview, the first three questions were repeated, thus allowing assessments of change in the panelists' conclusions, confidence in conclusions, and estimates of effect size magnitude. Participants were also asked about their general political beliefs and, in open-ended questions, about their reaction to the panel experience.

In the second phase of the study, the first drafts of the panelists' written papers were read by 14 post-Masters graduate students in psychology and education. The graduate readers took part in interviews before and after reading the first drafts that paralleled the interviews with the participants. The readers also completed a separate questionnaire concerning each first draft on which they made judgments about the reviewers' positions and the quality of the paper. More details on this phase of the study will be presented after the results of the interviews with the panel members are discussed.

Results: reviewer interviews

The first questions of interest involved the sources of the reviewers' predispositions. These impressions were gleaned primarily from the open-ended and nondirective responses of panelists during the phone interviews. I will state some of these results as conclusions general to all reviewers when, in fact, they are really hypotheses for a more broadly based and better-controlled study.

The most important source of predispositions for panelists was the outcomes of their own primary research. Hands-on experience with primary desegregation data appeared to form a central set of expectations for the results of any research on the same topic. Seeing – or in this case collecting and analyzing data – is believing. Panelists with primary research experience in the area appeared to give greatest, and perhaps disproportionate, weight to the outcomes of their own studies.

Because the present study was naturalistic and the data on the panelists' initial dispositions was retrospective, the assertion that out-comes of personal primary research *caused* dispositions is clearly speculative. It may also be supposed that initial dispositions led panelists to structure their primary research designs and analyses in a manner that made supportive results highly likely. However, two of the panelists explicitly stated that their beliefs about desegregation effects changed in response to data collection. Probably the most defensible assertion is that both processes exist in nature, that is, primary research influences beliefs and beliefs influence research design and analysis.

Also, there is much evidence that when initial beliefs are vague or tenuous, data collection will make a lasting impression on the ex-perimenter. Personal work on primary research is a highly salient event that is considerably more vivid than the research of others. The work of Tversky and Kahneman (1973) indicates that such events are not only overweighted in judgments but often form a preexisting structure (or schema) to which new information is assimilated.

and report preparation (Cooper, 1984). They are overlooked here only

A second source of predisposition was the disciplinary affiliation of the reviewer. Disciplinary affiliations appeared to be most important with regard to the selection of mediators of the effects of desegregation. Educators searched mainly for curriculum variables as mediators of the relation, psychologists offered mainly intervening variables associated with interpersonal interaction, and sociologists invoked mainly social-structure mediators. Less conclusively, disciplinary affiliations also evidenced themselves in predispositions about results. This may occur because of the reviewer's general faith in his discipline's level of analysis. To use an example other than desegregation, a sociologist might be more likely to agree with the statement "social class affects achievement motivation" than would a psychologist, who might see social class simply as a weak substitute for the "real" psychological determinant of achievement motivation, such as the amount of independence training that goes on in the family.

Finally, predispositions appeared to arise from the broader political and social belief systems of the panelists. Many topics in the social sciences relate to real-world problems, and certainly desegregation is one of these. The outcomes of hypothesis tests have implications for the validity of different world views. Conservative and liberal stances on general political issues can "filter" down to imply particular stances on testable research hypotheses. While the present study is only an indication of the consistency, but not causal interrelations, of general belief systems and specific interpretations of empirical data, cognitive consistency theories suggest the pressures toward congruence will work to keep general and specific beliefs consonant with one another (Abelson et al., 1968).

The observation that predispositions toward review outcomes are influenced by personal research, disciplinary affiliation, and general belief systems is commonsensible. The point needs to be made here, however, because it will shortly become evident that predispositions explained much of the panelists' reactions to their assignment. It appears that a description of the synthesis process would not be complete without clear reference to the role of prior beliefs.

The next set of questions dealt with the impact of research design on the utility of a study's results. Table 14.1 presents the panelists' rankings. The rankings reveal general agreement that research-design factors associated with internal validity most influence a study's utility. External validity factors were less important. The measurement of the outcome variable, in this case achievment, revealed much variability in its rated

Table 14.1 *Impact of research-design factors on the utility of a study's results*

Factors	Responses						$\bar{r}^a$
Experimental manipulation (definition of desegregation)	1	1	3	2	1	2	1.6
Experimental comparison (adequacy of control group)	3	2	2	1	2	1	1.8
Outcome measure (measurement of achievement)	2	6	1	3	4	6	3.6
Population generality	5	5	4	4	5	5	4.6
Ecological generality	5	3	5	6	3	4	4.3
Statistical analysis	4	4	6	5	6	2	4.5

Note: $^a\bar{r}$ = +.47 (Spearman correlation), ranging from r = −.29 to +.77.

importance. It appeared as both the most and least important design factor and only two panelists agreed on its ranking. The statistical analysis used in a study also showed variability in ratings of importance but the ratings were generally low. Several panelists mentioned that if a study had deficiencies in statistical analysis, these could be corrected after the fact.

A Spearman correlation between pairs of rankings revealed an average r of + .47. This number is not dissimilar from correlations found in broader studies of research-quality judgments (Gottfredson, 1978). The pair-wise correlations, however, ranged from −.29 to + .77. This finding led to a testing of whether disagreements about the impact of research-design factors on study utility were associated with disagreements about the effect of desegregation. To do this, participants were ranked in terms of their perceptions of the effectiveness of desegregation. Then, the difference in ranks between each pair of panelists was correlated with the correlation between their rankings of the design factors. The resulting Spearman r was −.78, indicating that those panelists who disagreed most about the effects of desegregation also disagreed most about relative impact of design factors on study utility. Of course, this is only a crude descriptive device and it cannot be determined from this information alone whether differences in quality criteria account for differences in interpretations of desegregation research, or vice versa, or whether both beliefs are a function of yet a third variable. However, this evidence does support the earlier assertion that dispositions toward specific empirical hypotheses cannot be understood in isolation of broader cognitive structures.

The final set of reviewer data involves the changes in panelists' attitudes toward desegregation. Before the panel began, three participants expressed a belief that desegregation had positive effects and none changed their mind. Two of three panelists who believed desegregation sometimes had no effect and sometimes had positive effects experienced no general attitude change. One participant changed his opinion from this equivocal position to the position that no conclusion could be drawn, due primarily to an enhanced appreciation of the complexity of the issue.

With regard to panelists' confidence in their conclusions, three participants found the experience enhanced confidence in their beliefs. For two participants, this change was dramatic. On a scale from zero (not confident at all) to 10 (totally confident), they moved from 2 to 6 and from 3 to 9. The third panelist showing enhanced confidence moved from 7 to 9. One participant lost a small, but perceptible, amount of confidence in his conclusion moving from 9 to 7 on the scale. Two participants reported no changes in confidence level remaining at 7 and 8 on the scale.

Next, the panelists estimated the magnitude of the desegregation effect. Three panelists revised upward their estimates of magnitude moving from "very small" to "small," from "small to moderate" to "moderate," and from "moderate" to "moderate to large." One panelist's estimate that the effect was "very small to small" did not change and two participants, who were reluctant to estimate an effect magnitude before the panel began, estimated the effect as between "very small" and "small" when their work was done. These results lead to a conclusion that there was some movement toward more positive impressions of the effect of desegregation. However, it is important to point out that a reading of the panelists' papers, when compared to their earlier writings, generally gives the opposite impression – that is, desegregation seems less impactful in the newer works. This assessment is supported by data on the graduate student readers' impressions before and after reading the papers, to be described shortly.

The conflicting impressions given by the phone interviews and the written papers provide an important insight into the estimation and interpretation of effect sizes. Cooper (1981) has argued that the sub-stantive interpretation of an effect contains two components. The first component is the mathematical estimation of the magnitude of the effect itself. On this estimate, the panelists achieved a high degree of cor-respondence. All of the panelists agreed that the effect was positive (i.e., desegregation enhanced black achievement) and the estimates ranged from $d = .04$ to $d = .17$, a difference of less than two months of gain on standard achievement tests. The estimate of effect probably captures this mathematical component and indicates that for half the panelists it was larger after the panel experience than before.

The second component of effect size interpretation, however, involves the choice of contrasting elements for purposes of comparison. That is, effects are rarely interpreted in a vacuum. Instead, they are contrasted with effects of a conceptually similar nature. In this case, panelists might ask themselves, "In comparison to other known educational interventions, how effective is desegregation?" It is this interpretation that appears to have been most prevalent in the panelists' written papers and, apparently, several panelists found the desegregation effect did not compare favorably with other forms of educational intervention. Put differently, for some, the panel experience may have raised their expectations concerning what the desegregation effect needed to be in order to be useful. When this second component is added to the mathematical evaluation of effects, the generally positive picture becomes somewhat negative for some panel members.

The estimates of effect also give some clues about whether the panel experience created consensus or dispersion of opinion. Clearly, there was as much disagreement among participants when the panel concluded as when it began, only after the experience, some panelists more firmly held their beliefs. However, there are some mitigating circumstances that offer consolation. First, the issue of desegregation is an exceptionally emotional one involving moral and political stances as well as the scientific perspective. Other issues may prove more amenable to efforts at consensus building through research synthesis and the panel format. Second, the members of the panel brought an unusually large degree of prior experience to their task. Their initial positions were well-thought-out, complex integrations of knowledge acquired over years of study. Any expectation of dramatic attitude change would have been unrealistic and contrary to research that indicates prior knowledge and experience with an issue makes attitude change more difficult (Wood, 1982).

Conclusion: reviewer interviews

In sum, hours of conversation with the panelists revealed that they probably hold disparate views on many social issues – in fact, they were chosen for participation based partly on their different perspectives. My impression was that the empirical data did create convergence in their thinking on the effects of desegregation though most of this occurred before the panel was convened, when the panelists' attitudes were more malleable. I think the panelists' positions would have been even more diverse had no data or prior synthesis activity taken place.

Finally, a potentially encouraging outcome of the panel concerns something that did *not* happen. Recent experimental evidence indicates that when people with conflicting beliefs are exposed to a set of studies containing conflicting results, attitudes can become even more polarized (Lord, Ross, & Lepper, 1979). Other research indicates that further thought about an issue, even in the absence of new information, leads to polarization in the direction of one's initial tendency (Tesser, 1978). There is little evidence that such attitude polarization occurred among the panelists. Two possible explanations for why panelists' beliefs did not show further dispersion can be offered. First, as noted before, the panelists entered this exercise with highly refined and rehearsed positions, limiting the opportunity for change in any direction. The second explanation is less encouraging. While the panelists began with differing opinions on desegregation's effectiveness, none of the panelists held the belief that desegregation had *negative* effects on black achievement. In other words, panelists disagreed about the existence or magnitude of positive effects while agreeing that the effect was not negative. The Lord et al. (1979) research demonstrated polarization among persons who believed the same intervention had opposite effects. It is impossible to tell whether or not the inclusion of panel members who believed desegregation had negative effects would have revealed evidence for polarization (by, for example, the negative group increasing its estimate of the negative effect size or showing enhanced confidence in its beliefs, paralleling the changes in confidence demonstrated by the positive panelists).

Results: reader reactions

Measures of change. The second phase of this study involved obtaining reader reactions to the six reviews. First, the fourteen graduate student readers were interviewed before reading the reviews. Several questions that they were asked concerned the readers' educational and topical background and general political beliefs. Four questions were identical to the repeated measurements obtained from the panelists and were meant to gauge the readers' beliefs about the effectiveness and mediators of desegregation and their confidence in these judgments. Also similar to

Table 14.2. *Graduate readers' beliefs about desegregation before and after reading the reviews*

Question	Before	After
What is the size of the desegregation effect?	4.41	2.58
	(2.57)	(1.38)
How confident are you that your belief is accurate?	6.00	7.00
	(1.92)	(1.36)
What variables of conditions mediate the effect?	6.46	8.93
(number mentioned)	(3.45)	(5.70)

Note: Standard deviations are in parentheses.

the panelists', these four questions were readministered after all six reviews had been read. The change in responses to these questions will be examined first.

The graduate readers' general beliefs about desegregation's effectiveness changed little as a function of reading the papers. Eight readers who initially felt desegregation enhanced black achievement did not change their belief, as did one reader who felt desegregation had no effect. Three readers who initially felt no conclusion could be drawn changed to an opinion that the effect was positive while two readers showed change from the latter to the former position. In contrast, the graduate readers' beliefs about desegregation as measured by three other indexes changed significantly. Table 14.2 presents the readers' (a) estimated effect size, (b) confidence in beliefs, and (c) number of suggested mediators of the effect.

In general, the reader's perception of the positive effect of desegregation dropped precipitously from before to after reading the reviews ($t(12) = -3.97, p < .004$). Before reading the reviews, the average effect size estimate was about "moderate," whereas afterward it was less than "small." Eight of ten readers who estimated the effect size both times revised their estimates downward. Interestingly, the readers' average magnitude of effect was considerably greater than the reviewers' estimate before reading the papers (4.41 vs. 3.00, respectively) but was smaller afterward (2.58 vs. 3.16). These figures reinforce the impression that the papers may have conveyed a less positive evaluation of the desegregation effect than did the reviewers' responses to the interview question.

With regard to the variety of reader opinions, it appears that reading the reviews created some convergence of beliefs – the standard deviation in effect estimates was about 2.5 before and 1.33 after reading the reviews.

However, this finding needs cautious interpretation because two readers who estimated "small" (3) and "moderate" (5) initial effect sizes did not offer an estimate after reading the reviews while two readers who initially left this question blank estimated "very small" (1) effects after reading the papers.

The graduate students' average level of confidence in their beliefs before reading the papers was identical to the reviewers' initial confidence levels (6.00). This would indicate that subjective confidence in beliefs about an empirical research area is not directly related (if at all) to objective expertise on the topic. However, after reading the papers, the students' confidence level tended to be higher (7.00; $t(14) = 1.66, p<.12$) but the level did not jump as much as did the reviewers' confidence (7.67).

Finally, reading the reviews led graduate students to cite more mediators of the effect of desegregation than they initially proposed, though statistically the effect only approached significance ($t(13) = -2.06, p<.07$). While about 6.5 mediators were mentioned on average before reading the papers, almost nine were mentioned after reading the papers. Nine readers enhanced the complexity of their beliefs about desegregation's effect.

It is important not only to note that the readers offered more mediators of desegregation effects as a function of reading the papers, but also to examine what kinds of mediators showed the greatest increase in number of citations. In order to find this out, a content analysis was conducted on the open-ended responses of readers to the question "What variables or conditions would you suggest that might mediate the effect of desegregation on black achievement?"

Figure 14.1 lists the 60 separate categories into which mediators were placed. The 60 categories were then reduced to 11 broader categories for statistical analysis. The 11 categories of mediators were: (a) the attitudes of the people involved in the desegregation effort, including parents, students, teachers, and school administrators; (b) the family and personal background of the students; (c) the geographic and cultural background of the community; (d) the characteristics of the school, (e) of classrooms, and (f) of teachers; (g) the measurement and type of achievement examined in the research; (h) conditions under which desegregation was accomplished; (i) the amount of resources available to a school district; (j) the number of and response to problems associated with moving students from one school to another; and (k), a miscellaneous category used for mediators that coders felt did not fit into any of the previous 10 categories.

I. *Attitudes* (support)
   of parents, white, black; of students, white, black; of teachers; of school administration; of politicians; of business; of clergy

II. *Student background*
   parent education; family relations; family size; social class, blacks, whites; achievement/ability, blacks, whites; age; self concept/personality

III. *Community background*
   area of country; urban vs. rural; size; historical conditions; media presentation

IV. *School characteristics*
   size; location; quality (curriculum)

V. *Classroom characteristics*
   size (teacher–pupil ratio; no. of teachers); seating (interaction) patterns; open vs. traditional

VI. *Teacher characteristics*
   ability; labeling (expectation) effects; training for desegregation; race

VII. *Achievement definition*
   measurement; subject matter; interpretation of measurement

VIII. *Desegregation definition*
   voluntary vs. forced; community involvement in implementation; need (distance) for busing; black–white ratio; length of implementation; who gets bused

IX. *Money* (expenditures)
   resources for teachers; other support services (personnel)

X. *Change of school problems* (confusion)
   preparation of students

XI. *Other*

Figure 14.1. Coding frame for moderators of desegregation effects.

The categories were developed by the principal investigator based on a reading of graduate students' responses. Then, each reader's responses were coded by two other judges. Their interjudge reliability across the 11 categories, as measured by Cohen's Kappa, was .74 when they coded the readers' prior beliefs and .76 when they coded the graduate students' responses to the question after reading the reviews.

Table 14.3 presents the results of this analysis. First, it should be noted that both prior to reading the reviews and after reading the reviews, the graduate students cited the attitudes of those involved in the desegregation effort as the most important influence on its effect. The two types of mediators that evidenced significant increases in citation from before to after reading the reviews were the two categories involving how achievement was defined and by what methods desegregation was accomplished.

Table 14.3. *Change in the number of mediators mentioned by readers in eleven categories*

Mediator category	Prior	Post	t-value	p-level
Attitudes	1.71	1.86		
Student background	1.11	1.39		
Community	0.86	0.56		
School characteristics	0.32	0.38		
Classroom characteristics	0.11	0.25		
Teacher characteristics	0.46	0.86		
Achievement definition	0.14	0.79	3.23	.007
Desegregation methods	0.96	1.75	2.27	.04
Resources (money)	0.46	0.25		
Moving problems	0.07	0.25	2.11	.06
Other	0.14	0.57		

Reading the reviews led the graduate students to place an increased emphasis on factors such as how achievement was measured and interpreted, what subject matter was under scrutiny, whether or not the desegregation effort was voluntary or forced, how involved the community was in its implementation, the need or distance of busing, the black–white ratio created by desegregation, the length of time between implementation and the assessment of outcome, and finally whether it was black or white children who got bused. There was also some indication that the readers placed greater emphasis on the need for planning and the avoidance of disruption after the reviews were read.

The next analysis involved relating the readers' background to their beliefs about desegregation before and after reading the reviews. These results are displayed in Table 14.4. Table 14.4 contains nine variables. The variable "topic familiarity" is a composite of the graduate students' year in graduate school and their responses to the questions, "How familiar are you with desegregation research?" and "How many scholarly articles related to desegregation have you read?" The intercorrelations among these items were .75, .81, and .83. The three items were only weakly related to the graduate students' answers to the question, "How familiar are you with research methodology?" (correlations ranged from $r = -.10$ to $r = .02$), so this response was left as a separate variable, as was the question asking readers to place themselves on the political spectrum. The last six variables on Table 14.4 should already be familiar. They are the graduate students' assessments of the direction and magnitude of the desegregation effect, their confidence in their beliefs, and the number of mediators they cited before and after reading the reviews.

Table 14.4. *Relations between students' background, prior and post-reading, beliefs about desegregation (All tests are based on between 9 and 13 degrees of freedom.)*

	Topic familiarity	Research expertise	Political beliefs[a]	Prior effect size[b]	Prior confidence	Prior mediators	Post effect size[b]	Post confidence	Post mediators
Topic familiarity	—	-.04	-.02	-.47	.48*	-.30	.35	.38*	-.24
Research expertise		—	.05	-.01	-.06	.10	-.45*	.00	.54**
Political beliefs			—	.01	.08	-.36	.39	-.35	.15
Prior effect size				—	.12	.51*	.01	-.53*	.07
Prior confidence					—	.06	.48*	.09	-.38
Prior mediators						—	-.12	-.19	.58**
Post effect size							—	-.22	-.38
Post confidence								—	-.26
Post mediators									—

[a]More liberal beliefs were given higher numerical values.

[b]Effect sizes were coded as negative values if the reader thought desegregation had negative effects. If absolute values were used, one trend emerged $-r$ with prior confidence = .45 ($p < .15$).

*.15 < p > .05.

**p < .05.

In examining Table 14.4, it should first be noted that the correlations are based on between only 9 and 13 degrees of freedom. Therefore, the tests have very poor statistical power and in some instances correlations will be mentioned that do not reach traditional levels of significance but are large enough to warrant attention in future studies.

With regard to the relationships between the readers' politics and their desegregation beliefs, no correlations between political beliefs and other variables was found to be significant or to produce a trend. The strongest relationships were between political beliefs and the size of the desegregation effect estimated after reading the papers. Specifically, the correlation of $r = .39$ indicates that more liberal readers estimated larger effects after reading the reviews. Before reading the reviews, the relation between political beliefs and effect size was near zero ($r = .01$). Although both of these figures are nonsignificant, the direction of change in the relation is revealing. If the data were building consensus by replacing abstract beliefs with objective outcomes, an opposite pattern of results would have been expected, that is, a disappearance of a relation between broad political tenets and beliefs about desegregation effects as a function of reading empirical reviews. Instead, something like a polarization effect appears to have occurred in that the readers' political beliefs may have guided their processing and interpretation of the data. Also, in future studies of this issue, it would be wise for researchers to ensure a wider range in initial political beliefs – in the present study readers predominantly described themselves as liberal. A less restricted range of beliefs might reveal a larger initial relationship.

The research expertise of the readers was negatively related to their effect size estimates ($r = -.45$) and positively related to the number of mediators they cited ($r = +.54$) after reading the reviews. Thus, it appears that graduate students with more research experience came to see a more equivocal and complex situation as a function of the information input, which is what one would expect an implication of research expertise to be.

Finally, familiarity with the topic of desegregation was positively related to the graduate students' confidence in their beliefs both before ($r = .48$) and after ($r = .38$) reading the reviews, but the relation was somewhat stronger at the first measurement. Possibly, the mitigated effect is a function of those graduate students who were unfamiliar with the topic showing increased confidence in their beliefs after reading the six reviews. Topic familiarity was also negatively related to effect-size estimates before reading the reviews ($r = -.47$). These data indicate that those readers least familiar with desegregation research had the higher expectations for desegregation's effect. Interestingly, after reading the reviews, topic familiarity was positively related to effect size estimates (r = .35). An examination of the raw data reveals that the beliefs about effectiveness of those readers who were most unfamiliar with desegregation research took the more precipitous drop from before to after reading the reviews. Again, this information substantiates the finding that familiarity with a topic is positively related to resistance to change.

Evaluations of individual reviews. The next set of analyses involved the graduate readers' evaluations of the individual reviews. One question asked the reader to estimate the reviewer's position on the direction of the desegregation effect; another question asked what the reviewer would estimate desegregation's effect size to be; and a third question asked the reader to list the reviewer's suggested influences on the impact of desegregation. Readers were also asked to gauge their own confidence in how accurate their interpretation of the *reviewer's* position was. The second set of questions asked the reader to make seven evaluative judgments about the review. These judgments included how clearly the problem was defined in the review, how exhaustive was the research covered in the review, how well the reviewer evaluated the strengths and weaknesses of desegregation research, how well the reviewer synthesized the separate studies into a coherent whole, and how clearly the review was written. Readers also gave an overall judgment of the review's quality and persuasiveness. Finally, readers were asked to make open-ended comments concerning their evaluation of the reviews.

The first analysis involved an informal content analysis of the open-ended comments offered by readers at the bottom of each evaluation sheet. This step was undertaken to get some idea of the subjective dimensions readers employed to evaluate the reviews, rather than those offered on the questionnaire itself.

The readers most often mentioned that a paper was either well or poorly organized. Second most frequently mentioned was writing style, in particular the author's ability or inability to keep the interest of the reader. Third most frequently mentioned was how well or poorly focused the paper was on the topic of interest. Fourth in order was how well or poorly the reviewers used citations to substantiate any claims made in their paper. After this, students evaluated the reviewer's attention or inattention to variable definitions and to mediating influences. Also mentioned were how well or poorly the reviewer described the methods of the individual desegregation studies and the methods of the review itself. Finally, the quality of the manuscript preparation, typically involving negative comments about typos or missing tables, was also mentioned by several of the readers.

To examine the responses to the closed-ended parts of the questionnaires, a factor analysis was first performed on the five judgments concerning specific qualities of the reviews. The factor analyses were performed separately for each review. They revealed that a single quality factor was probably present in all five judgments. The first principal component in each analysis accounted for between 58% and 83% of the variance in the 5 scores and other factors had high loadings by only single variables. When the first five questions were standardized and combined into a composite measure of review quality, this composite correlated with the reviewers' overall judgment of quality ranging from .84 to .96 across six reviews. Therefore, the composite measures of quality based on the first five questions were used in all subsequent analyses rather than the single measure.

The final analysis entailed an examination of the covariation between readers' evaluations of the quality and persuasiveness of a review and their perceptions of the reviewers' beliefs. To carry out this analysis, the readers' responses to the closed-ended items on the individual review questionnaires were correlated with one another as well as with several of the reviewers' answers to questions during the telephone interviews. These correlations were computed for each reader separately, the correlations for the 14 readers were then transformed to Z-scores and the Z-scores then entered into a one-sample t-test to determine if they were significantly different from zero. An example will clarify this procedure. Each reader made six quality judgments, one for each review, and six judgments of the persuasiveness of the reviews. Therefore, for each reader a correlation was computed, based on six paired observations, which described the direction and strength of the relation between quality and persuasiveness judgments for that reader. This procedure was carried out for each reader and then the set of 14 correlations were transformed to Z-scores to normalize their distribution. Finally, by testing whether the average Z-score was significantly different from zero, it could be established whether or not a relation between the two judgments could be inferred from the sample of readers.

Figure 14.2 displays the significant relations between the readers' perceptions of the individual reviews and selected reviewer characteristics. In interpreting these relations, it must be kept in mind that they are associational in nature, so inferences about causal direction and spuriousness must be made with extreme caution.

The *quality* of a review was correlated
    (a) positively with the reader's confidence in its interpretation ($\bar{Z} = .42, p < .02$)

The *persuasiveness* of a review was correlated
    (a) positively with the reader's judgment of its quality ($\bar{Z} = 1.05, p < .0001$)
    (b) positively with the reader's confidence in its interpretation ($\bar{Z} = .66, p < .001$)
    (c) positively with the reader's judgment of the number of mediators it mentioned ($\bar{Z} = .32, p < .05$)

The *effect size* in a review was correlated
    (a) positively with the reviewer's stated effect size ($\bar{Z} = .92, p < .0001$)
    (b) positively with the reviewer's politics ($\bar{Z} = .32, p < .02$)
    (c) negatively with the reviewer's own confidence in their interpretation ($\bar{Z} = -.76, p < .04$)
    (d) negatively with the reader's judgment of the number of mediators it mentioned ($\bar{Z} = -.92, p < .01$)

The *number of mediators* in a review was correlated
    (a) positively with the reviewer's confidence in their interpretation ($\bar{Z} = .62, p < .0001$)
    (b) positively with the reviewer's politics ($\bar{Z} = .55, p < .0001$)

Note: All data are correlational but are repeated under only one heading for ease of presentation.

Figure 14.2. Significant relations between reader perceptions of individual reviews and reviewer characteristics.

Of foremost interest are those perceptions of reviews that correlated with judgments of quality and persuasiveness. It was found that the quality of reviews was not related to the substantive position of the reviewer, such as the perceived effect size or number of mediators offered. Again, it must be emphasized that the sample of both panelists and readers were all on the same side of the issue (i.e., no one felt desegregation had negative effects). Had a wider range of beliefs been represented, a relation between judged quality and substantive position might have emerged. Instead, reviews judged to be of higher quality were those which the readers felt the most confidence in the accuracy of their interpretation of the reviewers' position, regardless of what that position was.

The persuasiveness of a review was positively correlated with its quality, with the reader's confidence in its interpretation and with the number of mediators the reader thought it mentioned. This last relation, indicating more persuasive reviews were those seen as mentioning more mediators, is of special interest because it indicates a relation between persuasiveness and complexity. It would be important to know if this relation is general across all topics or if it holds only for topics where readers are predisposed to believe the relation under study is very complex.

The magnitude of the desegregation effect a reader thought a review espoused was positively related to the reviewers' stated effect size and to the liberalness of the reviewers' stated political beliefs. Effect size perceptions were also negatively related to the reviewers' stated confidence in their interpretation and to the number of mediators a reader thought the review mentioned. Finally, the number of mediators a reader thought a review mentioned was positively associated with the reviewers' confidence in their interpretation and with the reviewers' politics.

To summarize the results of the second phase of this study, the graduate readers showed greater flexibility in their attitudes than the reviewers, due undoubtedly to differences in the two groups' initial states of knowledge. In general, readers' beliefs became more congruent with the reviewers' beliefs and more complex as a function of reading the papers. What was not examined, however, is whether under natural circumstances readers would have chosen to expose themselves to the variety of opinions contained in these papers or whether they would only seek out papers that would confirm or bolster their initial positions. This latter phenomenon, called *selective exposure*, is a source of controversy in social psychological research.

The analysis of readers' backgrounds found little initial bias due to political beliefs but some indication that increased knowledge of the topic also led to increased congruence between general political beliefs and beliefs about desegregation. This may indicate the presence of the phenomenon mentioned earlier—that when people are confronted with a smorgasbord of empirical findings they give greatest weight to those that are consistent with prior beliefs.

With regard to the evaluation of individual reviews, these appeared to be relatively free from the influence of initial topical beliefs. Quality judgments covaried with confidence in interpretation. Judgments of the persuasiveness of a review covaried with quality, confidence in interpretation, and number of mediators mentioned.

Conclusions

The basic principles of attitude change appear to apply to the process of empirical knowledge synthesis. Rather than being an activity of a qualitatively different order, the attitude-relevant aspects of research reviewing, as exemplified by NIE's panel, are probably best understood by noting the special characteristics of the people and circumstances involved and by applying established principles to this unique situation.

First, the desegregation panelists began their synthesis task with a great deal of prior knowledge, as do most research reviewers. This knowledge is not only great in magnitude but it is also well organized in a complex structure. These characteristics of reviewers will lessen the possibility of change in basic beliefs because the synthesizer will (a) encounter few arguments which are truly novel and (b) have a cognitive schema with which to integrate or argue information that is new.

Readers of research reviews who bring less tenacious beliefs to the topic area, such as the graduate students in this study, are more likely to experience attitude change and enhanced complexity of beliefs. The amount and direction of this change apparently will not only be a function of the reviewer's conclusions and treatment of the relevant material, but also of the effectiveness of the reviewer's presentation, in particular the organization and style of the manuscript.

Aside from the characteristics of the actors in the review process, the empirical character of research syntheses, like the question of the effects of desegregation, is also critical to understanding related attitude change. Scientific studies claim a certain degree of objectivity for their results, and by implication assume that identical tests of the same hypothesis will lead to identical, or at least similar, results. Yet, sets of empirical studies yield varying, often conflicting findings. This disparity may result because methods are different, hypotheses are not really commensurate, or the assumption of objectivity is false at the start.

The diversity of results often found in a set of empirical studies will inhibit attitude change in its consumers. If an initial opinion is minimally reasonable, an examiner of the related research will find some studies that confirm the initial belief. Obviously, the diversity in results will also greatly impede the ability of research to create consensus among reviewers or review readers. In the instance of less knowledgeable consumers, like the graduate readers in this study, the diversity of results may lead to the formation of attitudes consistent with other more generally held beliefs (e.g., political philosophy).

Finally, even when a certain degree of consensus is reached on the objective outcome of a set of studies – in this case the size of the desegregation effect – the varying perspectives of reviewers and readers can still create discrepancies in the subjective utilities that are used to interpret the findings. Thus, while a great deal of agreement might be reached on the observation that an 8-ounce glass contains 4 ounces of water, there can still be much disagreement about whether the glass is half empty or half full.

It is this last point which speaks most directly to studying the social psychology of education in general. Many problems in education require both objective measurements and subjective interpretations of what the measurements mean. Questions like "Is a teaching method that fosters independent learning better than one that maximizes achievement?" or "Is the cost of a program justified by its academic outcomes?" are not answerable with data alone. Researchers cannot resolve these debates – they can only help the debaters ground their arguments in more precise and reliable information (e.g., How much independence is gained by a teaching method? How much added knowledge does a program buy?). When the researcher moves from informing debaters to joining the debate, that individual moves from the role of researcher to that of advocate.

Of course, the distinction between these roles is not as clear as it sounds. Often the choice of problems and how they are to be studied can be as value-laden as how data are interpreted. For instance, in assessing the effects of desegregation, its impact on white as well as black students' achievement, or on housing patterns might lead to different conclusions about the treatment's effectiveness. Thus, social psychologists of education will be challenged at every stage of a research endeavor to remain aware of when they are acting as knowledge seekers and when as advocates.

If this assessment of the research-synthesis process in educational research seems disheartening it is only because the expectations for modern-day social science may be too high. It is unreasonable to consider a failure anything less than complete agreement among scholars. It is also unreasonable to overlook those aspects of a problem upon which agreement has been reached: NIE's panelists achieved remarkable consensus on the magnitude of the desegregation effect.

Also, it should be remembered that the development of new techniques for increasing the objectivity of research synthesis, such as computerized literature searching and meta-analysis, is occupying the time of many social science methodologists. Using these techniques, as the panelists did, probably led them to greater agreement than would have been the case otherwise. It is likely that further refinements in method will lead to more consensus and, just as important, better understanding of why disagreement occurs.

Finally, philosophic debates within the social sciences are helping to define the limits of objectivity, and as such will help define when a research synthesizer is speaking as a scientist and when as a citizen.

In sum, the convening of NIE's panel on desegregation and black achievement proved to be an exciting natural laboratory for the study of knowledge synthesis. It would serve the purposes of both the social science community and the general public if efforts of this sort were continued in the future. Social scientists would learn about basic social psychological processes and how they influence their own activities. The general public would learn more about what to expect from social science products and how best to interpret them. Knowledge synthesis is more meaningful if it is accompanied by descriptions of the process that brought the synthesis about.

References

Abelson, R. P., Aronson, E., McGuire, W. J., Newcomb, T. M., Rosenberg, M. J., & Tannenbaum, P. H. (Eds.). (1968). *Theories of cognitive consistency: A source book.* Chicago: Rand McNally.

Cooper, H. M. (1981). On the significance of effects and the effects of significance. *Journal of Personality and Social Psychology, 41*, 1013–1018.

Cooper, H. M. (1984). *Integrative research reviewing: A social science approach.* Beverly Hills, CA: Sage.

Gottfredson, S. (1978). Evaluating psychological research reports. *American Psychologist, 33*, 920–934.

Lord, C., Ross, L., & Lepper, M. (1979). Biased assimilation and attitude polarization: The effects of prior theories on subsequently considered evidence. *Journal of Personality and Social Psychology, 37*, 2098–2109.

Schneider, J. (April 1983). Overview of research on effects of desegregation on achievement. In P. Wortman (Chair), *An analysis of methodologies used in synthesis of research on desegregation and student achievement.* Symposium conducted at the meeting of the American Educational Research Association, Montreal, Canada.

Tesser, A. (1978). Self-generated attitude change. *Attitudes in experimental social psychology.* New York: Academic Press.

Tversky, A., & Kahneman, D. (1973). Availability: A heuristic for judging frequency and probability. *Cognitive Psychology, 5*, 207–232.

Wood, W. (1982). Retrieval of attitude-relevant information from memory: Effects on susceptibility to persuasion and on intrinsic motivation. *Journal of Personality and Social Psychology, 42*, 798–810.

Author Index

365

Subject Index

ability, 17, 18, 19, 20, 22, 28, 29, 31, 44,
    60, 183, 186, 245, 248, 261, 264, 266,
    285, 297, 298, 300, 313, 318, 321
  affective reactions to, 44
  as causal attribution, 25, 39, 40, 41, 45,
    49, 50, 54, 56, 62, 140, 238, 246, 249,
    250, 252
  cues, 41, 44, 60–2
  differentiation of, 241–3
  dimensions of, 42–3
  as failure attribution, 30
  self-concept of, 243, 245, 246, 250
  social comparison of, 243, 244
  as success attribution, 20, 21, 24, 29, 33,
    34, 57
  teacher beliefs about extrinsic vs.
    instrinsic, 241
  ability stratification system, 242
achievement, 19, 21, 30, 32, 33, 220, 237,
    239, 240, 241, 247, 248, 251, 252, 253,
    257, 259, 269, 278, 290, 291, 292, 293,
    296, 298, 315, 343, 347
  attributions, 140–1, 246
  behavior, 250
  black, 344, 349, 363
  cognitive processes for motivating, 225,
    249
  controversy and, 214
  differentiated, 290
  effect of cooperative learning methods
    on, 154–5, 157, 158–69
  effect of Jigsaw teaching on, 156
  effect of Team Assisted
    Individualization on, 162, 163–4, 168
  measuring school effectiveness, 237, 239
  in minority children, 341–2
  minority motivation of, 4, 53–6, 156
  motivation of, 235–6, 237, 243, 244, 245–6
  student, 158, 160, 168
  teacher expectancy and student, 96, 103
action, 70, 71

affect, 28, 45, 132
  outcome-dependent, 24, 25, 43
  racial differential displays, 123
  as source of attributional cues, 49, 60–2
  teacher, 60–2
affective reactions, 24–9, 60–2, 132
  dimensionality of, 25–6, 28–9, 43–4
  racial differentiation, 117
  unitary, 25–6, 27, 28
anger, 24, 26, 27, 62, 321, 326, 330, 332,
    333, 337
  as affective reaction, 43, 44, 45
  as attributional cue, 48–9, 59, 60
antecedents of causal attributions, 59
aptitude, see ability
attitude, 19, 138, 139, 145
  cognitive and affective model of, 68
  definitions and perspectives, 68
  during classroom transitions, 83
  effects of Team Assisted
    Individualization on, 167–8
  measures of, 68, 69, 70, 71
  as outcome measure, 69
  polarization, 350
  racial differentiation of, 116–17
  study of, 4
attitude-behavior relationship, 4, 66–7, 69
  causal association, 66–7, 68–9
  correlation during classroom
    transitions, 83
  correspondence of variables in, 70, 71
  individual emphasis, 70
  methodological vs. mediational
    perspectives, 70, 73
  methodology to study classroom, 74–7
  multiple vs. single act criteria, 69, 70
  ordering of, 67
  results of study of, 78–82
  suppression of discrepancies, 81
attitude change, 205, 206, 211, 213, 343,
    348, 349, 360, 361

374

self-esteem, 20, 39, 45, 57, 59, 60, 62, 156, 174, 182, 184, 216–17, 239, 240, 247, 251, 321
  ability level in conflict and, 216–7
  and affective reactions, 44
  black, 59
  enhancing minority, 62
  role of feedback in influencing, 108
  teaching methods to enhance, 62
  effects of Team Assisted Individualization process on, 160
self-evaluation, 235, 237, 240, 249, 252
  attributions for, 246
  as outcome of social comparison, 244
self-fulfilling prophecy, 5, 91, 92, 93, 112, 189, 269, *see also* expectancy
self-monitoring, effect on attitude-behavior relationship, 70
shame as affective reaction, 43, 45
situational context, 70
  meaning of, 294–5
social cognition, 9, 39
social comparison, 242, 244–5, 248, 250, 252, 293, 297–8, 299
social context of computing, 317
social learning theory, 7
social psychology of education, definition of, 1–3
socialization outcomes, 318, 321, 323, 329, 333
stability, 10–11, 19, 21, 22, 27, 29, 32, 53, 56, 250
  affective reaction to, 44
  as causal attributional dimension, 33, 41–3, 45, 246
  as factor of success and failure, 55–7, 59, 140–1
stereotyping, 177, 179
strategy, as attribution, 54, 55, 56, 57
  of mastery-oriented student, 246, 250, 252
  processing, 30, 237
  research, 343
  student, 250, 252
  teacher, 61–2, 82, 83, 199
student choice, 237, 243, 248, 253
student classroom behavior, 66–84
  callouts, 71, 75
  evaluation of teacher, 68
  hand-raising, 71, 72, 75, 79–80, 82, 83
  involvement-attitude correlation, 81–2
  verbal responding, 80,82
  volunteering, 71, 82
Student/Teacher Interactive Learning Environment project, 111–2

Student Team Achievement Divisions (STAD), *see* cooperative learning methods
success, as a function of stability, 57
  attributions to, 41, 57
  dimensional placement of by race, 57
  unusual expectancy shifts in, 184
success and failure, 3, 10, 24, 28, 32, 44, 59, 236, 243, 246, 250, 252, 259, 260, 261, 264, 277, 278–9, 282, 290, 298, 299
  affective reactions to, 24–25, 43–44
  attributions of, 30, 31, 47, 56–7
  causal attributions about, 17, 20–1, 33, 34, 48–9, 140–1, 240, 247
  causal dimensions of, 41–3, 44–5, 55–6
  in competitive structures, 238
  as factor in interracial interaction, 125–6
  meanings for culturally diverse groups, 53–5
  minority attributions about, 46–7
  role of effort in, 59
symbolic interactionism, 67–8
sympathy, 44, 45, 48–49, 62
  as attributional cue, 59
  cue to minority students, 60–1
  as low-ability cue, 60–1
  low ability linkage, 48–9
synthesis techniques, 343

task, difficulty of, 17, 18, 19, 20, 21, 22, 25, 28, 31, 40, 41, 45, 46, 49, 50, 56, 57, 61–2, 246, 261, 267, 279, 280
  engagement, 237, 240, 260, 267, 269, 271, 272, 273, 280, 281, 285, 299, 300
  "flow," state of, 264
  introductions, 269–85
  meaning, 295
  specialization, *see* cooperative learning methods
teacher expectancy, 41, 141, 242, 252, 257, 269, 271, 272, 280, *see also* meta-analysis to study four-factor theory of mediation of teacher expectancy effects
  for minority students, 60–2, 91–2
teacher expectancy effects, 5, 91–2, 140–1
  mediating behaviors, 100, 106
  mediating factors in, 102, 107
  mediation of, 92, 93–5, 109–10, 111–2
  outcome variables, 103–5
Teacher Expectations and Student Achievement in-service training model, 111